FOREVER VIETNAM

A VOLUME IN THE SERIES

CULTURE, POLITICS, AND THE COLD WAR

edited by
Christian G. Appy

OTHER TITLES IN THE SERIES

James T. Fisher, *Dr. America: The Lives of Thomas A. Dooley, 1927–1961*

Daniel Horowitz, *Betty Friedan and the Making of "The Feminine Mystique": The American Left, the Cold War, and Modern Feminism*

Tom Engelhardt, *The End of Victory Culture: Cold War America and the Disillusioning of a Generation*

Christian G. Appy, ed., *Cold War Constructions: The Political Culture of United States Imperialism, 1945–1966*

H. Bruce Franklin, *Vietnam and Other American Fantasies*

Robert D. Dean, *Imperial Brotherhood: Gender and the Making of Cold War Foreign Policy*

Lee Bernstein, *The Greatest Menace: Organized Crime in Cold War America*

David C. Engerman, Nils Gilman, Mark H. Haefele, and Michael E. Latham, eds., *Staging Growth: Modernization, Development, and the Global Cold War*

Jonathan Nashel, *Edward Lansdale's Cold War*

James Peck, *Washington's China: The National Security World, the Cold War, and the Origins of Globalism*

Edwin A. Martini, *Invisible Enemies: The American War on Vietnam, 1975–2000*

Tony Shaw, *Hollywood's Cold War*

Maureen Ryan, *The Other Side of Grief: The Home Front and the Aftermath in American Narratives of the Vietnam War*

David Hunt, *Vietnam's Southern Revolution: From Peasant Insurrection to Total War*

Patrick Hagopian, *The Vietnam War in American Memory: Veterans, Memorials, and the Politics of Healing*

Jeremy Kuzmarov, *The Myth of the Addicted Army: Vietnam and the Modern War on Drugs*

Robert Surbrug Jr., *Beyond Vietnam: The Politics of Protest in Massachusetts, 1974–1990*

Larry Grubbs, *Secular Missionaries: Americans and African Development in the 1960s*

Robert A. Jacobs, *The Dragon's Tail: Americans Face the Atomic Age*

Andrew J. Falk, *Upstaging the Cold War: American Dissent and Cultural Diplomacy, 1940–1960*

Jerry Lembcke, *Hanoi Jane: War, Sex, and Fantasies of Betrayal*

Anna G. Creadick, *Perfectly Average: The Pursuit of Normality in Postwar America*

Kathleen Donohue, ed., *Liberty and Justice for All? Rethinking Politics in Cold War America*

Jeremy Kuzmarov, *Modernizing Repression: Police Training and Nation Building in the American Century*

Roger Peace, *A Call to Conscience: The Anti-Contra War Campaign*

Edwin A. Martini, *Agent Orange: History, Science, and the Politics of Uncertainty*

Sandra Scanlon, *The Pro-War Movement: Domestic Support for the Vietnam War and the Making of Modern American Conservatism*

Matthew W. Dunne, *A Cold War State of Mind: Brainwashing and Postwar American Society*

Patrick Hagopian, *American Immunity: War Crimes and the Limits of International Law*

FOREVER VIETNAM

***

How a Divisive War Changed American Public Memory

***

DAVID KIERAN

UNIVERSITY OF MASSACHUSETTS PRESS
Amherst and Boston

Printed in the United States of America

ISBN 978-1-62534-100-6 (paper); 099-3 (hardcover)

Designed by Sally Nichols
Set in Adobe Minion Pro
Printed and bound by Maple Press, Inc.

Library of Congress Cataloging-in-Publication Data

Kieran, David, 1978–
Forever Vietnam : how a divisive war changed American public memory / David Kieran.
pages cm. — (Culture, politics, and the Cold War)
Includes bibliographical references and index.
ISBN 978-1-62534-100-6 (pbk. : alk. paper) — ISBN 978-1-62534-099-3 (hardcover : alk. paper)
1. Vietnam War, 1961–1975—Social aspects—United States. 2. Vietnam War, 1961–1975—United States—Psychological aspects. 3. Vietnam War, 1961–1975—Influence. 4. Memory—Social aspects—United States. 5. Collective memory—United States. I. Title.
DS559.8.S6K54 2014
959.704′31—dc23
2014008141

British Library Cataloguing-in-Publication Data
A catalogue record for this book is available from the British Library.

For Emma

★★★

CONTENTS

ACKNOWLEDGMENTS

Only a person who has never written a book could believe that authors' expressions of debt and gratitude are hyperbolic. So many people have helped me as I have worked on this project, and I am grateful to each of them for the large and small ways they made this book possible. My gratitude begins in the American Studies Department at George Washington University. Jennifer James was a tough, realistic, and discerning mentor who balanced her demands for intellectual rigor with offers of compassionate encouragement. We should all hope to be so good to our students. Melani McAlister and Jim Miller taught me how cultural studies and policy fit together and always urged me to think about why my writing mattered. Jim Horton and Kathleen Anderson Steeves gave me a fellowship at the Center for Public History and Public Culture that allowed me ample time to write. Kip Kosek and Marshall Alcorn asked critical questions. Barney Mergen, Phyllis Palmer, Terry Murphy, Chad Heap, and Tom Guglielmo taught me what American Studies was and how to practice it. Tim Bauer, Kathleen Brian, Julie Passanante Elman, Ramzi Fawaz, Joshua Fisher, Sandra Heard, Kyle Riismandel, Stephanie Ricker Schulte, and Laurel Clark Shire cared about their work, the work of their colleagues, and each other in equal measure. This is what a scholarly community should look like. I am especially indebted to my writing group of Lars Lierow, Kevin Strait, and most of all Jeremy Hill. Over the years, no one has had more conversations with me about or read more drafts of this project than Jeremy, and every comment he made improved the work and helped keep me sane.

I was fortunate in so many ways for the personal and professional growth I experienced during a postdoctoral fellowship at the American Culture Studies program at Washington University in St. Louis. Randy Calvert, a political scientist who is really an American Studies scholar at heart, pushed me to think more deeply about the policy implications of my arguments. Wayne Fields, more than anyone I have met, has a remarkable ability to ask one crystalizing question that moves a work forward and embodies the model of the publicly engaged scholar and teacher; we should all strive to cultivate his combination of humility, compassion, and intellectual commitment. Heidi Kolk became my thought partner in many ways, and one of the highlights of my professional life has been teaching a course on American remembrance with her. Matt Mancini was a tireless supporter. Matt Wilkens read drafts and made me think about new possibilities. Dave Walsh solved my technology problems. Tina Marti, Brenda Laymance, and Debra Kennard made the trains run on time.

Franklin & Marshall College has been an ideal place at which to complete this book. Alison Kibler may be the best department chair in academia. She not only scheduled my courses so that I had time to write but also helped me learn how to balance teaching so that I could finish the book. When I was coming in at five in the morning to write, she brought me coffee and donuts. Van Gosse read the entire manuscript and made important comments, and Dennis Deslippe always had time for conversations about recent American culture. Greg Kaliss read drafts and offered much-needed encouragement and, along with Leigh, fed me. Carla Willard let me borrow her dog, Max, when I was having a tough day and always believed in me. David Schuyler and Louise Stevenson modeled an enduring commitment to scholarship and teaching. Meg Massey in the Shadek-Fackenthal library's interlibrary loan office amazed me with her ability to track down obscure sources. Doug Anthony, Lisa Stillwell, Sue Mennicke, and the rest of the Posse kept me sane.

Many colleagues from other institutions also helped make this book possible, but three were most important. Kristin Ann Hass wrote the book that made me want to go to graduate school and offered advice and support as our scholarly interests became even more closely aligned. Four years ago I e-mailed Rebecca Adelman out of the blue because her work sounded interesting, and I am thrilled that we've become friends. She read my entire manuscript and offered critical insights as I finished my manuscript a month after she finished hers. Ed Martini has supported this project from the beginning. His thorough reading of the completed manuscript made it a better book, and I am grateful for his insight and his friendship. Ed introduced me to Clark Dougan, Chris Appy, and the University of Massachusetts Press. Clark believed in this project from our first conversation in 2008 and has been a steady hand and calming influence. He also made sure that the manuscript got a rigorous review. Erika Doss and Patrick Hagopian offered detailed, insightful, and challenging comments that made the book so much stronger. Lawrence Kenney's copyediting made the book more readable.

This book has depended on material from more than a dozen archives, and I am grateful for the funds from Washington University in St. Louis, Franklin & Marshall College, and the American Heritage Center at the University of Wyoming that allowed me to travel to most of them. Eric Leonard at Andersonville National Historic Site and Barbara Black at the Flight 93 National Memorial always made time and space for me, even as they were busy running historical sites. I am grateful to the archivists at the Daughters of the Republic of Texas Library, Mokie Pratt Porter and Mark Leepson at the Vietnam Veterans of America, Bill Davis at the National Archives, Rich Baker and Terry Foster at the Army Heritage and Education Center, and Jill Severn at the Russell Library. Jill tracked down documents that appear in these pages; so did Catherine Kisluk at the National Park Service's Denver Service Center; Tom Converse at Columbus State University; Rachael Altman and Debbie Wheeler at the Bush Presidential Library; Brian McNerney at the LBJ Presidential Library; Tom Shelton at the University of Texas, San Antonio; and Amy Canon at the San Antonio City Archives. Irene Garza helped me look for sources, too. The Provost's Office at Franklin & Marshall provided me with funds to hire Leah Brenner, who cheerfully checked every footnote, saving me a tremendous amount of time and more than a little embarrassment.

A version of chapter 4 originally appeared as "Humanitarian Intervention: Cultural Remembrance and the Reading of Somalia as Vietnam," in *Media and Mobilization: The (de)Mobilizing Effects of Media Portrayals of Human Rights Activism*, ed. Tristan Borer (London: Zed Books, 2012). A segment of chapter 6 was published as "'It's a Different Time. It's a Different Era. It's a

Different Place': The Legacy of Vietnam and Contemporary Memoirs of the Wars in Iraq and Afghanistan," in *War and Society* 31.1 (2012): 65–84. © Maney Publishing (www.maneyonline/war). I am grateful to each publisher for permission to republish this work.

My most important debts are personal, and so I save them for last. I was fortunate to grow up in a family in which education was important. My father, Richard Kieran, wasn't around for my graduate school years and what came after, but he would have loved hearing about every aspect of the research, writing, and teaching. My mother, Mary Anne Kieran, has been a tireless cheerleader for this project. So have my aunt, Kathy Dolley, and my sister, Kathleen Kieran. I was lucky to marry into a wonderfully supportive family that includes Susan Gilmore, Elsbeth and Jamie Iannone, Carrie and Rob Wagner, and Sam, Megan, Marshall, and Nora. Many friends deserve thanks, but Anne Litchfield and Sasha and Eduardo Nunes in particular have cared about this book, and for me, since the beginning.

Because they are the deepest my final thanks go to Emma Gilmore Kieran. A lot has happened over the decade since we packed up and headed south so that I could start graduate school. But one thing that has been constant has been her support for me. For more than a dozen years—from the beginning of graduate school through years of a long-distance marriage to the nights and weekends I was cooped up in my office writing—no one has done more to sustain me personally and professionally, and she has done it while achieving personal and professional successes of her own. My debts to her are far too vast to be explained in one paragraph. So I will only say thank you and tell her, once again, how lucky I am.

FOREVER VIETNAM

★★★

INTRODUCTION

"I KNOW WHAT IT'S LIKE"

On September 9, 2010, Tony Sklock and his wife, Linda, visited the temporary memorial to Flight 93, the hijacked airliner that had crashed in rural Pennsylvania on September 11, 2001, when some of the passengers and crew attacked the hijackers. The National Park Service (NPS) had recently moved the memorial to a rusting Quonset hut overlooking the crash site and the construction of the permanent memorial scheduled to open a year later. Inside the hut there were panels explaining the events of September 11 and the recovery effort, pictures of the passengers and crew, plans for the permanent memorial, and a segment of the original temporary memorial fence. Hanging from the fence were items that the volunteer ambassadors at the site had chosen from among thousands in the memorial's collection to represent the diversity of objects left by visitors. Among them were two patches memorializing servicemen killed in Iraq, one of which declared, "All Gave Some . . . Some Gave All" and the other entreating viewers to "Never Forget." There was also a set of dog tags left by a wounded veteran and a hat declaring the owner to be an air force veteran of the Vietnam War. One of the volunteers had chosen to display this object because her son had deployed shortly after September 11. The NPS provided white five-by-seven-inch index cards on which visitors could record their thoughts and assured them that "your response will become part of the tribute collection of the Flight 93 National Memorial." Tony Sklock wrote on his card, "I'm very honored to be here and see the memorial. I know what it's like to sacrifice our lives for peace. Vietnam Veteran, 1970, 25th Infantry Division."

This collection of items, the choices made by the volunteer ambassadors and NPS officials, and Sklock's message raise critical questions about the intersections of the legacy of Vietnam, memorialization, and foreign policy in the contemporary United States. Why would a Vietnam veteran make a point of visiting the memorial and in addition use that visit to make a claim about his own experience? How does that claim rely on his reimagining of both the American experience in Vietnam and the events aboard Flight 93? Why would volunteers choose items that link the crash of Flight 93 to both the Vietnam War and the wars that followed the attacks of September 11? What does it mean that the NPS officially sanctioned those links by displaying the items at the memorial? And most crucially, why does it matter that Sklock and the volunteers adapted a memorial practice familiar from the Vietnam Veterans Memorial?

The answers to these questions are complex. Sklock's card implicitly claims that Vietnam veterans' experience somehow parallels that of Flight 93's celebrated dead, that he, too, "know[s] what it's like to sacrifice our lives for peace." Yet it is not immediately clear that there are, in fact, many parallels between the two groups. Sklock was a soldier, while the passengers and crew were civilians. Sklock fought in a controversial war waged to preserve America's global dominance during the Cold War, a war marked by deceit and flawed policymaking. The people aboard Flight 93 acted to save their own lives and those of civilians on the ground and had only the barest understanding of the political contours of the terrorist attacks in which they were caught up. Sklock's identification of his service in the Twenty-Fifth Infantry Division in 1970 hints that he likely participated in the invasion of Cambodia, a controversial escalation of an already unpopular war that generated widespread protests, including, infamously, those at Kent State University that culminated in the killing of four students by the Ohio National Guard.[1] The September 11, 2001, attacks reinvigorated narratives of American exceptionalism and support for American interventions abroad. Everyone aboard Flight 93 died, while Sklock survived. And perhaps most important, while the dominant memory of Vietnam posits, somewhat erroneously, that the nation ignored Vietnam veterans, many Americans immediately celebrated Flight 93's passengers and crew as models of patriotic heroism.

Sklock's card does not recognize inherent similarities between the two events but asserts that they exist. In writing what he did, he seeks to correct the last of these differences—the understanding of Vietnam veterans as marginalized and unappreciated—by aligning his own service with the events aboard the hijacked airliner. His appropriation of the Flight 93 Memorial contributes to a long-standing revisionist narrative that obscures the imperialist origins of the Vietnam conflict and America's devastation of Vietnam through claims that it was waged for peace and that American soldiers made the primary sacrifices.[2] Sklock's card reveals, however, that the recuperation of the Vietnam veteran remains tenuous and must be consistently reasserted. The items displayed at the memorial that link the Iraq War to the events of September 11 affirm the appropriateness of another controversial intervention in spite of the discredited connection between Iraq and the September 11 attacks. The patches remind visitors that "some gave all" and implore them to "never forget." These all are hedges against anxieties that the public mistreatment of Vietnam veterans, apocryphal though it may be, will repeat itself.[3] Taken together, the items show how hard Americans continue to work to resolve the Vietnam War's enduring trauma and prevent its recurrence. Moreover, they show that Americans have done this work at other meaningful sites of American memory by revising and redeploying memorial practices central to Vietnam's remembrance.

This book argues that the evolving and contested memory of the American War in Vietnam has shaped Americans' commemoration of other events in ways that inform their understanding of themselves, the nation, and the global interests and obligations of the United States. Sklock and the volunteer ambassadors who selected items to display at the Flight 93 Memorial are hardly unique. Over the past fifty years, the recalling, revising, and redeploying of the memorial practices and tropes central to the remembrance of Vietnam became the primary means through which Americans made remembrance of other events into vital spaces for debating issues about war, militarism, foreign policy, and veterans' affairs.

This process has addressed two kinds of questions that have been central to post-Vietnam culture in the United States. The first have been about the Vietnam War itself: Was the war a chaotic disaster beset by inequality, atrocity, and brutal violence that demands a rethinking of American militarism? Was it a well-intentioned, nobly fought conflict that was poorly managed and unsupported and should inspire a recommitment to exceptionalist narratives and interventionist policies?[4] Have its veterans, including those who remain unaccounted for in Indochina, received appropriate recognition? The second set of questions has been about U.S. foreign policy in the aftermath of the Vietnam War: Under what circumstances should the United States intervene? How should it do so? How should the public respond to such interventions?

These questions have been so persistent because of the Vietnam War's traumatic impact on American culture. It was, the literary critic John Hellman has argued, "the disruption of the American story."[5] If Kristin Hass's claim that Vietnam "proved challenging to a consistent understanding of American wars as virtuous" is somewhat understated, the cultural historian Katherine Kinney is more explicit: "Vietnam is the traumatic site which violates all images and assumptions of American identity."[6] The reasons are well known. A war that was begun and continued for dubious reasons, that was managed by dissembling policymakers, that was vigorously protested by much of the public, and that the United States lost dealt a tremendous blow to visions of the United States as a noble, unified, powerful nation. The atrocities that occurred as a matter of course and of official policy throughout the war undermined declarations that the war was morally justified and that the military was honorable.[7]

The Vietnam War generated new and troubling questions about the nation, the military, and the role of the United States in the world, and it is difficult to overstate how central the project of recovering from the war has been since the fall of Saigon in 1975. These efforts have focused on new problems, including veterans' mental health and the recognition of post-traumatic stress disorder (PTSD), anxieties about Agent Orange, and the unprecedented interest in American servicemen's unrecovered remains.[8] They have also increasingly demanded the uncritical, depoliticized celebration of Vietnam veterans as part of what Patrick Hagopian has called "a therapeutic discourse of wounds and healing [that] began to supersede other ways of remembering the war."[9] Political and military leaders, meanwhile, persistently avow that future military interventions will not repeat the errors of Vietnam, though exactly what those errors were continues to be contested. Many Americans have come to view the war as a disaster from the outset, marked by American hubris and a fatal overreliance on military power that demonstrates a need for more circumspection in the use of military power.[10] Between the 1980s and the midpoint of the Iraq and Afghanistan wars, however, American culture began to evince a renewed faith in American militarism and the exceptionalist narratives that presented the United States as a morally upright, benevolent superpower able to effectively use military power to achieve its global interests and fulfill its ambitions.[11]

Americans' remembrances of Vietnam in myriad cultural locations, including novels and memoirs, memorial sites and political speeches, films and museum exhibits, have provided a key means of constructing and negotiating these narratives. These efforts required new practices and representational strategies, most notably the design of the Vietnam Veterans Memorial and the practices that emerged there, but also, for example, new styles of war memoir.[12] They have shaped Americans' memorialization of other wars as well; as Hass explains, "The crisis of patriotism produced by the Vietnam War created a need to reassert U.S. nationalism in particular terms, and . . . honoring the memory of American soldiers who served in Vietnam inspired a demand to produce more memory of more soldiers. War memorials on the [National] Mall emerged as important sites at which to do just this."[13] Yet as Sklock's message reveals, Americans have also turned to other sites of memory, ones that ostensibly have nothing to do with Vietnam, and recalled and revised memorial practices and discourses central to Vietnam's legacy to use those sites to answer the critical questions of Vietnam's aftermath.[14]

To explore how they have done so, I examine the recent remembrance of six events, three of which are historically antecedent to the Vietnam War and three subsequent to it: the incarceration of Union troops at Andersonville Prison during the Civil War; the experience of combat in the Second World War; the siege of the Alamo during the Texas revolution in 1836; the American intervention in Somalia in 1993; the crash of United Airlines Flight 93 on September 11, 2001; and the Iraq and Afghanistan wars. These are disparate events, as unrelated to each other as they are to the Vietnam War; and yet they belong together in this study for four reasons. First, the remembrance of each was constructed or revised in the wake of Vietnam and amid controversies over foreign and domestic policy that themselves follow from and are central to Vietnam's legacy. Second, each demonstrates how Americans have invoked divergent, at times competing legacies of Vietnam and used the practices and narratives through which those legacies have been constructed to define the event's contemporary import. Third, these six examples, which encompass the sweep of American militarism from 1836 to 2011, show not only the range of sites to which Americans have turned as they have sought to make sense of and recuperate from the Vietnam War but also how deeply Vietnam's legacy has saturated American culture; it has reshaped the remembrance of events both long celebrated, like the Second World War, and briefly controversial, like the Somalia intervention, and has done so for periods that ranged from a few days, as at the Alamo, to several decades, as at Andersonville. Finally, the examples reveal that the use of practices central to Vietnam's legacy to remember other events has, with a few exceptions, worked to resolve the anxieties of post-Vietnam culture in ways that affirm the continued embrace of American militarism, truncate debates about the wisdom of American military interventions, and obscure not just the violence done during those interventions but also its impact on both those who commit it and those who endure it.

This book joins a rich body of scholarship on the Vietnam War and its legacy. Yet it is neither a history of the war nor, strictly speaking, an analysis of how it has been remembered.[15] Neither is it a comprehensive history of any of the six events whose remembrance I analyze, for each has been well studied by others. Rather, I build on this scholarship by asking how Vietnam's remembrance has impacted American memorial practice generally, and how its legacies have shaped the most important political debates of the war's aftermath. I go beyond pointing out that much debate about post-Vietnam military culture is "about Vietnam." Tracking the seemingly automatic comparisons of Vietnam to proposed military interventions, or noting, for example, that more recent memorials do or do not look like the Vietnam Veterans Memorial are important undertakings, but they don't tell the complete story. Neither does noting that cultural texts and sites of memory participate in specific policy debates. In the chapters that follow, I show how various stakeholders used Vietnam's legacy to craft that participation in culturally legible ways. My goal in this book is to illuminate the wider story of how the remembrance of one event has created the conditions according to which Americans have meaningfully remembered other, seemingly unrelated, events.

In studying how Vietnam's legacy has shaped remembrance of other events, I follow the work of memory studies scholars who have investigated similar patterns in other contexts. Andreas Huyssen, for example, analyzes the impact of Holocaust remembrance on Argentinian memorials to victims of the military junta and identifies a "global politics of memory" in which the "productive inscription of certain tropes and images, ethical and political evaluations. . . . functions like an international prism that helps focus the local discourse about the *desaparecidos* [the disappeared] in both its legal and its commemorative aspects."[16] I also draw on the formulation of Jay Winter, the foremost historian of war and memory, who writes that "the [European] survivors of the First World War [represent] the first (though not the last) 'generation of memory' in the twentieth century" because "the images, languages, and practices which appeared in the aftermath of the Great War shaped the ways in which future conflicts were imagined and remembered."[17]

The same is true about the remembrance of the Vietnam War in the United States. Vietnam's legacy supplied the narratives and memorial practices through which Americans have transformed other sites of memory into spaces in which they could tell stories about Vietnam and its aftermath and engage with critical questions of post-Vietnam American culture.[18] Through this deeply political process, Americans have engaged in larger debates about foreign and domestic policy in four ways. First, in limited cases they have challenged dominant, celebratory narratives of American militarism that posit the atrocity, trauma, and dissent surrounding Vietnam as an aberration and other American wars as noble and necessary by remembering those wars in ways that accord with dominant understandings of Vietnam.[19] Second, they have encouraged recuperation from Vietnam's trauma by revising the remembrance of historically antecedent events in ways that legitimize revisionist narratives of Vietnam, celebrate the Vietnam War itself, and reassert the value of militarism and interventionist foreign policies. Third, Americans have responded to post-Vietnam military engagements by alternately constructing them as being like or unlike Vietnam in order to define as acceptable only those unilateral military interventions that support a narrow set of national interests that perpetuate U.S. empire. Finally, they have revised memorial practices that initially expressed critiques or ambivalence about service in Vietnam in ways that foster a depoliticized, uncritical celebration of the military.[20]

With the exception of the first of these debates, such remembrances have sought to resolve the anxieties about race, class, and gender and about the place and role of the United States in the world that are central to the Vietnam War's traumatic history. Such anxieties may surface in diverse ways, whether in the racialized representation of the Vietnamese, the racial and economic inequalities of the military, worries about American manhood given the outcome of the war, and related fears of national powerlessness.[21] The use of the tropes and narratives central to Vietnam's remembrance has made other sites of memory into spaces for responding to these preoccupations, whether in the case of activists working on prisoner of war and missing in action (POW/MIA) issues to further a narrative of the ruptured family at Andersonville or in veterans' efforts to articulate a white, male, working-class patriotism at the Alamo or the Flight 93 Memorial.

My focus on how veterans, their families, government officials, politicians, and others have constructed these memories is informed by theorists who view remembrance as a process in which individuals and groups construct narratives of the past in order to engage with the central issues of their cultural moment. As the historian Fitzhugh Brundage explains, "For individuals and groups alike, memory forms an essential component of their social identity. . . . Groups invariably fashion their own image of the world and their place in it by establishing an accepted vision of the past, a sort of genealogy of identity."[22] Remembering, he insists, is deliberate and involves "the active labor of selecting, structuring, and imposing meaning on the past rather than the mere reproduction of inherent historical truths."[23] Jay Winter agrees, explaining that the term *remembrance* is preferable to *memory* because "to privilege 'remembrance' is to insist on specifying agency, on answering the question who remembers, when, where, and how?" "Collective remembrance," he continues, ". . . points to time and place above all, to evidence, to traces enabling us to understand what groups of people try to do when they act in public to conjure up the past."[24] Following these injunctions, I am interested not only in identifying the choices particular stakeholders have made as they mobilized Vietnam's legacy to remember each event but also in untangling the political stakes and consequences of those choices.

I analyze widely available sources, including best-selling memoirs and nonfiction narratives, museum exhibits, and memorials as well as archival materials, some of which have gone previously unexamined, including museum scripts (that is, the narrative plans for museum exhibits), NPS planning documents, remarks made by political leaders, and items left at the Flight 93 Memorial. I also rely on media coverage to recreate moments, such as the opening of the National Prisoner of War Museum at Andersonville and the Vietnam veterans' vigil at the Alamo in 1985, and to place these acts of commemoration in their historical context. I inspect government documents, including the *Congressional Record*, transcripts of congressional hearings, internal documents of congressional committees, and papers from the United States Army, to delve into larger, ongoing debates about the military, veterans, and the country's global responsibilities.

In many cases the archival record shows that individuals explicitly remembered events in ways that drew on Vietnam remembrance and entered into debates about the war. For example, Sklock's note is but one of many similar items at the Flight 93 Memorial, and the producers of the Public Broadcasting Service (PBS) drama *The Andersonville Trial* (1970) actively promoted the program as a commentary on Lt. William Calley's trial for murder in the aftermath of the My Lai massacre. In other cases, the influence is less clearly articulated, and I rely on discursive analysis to show the more subtle ways in which Vietnam's legacy has shaped Americans' remembrance of other events. For example, I probe the affinities between Vietnam memoirs and Second World War memoirs written after Vietnam that enabled the latter texts to challenge dominant understandings of the earlier war. I do the same with neoconservative rhetoric that applied revisionist remembrances of Vietnam to promote more aggressive foreign policies in the 1980s and the commemorative rhetoric that simultaneously surrounded the Alamo. Combining these methods, I reveal that Americans' use of Vietnam's remembrance to talk about other events and vice versa represents a key way in which citizens have sought to heal, both individually and nationally, the damage that the war visited on American culture.

The book begins with a survey of how, starting in 1965, Americans have persistently used Andersonville's remembrance to address troubling aspects of Vietnam's legacy. The infamous Civil War prison, in which thousands of Union prisoners of war died, reentered the American imagination when an African American Green Beret who had been killed in Vietnam was buried there after being denied that right in his hometown, where the cemetery was segregated. Coverage of the episode affirmed narratives of African American military citizenship by casting Andersonville as a space in which the federal government's appropriate memorialization had previously righted southern injustices against American soldiers, thereby validating contemporary rhetoric of a nation aware of the costs of war, appropriately honoring its dead, and thus not engaging in military adventurism.

The chapter then turns to the promotion and reception of *The Andersonville Trial,* a drama specifically marketed by producers and understood by reviewers as a comment on Calley's trial and an indictment of a culture that enabled such violence but refused to take collective responsibility for it. The chapter next interrogates a shift in the curation and use of Andersonville, a National Historic Site, from its initial invocations in support of President Richard Nixon's Vietnam policies through a moment in which NPS interpretation spoke to post-Vietnam war weariness to its increasing appropriation by POW/MIA activists, who used the site's prominence to call for continued action on POW/MIA issues. The chapter closes with an analysis of Andersonville's National Prisoner of War Museum, which presents a revisionist remembrance in which the Vietnam War was dominated by Vietnamese brutality and American suffering.

In the second chapter I discuss remembrance of the Second World War from the late 1970s to the mid-1990s. During this period, medical literature posited that many Second World War and Korean War veterans suffered from symptoms of chronic PTSD identical to those plaguing Vietnam veterans. This revelation led to vigorous legislative debates over the extension of readjustment counseling benefits to older veterans; while veterans' groups and liberal legislators saw this as a necessity, some conservatives saw it as fiscally unwise and, moreover, refused to believe that older veterans continued to suffer from combat-induced mental health issues. In the midst of these debates, three of the most important memoirists of the Second World War redeployed the language and tropes of Vietnam memoirs to cast their experience as similarly traumatic, constructing a set of narratives that buttressed claims that older veterans were long suffering.

I next turn to the Alamo, the venerated shrine in San Antonio at which 187 men died defending the site in the most notable battle of the Texan war for independence in 1836. In the 1980s both conservatives, worried about the Vietnam syndrome, and Vietnam veterans, angry about what they perceived as their marginalization, seized upon the Alamo and its unquestionable place in the pantheon of American patriotism as a central site for recuperation. I first consider how speakers' rhetoric and media coverage surrounding the Alamo's 150th anniversary in 1986 borrowed from the language of Vietnam revisionists and proponents of a renewed commitment to interventionist foreign policy. Figures like Norman Podhoretz, a leading neoconservative who was the longtime editor in chief of *Commentary* magazine, and Nixon, for example, painted Vietnam as a well-intentioned if misbegotten war and argued for a renewed commitment to American militarism. In the same moment, media coverage of the Alamo commemoration, including the sesquicentennial keynote address by then–Vice President George H. W. Bush, cast the defenders of the Alamo as historical examples of that neoconservative interventionism. This rhetoric, which borrowed from and echoed that of Podhoretz, Nixon, and others, interpreted the defenders as American men who had gone to Texas solely to assist a struggling nation free itself from a despotic ruler, a rewriting of Alamo memory that postulated a historical precedent which retroactively validated the Vietnam War as a noble and necessary undertaking.

I next tell the story of the Last Patrol, a veterans' organization founded by two singer-songwriters who led a march and vigil at the Alamo over Veterans Day weekend in 1985. Ostensibly an effort to raise POW/MIA awareness, it in fact aimed to establish a positive image of the Vietnam veteran and demand improved government services. The Last Patrol rewrote Alamo memory according to the participants' recollection of their service, recalling the Alamo defenders as being politically disengaged, knowingly fighting a losing battle, and fighting for their comrades rather than for any larger cause. For both groups, revising the memory of the Alamo established a historical precedent that legitimized their understanding of Vietnam and their contemporary political imperatives.

The final three chapters highlight Vietnam's significance in American remembrance after the end of the Cold War. Chapter 4 addresses Americans' misgivings about the possibility of military commitments to ensure human rights in the 1990s. The most noteworthy literature about the Somalia intervention in 1993 that killed nineteen Americans, especially Mark Bowden's best-selling *Black Hawk Down*, drew on the tropes and narratives central to recent popular and critically acclaimed memoirs that had construed the Vietnam war as a well-intentioned mistake. In doing so, this literature called into question the notion that U.S. military power could or should be used in multilateral peacekeeping operations.

The fifth and sixth chapters deal with the global war on terror. Chapter 5 examines the remembrance of Flight 93, the jet hijacked on September 11, 2001, that failed to reach its destination because of a passenger revolt. Portrayals of the passengers and crew on that plane see them as archetypal Americans and models for the interventionist foreign policy that defined the global war on terror declared by the administration of President George W. Bush. That language relies on the themes and motifs of post-Vietnam films to construct the people aboard Flight 93 as American bodies fully recuperated from the Vietnam syndrome—strong, fearless, and willing to intervene forcefully to protect themselves and others.

I then turn to both informal and formal memorialization of the crash site, showing that veterans of Vietnam and the more recent wars in Iraq and Afghanistan have persistently appropriated the site as a space in which they can affirm their own patriotic citizenship by aligning themselves with those who died aboard the plane. Such preemption, however, required that they revise the act of remembrance most central to the Vietnam Veterans Memorial, that is, the leaving of objects. While the Vietnam Veterans Memorial has been a place where diverse views about the war have been articulated, veterans and military families who visited and placed objects at the temporary Flight 93 Memorial nearly universally did so in order to warrant their service as noble, patriotic, and in the nation's best traditions. The result was the transformation of the Flight 93 Memorial into a militarized site that endorses interventionist foreign policies. These uses of Flight 93's remembrance continue, I argue, at the permanent memorial, which borrows from but revises elements of Maya Lin's design at the Vietnam Veterans Memorial in ways that enable a similar experience for visitors even while protecting the dominant narrative of heroic patriotism.

Finally, I examine competing mobilizations of Vietnam's legacy within debates over the Iraq and Afghanistan wars. I begin by showing that opponents of the troop surge of 2007 in Iraq invoked a remembrance of patriotic, morally justified anti–Vietnam War activism by well-known liberals—particularly that of Martin Luther King Jr.—to vindicate their rejection of Bush administration policies. I then turn to memoirs written by Iraq and Afghanistan veterans between 2005 and 2009 to uncover how they invert key scenes of the most important Vietnam memoirs in ways that distance the contemporary military and the current wars from critiques that rely on comparisons to Vietnam. Through such distancing, I contend, the memoirs obscure the wars' violence, construct them as acceptable, and assert that the military is an essential institution in American public life.

Taken together, the chapters demonstrate the frequency with which Americans have employed the narratives and memorial practices central to Vietnam's legacy to make the remembrance of other events useful within the debates about foreign policy and veterans' affairs that have dominated the post-Vietnam era. They also reveal that the rare moments in which the potential of Vietnam's remembrance to critique American militarism created the conditions under which veterans could seek better services or Americans could vigorously debate the morality and wisdom of U.S. foreign policy have been overshadowed by its mobilization and revision in ways that validate a foreign policy defined by aggressive, unilateral interventionism and the continued celebration of American militarism.

In untangling Americans' reliance on the legacy of Vietnam as they remember other events, I want to delineate more fully the contours of many Americans' enduring embrace of militarism, often uncritical acquiescence to the use of military force abroad, and continued failure to acknowledge the crises that those interventions prompt in the lives of veterans, their families, and the civilians who experience them. My argument is not inherently antimilitary or anti-interventionist. Nor do I argue against remembering the wars fought by the United States and the soldiers who fought in them. The military is a crucial institution in the nation's culture, there are times when military force is not only justified but necessary, and the sacrifices of those who serve are worthy of recognition. Belief in such certainties, however, does not absolve Americans from the need to have difficult conversations about how the United States might use its military power less cavalierly and about the global impact of the use of that power. Neither can it prevent Americans from acknowledging that recognizing soldiers' sacrifices requires effectively confronting the postwar struggles that many veterans face. My hope is that the book's illuminating of one way in which Americans have at times encouraged but often prevented these conversations over the past fifty years will lead to more robust and candid debate about these issues in the next fifty.

CHAPTER 1

"HOW FAR IS ANDERSONVILLE FROM VIETNAM?"

Vietnam Revisionism and Andersonville National Historic Site

On April 9, 1998, Sen. John McCain (R-AZ) delivered the keynote address at the dedication of the National Prisoner of War Museum at Andersonville National Historic Site, the former Confederate prison site in southern Georgia. McCain told the story of Lance Sijan, an air force pilot shot down in Vietnam in November 1967 and taken captive on Christmas Day a month later. "Interrogated repeatedly," McCain explained, "he refused to say anything" and "was savagely beaten for his silence, kicked repeatedly and beaten with a bamboo club."[1] Ministered to by his fellow soldiers, who "talked quietly to him of his courage and faith," Sijan eventually died at the hands of his captors.[2] McCain exhorted all Americans to "carry his dignity with you. Keep his memory alive, confident in your faith that almighty God blessed him and gave him the strength to prevail over his enemies."[3] After the ceremony a woman who in childhood had worn a POW/MIA bracelet engraved with McCain's name hugged the senator. The next day a local newspaper columnist mused, "While I was celebrating my first birthday with my family, [McCain] was there, not knowing if he would ever get back to his."[4]

McCain's speech and the public response to it demonstrate that Andersonville is a site at which the dominant story of the Vietnam War prisoner of war experience, one that has long been central to revisionist remembrances of the war, has been validated.[5] His rhetoric and the media coverage of it hit familiar notes: in Vietnam brutal savages tortured unfalteringly patriotic Americans; at home, wives worried in agony, and patriotic youngsters kept a hopeful vigil.[6] The dedication was not the first moment in which the larger claims of post-Vietnam POW/MIA activists were validated at Andersonville. McCain failed to call for the "fullest possible accounting" of missing servicemen, but otherwise his remarks fit neatly into activists' and officials' nearly two-decade-long history of using Andersonville to affirm Vietnam-era POWs' sacrifices and suffering, legitimize the myths central to the POW/MIA movement, and call for or promise continued efforts to locate missing Americans.[7]

That activists would so use Andersonville, designated by Congress as the national memorial to prisoners of war, is not surprising. Andersonville's gruesome history—reports vary, but some twelve to thirteen thousand Union soldiers died there in conditions so horrid that the prison commandant, Capt. Henry Wirz, was executed for war crimes—has made it attractive in this regard, as it raises questions about the nature of prisoners' experience, moral responsibility, and public commemoration while telling a story whose horrific details are rivaled perhaps only by remembrances of Vietnam.

However, these uses were neither predetermined nor automatic. For Andersonville to become such a space, Americans had to bring to it, and construct its memory according to, the narratives that simultaneously dominated their thinking about Vietnam. I examine here how the changing remembrance of the former Civil War prison and the remembrances of other wars that have taken place at the site have enabled evolving critiques of American policies regarding Vietnam.[8] After beginning with the story of a Green Beret whose burial at Andersonville in 1966 assuaged fears that the nation insufficiently recognized African American soldiers' sacrifices in Vietnam, I turn to the PBS production in 1970 of Saul Levitt's play *The Andersonville Trial* (1958), which the network explicitly publicized as a commentary on both the My Lai massacre and a culture that sought to wash its hands of responsibility for the atrocities of the war. Americans' use of Andersonville to respond to the injustices of the war shifted, however, with the official establishment of the Andersonville National Historic Site in 1970. Although the NPS's curation initially intimated that the war had been futile, beginning in the 1980s and most markedly since the opening of the National Prisoner of War Museum in 1998 activists have insistently used the park, often with NPS sanction, to validate the POW/MIA movement's revisionist account of Vietnam. Together, these three moments demonstrate that Andersonville has been a place at which Americans have abandoned a critical interrogation of the racially problematic and imperialist policies central to the war and embraced a remembrance that emphasizes American suffering, vilifies the Vietnamese, and celebrates American militarism.[9]

"Surrounded by the Graves of Other American Fighting Men"

On May 27, 1966, the Friday before Memorial Day, the name Pfc. Jimmy L. Williams, Wetumpka appeared third from the top in the *Birmingham News*'s weekly list of Alabamans killed in Vietnam.[10] Sandwiched between Victor R. O'Neal, from Birmingham, and Sammy A. Barga, from Anniston, the name might ordinarily have passed without notice. Williams was one of nearly 150 American servicemen killed that week in Vietnam and one of more than 1,100 Alabamans who would ultimately die in the war, many of them from similarly small, rural communities like Pittsview, Eight Mile, and Mulga.[11] Within a few days, however, Wetumpka refused to bury Williams, an African American, in its segregated cemetery. That decision, by making visible the persistent racial inequality that marked the nation and the war, threatened to upend claims that the United States appropriately honored its fallen soldiers. This danger was avoided when Williams's casket was lowered into plot E-163 at Andersonville National Cemetery, a site that newspapers established as representing the nation's historical fulfillment of its promises to soldiers and its capacity to overcome past injustices.

Memorial Day weekend in 1966 was not a promising time for supporters of the war. News of the Twenty-Fifth Infantry Division's successful operation in the Central Highlands paled next to reports of record casualties, accounts of violent student protests in Hue, and stories of Buddhist monks sending President Johnson letters written in their own blood and staging public self-immolations.[12] At home, the news was hardly better. In New York white-robed protesters led a mock funeral procession for the war's dead in Central Park, and Congress began investigating draft inequality.[13] An editorial in the *Mobile Press-Register* captured the national mood: "Nowhere in its history has the United States been bogged down in a situation identical in miserable aspects."[14]

Johnson sought to use the holiday to shore up support for the war, connecting the sacrifices of "Americans [who] will be fighting and dying in Vietnam on this Memorial Day, 1966, in fulfillment of our commitment to freedom" to their predecessors who "gave their lives that men might live and prosper in freedom." He declared, "We shall not forsake their sacrifice. We shall—because we must—persevere."[15] At the Tomb of the Unknowns in Arlington National Cemetery Johnson hailed the valor of Americans in Vietnam, saying, "On this Memorial Day it is right for us to remember the living and the dead for whom the call of their country has meant much pain and sacrifice."[16]

The setting was deeply symbolic, as the Tomb of the Unknowns had long been a place where the nation met its obligation to remember fallen soldiers. Johnson's wreath laying there underscored Pentagon reports that "the Viet Nam war is without a single unknown American fallen in battle."[17] This story, along with a cartoon of Uncle Sam in the *San Francisco Examiner,* his head bowed as he faces a military cemetery and announces, "None is unknown to me," buttressed Johnson's efforts to evoke a righteous nation solemnly aware of its sacrifices and not cavalierly engaged in military adventurism.[18]

Similar rhetoric appeared in other newspapers across the country. The *Examiner,* observing that "this nation was born in battle. . . . [and] in the hearts of men who prized liberty enough to die for it," asked, "And how about those in Vietnam who are still paying? Is not Memorial Day an appropriate time to reflect on them and the duty they are so bravely discharging in their country's behalf?"[19] The *Philadelphia Inquirer* opined, "Memorial Day means a little more this year" because "each day boys are dying and another name is added to an honor roll in a township or city."[20] The *Boston Globe* reminded its readers that "caskets containing American bodies are arriving home by plane every day, and in thousands of homes today's grief crowds out all others."[21] The *New York Times* pointed to the holiday's origins in remembering both Union and Confederate dead as evidence that whatever "conflict of minds over Vietnam" existed, "for those who died in that faraway land all conflict is over. They rest in peace and in honor."[22] Around the country, rhetoric about appropriate remembrance on Memorial Day served as a means of sidestepping political debates about the war.

African American newspapers used the holiday to valorize black Americans' military service. For many African Americans, service in Vietnam continued long-standing traditions that viewed military service as both evidence of and an avenue leading to national belonging.[23] As James Westheider argues, "African-Americans often welcomed their assignment to Vietnam in the early days of the war" because "it was . . . the first in which African-Americans ostensibly had the same opportunities as whites."[24] This led, he contends, to portrayals of African Americans as "good soldiers," men who "just did their jobs to the best of their abilities and did not question too deeply the war itself or the basic fabric of American society."[25]

If the fissures that later became fractures in African American support for the war—uneasiness with draft inequality and death rates chief among them—were apparent, newspapers also endeavored to bolster African Americans' reputations as "Good Soldiers."[26] The *(Baltimore) Afro-American,* which, Lawrence Eldridge writes, generally "held its nose over Vietnam," ran a front-page story about African American graduates of West Point.[27] The *Chicago Defender* declared, "Memorial Day belongs to the Negro too—for there were 200,000 Negroes fighting the Civil War, with many being cited for valor," and "Negro men" from all wars "are at last being credited for their valor."[28] Like other papers, these implied that regardless of any doubts one might have about the war, appropriately acknowledging those who fought in it was a patriotic obligation.

As the *Examiner*'s cartoon and photos of Johnson's wreath laying demonstrate, national cemeteries became the most appropriate sites of such recognition. Several major newspapers showed flag-decorated gravestones and people visiting cemeteries.[29] On Memorial Day the front page of the *Washington Post* showed a marine honor guard burying a Vietnam casualty "as the nation prepares to honor the military dead from past and present conflicts" and described a wreath laying at the grave of a former Tomb of the Unknowns guard who had chosen his own gravesite before deploying to Vietnam.[30] Cartoons amplified this theme: in the *Mobile Register,* a flag flying at half staff among white crosses; in the *Afro-American,* a gigantic wreath labeled "Viet Nam Casualties" hovering over rows of white crosses, under which a caption reads, " 'That They Have Not Died in Vain' Our Memorial Day Prayer"; in the *Chicago Defender,* the spirit of a presumably African American soldier salutes Uncle Sam and speaks to him: "Sir, Tell Them Ours Is a Country to be Proud Of."[31]

Eight hundred miles south of Arlington National Cemetery, at Andersonville, this narrative was being sorely tested. Others have noted the broad outlines of the controversy that began when military pallbearers escorted Williams's casket from Vietnam to the W. T. Goodman Funeral Home in Wetumpka. When Williams, a paratrooper in the 173rd Airborne, died in combat on May 19, the mayor of the town, a local barber named Demp Thrash, told the family that both the African American and white sections of the local cemetery were full. He offered the Williams family a plot reserved for the indigent on the graveyard's fringes, while another, private, cemetery announced that it practiced rigid segregation.[32] Over the next four days, newspapers exploded with echoes of the claims about patriotism, remembrance, and African American military service that appeared in that weekend's news. When Williams was finally buried at Andersonville, media coverage construed the space as one at which the South's historical injustices toward American soldiers had been and could again be assuaged through appropriate remembrance.

Thrash at first defended himself and Wetumpka, which had "received many calls from around the nation asking if the city had denied its war hero a proper burial place," by saying that the town had "never had any racial trouble" and that "white and colored people live next door to each other in harmony."[33] Moreover, he embraced the rhetoric of race-blind military citizenship, saying he had "full respect for any man, white or colored, who dies serving his country."[34] Wetumpka's racial politics were not that rosy, however. A year earlier, the local NAACP chapter had reported that "the most outstanding achievement [in 1965] was to get a branch operating in Elmore County again" but that "there are still many who are reluctant to join. . . . There still seems to be great fear for some to belong to the organization."[35] That fear was not shared by the Williams family, however, because as of April 1968 three of Jimmy Williams's siblings were members of Elmore County's NAACP Youth Council.[36] Indeed, the refusal to bury Williams was likely retribution for their activism.[37] On May 25, Fred Gray, a civil rights activist and the pastor of the church where Williams's funeral was to be held, telephoned the Washington bureau of the NAACP to report that "the difficulty confronting the Williams family is due to its efforts to desegregate the schools" and that "this is one of the few families that have been willing to seek the right for their children to attend desegregated schools."[38] Certainly, the townspeople didn't seem to be welcoming Williams's body with open arms. The mayor told an army survivor's assistance officer that "some niggers own graves in the colored section which they trade back and forth. Why don't you go talk to them?" Gray reported that "one of the [Williams] children indicated that a white boy said 'it should have been you who was killed.' "[39]

Williams's death became a national issue because it showed Wetumpka's failure to meet the national obligations that the Good Soldier discourse required on Memorial Day in 1966. People across the nation quickly tied the matter to the larger civil rights movement. "It really hurts," Williams's mother told reporters, "not to have him recognized as a first-class American citizen in death. . . . In all his life in Wetumpka the white people never recognized him as one."[40] A mourner at his wake told a reporter from the *New York Times* that "I think when a soldier goes off and gives his life for another country, then his people should have freedom here."[41] Williams's mistreatment became a symbol of the South's enduring racism and its larger failure to meet national obligations.

The sense of injustice was amplified by newspapers' mobilization of an already established idealization of the Green Berets to situate Williams within a narrative that linked racial progress, masculinity, and military service.[42] *Jet* magazine showed Williams in his beret and called him a "Negro hero"; in newspapers he was called a "Green Beret paratrooper," a "Special Forces pfc.," "a Negro Special Forces paratrooper," and "a member of the elite Green Beret corps."[43] On a weekend when the government trumpeted the lack of unknown dead in Vietnam, Williams's mother told reporters, "I do not want my son buried in some out of the way place for unknown people. . . . My son was not a shoeshine boy like his father. He was a soldier, a paratrooper in the Green Berets."[44] The tragedy here was less that Williams had died than that his sacrifice had gone unappreciated and, more broadly, that the nation had violated its promise to servicemen.

The controversy quickly reached the White House. On May 27 the Williams family sent a telegram that explicitly positioned Williams within the Good Soldier theme, explaining that he had "lost his life in defense of his country in Viet Nam" and calling on Johnson to keep his promise that the nation would respect its fallen soldiers: "We know that this narrow-minded and shameful conduct has no place in the Great Society that you are trying to build for all our country's people."[45] The telegram closed by demanding that Johnson "direct that he be buried in one of our national cemeteries with the affection and respect that our nation gives to its sons who died in battle."[46]Another letter, written by Jamie McCracken, a New Yorker, asked whether Alabamans were "so blind until they can't see that this negro soldier died for black as well as the white" and reminded Johnson that "our ex-president asked us the young people of America 'to ask not what our country can do for us, but what we can do for our country.' This young man answered by giving his life, now it is time to ask what his country can do for him." Alice Wildermuth, from Illinois, similarly wrote, "I am white but I think anybody who dies in Viet Nam should have a hero's burial regardless of his color."[47] From Hollywood, no less a figure than John Wayne telegrammed that "a national disgrace has just taken place in Wetumpka Alabama. It is criminal that Private First Class James L. Williams of our special forces, an American citizen, who has made the supreme sacrifice—killed in action fighting an American war—now denied burial in his home town."[48]

Like the Williams family, McCracken, Wildermuth, and Wayne viewed the controversy as contradictory to the moment's prowar rhetoric. The White House immediately began working to put out the fire. On May 31 a staffer named Ervin Duggan wrote a memo to Douglas Cater, Johnson's special assistant, saying, "We might consider some gesture by the President or the Administration when unfortunate messes like this one in Wetumpka, Ala., occur."[49] Three days later Cater directed the Defense Department to inform him of "any way we can act to avert this kind of disgrace before it provides international news copy?"[50] The resolution of the episode, like the outrage that accompanied it, intersected with larger discourses of appropriate remembrance. The day after receiving the family's telegram, one of Johnson's advisers, Harry McPherson, assured the Williams family that "the United States Army will provide a burial site for your son in a national cemetery. There he will lie with others who have given their lives for their country. . . . [T]he burial ceremony will be conducted with full military honors on Memorial Day."[51] McPherson further explained that "America is humbly proud of these men, and within our lifetime we shall see the redemption of their deaths in a nation without bigotry."[52] Bill Moyers, Johnson's press secretary, wrote a similarly reassuring letter to Wayne.[53] Already, Williams was being reincorporated within the nation in accordance with the moment's defining rhetoric.

That Williams was buried at Andersonville helped buttress claims of an egalitarian nation. While his family chose it over Arlington because it was closer to Wetumpka, media coverage constructed Andersonville as a space in which Williams's identity as a patriotic soldier embraced by the nation was ensured despite an enduring history of southern indifference.[54] As a national cemetery, Andersonville fit Williams's death neatly into the larger story recounted by the weekend news coverage and the Johnson administration, replacing images of local injustice with those of national homage. References to the site's history dwelled little on the South's legacy of slavery and racial inequality, as might be expected, and instead emphasized a history of Americans rectifying soldiers' mistreatment through proper memorialization.[55]

A headline in the *Philadelphia Inquirer* hinted at salvation, proclaiming "Dixie Negro GI Saved from Pauper's Burial," and almost every article aligned Williams's burial with the weekend's larger script of appropriate memorialization.[56] Articles mentioned that "military pallbearers, honor guard, bugler and rifle salute will accompany graveside rites" and that "a crack honor guard from the 175th Infantry Brigade at Ft. Benning, Ga. gave Williams . . . a burial with full military honors."[57] The *Augusta Chronicle* wistfully predicted that "taps will echo over historic Andersonville National Cemetery Memorial Day. . . . A rifle salute will crackle across the still countryside. A bereaved mother will be presented an American flag, symbol of the freedom her G.I. son died fighting to preserve in Viet Nam."[58]

References to the space itself, as a national cemetery, likewise folded Williams's burial into the weekend's larger portrayal of a country that met its patriotic obligations. Photographs of an integrated honor guard carrying Williams's flag-draped casket into Andersonville, including one on the front page of the *Los Angeles Times* under the heading "Burial on Memorial Day," visually and verbally connected his burial to others that had appeared in American newspapers that week and warranted that Williams and his family had achieved their rightful place as citizens and patriots (fig. 1.1). Several newspapers explicitly incorporated Williams and his family within the nation. "Williams, whose parents were told there was no space except a pauper's grave in the segregated Wetumpka City Cemetery, was buried in Section E Grave 163, surrounded by the graves of other American fighting men," the *Atlanta Daily World* wrote, adding, "The flag he died fighting for May 19 was presented to his mother."[59] The *Columbus (Ga.) Ledger* framed the burial as evidence of the Williams family's inclusion within the nation, reporting that "the Williams family will be among countless Americans who will pause to honor the nation's military dead on Memorial Day."[60] Similarly, the *Augusta Chronicle* wrote, "Williams, a lad of 19 years, will be buried with full military honors as have thousands of Americans who will be remembered Memorial Day for

FIGURE 1.1. Jimmy Williams's funeral procession, Andersonville National Cemetery, May 30, 1966. Coverage of the funeral drew on remembrances of Andersonville as a site where wrongs committed against American soldiers had been corrected through appropriate memorialization. Bettman/Corbis

the supreme sacrifice they made for the nation. The John Williams family will shed tears along with countless other Americans as the nation pauses to honor its military dead."[61] The army itself made a similar claim when Alfred B. Fitt, the army's special assistant for special functions, wrote a Chicagoan who had complained to the White House, saying, "It is unfortunate that discrimination should have pursued this soldier even after death, but his body now rests where race, color, creed or rank make no difference, and all are honored equally for their service to the United States."[62] These ceremonies and claims apparently served their purpose, as the *Boston Globe* reported that "Mrs. Williams, who said she wanted her son buried as an American, not as a Negro, told a reporter, 'I'm satisfied now that he's been shown respect and given a decent burial.'"[63]

Coverage of Williams's burial helped sustain the weekend's larger claim that the country did not dismiss and in fact appropriately honored American sacrifices in Vietnam. Several newspapers, however, went further, constructing Andersonville as a site at which this tradition of appropriate memorialization was already evident because the cemetery had restored the honor of soldiers wronged by the South. Many articles recalled Andersonville's sordid past, calling it, for example, "the site of the infamous Confederate prison where thousands of Union soldiers died."[64] Readers would likely have recognized such a reference, as Andersonville already lived in the national imagination as a symbol of Southern injustice toward American soldiers; the *New York Times* review of MacKinlay Kantor's novel *Andersonville* (1955), for example, called the prison a "long, smoldering hell" and recalled its "unspeakable horror."[65]

Transforming the landscape from one of horror to one of peace, newspapers made clear that Williams was being buried in a space that the nation had, through appropriate acts of memorialization, reclaimed from Southerners who had brutalized American soldiers. The *Boston Globe* reminded its readers that "the gently rolling hills of the national cemetery are the resting grounds for almost 13,000 Union soldiers who died in the Andersonville Confederate prison."[66] The *Baltimore Sun* described "row upon row of white marble slabs marking graves of northern soldiers who died by the thousands in the Confederate stockade here 100 years ago."[67] Even southern papers adopted this posture, publishing versions of an Associated Press article describing the "tiny American flags, in recognition of Memorial Day, [that] dotted the Union graves in the National Cemetery, where about 12,000 prisoners died in the old stockade" and going on to note that "from June to October 1864 nearly 10,200 soldiers died in the Confederate compound."[68] The fact that "big monuments from Northern states dot the landscape in commemoration of the dead" alluded to a memorial tradition that corrected these injustices. In pointing out that Williams had been "buried . . . with military honors amid thousands of graves," the article equated his story with that of an earlier generation who had served their country and been mistreated but ultimately were honored.[69]

In 1966 the attention given to Williams's death and burial returned Andersonville to Americans' imagination in ways that helped bolster the Johnson administration's larger view about the Vietnam War's validity and necessity. If the controversy over Williams's burial threatened the narratives of African American military citizenship and sacrifice simultaneously being mobilized to ensure broader acquiescence to the Vietnam War, his interment at Andersonville literally situated him within a landscape that attested to the country's awareness of the costs of war and its intolerance of the injustices that the South had historically visited on American soldiers. Four years later, however,

Andersonville's return to the American imagination would be a means of criticizing what had become for many an unpopular and unjust war.

"You See This on the Same Box Where You See the News of Today"

Lewis Freedman had a long history in television. A former producer at CBS, he had been recruited by New York Public Television shortly after the creation of PBS and then, in 1969, by KCET, the public broadcasting affiliate in Los Angeles, where his task was "to supply PBS with a much-needed drama series. The result was *Hollywood Television Theater*," which would provide minimally adapted stage plays that "stimulated the intellect and imagination of the audience . . . [and] with which the audience felt comfortable."[70]

The series, funded by a Ford Foundation grant, was announced in the major Hollywood trade sheets, *Daily Variety, Entertainment World, Hollywood Reporter,* and *Weekly Variety,* on January 14, 1970.[71] Freedman chose Saul Levitt's play *The Andersonville Trial* (1958), a courtroom drama whose Broadway premier had starred George C. Scott, as the first production of the series. The play told the story of proceedings in 1865 against Henry Wirz, Andersonville's commandant and the only American to be executed for war crimes, and had originally been widely understood as a commentary on the Nazi war crimes trials.[72] In its review of the play, the *New York Times* wrote that "the essential question is this: does a military officer have a moral duty to refuse an order that he regards as inhuman?"[73] For the *Times,* Wirz was the villain. Noting that the prosecutor "argues . . . that for humanitarian reasons Wirz should have disobeyed the orders of his superiors to save the lives of the men herded into the Andersonville Prison," the review concludes by declaring him "guilty as charged."[74] The sense that the play cast Wirz as bearing moral responsibility for the prison's brutality likely contributed to some southerners' ire. E. L. Forrester, the unreconstructed Georgia congressman whose father had been a guard at Andersonville, asked the House Un-American Activities Committee (HUAC) to investigate Levitt and filed the resulting report along with a pamphlet-sized summary of Henry Ford's *The Global Jew.*[75] In Atlanta and Birmingham, sponsors who "[did] not wish to sponsor anything that may be of a controversial nature" canceled the play.[76]

In 1970, however, *Hollywood Television Theater*'s version of Commandant Wirz received a somewhat more sympathetic reception, perhaps because Freedman and his staff explicitly sought to encourage Americans to think critically about the moral and political issues raised by the plight of a young second lieutenant, William Calley, on trial for his life at Fort Benning, Georgia. The production and reception of *The Andersonville Trial* thus marked a moment when Americans simultaneously turned to the remembrance of Andersonville to make sense of Vietnam and applied their understanding of Vietnam to shape their view of Andersonville.[77] Reviewers who read the play through the lens of the My Lai massacre were softer on Wirz's character than the *Times* had been twelve years earlier; his actions remained reprehensible and inexcusable, but he now became a victim of an unjust system for which all Americans shared responsibility.

Freedman announced that this first production of the series would be shown on February 25, 1970. He said the drama had "powerful roots in both the American past and the American present" and, mirroring the language of the original reviewers, held that it "raises questions familiar today as it explores the agonizing conflict between military authority and personal responsibility."[78] This was an issue with which Americans had lately become familiar. Three months earlier Seymour Hersh had broken a story about a company in the Americal Division that had reportedly executed hundreds of Vietnamese civilians in the village of Son My, also known as My Lai (4).[79] Questions quickly arose regarding whether Lt. William Calley, the soldier most closely associated with the event, could defend himself by claiming to have been ordered to commit the murders.[80]

Many Americans had larger questions. "The story of the massacre progressively evolved into a story about Americans," Kendrick Oliver notes, "about the burden of blame carried by Calley, Medina and their men, and about the wider distribution of guilt upwards, through the ranks of those who had managed the war, and horizontally across American society as a whole."[81] To many, the thought of prosecuting Calley reeked of hypocrisy. Michael Belknap writes, "Americans seemed inclined to assign responsibility for whatever happened at My Lai (4) to the Vietnam War itself rather than to the men of Charlie Company," and many felt that "Lieutenant Calley should *not* be standing in the dock of a military court."[82] Within weeks of the publication of Hersh's account, more than half of the country viewed Calley as a scapegoat for the larger moral failings evident in the conduct of the war, and a substantial number wondered along with a *New York Times* op-ed piece whether "this nation, outraged and sickened by the massacre at Songmy, [can] now deal calmly and fairly with those accused of the atrocity? Will the massacre . . . now be followed by a lynching?"[83]

Freedman and his staff explicitly cast *The Andersonville Trial* as a national opportunity to explore the tension between Americans' horror, desire for justice, and uncertainty about whether Calley had become a sacrificial lamb for an army and a country unwilling to acknowledge the immorality of the war. Freedman first sought to schedule the play's premier to coincide with the beginning of Calley's trial. Two weeks after the military judge Reid Kennedy scheduled a date of Monday, May 18, to commence the trial, Freedman informed all PBS stations that "the play will be broadcast uncut in color over 184 non-commercial stations of the Public Broadcasting Service's network on Thursday night, May 14, from 8:30 to 11 p.m."[84] After a March scheduling conflict with the Eastern Educational Network, which wanted to run the premier in a less desirable Friday evening slot that Freedman complained would "certainly lessen the impact of the play," the premiere was moved to 8:00 p.m. on Sunday, May 17, the night before the trial began.[85] Many stations planned to repeat the program the next week, with KCET slotting it into the prime-time slot each night.[86] Had Judge Kennedy not postponed the opening of the trial to August 24 and then to November, *The Andersonville Trial*'s premier would have concluded in time for viewers to switch to late local news coverage of the trial.

Although the premier ultimately did not coincide with the trial opening, Freedman and Scott, who was making his directorial debut with the play, made every effort to connect the two. A lengthy press release setting the premier for May 14 and 15 announced, "'History repeats itself' is an old cliché, but if you compared the headlines of 1863 with the newspaper banners we read today, there would be surprisingly little difference" and quoted Freedman's observation that "day after day, in the newspapers and magazines of this country, there are stories and ideas discussed that are reflected and dramatized in this play," including "the responsibility of the military."[87] Freedman then made the comparison explicit: "*The Andersonville Trial* is not a period piece. . . . Considering the events in Vietnam, it's just as important and timely today as it was then."[88] He further explained, "Questions raised in 1863 [*sic*] at this trial are now being asked again, more than a century later. 'War criminal,' 'crimes against humanity,' even the concept of collective guilt is current. . . . Television brings 'The Andersonville Trial' home to everyone in every corner of the world. You see this on the same box where you see the news of today."[89]

Other materials followed suit. A letter of April 27 to member stations included a *Los Angeles Times* article about Scott's directorial debut in which Scott explained that the play was "more pertinent today—to 1970—than it was to 1959, when I did it on Broadway. This was the first trial of a war criminal, where the term was coined. In that light and in the light of Vietnam, here's a play happening 100 years ago that could come out of the headlines of today's paper."[90] An accompanying press release quoted Freedman as explaining, "The questions raised by the play are familiar to all of us. They . . . are being asked again today in relation to My-Lai in South Vietnam."[91] The *New York Daily News* reported that Scott "thinks the play is more pertinent today than it was back in 1959—this because of the obvious parallel between the pending trials of the officers accused in the My Lai massacre."[92] Scott averred that, compared to earlier comparisons to Nazi trials, "it's much closer to home with My Lai."[93]

These efforts to situate the play continued in its rebroadcasts. In February 1971 Calley was undergoing a psychological examination at Walter Reed Army Medical Center. During the preceding month, the defense had called "witness after witness" who, as the *New York Times* reported in January, "show[ed] that Lieutenant Calley was acting under orders and that higher officers knew what was happening. . . . The question here, then, is whether the order, if that is what it was, to kill everything was one that a prudent man should obey."[94] The *Times*, like a growing number of Americans, seemed inclined to believe Calley. An article of January 15 noted, "All the evidence heard so far has indicated that the military gave no thought to the care of civilians."[95] Two months after *The Andersonville Trial* was rebroadcast, three-quarters of Americans believed Calley had been following orders, and seven in ten felt he had been unfairly singled out.[96]

Again, PBS contributed to this assessment in its marketing materials, urging member stations to advertise the play as "the courtroom drama of one hundred years ago that echoes today's headlines" and to ask viewers whether "an individual [has] the right to disobey military commands he considers unjust."[97] Other promotional materials remarked that "the plea that he was 'only obeying orders' which he 'could not disobey' echoes today's headlines and provides the play with its basic conflict" and that whether "a moral man must rebel against barbaric or inhumane orders, even one within the framework imposed by military discipline . . . is the moral dilemma on which the play pivots."[98] These parallels were made visual in the *New York Times* for

February 2, 1971, which featured a portrait of Wirz shown from the shoulders up and facing slightly to the right while giving a thousand-yard stare. The image recalled Calley's appearance on the covers of *Time* and *Newsweek* two years earlier. The paper asked, "Was or wasn't the commandant morally responsible for the death of his charges?"[99]

PBS seemed largely content to simply point to those parallels without intimating how viewers should interpret them. But Freedman occasionally tipped his hand, first when he mentioned "collective guilt" in the press release and more publicly in his essay "How Far Is Andersonville from Vietnam," which appeared in the *New York Times* the morning of the premier. He began by reasserting the historical parallels, writing that "today, the play has unbelievable immediacy" and that "when Richard Basehart, as Wirz, cries out that the prisoners were like rats trying to escape and prosecutor William Shatner seizes upon that statement as the measure of Wirz's inhumanity, we are suddenly in Southeast Asia dealing with an alien and exotic enemy."[100]

Freedman did not stop there. He indicted the entire nation for its complicity in the My Lai massacre: "But most important of all is the crux of the defense. Captain Wirz declares over and over that he was simply obeying orders, that he had no choice, that he would have been shot for treason if he hadn't obeyed. As we listen to him, and are moved, we also hear the voices in today's news. It is not only the officer of the Confederacy, it is the officer in our own Army, it is the student on our own college campus, it is ourselves, caught in today's dilemmas."[101] To Freedman, Wirz was not only a pitiful if sympathetic character singled out from a culture that shares responsibility but also every American who had acquiesced to the war. He made this point clearly in his closing paragraph, which quoted from T. S. Eliot's "The Waste Land": "What is not ambiguous, and never was, is the closing line—as vivid and accusatory on this page today as it was 50 years ago: You! Hypocrite lecteur—hypocritical reader—mon sembable—you who are exactly like me—don't pretend we are talking about somebody else—mon frère—it is you who are on trial—my brother!"[102] Freedman, writing in the most influential newspaper in the country, did more than simply publicize his play as an opportunity to reflect on My Lai; he asked Americans to think about it in accordance with the growing sentiment that Calley had been singled out and that the impossibility of refusing an order reflected a culture that condoned and enabled the war.

Similar utterances dominated media coverage of the premier. Probably owing to PBS's publicity campaign, most reviews referenced My Lai and the question of whether a soldier could be condemned for following orders. In a sign of how much the Vietnam comparison had changed Americans' approach to Andersonville's legacy, in Atlanta—where ten years earlier the play had been too incendiary for public performance but only a little more than one hundred miles from Fort Benning, where Calley was to be tried—the *Journal and Constitution* quoted Freedman's interview at length and ran a cartoon rendition of the play's defining confrontation.[103] Several papers situated the program squarely within the broader public sentiment that simultaneously recognized Calley's personal actions as reprehensible and the moral culpability extending far beyond him. *Entertainment World*, which wrote that the play looked "piteously straight at My Lai and every day since," "cuts with a slap of recognition," and was "numbingly relevant," found that "in the final confrontation. . . . [Wirz] is destroyed, and the very military system, the right, in fact, of the state to demand blind obedience, is triumphantly assailed."[104]

The *New York Times* wrote that "last night the issue of the individual moral responsibility of a soldier was associated with the massacre at Mylai." The article found that the prosecutor's and the defense attorney's "mutuality of doubt over the proceedings" and the conclusion, in which "Captain Wirz ultimately is to be hanged, if only because in war the victors and not the losers decide what is moral," called into question the very nature of justice in a military trial.[105] In the *Detroit Free Press* the reviewer Bettelou Peterson called the play "gripping drama, relevant today with its moral dilemmas and arguments" and observed that My Lai was symptomatic of the Vietnam War's larger failings: "There are echoes of My Lai, of Cambodia, of the whole frightening picture of war and what it does to men."[106] Peterson thereby condemned not Wirz or Calley but the entire enterprise that enabled and encouraged the violence and then denounced it: the defense attorney "sees the futility of a pre-tried case," and Wirz himself has the "weakness of a man bred to inviolability of orders."[107] In saying that Wirz is "bred," she makes his atrocities not wholly his own fault; in concluding that "the audience, too, becomes the people involved," she repeats Freedman's contention that war crimes are national sins.[108]

The *Boston Globe* made the most explicit comparisons, publishing a review on May 18 and an editorial the next day. Like other critics, the *Globe* reviewer read the play as an analogue to the injustices being visited on Calley: "Even in the midst of the unspeakable barbarities and inhuman condition so graphically described in the testimony, disturbing points were raised about the extent of the guilt of a man who had to 'follow orders' or himself be sacrificed. As his attorney hammered home, time and again, how can 'obedience' be equated with 'conspiracy'?"[109]

These arguments were being made simultaneously about My Lai. No one disputed that Calley was responsible for committing atrocities; just as surely, though, few Americans believed him to be the lone villain. The *Globe* made this more clear in its editorial of May 19, "The Excuse of Obeying Orders," which contended that "the moral question continues to plague the thoughtful. Should an individual disobey a command which offends his conscience? Is discipline, however necessary to an army, so praiseworthy? What of those who use outrageous orders?" It then asked, "But why should such moral conflicts be imposed on any individual?"[110] Here, the *Globe*'s editorial board joined other reviewers and a public that were both skeptical of claims that Calley was an individual bad actor and sympathetic to the claim that the fault was systemic and that responsibility lay with those who forced individuals to confront untenable orders.

The Andersonville Trial won an Emmy in 1970 and was widely celebrated as PBS's successful opening salvo in the prime-time drama market.[111] At a moment when Americans confronted unsettling questions about American soldiers' atrocities in Vietnam, Freedman portrayed Wirz's war crimes trial as an opportunity to confront lasting questions about shared moral responsibility during war. Both he and the reviewers who raved about it read the play as an indictment of a military and a culture that was complicit in but sought to distance itself from the war's larger barbarity. In the coming decades Andersonville remained central in Americans' thinking about the Vietnam War, but their use of its remembrance to interrogate their own culpability for Vietnam's horrors steadily gave way to a revisionist narrative that emphasized American suffering.

"Such Adversity and Deprivation Should Count for Something"

In the spring of 1973 Jean Swearingen, a planner at the NPS's Denver Service Center, was consumed with preparing the interpretive prospectus of the newly created Andersonville National Historic Site. The site had been established in October 1970, when legislation shepherded through Congress by Rep. Jack Brinkley (D-GA) and Sen. Richard B. Russell (D-GA) ended a lengthy process in which, first, the army, which had previously controlled the place, sought to off-load it, then a regional planning commission aborted its community development plan for increasing tourism, and finally the NPS reluctantly took possession even though it initially had little interest in doing so.[112]

Most of the NPS staff who read Swearingen's prospectus liked it. John Jensen, the superintendent of Andersonville, despite "violently disagree[ing]" on the question of living historical interpretation, called it "the best 'rough draft' I've seen."[113] But Jerry Lowery, Andersonville's seasonal historian, was less congratulatory:

> This entire report leaves the reader with the impression that Andersonville National Historic Site is to leave the visitor in "tears" as he completes his visit. . . . I do not agree with this method of interpretation of a Memorial to Prisoners of War.
>
> I believe today, with the Viet Nam conflict coming to a close and prisoners of our most recent war returning home, that most of the populace of this country have a good idea of the atrocities of prisoners of war camps.

Lowery mentioned the Bataan Death March and the Korean conflict in his memo, but it was Vietnam that persuaded him not to pay too much attention to prisoners' tribulations. Lowery was the lone dissenter, apparently, in concluding that "a park should not only be informative but also 'fun.'"[114] Jensen handed the memo off with a shrug—"maybe a valid feeling"—and Swearingen wrote in the margins, "[I] cannot agree that this prison is enjoyable, 'fun,' or cute."[115]

Lowery's comment and the response to it highlight that if the establishment of Andersonville was not entirely prompted by the war in Vietnam, the NPS's initial efforts to curate Andersonville were shaped by the cultural politics of the post-Vietnam years. Although Lowery wanted the park to soft pedal the experiences of prisoners, Swearingen and others viewed it as an opportunity to speak to the larger sentiment of war weariness and futility that pervaded Vietnam's immediate aftermath. This largely antiwar sentiment, however, existed in tension with other uses of the site as the discourse surrounding prisoners of war shifted after the war. Andersonville's enabling legislation echoed both the Nixon administration's Go Public campaign, which called on Americans to support the war because of American POWs' suffering in

Vietnam, and Memorial Day celebrations that in the 1970s curried support for Nixon's expansion of the war and in the 1980s called for continued efforts to locate prisoners and missing soldiers' remains. In the 1990s, the National Prisoner of War Museum's layout established the Vietnam POW story as marked by exceptional depravity and suffering. These uses of Andersonville overwhelmed the NPS's initial effort to align interpretation with post-Vietnam sentiments of futility and antimilitarism and instead fully embraced narratives of POW/MIA suffering and of Vietnam as a righteous war waged against a barbarous enemy.

ANDERSONVILLE BECAME A NATIONAL HISTORIC SITE AT A JUNCTURE when the public was giving increased attention to Americans held captive in Vietnam.[116] Shortly after taking office, Nixon and his administration sought to build support for the flagging war effort through the Go Public campaign, whereby, as H. Bruce Franklin has argued, "the issue of POWs and MIAs would serve mainly as an indispensable device for continuing the war"; it offered "a purely 'humanitarian' question to transform the peace negotiations into a stage for displaying the inhuman features of the enemy."[117]

Three years earlier, in 1967, the then-retired ex-congressman Forrester, who, as noted, had asked HUAC to investigate Levitt, exploited Andersonville to legitimize support for the Vietnam War.[118] As the keynote speaker at the site on Memorial Day that year, Forrester recalled the suffering of both Union and Confederate prisoners, men who died "from stark hunger" and "found the price of rats exceedingly high." He presented a reconciliationist account that paid "tribute to those boys of all of our wars, who fought for right as they knew the right."[119]

This vision of national unity was central to his use of Vietnam POWs to critique the antiwar movement. Exactly a year after Jimmy Williams was buried, Forrester went to Andersonville not to reckon with the war's racial inequalities and recognize African American manhood but to racialize the Vietnamese as "a fanatical and relentless foe"; at the same time, he infantilized American troops as "our best beardless youths [who] have given their lives, because their country called" before linking them to their predecessors, "all of those boys fighting for love of home and country, and in order that we might live."[120] American captives supplied Forrester's example, as he described the "pictures of our boys who had been shot down, and were being paraded, spit up, beat and mistreated by a savage foe. They are taking the blows for you and me. A few nights ago, an American family were sitting in their homes and saw with their own eyes, their own son, wounded by the enemy."[121]

Foreshadowing not just the Go Public campaign's efforts to seize the POW issue from the antiwar movement but also a later discourse that Natasha Zaretsky has shown "consistently identified the captured soldier with . . . the affective ties of the family" and "portrayed America as victim rather than aggressor," Forrester, misrepresenting the antiwar movement's aims, declared that supporting the Viet Cong in light of such images was unconscionable.[122] "The blood of our boys are [*sic*] on [the antiwar movement's] hands," he complained; "those acts are treasonable."[123]

Until the end of the war Andersonville remained a space that contributed to the mobilization of the prisoner of war story on behalf of the Nixon administration's war plans. As Kenneth Foote writes, "Andersonville was dedicated at the very moment when the POW and MIA debate was being used as a rallying point to sustain support for the Vietnam War."[124] Analyzing the enabling legislation that opened the way for Andersonville to become a historic site, Benjamin Cloyd writes, "The harsh lessons being learned once again in Vietnam about the suffering of prisoners of war prompted the Senate's understanding of Andersonville as an important opportunity to recognize permanently the 'grim' reality of the 'story of captivity.' Although Vietnam never received explicit mention, the universal language with which the Senate discussed the bill clearly reflected the impact of that terrible war and provided a powerful incentive to support it."[125]

Foote and Cloyd are correct that Vietnam was an unmentioned influence, but the language was not quite "universal." The Senate report, in describing the prisoners at Andersonville, insisted that "the story of captivity is often as grim as the story of war itself. Men, isolated from their comrades, and lonely for their loved ones, must be strong in mind and spirit to endure such circumstances. Andersonville can tell that story." This is precisely the language that, as Zaretsky shows, dominated discussion of Vietnam POWs: they were husbands, fathers, and sons who endured with stalwart patriotism.[126] And in case readers were likely to mistake its comments as being solely about the Civil War, the report abruptly shifted from past to present tense: "It is the undaunted spirit of men such as these that keeps America the Nation that it is."[127] Here, Andersonville's remembrance validated the Nixon administration's imperatives by mobilizing and thus legitimizing the language of domestic suffering and patriotic stoicism that dominated the administration's prowar rhetoric.

This was hardly the only instance in which Andersonville was used to buttress the Vietnam policies of the Nixon White House. On Memorial Day 1970 Rep. Jack Brinkley (D-GA) echoed Nixon's calls for "peace with honor" and his disdain for antiwar activism, intoning, "How we all pray that our Commander-in-chief will be granted the wisdom, and the unity at home, which will enable him to bring our boys back with our national honor unsullied."[128] Recalling both Nixon's silent majority and construction workers' choreographed assault on antiwar activists in New York, Brinkley praised "'Hard Hat' people" who "marched with flags" and "showed disgust for *anti*-American demonstrators." He compared those who acquiesced to antiwar sentiment to Neville Chamberlain and critics of the war to Hitler.[129]

Rhetoric in this vein continued over the next two years. In 1971 Rep. Dawson Mathis (D-GA), who called the war a mistake from the outset, nonetheless dismissed the Vietnamese as "the revolutionaries of 1971 [who] have nothing to lay on the line but their dirty feet and a book of Chairman Mao's quotations." He "declared that he supported the President's policy of orderly withdrawal and asked fellow Georgians to support him in this belief."[130] A year later Rep. Fletcher Thompson (R-GA) stated, "The President had about succeeded in the Vietnamization of the war before the massive offensive was launched by the Communists about nine weeks ago. But had Mr. Nixon not taken the blockade action of North Vietnam ports and committed our country to more air power, then many lives would already have been lost."[131] In these speeches Andersonville became a site at which national unity turned on a shared commitment to prolonging the Vietnam War as much it did as on remembering the nation's war dead.

By the time Swearingen was writing her interpretive prospectus in the spring of 1973, however, the Paris Peace talks had resulted in plans for a withdrawal by the United States, the return of POWs, and a combined sense of war weariness and futility regarding South Vietnam's future. In April, R. W. Apple wrote in the *New York Times*, "The issue of control of South Vietnam, which was what the war was all about, was fudged in Paris, and seems likely now to be resolved by military means."[132] This was neither an optimistic nor a minority view; a few months earlier, a *Times* editorial had judged that "it is futile to expect a tidy end of this messy conflict," and "nothing could be more auspicious for starting Mr. Nixon's second term than . . . extricat[ing] the United States at last from the cruel and costly Southeast Asian quagmire."[133] The POW narrative had shifted accordingly. Since at least 1972, Michael Allen has shown, many Americans had felt that "the plight of the POWs only added to the list of reasons to end the war."[134] The Nixon administration and returning POWs responded to these anxieties by proclaiming that the sacrifices had been worthwhile because they had achieved peace; a *New York Times* piece from February 1973, for example, reported that "former American prisoners of war insisted . . . that their years in captivity had not been in vain" but also noted, "That view is not completely shared even in their own families. As one wife put it recently, 'It's hard to believe that eight years was worth it.' "[135]

The latter sentiment informed Andersonville's first interpretive plan, which thought it essential that visitors "see that *they* have it in their own power to prevent" camps like Andersonville.[136] The plan for the visitors' center included an entryway designed to "lead to an intense thought about the horrors of war" and a Mood Room in which "the peculiarly depressing dinginess of the room will tend to slow down visitors' thoughts, creating feelings of physical and mental constriction."[137] Likewise, the fifteen-minute audiovisual program that would follow the Mood Room reinforced earlier celebrations of POW exceptionalism and endurance with an explicit call for the public to commit to making those sacrifices worthwhile:

> A person can go to war, knowing why, imagining what it will be like. He can imagine being wounded, and even dying. But he cannot see himself incarcerated, confined, and totally degraded, both physically and mentally. . . . The purpose of this program must be to share with the viewer some of the suffering of the prisoners at any time, in any period. The viewer should leave this area with a greater awareness of man's ability to overcome extreme adversity—but also with the conviction that such adversity and deprivation should not be without purpose, without meaning, without value. The sacrifices made should count for something. They should not be in vain. At the same time, the theme of this audiovisual presentation should suggest a feeling of hope—hope in man's ultimate capacity to live in harmony.[138]

The nearly desperate tone of the passage, together with its demand that sacrifices "should not be without purpose, without meaning, without value," echoes the moment's war weariness; the prospectus concluded that "people should leave this place with a sympathy for . . . the futility of war."[139] In making this sentiment the guiding interpretive principle, the NPS constructed Andersonville as a site that affirmed the larger sentiment that the Vietnam War had been meaningless.

Although the Mood Room was never built, such language shaped the park's interpretation and use throughout the 1970s. On Memorial Day in 1975 protestors appropriated the space and declared, "Our presence today is a silent symbol that we do not intend to join the Pentagon's Dance of Death. We will not bow obediently to our nation's priority on destruction."[140] Seven months after Saigon fell on April 30 that year, the NPS held its first Christmas tree lighting at the site, which featured Dale Doss, who had been held captive in Vietnam, and Congressman Brinkley.[141] Inviting Brinkley, John Flister, the superintendent at Andersonville, offered that he "might mention that we at the Park stress the fact that this will be a Christmas when our American men are not at war."[142] The dedication in 1976 of the Georgia POW Memorial, a sculpture created by William Thompson and installed in the cemetery, included nods to Vietnam veterans, but in the context of healing and respect for their service.[143] How much the sentiment surrounding the site had changed in a decade is evident in the speech Rep. Charles Hatcher (D-GA) gave on Memorial Day in 1980: "The young people of today have not known war, and I pray with you they never will. And while it is almost beyond the imagination of these veterans to tell the young what it is like, and beyond the imagination of those who have lived in peace to understand war, they must try. For unless we remember and learn from the mistakes of the past, we are doomed to repeat them. Unless we pause to reflect on the sacrifice of the men we commemorate today, we will send more behind them, mindless of the lessons to be learned from war."[144]

Hatcher's references to "mistakes" and the possibility of "mindless" intervention are a pointed censure of Vietnam, one very much at odds with his predecessors' calls for continued support of the war. At least one visitor felt that the site was a counterweight to early exploitations of the Vietnam POW, writing to Flister in June 1977 that "a memorial to the honor of all Prisoners of War for all wars" was "a very commendable gesture, especially in the light of our nation's most recent utilization of POWs as pawns in a strategic chess-game, or to be simply forgotten."[145]

Perhaps the most notable shift away from the use of POWs and MIAs to justify the war came in 1978, when the family of Bobby Jones, a flight surgeon who had perished when his F-4 Phantom jet fighter was shot down in 1972, placed a memorial stone at Arlington that was identical to a standard gravestone but for the words "In Memory" over his name. Jones was likely one of the missing whom the United States declared "presumed dead" in the 1970s.[146] This marker is one of few memorials to a man missing in Vietnam and stands in contrast to the POW/MIA movement's general antipathy toward any gesture that suggested closure.[147] To memorialize Jones with the same stone as those used to mark the graves of people who were actually buried seemed to signal acceptance that his body was permanently missing.

Such acceptance did not, however, characterize the larger POW/MIA movement, and by the 1980s ceremonies at Andersonville became moments at which the mission "to interpret the role of prisoner of war camps in history" was pressed into service to authenticate calls to locate American remains and men presumed held captive. Although the history and politics of the POW/MIA movement are too vast to summarize here, several scholars have pointed out that the post-Vietnam period has been marked by an unprecedented demand that the United States rescue or recover the remains of unaccounted-for U.S. troops.[148] The notion that the Vietnamese government has impeded efforts at recuperation or even kept American prisoners after the end of the war has shaped a memory of the conflict that underscores Vietnamese leaders' inhumanity, American leaders' indifference, and American soldiers' victimization. As Allen explains, "MIA activism was . . . a means to address the pain and anger [the war] still caused, and a weapon with which to attack those deemed responsible . . . at home and abroad."[149] It is nearly impossible to overstate the movement's impact on post-Vietnam American culture. Allen's claim that "belief in POW/MIA abandonment was so serious and widespread as to alter U.S. politics and foreign policy over four decades" is hardly an exaggeration; neither is Edwin Martini's judgment that "the myth . . . became an uncontrollable creature that would create policy dilemmas for all future administrations."[150] And, as Allen and Franklin have shown, the myth's endurance relied on the combined efforts—sometimes in concert, other times in tension—of government figures and grassroots activists, particularly the League of American Families.

During the eighties and nineties, the POW/MIA myth flourished at Andersonville. Between 1984 and 2000 half of the Memorial Day keynote speakers were former Vietnam prisoners, POW/MIA activists, or legislators and bureaucrats invested in the movement's affairs. Several made explicit calls for action on POW/MIA issues. Consequently, it is not enough to say, as Cloyd has, that Vietnam was frequently cited at Memorial Day celebrations or that "Andersonville's tragic history did (and does) not matter nearly as much as the prison's redefined role as a national mourning ground for all American prisoners of war."[151] These observations are correct, but they don't fully explain the post-Vietnam politics that shaped those uses.

Furthermore, these celebrations were forums at which activists and politicians conjoined revisionist narratives of Vietnamese brutality and American indifference with demands for and assurances of continuing efforts to recover prisoners and remains in Southeast Asia, assertions that the National Historic Site's substantial cultural capital helped legitimate. In 1984 the official program featured Orson Swindle, who, after being shot down and taken prisoner, had been "subject[ed] to abuse and isolation by his captors."[152] His speech was rife with familiar revisionism: "No American fighting man had ever fought under such terrible conditions as in Vietnam, and . . . we weren't allowed to win the war although we won every battle," he complained, insisting that "the search for the estimated 2,500 MIAs must continue."[153]

Three years later the speaker was Hervey S. Stockman, another former Vietnam POW and president of NAM-POWs, an organization of former Vietnam POWs.[154] However, the park most deeply embraced the notion that American soldiers were potentially still held captive and that a full accounting was necessary in 1988. That year Andersonville, after a long, unbroken succession of keynote speakers who were male veterans and male government officials, for the first time chose a woman, Barbara Smith, to fill that role.[155] Smith was the wife of an airman missing in Vietnam and had become deeply involved in two organizations, the League of Families of American Prisoners and Missing in Southeast Asia, and in the efforts to construct the national POW/MIA museum at Andersonville.[156]

Smith's appearance as well as the program as a whole that year not only marked a reimposition of the rhetoric of domestic sacrifice that had defined the culture of POWs and MIAs during the Nixon years but also put the NPS's imprimatur on the movement's central thesis. Newspaper coverage leading up to the event recorded that details of Hubert Smith's disappearance, Barbara Smith's lengthy vigil and activism, and the recent potential recovery of her husband's remains.[157] More significant, the service itself attested to the enduring, multigenerational suffering of POW/MIA families: "Five year old Breana Johnson, dressed in Sunday best, was the last in the long procession that came to the rostrum. Escorted by two sharply dressed members of the Georgia Southwestern College Army ROTC Honor guard, she carried a wreath in honor of U.S. Servicemen who died or were held prisoner of war in Vietnam—including a grandfather she never knew."[158] The spectacle of an MIA's granddaughter publicly remembering a man "she never knew" drew attention to the issue's ongoing lack of resolution while attesting to American innocence. In this ceremony, the Vietnam War's most obvious victim was a five-year-old American girl.

In her speech Smith unsurprisingly reiterated familiar notions as she "reminded the audience that, of the 2400 men we left behind as Prisoners of War in Vietnam . . . we have reports of less than 250."[159] She repeated old myths and manufactured numbers, both in the notion that Americans had been "left behind" as prisoners and in the figures she offered, which, as Allen and Franklin demonstrate, stemmed from the Department of Defense's merger in 1980 of the categories "Killed in Action / Body Not Recovered" with the designation "Prisoner of War" and "Missing in Action."[160] Repeating them at the site designated "to interpret the role of prisoner-of-war stories in history," however, certified them as credible. In addition, the larger ceremony too, which featured an honor guard, wreath laying, and official remembrance of "those still listed as Prisoners of War in southeast Asia," officially sanctioned the league's insistence that Americans remained captive in Vietnam.[161] Indeed, the next day's *Americus Times-Recorder* showed Smith "among friends," embracing the superintendent and the head ranger.[162]

The focus on Vietnam returned two years later, in 1990, in the person of Rep. Pete Peterson (D-FL), himself a former Vietnam POW, as the keynote speaker. The next year, Deputy Assistant Secretary of Defense Alan C. Ptak, whose portfolio included the recovery of MIA remains, provided another instance of remembrance at Andersonville that stoked the POW/MIA movement's mythology. Referring to researchers' and activists' claims from the early 1990s that Soviet documents proved that Americans had remained imprisoned in Vietnam or, worse, in the Soviet Union, Ptak "revealed that he had recently returned from a mission to Russia where he sought the support of that country in helping locate any possible American military held prisoner there, as well as the bodies of any MIAs." He went on to say, "Russian promises will not be enough to satisfy us. We will be rigorous in our demand for, and analysis of, the results."[163] Here again, Andersonville's mission to document the POW experience in the United States gave official sanction to a myth in which prisoners remained alive and were victims of the nefarious plots of America's enemies.

Calls for continued attention to locating POWs and the remains of MIA continued at Andersonville at least until 2000, when Gen. Paul M. Lee of the Marine Corps "encouraged those present to press government officials until 'a full accounting of all MIAs is made real.'"[164] In the mid-1990s, however, another narrative arose, one that likewise mobilized Andersonville's interpretive mission to validate claims of American victimhood and Vietnamese brutality amid anxieties about the potential normalization of relations with Vietnam.[165] In this version of events, Andersonville was juxtaposed with Vietnam in ways that made the latter the most egregious example of captive Americans' suffering.

The Memorial Day address in 1994 by Adm. James Stockdale, fresh off his vice presidential campaign of 1992 and recently named cochairman of the efforts to build the National Prisoner of War Museum, is exemplary. Given the ominous cultural location that Andersonville had long occupied, making Vietnam worse was a tall order, but Stockdale made it clear that although the number of Civil War soldiers who died in POW camps was equal to the total number of deaths in Vietnam, his generation of POWs had it much worse: "The deaths [in Civil War prisons] were tied almost exclusively to poor sanitation and contagious diseases. I sensed nothing like the purges I and some of you have been through, where they isolated one prisoner after another and tortured him, choked him, shut off his blood circulation, sometimes broke his bones. . . . In a book about the trial of Andersonville's stockade commandant Captain Henry Wirz, I saw incompetence, I saw neglect, but I didn't see conspiracy, the crime he was executed for."[166]

Stockdale's comments juxtaposed a familiar reconciliationist view—that terrible conditions caused inevitable suffering—with one in which sadistic Vietnamese torturers caused intentional suffering.[167] Saying that "neglect of prisoners and indifference toward [prisoners] grew to be Standard Operating Procedure in [Civil War prisons]," he became almost wistful: "God, how I wish I could have had a little of that neglect and indifference. . . . Coercion and torture were used to intimidate. . . . To the die-hard leaders went years of solitary confinement and isolation. . . . Andersonville got down to about one guard to thirty or forty prisoners; I spent two years in a compound with 13 tiny cells, in leg irons and solitary throughout, and the 11 of us prisoners there were watched by two officers and 33 guards."[168] And if the facile comparison to Andersonville's well-known horrors weren't sufficient to vilify the Vietnamese, Stockdale described another prisoner who "had served time in a Nazi prison" who found that while "the Nazis wanted nothing from us," the Vietnamese sought to produce "wear and tear on your nervous system."[169] That Vietnamese prisons were worse than Andersonville and the Vietnamese more cruel than the Nazis dovetailed with the dominant discourse of Vietnamese sadism and American suffering that has long been central to the POW/MIA movement's revisionism.

The cultivation of Andersonville to certify the paramount narrative of the Vietnam POW experience and make it the defining story of American captivity continued over the next decade. In 1998 Rep. Sanford Bishop (D-GA) didn't go as far as Stockdale, but he nonetheless equated Andersonville and the "Hanoi Hilton," the infamous POW camp in North Vietnam.[170] In 2003, when the program commemorated the thirtieth anniversary of the POWs' return in 1973, the media coverage described the appearance of Dick Stratton, who "in March, 1967, . . . was forced by his captors to appear at a press conference in Hanoi" at which he "appear[ed] hollow-eyed and bowing like a mechanical man."[171] These uses of Andersonville to both officially sanction the POW/MIA movement's defining mythology and to make Vietnamese brutality and American POWs' suffering in Vietnam exceptional within the larger POW story would continue when the National Prisoner of War Museum opened in 1998.

"Visitors Can, for a Moment, Get a Sense of the Isolation and Loneliness"

On January 20, 1999, Superintendent of Andersonville Fred Boyles wrote, "For the first time in 28 years the park has met its Congressional Mandate."[172] This was the result, Boyles wrote, of "the long awaited building completion and dedication of National Prisoner of War Museum" (*sic*).[173] Over the next two years more than 300,000 people visited the museum.[174] Academic and popular reviewers have found much to commend about the exhibits, which seek to show the common experiences endured by prisoners of all wars.[175] The exhibits lead visitors through rooms that begin with the service members' initial capture, describe various facets of their incarceration, and conclude with either their escape or liberation. Cloyd is more equivocal, calling the museum "a triumph for the National Park Service" but criticizing its "idealized interpretation" and celebration of American wars; he locates it within "the ongoing desire of Americans to patriotically remember, and admire, the sacrifices of past soldiers."[176] I don't wish to underestimate the struggles of POWs or to quibble with the museum's many successes. Yet I build on Cloyd's observation by arguing that as the museum seeks to convey commonalities across the history of warfare, it constructs the suffering endured by American captives and their families and the wanton brutality meted out by the Vietnamese as exceptional by reproducing familiar revisionism.

The entrance to the "Capture" room, for example, features a photograph of a Vietnamese soldier leading a captured U.S. pilot and a quote from Spike Naysmyth's memoir, *2,355 Days: A POW's Story* that describes the POW as "cornered prey."[177] The image appears again in the museum's next section, "Journey to Camp," with a caption that reads, "An injured American pilot is led under guard through Hanoi."[178] This graphic, apparently used in place of a *Time* magazine photograph from 1973 that displays a "POW being heckled in a Vietnamese village," is the exhibit script's only entry for the theme "Public Humiliation."[179]

While the artifacts do not present the experiences of prisoners in other wars as being easy—for example, the "Journey to Camp" room evokes the Bataan Death March and includes images of Americans who died during it—this photograph is implicitly juxtaposed with the exhibit's quotation of a Geneva Convention mandate from 1929—that prisoners "must at all times be humanely treated and protected, particularly against acts of violence, insults and public curiosity"—in order to certify that during the Vietnam War, Americans needlessly suffered because of extraneous Vietnamese sadism.[180] An exhibit tag that acknowledges the cruelty of other enemies in other wars—again, for example, that of the Japanese during the Bataan Death March—notes that "using the international press [for propaganda purposes] was common during the Korean War and, to an unprecedented degree, during the Vietnam War as well."[181]

The museum's distinction between Vietnam and other wars, in which the latter, while never pleasant, were not marked by the captors' sheer depravity, continues throughout the museum, and the effect is to acknowledge how terrible captivity during other wars was while establishing Vietnam as especially brutal. The room titled "Camp Life" describes several prison camps' informal economies, through which prisoners obtained items from Spam to raisins, and shows a German guard negotiating with an American prisoner and the prosthetic arm and eyeglasses that American prisoners received in German camps.[182] In contrast, Vietnamese prisons are presented as lacking even rudimentary materials: "For POWs held in Vietnam, basic toiletries were rare commodities. While toothbrushes and toilet paper were fairly standard items, the toothpaste and soap belonging to former POW Vernon Ligon, Jr. were, in his words, '"going away" presents by the North Vietnam Communists and were *not* a normal POW fare.' "[183]

These juxtapositions demonstrate Vietnamese captors' needless inhumanity, as evidenced by their withholding of simple items that implicitly could have been provided earlier, and duplicity, shown in what is presumably their efforts to ensure that a prisoner preparing to meet his superiors, family, and the media appeared to have been well treated. Similarly, in the communications room, visitors learn about the newspapers produced in German POW camps and the crystal radios with which prisoners could listen to the British Broadcasting Corporation but discover that in Vietnam prisoners resorted to a forbidden tap code, "choosing to risk torture rather than give up their lifeline" in order to teach each other "how to uphold the code of conduct during torture sessions."[184] Similarly, a description of prisoners' use of codes offers a vaguely bureaucratic explanation that "during World War II, MIS-X coordinated the use of letter codes with its British counterpart, MI-9," but "during Vietnam, letter codes were used . . . to report on the use of torture by the North Vietnamese and to provide updated lists of the prisoners held in Hanoi."[185] In the next room, where visitors learn that while the families of Korean War POWs faced "tight censorship rules [that] restricted what they heard" and "months passed before they learned that their loved ones were alive but being held by the North Koreans," Vietnam again appears as worse because "POW families became aware that their loved ones were treated as 'war criminals' and subjected to torture."[186] As the repeated references to torture indicate, these representations cumulatively construct Vietnam as exceptional in its horror.

Nowhere is this claim more explicit than in the exhibits "Those Who Wait" and "Privation," both of which are dominated by Vietnam and enforce familiar claims about Vietnam POWs and their families' suffering. The entry to "Those Who Wait," which features Sybil Stockdale's quote, "Living through day after day of wondering and never knowing if Jim was alive became a way of life," superimposed on a photograph of Stockdale's family at Christmastime, recalls long-standing accounts of POW families' agony, as does the earlier reference to the families' awareness of their loved one's torture.[187] This is a sentiment that the NPS intentionally embraced in the room's defining artifact, a ten-minute video presentation of interviews with former POWs and their families. A "montage of candid shots and home movies sets the stage of home, hearth and family," but then the presentation shifts to "starker imagery": "The same men we saw moments ago as husband, fathers, sons and brothers are now POWs. From this point forward, the show traces the stories of approximately six POW families and chronicles their struggle to endure successive months and even years of separation and uncertainty. Two points of view are constantly juxtaposed: that of the man in prison longing for home, and that of his family wondering if he will come home alive."[188]

The designers made a point of noting that "care should be taken to include all wars," and the film does include stories from the Second World War and Korea.[189] It thereby enables visitors to read the experience of earlier wars through a construct that emerged during the Vietnam War and has dominated remembrance ever since. At the same time, the design plan emphasizes Vietnam:

> For example, we will see Vietnam POW Richard Stratton saying that his wife Alice had the more difficult struggle of the two. . . . We then see Alice Stratton describing the challenges of raising the children alone, of breaking the comfortable mold of the Navy wife who didn't rock the boat, all the while lobbying to let the public know about the mistreatment the Vietnam POWs endured. The children of POWs will have their voice to, [*sic*] describing what it was like to miss their daddy, maybe even forget what he looked like. The show deliberately avoids scenes of reunion.[190]

Much like the NPS's selection of Barbara Smith as a speaker, the video presentation and the extensive coverage of activism by the National League of Families helps sustain the popular view that Vietnam's suffering extended to families, who "had the more difficult struggle," as well as across generations and that the government was unresponsive. The exhibit thus demands the continual recognition and reaffirmation of the idea that Vietnam's trauma remains unresolved.

The "Privation" room even more emphatically constructs Vietnam as exceptional in the suffering it visited on captive soldiers. Despite containing some artifacts from Andersonville and explaining that during the Second World War "Americans were held in contempt by their [Japanese] guards and frequently subjected to random brutality," other wars are largely absent or presented as paling in comparison to Vietnam. This comparison is not because other wars were less horrific or because Americans were less interested in them; as Susan Carruthers has written, after Korea "homecoming soldiers faced ceaseless entreaties to elucidate communist brutality, the more gruesome their stories—or emaciated their bodies—the better" and that "accounts of camp life spared their readers no detail" of gruesome tortures.[191] The room does portray a reeducation session and mentions that "POWs in Korea were left for hours with their feet frozen in ice to 'reflect' on their crimes."[192] Yet even as it recounts this painful torture, the exhibit again casts Vietnam as having been worse, explaining in the next sentence, "The Viet Cong had their own techniques, including painful rope torture sessions and forcing prisoners to wear manacles and leg irons for days at a time."[193] The difference is small but significant: the Koreans made Americans suffer for hours, the Vietnamese for days.

The Vietnam War dominates this room, offering a sharp contrast with the "Morale" room, which follows it and features no Vietnam-era items—implying, perhaps, that Vietnam was so dire that maintaining morale was nearly impossible. The Vietnam POWs' isolation and torment are presented at the entrance to "Privation" through a large photograph of the prisoner Ted Triebel and James Stockdale's words that he has become "so despondent" from being in a "private hell" that he faces "all by myself."[194] Inside the room are pen-and-ink drawings of the stress positions that Vietnamese guards forced American prisoners to assume, descriptions of the Hanoi Hilton as "a virtual dungeon" in which Americans were subjected to "particularly brutal interrogation session[s]," a set of North Vietnamese manacles that "cut into the prisoners' flesh and left deep and painful bruises," and a list of Vietnamese prison rules that describe Americans as "the blackest criminal[s] that this country has ever seen."[195] This list doesn't appear in the plan for the exhibit, which instead calls for the reproduction of a sign listing the rules of a camp in Santo Tomas, the Philippines, during the Second World War.[196] The rules that do appear are apparently reproduced from the memory of the former POW "Lt. Cmdr. Charlie Plumb, a Navy pilot," who had "ample time to memorize camp regulations." Here, the cultural capital of the former POW, rather than an actual artifact, guides the presentation of Vietnamese atrocity.

The room's principal features, however, are replicas of two Hanoi Hilton cells and a bamboo tiger cage (figs. 1.2, 1.3). The first cell features a mannequin clad in striped pajamas and shackled to a concrete bunk. Notably, the mannequin's solitude contrasts with a picture on the other side of the room of a Second World War POW in solitary confinement but whose cell contains amenities, including reading materials. Museum visitors can enter the second Hanoi Hilton cell. The exhibit designers intended for this " 'Alcatraz' cell" to allow visitors to momentarily experience "the isolation and loneliness experienced by POWs held captive under such conditions." The exhibit is multisensory, including "the sounds a prisoner might have heard during the course of a day . . . guards, interrogation, [and] handcuffs."[197] This exhibit is unique in that nowhere else in the museum can a visitor fully occupy the position of a prisoner and experience a simulacrum of the trauma conveyed by the quotation from Winston Churchill that frames the entrance to the museum: "Prisoner of War! . . . You are in the power of your enemy! You must obey his orders, go where he tells you, stay where you are bid, await his pleasure, possess your soul in patience."[198] These two cells make the Vietnam POW experience the defining experience of American captivity by intimating that its horrors exceeded those of other wars. These cells were clearly compelling, as *U.S. News and World Report*, the *Christian Science Monitor*, and the *Atlanta Journal-Constitution*, the *Orlando Sentinel*, and other papers mentioned or included images of them in coverage of the opening of the museum.[199]

The "Privation" room does more, however, than define the Vietnam War as most representative of the suffering endured by American POWs. In keeping with the rest of the museum's emphasis on the Vietnamese penchant for torturing Americans, the room emphasizes Vietnamese prison guards' sadistic brutality. This is evident in the references to "interrogation" and a "dungeon" and in the manacles and the titles of the videos available in the room. Here again, the contrast with Korea is instructive. While the titles of the videos about that war emphasize the brutal conditions, only two mention "solitary confinement" or "summary execution." Five of the Vietnam videos use the word "torture" in the title; another is entitled "Russian Roulette as Interrogation Technique."

FIGURE 1.2. Replica of a cell at the "Hanoi Hilton," National Prisoner of War Museum, Andersonville National Historic Site. Visitors can enter the cell and "for a moment, get a sense of the isolation and loneliness experienced by POWs held captive under such conditions." The only space in the museum in which visitors can have such an experience, it contributes to the museum's presentation of the Vietnam War as exceptional in the brutality it visited on American servicemen. Photograph by the author.

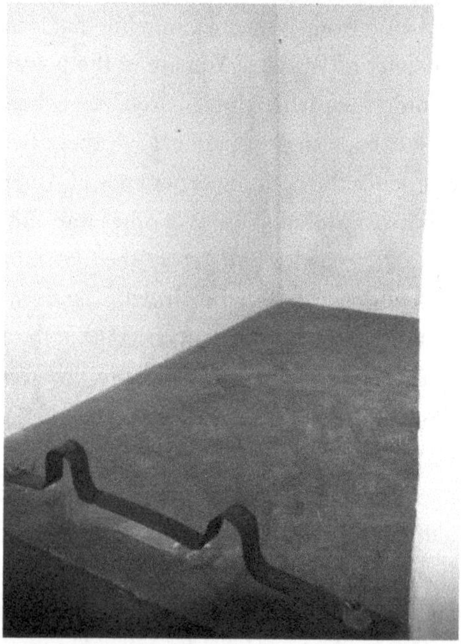

FIGURE 1.3. Replica of a cell at the "Hanoi Hilton," National Prisoner of War Museum, Andersonville National Historic Site.

This last title is a reminder that while Americans captured in Vietnam surely endured torture, it is also the case, as H. Bruce Franklin argues, that some of the most troubling images of violence committed by Americans in Vietnam have over the past several decades been recast as violence visited on Americans.[200] Franklin sees the revision of Eddie Adams's photograph of a South Vietnamese police chief executing a Viet Cong suspect during the Tet Offensive as the most egregious example of this rewriting of American violence. As he shows, "this image, with its roles reversed, would be transformed into the central metaphor of a Hollywood production crucial to reimaging the history of the Vietnam War and its prisoners of war" when it was inverted in the Russian roulette scene in *The Deer Hunter* and, later, in other texts in which Vietnamese soldiers similarly killed Americans.[201]

A similar inversion occurs in an interview of the former POW Querin Herlick: "They would make me kneel in front of the Viet Cong Major for questioning sessions," he explains; when he refused to provide information,

> he showed me the .38, took all his rounds out but one, he put it in, he spun the chamber, and threw it to a Private next to me, and he put it to my head. And he said, "I'm going to ask you again." And I gave him name, rank, and serial number. And, ah, at that point he pulled the trigger. And I said, "Uh-uh. I'm not going to be wasted in this jungle like this." So I began to lie. . . . and I repeated the questions and my answers very loudly because the two enlisted men were together in a hole about 20 feet away, and so they knew every question and answer before it became their turn for the sessions.[202]

Herlick's testimony is impossible to validate or discredit; what is important about it is that by including it, the museum, again in its official status as a National Historic Site, uses its cultural capital to support a revisionist narrative of the Vietnam War, one that silences histories of American-sponsored violence while affirming stories of Vietnamese sadism and American innocence, ingenuity, bravery, and selflessness.

The tiger cage similarly accomplishes such revision. A drawing that places the viewer in the captive's position explains that Nick Rowe, a Green Beret, "spent . . . five years of his life in a tiger cage. Two of those five were spent in solitary confinement."[203] Rowe is represented as the victim of sadists, men who wished to "break a POW's will during the Viet Cong's indoctrination process" by placing him in a cell "just long enough to fit a man lying down, not high enough to let him stand."[204] In portraying this violence as being inflicted only on Americans, the museum's description of the tiger cage maintains the silence around similar atrocities perpetrated by the South Vietnamese allies of the United States. As Franklin notes, one of the issues that stoked antiwar sentiment in the late 1960s was Americans' awareness of South Vietnam's "appalling prison camps" and, in particular, "the notorious tiger cages of Con Son Island, where the few survivors were almost all permanently disfigured and severely crippled by torture."[205] Franklin's point is important to understanding the museum's full participation in validating the overriding narrative of Vietnam POWs. Rowe spent a comparable amount of time in the cage before escaping, and the fact that he appears to be relatively healthy in a photograph taken "just after his escape" confirms the American soldier's masculine toughness that is central to POW mythology.[206]

The museum's curatorial choices draw upon familiar components of revisionist Vietnam history to establish that war as exceptional. However bad earlier wars or captors may have been, the exhibit repeatedly asserts, the Vietnam War and the Vietnamese were worse because depraved sadists wantonly flouted the rules of civilized warfare and took pleasure in the suffering visited on innocent U.S. soldiers and their families. In making this the war's primary tragedy, the impact of the conflict on the Vietnamese is forgotten, and, more important, the righteousness of the Vietnam War in particular and American militarism in general is confirmed.[207]

These emphases within Andersonville's remembrance were not preordained. As its significance early in the Vietnam War reveals, Andersonville at one point offered an opportunity to censure American involvement in Vietnam. Through programmatic and curatorial choices, a revisionist discourse came to dominate American remembrance of Vietnam at Andersonville. How deeply Andersonville has become a key site for such discourse is evident in JoAnne Shirley's keynote address at the POW/MIA recognition day ceremony held at the site on September 15, 2010. Shirley is the sister of Bobby Jones, the pilot who was shot down in 1972 and whose memorial stone was installed at Andersonville in 1978. If Jones's marker was at least a tacit admission of his death, it was not one that Shirley accepted. In the intervening years she had become a key figure in the POW/MIA movement and a major voice in the National League of Families and in making Andersonville a site for voicing POW/MIA issues.[208]

Her speech was a tour de force of the POW/MIA culture's suspicions and anxieties. She complained, for example, that Democratic administrations had "made it difficult to gather information" and left her in "a position of begging"; that the military had refused to DNA test all of the evidence; and that the villagers who found it had disappeared.[209] Although the air force confirmed Jones's death with archaeological evidence in 2008, Shirley didn't accept it.[210] The discovery of Jones's "blood chit," an identification tag carried by airmen, provided not relief but evidence of conspiracy. In 2008, when it had been found, Shirley told a Georgia newspaper that it was "verification that he's not a prisoner, he probably didn't suffer, he was probably killed on impact," an item that "takes away that wondering, 'What if? What if?' "[211] In 2010, though, her suspicions returned with a vengeance. "How could there be a blood chit, and no remains?" Shirley asked the crowd before giving them the answer provided by one of her advocates, the Georgia congressman Nathan Deal: "Nathan thinks that the blood chit was planted."[212]

Shirley's address demonstrates how deeply remembrance at Andersonville intersects with Vietnam's legacy, and how much it has changed in the forty years since Jimmy Williams's death. NPS planners' initial interest in enabling Americans to engage critical views of America's involvement in Indochina steadily gave way to officially sanctioned programs and curation that first buttressed Nixon-era justifications for continuing the war and then POW/MIA activists' claims that Americans had been brutalized and then abandoned in Southeast Asia. Repeatedly made to speak on behalf of Vietnam, Andersonville has come to legitimate notions of American innocence and Vietnamese guilt that have long been central to revisionist justifications of the war and the maintenance of exceptionalist narratives of American militarism.

CHAPTER 2

"WE VETERANS OF MASS MURDER AND STUPIDITY"

Older Veterans' PTSD and the Narration of Combat in Post-Vietnam Memoirs of the Second World War

IN THE EARLY 1980S, POLICE OFFICERS BROUGHT A VETERAN WHO HAD smashed his furniture and threatened his girlfriend at gunpoint to the Veterans Administration (VA) hospital in Milwaukee. He confessed to James Hamilton, the hospital's medical director, that following a night of drinking he had "vividly relived . . . a fellow Marine killing an old native woman for no obvious reason."[1] This was not the only disturbing incident of the veteran's tour: a few weeks after the first incident he had watched as a local woman who "apparently thought he was going to kill her child . . . slit the baby's throat herself."[2]

In 1982, when Hamilton's article about the veteran appeared in the *Bulletin of the Menninger Clinic,* the story fit quite nicely into the prevailing narrative of Vietnam veterans' experience. In the war's aftermath, veterans publicly sought help, confessed to atrocities, and lobbied the American Psychological Association to recognize post-traumatic stress disorder (PTSD).[3] By the 1980s, the horrors Vietnam veterans had witnessed and the psychological damage they suffered defined their experience.

The veteran described by Hamilton, however, was fifty-five years old, and his nights were troubled by memories of what he had experienced at

Okinawa. His was not an isolated case. Throughout the 1980s, psychiatrists, psychologists, and social workers published similar vignettes, relating tales of a veteran who suffered nightmares of machine-gunning a group of teenage boys whom he mistook for enemy soldiers; of another no longer able to make himself sleep by stroking a locket that he had taken from an unarmed enemy soldier whom he had killed; and of a veteran filled with shame by "a picture of himself and his buddies that had found its way into newspapers and that showed them holding the severed heads of their enemies."[4] These vignettes were anecdotal evidence amid clinicians' growing realization between 1979 and 1996—roughly the period between the official recognition of PTSD and the fiftieth anniversary of the end of the Second World War—that older veterans struggled with the disorder at rates that rivaled those of Vietnam veterans.

These realizations became politically controversial, as legislators debated whether older veterans deserved access to the mental health treatments that Vietnam veterans had struggled to achieve. Central to the debate was a nearly decade-long effort to open to older veterans the VA Vet Centers that had been created specifically for Vietnam veterans. The debate was not, however, simply about resources; it was also about the legacy of the Second World War. That is, did revelations about the continuing mental health struggles of Second World War veterans undermine the discursive separation of the two wars—one the noble mission that demanded enduring veneration, the other the misguided quagmire that demanded public healing—that had long been central to their public remembrance? Had there, in fact, been no "good war"?

The most important Second World War memoirists of this period asserted that this was indeed the case. However supportive of the need to wage the Second World War, E. B. Sledge, Paul Fussell, and William Manchester affirmed that they had suffered in ways nearly identical to the men who fought in Vietnam. In his memoir *With the Old Breed: At Peleliu and Okinawa* (1980) Sledge called the war "brutish, inglorious, and a terrible waste"; sixteen years later, Fussell's *Doing Battle: The Making of a Skeptic* (1996) referred to the so-called Greatest Generation as "we veterans of mass murder and stupidity"; and in *Goodbye, Darkness: A Memoir of the Pacific War* (1979) Manchester describes the nightmares about the war he began to have twenty-three years after coming home.[5]

Scholars have noted that revisionist views of the Second World War emerged in the post-Vietnam moment, and particularly in these three memoirs.[6]

Unrecognized, though, is that the capacity of Fussell, Sledge, and Manchester to make these claims relied on both the cultural work that Vietnam memoirs had done during the 1970s and their appropriation of that literature's tropes, strategies, and language. My interest in this chapter lies not in offering new interpretations of Vietnam memoirs or in pointing out that post-Vietnam memoirs of the Second World War challenge that conflict's dominant remembrance but in showing how key scenes in the former shaped the latter.

Trauma theorists explain that an individual's capacity to testify about trauma—the psychic response to an event that devastates an individual's foundational, though culturally constructed, ideas about himself or herself and his or her society—requires an audience that "know[s] the 'lay of the land'" and is able to "make [it]self known as one who knows" about such traumas.[7] As Leigh Gilmore stipulates, survivors must affirmatively answer two questions: "Can language be found for this experience? Will a listener emerge who can hear it?"[8]

Vietnam's remembrance enabled Second World War memoirists to find that language and thus those listeners. As the literary critic Philip Melling points out, "In the later years of the 1970s . . . the Vietnam veteran came to be regarded as a genuine witness whose right to testify publicly was seen as a worthwhile calling," and cultural products that meditated on Vietnam's brutality and on returning veterans' struggles were central to the war's legacy.[9] These representations created the conditions through which Americans became able, whether in VA examination rooms, congressional hearing rooms, or their living rooms, to hear similarly traumatic narratives of the Second World War that challenged that war's dominant remembrance. Most important, Vietnam memoirs supplied the language and tropes through which Second World War memoirists could voice such a challenge. Appropriating and redeploying the language of Vietnam memoirs, Sledge, Fussell, and Manchester revealed that combat in the Pacific and in Europe was disturbingly similar to that in Vietnam in its brutality and enduring psychological impact; in doing so, they helped legitimize medical and political discourses that presented the two wars and their veterans as fundamentally alike.

"Even Vietnam Didn't Tell Us It Could Last So Long"

Around the time Hamilton was interviewing the Okinawa veteran in Milwaukee, Merrill Lipton, a psychiatrist at a VA Medical Center in Temple, Texas, and his colleague William Schaeffer, a social worker, began noticing that their patients, most of whom had passed retirement age, had begun sounding a lot like Vietnam veterans—recalling "wartime events during which they were numb to the horror around them," professing "unreasonable guilt" at their actions, and reporting "nightmares, irritability, anxiety, depression, and daytime ruminations."[10] Drawing on the model of the "'rap groups' of Vietnam Veterans," Lipton and Schaeffer organized therapy sessions for these older men, who quickly became comfortable sharing difficult stories and helping each other come to terms with their violent experiences.[11] Several hundred miles to the east, at the VA Medical Center in Jackson, Mississippi, psychologists treating an anxious, alcoholic Second World War veteran who had nearly been killed in an attack on his ship found that methods originally used to treat Vietnam veterans could be applied "effectively in treating older combatants with fears of long duration."[12] And nearly a thousand miles north in Washington, D.C., VA psychologists told the Senate Veterans Affairs Committee that Second World War veterans "who were in heavy combat or who were exposed to other stressful situations . . . are experiencing problems which are similar to those of Vietnam veterans suffering from post-traumatic stress-disorder."[13] Nearly twenty-five hundred Second World War veterans, they reported, had already sought help at VA Outreach Centers.[14]

These were but three instances of researchers' increasing awareness after PTSD's official recognition as a psychological condition in 1980 that although Vietnam veterans suffered in greater percentages and with greater severity, a staggering number of elderly veterans were also haunted by what they had seen and done decades earlier. Legislators heard, for example, that "many World War II, Korean, and Vietnam veterans have struggled with this condition for years attempting to find ways to live normal lives."[15] That PTSD deeply affected Second World War veterans had become so widely accepted by the fiftieth anniversary of the war that older veterans were sometimes regarded as suffering more substantially even than Vietnam veterans.

The discovery that older veterans shared Vietnam veterans' struggles troubled the dominant remembrance of the Second World War, but it did not translate into unequivocal government support of treatment of those older veterans, particularly at the readjustment counseling centers Congress had created for Vietnam veterans in the early 1980s.[16] Several times in the 1980s and 1990s, liberal senators who viewed opening the centers to older veterans as a moral obligation proposed such legislation over Republican objections, only to have it routinely stripped from final legislation. Conservative opponents of these measures, by contrast, argued that they wasted money, but these debates were not simply about fiscal responsibility and the most useful apportioning of scant resources for an aging population, as conservatives also maintained that veterans of wars that had been over for decades didn't need readjustment counseling. These discussions were thus part of a larger debate about the Second World War's legacy, because determining that that war's veterans suffered in ways similar to, and could benefit from the treatment protocols designed for, Vietnam veterans amounted to defining Vietnam not as aberrant, but as the model of American militarism.

LIPTON AND SCHAEFFER AND OTHERS WHO RECOGNIZED PTSD IN OLDER veterans did so in a culture that closely, if not universally, associated the condition with Vietnam veterans. Initially, in fact, this notion met with some resistance amid assertions that whatever suffering older veterans had endured paled in comparison to that of Vietnam veterans, who had faced unconventional combat while deployed and social marginalization after their return. "Vietnam syndrome is considered similar to . . . 'combat fatigue' among World War II veterans," the Associated Press reported in May 1981. "But experts say the emotional wounds of Vietnam run deeper."[17] Senate hearings echoed these sentiments. In 1984 the Vietnam veteran Max Cleland, who had been the VA administrator during the administration of President Jimmy Carter, told the Senate Veterans Affairs Committee, "I think that it is not that the Vietnam veteran underwent any particularly greater stress in combat. But I think part of what I have learned about it is stress back here became pretty severe because of the absence of one basic element, and that was public support to help one deal with that."[18] A year later, the *New York Times* described one Vietnam veteran and outreach center counselor's recollection that "a World War II veteran came to the center and told him: 'I know that you never got your parade. I know that you can't sleep at night cause you're afraid you'll have nightmares. I still get nightmares. I know what you're going through, because I've been there—I'm still going through it'" only to undercut this undeniable moment of transgenerational solidarity by saying that "Vietnam was a different war."[19] Such claims recited a familiar story of Second World War veterans as having had few difficulties and much support and hence as qualitatively different from Vietnam veterans.[20]

This sentiment, however, was increasingly overwhelmed by research demonstrating that Second World War veterans suffered significantly and in ways identical to those of Vietnam veterans. Moments after Cleland's testimony, in fact, Arthur Arnold, the head psychiatrist at the Phoenix VA Medical Center, told the committee he had "seen a number of World War II veterans who have a clinical syndrome indistinguishable from the PTSD of Vietnam veterans. . . . some of them have had symptoms which they have attempted to conceal for more than 30 years."[21]

Arnold's testimony reflected a growing medical consensus. By the 1990s, researchers confidently declared not just the existence of the problem but its staggering prevalence: that "those who have looked systematically for evidence of PTSD in World War II combat veterans have had little difficulty finding it," that "veterans of [World War II and Korea] suffer from the same symptoms that have been so well documented in Vietnam combat veterans," and that although "a great deal of attention has been focused on PTSD in the Vietnam-era veteran population . . . many World War II and Korean Conflict veterans suffering from PTSD must have their needs addressed."[22]

The years in which these studies were performed and these claims made, however, were not marked by smooth progress toward this consensus, nor did discussion about how to address the matter end when it was reached. Researchers debated, for example, whether similar symptoms arose from similar experiences and called for the same treatment.[23] Comparing the two populations became an imperative in the second half of the eighties.[24] One of the most important and frequently cited studies, conducted by the Duke University School of Medicine and the Durham, North Carolina, VA Medical Center, studied forty-four veterans of the two wars who had been diagnosed with PTSD and determined not only that Vietnam veterans "exhibited significantly more severe PTSD, depression, and global severity of illness" but also that the events described as most traumatic differed markedly between the two groups.[25] Asked to describe the war's "most upsetting events," veterans of both wars gave responses that might be expected; approximately equal numbers, for example, cited seeing a dead body or feeling guilty at surviving when their friends did not.[26] Yet while one-third of the Vietnam veterans chose "sight of mutilated bodies" or "observing or taking part in brutality" as most traumatic and one-fifth chose witnessing a child's death, not a single veteran of the earlier war identified such incidents as traumatic.[27] Researchers concluded that "WW2 combat veterans may have perceived their trauma . . . as being more related to events that threatened their own physical integrity or freedom, whereas VN veterans appear to have been struggling with traumatic experiences related to interpersonal issues," notably "their own destructive impulses."[28] The study thus acknowledged a similar level of suffering by both groups but reestablished the two wars as morally dissimilar.

Other studies reached different findings. In 1990 the Department of Veterans Affairs produced the first volume of *The Long Journey Home: The First Progress Report on the Department of Veterans Affairs PTSD Clinical Teams Program.* Nearly equating the Second World War and Vietnam cohorts' experiences, it showed that around 70 percent of the veterans were traumatized by "being exposed to death and dismemberment" and 40 and 49 percent, respectively, of Second World War and Vietnam veterans were traumatized by "killing others."[29] Perhaps of most import, though, the study asked veterans "whether they had ever witnessed or participated in behavior that they believed to be 'morally wrong,'" concluding that such behaviors were epidemic and that "it is important to recognize, furthermore, that these experiences are not unique to Vietnam veterans. Although World War II veterans did not report participating in abusive violence (5.4%) as frequently as other veterans did, a substantial percentage reported having witnessed such violence (31.1%)."[30] More than the Duke study, then, *The Long Journey Home* insisted on a transgenerational parity of veteran experience that challenged ascendant understandings of the Second World War; when the study's third volume appeared in 1993, the authors, Alan Fontana and Robert Rosenheck, confidently declared that age seemed to mitigate PTSD symptoms, but "the similarity of relationships between traumatic exposure and symptoms across wars testifies to the generality of the effects of these experiences"; their results, they maintained, were "likely to be applicable to modern warfare in general."[31]

These resemblances in symptomatology, and particularly the recognition that participation in or witnessing of violence and brutality produced symptoms, was more thoroughly established in "Long-Term Sequelae of Combat in World War II, Korea, and Vietnam: A Comparative Study," another study by Rosenheck and Fontana. Noting that Vietnam veterans formed the sample for most PTSD studies, they embraced earlier hypotheses that "suggested that both the guerilla nature of combat in Vietnam and the public controversy surrounding the war resulted in a degree of social alienation and psychological stress among Vietnam veterans that was relatively uncommon among veterans of World War II." They hypothesized that "specific war zone experiences and traumas would differ among combat veterans of the three wars," as would "social maladjustment problems."[32]

Their study of more than two thousand veterans confirmed elements of both the Duke study and *The Long Journey Home*, identifying Vietnam veterans as both more deeply affected by PTSD and more likely to have been traumatized by complicity in atrocities.[33] Yet the *causes* of PTSD were, again, similar in the two groups, with nearly equal numbers of each describing as traumatic incidents in which they "saw troops killed," "sat with the dying," were "horr[ified] at death and dismemberment," and were "horr[ified] at the stream of human remains."[34] And while about six times as many Vietnam veterans as Second World War veterans admitted to *perpetrating* atrocities, nearly a third of the older veterans had been traumatized by *witnessing* such acts.[35] These results contributed to a growing consensus that the similar postwar experiences of veterans of both wars emerged from their having witnessed similarly gruesome events. As three counselors from Mountain Home VA Medical Center in Tennessee declared in 1994, "Although the post-traumatic stress program staff agreed with the contention that Vietnam was by far the most morally suspect war in which America engaged in modern times and that it created the most problems for those who fought in it, we were surprised to learn how many World War II and Korean Conflict veterans expressed distress over the brutality and violent acts they had committed or observed during their own tours of duty."[36]

The growing sense that veterans of the two wars were equally traumatized and for similar reasons was not lost on members of Congress. In the 1980s witnesses before the House and Senate Veterans Affairs Committees repeatedly noted that older veterans suffered from PTSD and were seeking treatment at Vet Centers; during a meeting on July 21, 1987, discussing Vet Centers, Senate staffers learned that at "all mental health facilities" older veterans composed a "good chunk of visits," and that the VA made "no effort to look for them" because they "come by word of mouth."[37] By 1991 a Senate Veterans Affairs Committee report argued that these "numbers indicate an obvious unmet need among them [older veterans] for the services provided by Vet Center staff and, in turn, clearly demonstrate the need for legislation authorizing Vet Centers to provide services to them."[38]

Getting funding for this purpose proved nearly impossible. From 1984 through 1995 Democrats regularly introduced, against Republican opposition, legislation expanding VA Readjustment Counseling to veterans of the Second World War and the Korean conflict only to have the provision removed or, when it passed, fail to become law before finally passing in the Veterans' Eligibility Health Care Reform Act of 1996. The debates reveal the extent to which the recognition of Vietnam veterans' suffering threatened the predominate remembrances of the Second World War.

To Senate liberals, the expanding of Vet Center funding to older veterans addressed a public health crisis and met a moral obligation. The senators were eventually, though not initially, supported in their efforts by major veterans' organizations, who seemingly felt Vietnam service members had received special treatment. In 1990 the American Legion complained of "an enormous gap in what should be VA's obligation to provide care on an equitable basis for all those who suffer from PTSD," while the Disabled American Veterans called it "patently unfair to deny [older] veterans the full array of [VA] mental health services."[39] Like the professional journals, such testimony served to de-essentialize Vietnam veterans' experience; like the media coverage that came later, it also made veterans of the Second World War the original but forgotten victims of PTSD.

Readjustment counseling was, by congressional designation, restricted to Vietnam veterans, and older veterans had legislative opponents as well as allies, namely, conservative committee members who viewed the expansion of Vet Centers as a misuse of limited funds and a treatment in search of a malady. The contours of this debate became apparent in the summer and fall of 1987, when the Senate debated a Veterans Affairs Bill that included "Readjustment Counseling Program Improvements," which would have allowed "any veteran who served on active duty during World War II or the Korean Conflict" to request counseling to "[*overcome*] *any psychological problems associated with such veteran's or person's service during such period.*"[40]

This language was introduced over the objections of the VA, which declared, "We find no rationale to extend eligibility for this program to World War II and Korean Conflict veterans for their 'readjustment' to civilian life. These conflicts ended 30 to 49 years ago."[41] Senate Republicans adopted this position as well. On July 16, 1987, Anthony Principi, the chief counsel to Republicans on the Veterans Affairs Committee, wrote that he was "especially concerned about expanding entitlement and/or eligibility for this program at a time when veterans who fought in World War II, Korea, or Vietnam are, in certain cases, having difficulty receiving hospital or outpatient health-care services because of limited resources."[42] This memo was never sent, but its sentiment framed Sen. Frank Murkowski's (R-AK) message on the Senate floor that, given the age of earlier veterans, the money was better spent on geriatric services; and that anyway "most of these veterans . . . have readjusted to civilian life over the last 40 years."[43] Murkowski's chief point may have been financial, but he was also skeptical about Second World War veterans' claims; "That this body would tell a combat veteran of World War II that he cannot receive treatment for medical problems . . . but he can go down to the local vet center and participate in a rap session to readjust to civilian life . . ." Murkowski explained, "is bizarre."[44]

His colleagues shared this suspicion. Jesse Helms (R-NC) said, "This expansion is untenable. These veterans at this point in their lives need scarce Government funds spent on hospital and nursing home care much more than they need Government paid psychological counseling to help them 'readjust to civilian life' 35 to 45 years after their return from battle."[45] Helms may have required quotation marks in the *Congressional Record* to convey his incredulity; Sen. Alan Simpson (R-WY) did not: "As for extending these services to veterans of our earlier wars, I must honestly ask, 'Why?' How many decades should be set aside to readjust to civilian life? Armistice was declared in the Korean Conflict in 1953—34 years ago—and World War II ended 42 years ago. Yet this bill proposes that veterans of those wars be eligible for counseling to help them readjust to civilian life. . . . These veterans of Korea and World War II seem to have done a fine job of adjusting up to this point."[46] Although they implied that sufficient care was available at VA hospitals or through Medicare and Medicaid, Murkowski, Helms, and Simpson thought the matter went beyond fiscal discipline.[47] To them, the very notion that counseling was necessary bordered on the absurd.

Sen. Alan Cranston (D-CA), the committee's ranking Democrat, was not, however, an insignificant opponent. He took to the Senate floor each time the provision came up, twice quoting Arnold's testimony from 1981 and reading into the record a *Los Angeles Times* article about PTSD in Second World War veterans.[48] And he became increasingly vigorous. In 1988 the issue was once again introduced as part of a bill titled "Veterans Benefits and Healthcare Amendments of 1990." In March, Arthur Blank, the head of the Readjustment

Counseling Service, wrote a memo that the committee staff apparently never delivered to the senators; it was filed with a Post-it note reading, "Highly confidential; never submitted."[49] Yet Blank's conclusions offer crucial insight into both the scope of the problem and the possible solutions. "World War II and Korean veterans come to the vet center even knowing that the center is established for Vietnam era veterans," Blank wrote. "It appears that some . . . veterans who come seeking help are those with previously undiagnosed and untreated PTSD, who therefore have related readjustment problems."[50] These men were coming of their own accord, "based on what they have heard about readjustment counseling services from Vietnam veteran friends or family members. Some cases are World War II veteran fathers . . . of Vietnam veterans."[51]

Blank then proposed expanding Vet Center coverage to include Second World War and Korean conflict servicemen. Such an initiative, he claimed, would not only "utilize the talent and experience of readjustment counseling staff for the benefit of war veterans of other than the Vietnam era" but also "end what has gradually become an artificial and unnecessary exclusion of non-Vietnam War veterans from readjustment counseling services."[52] "There are," Blank concluded, "no major disadvantages to this proposal," cost included, as Blank "expect[ed] to implement this proposal within existing resources."[53]

Blank's report, like Principi's memo in 1987, was apparently never made available to the committee. But when the expansion of readjustment counseling came to the Senate floor later that year and was again opposed by Republicans, Senator Cranston was upset, declaring himself "unable to understand the opposition to making these services available to those veterans who may need counseling."[54] Two years later, he railed at length about Republican intransigence and the need for the provision:

> The need of veterans of wars prior to Vietnam for vet center services is not a hypothetical concept. . . . Whether we in this Chamber choose to acknowledge it or not, veterans from earlier wars do suffer—often times many, many years later—from psychological readjustment problems directly related to their experiences in combat. And having psychiatric care available in conventional hospital settings is well and good, but it is not enough. There are many that we can reach only through community-based treatment and outreach programs such as vet centers. . . .

> Mr. President, denying that older veterans or post-Vietnam veterans may need readjustment counseling directly contradicts everything we have learned over the years about wars and the psychological effects on those who fight them.[55]

Cranston's remarks directly rebuke Helms and Simpson. Beyond his contention that the suffering of older veterans was incontrovertible and that making treatment accessible to them was a "fundamental obligation," his reference to "everything we have learned over the years" privileged Vietnam as the initial site of knowledge about PTSD. He made the same point a few months later when he said, "It would be most misguided, based on differences between Vietnam and other wars, to fail to recognize the basic value of Vet Centers and readjustment counseling to combat veterans" and that counselors experienced in treating Vietnam veterans were best prepared to help older veterans.[56] Like Rosenheck's and Fontana's work, Cranston's speeches effectively universalized the psychological impact of combat in terms that had been defined through research on and advocacy by Vietnam veterans.

Senator Simpson would have none of this. Although he presented himself as both an army veteran—he had spent two years stationed in Germany during the mid-1950s—and a "very proud" member of several veterans' organizations, he was skeptical of expanding veterans' services.[57] He repeatedly called for means testing of veterans and for prioritizing the treatment of service-connected injuries over those that were not. Simpson also remained wary of powerful veterans' organizations, which he suggested sought to squeeze more resources out of a strapped government. He summed up his position in a press release in 1987: "Show me a veteran fighting or injured in combat and I say, 'Write the Ticket.' . . . But most veterans who benefit from VA medical care are not even receiving treatment for service-connected conditions. And even those veterans who receive treatment for service-connected conditions may not be receiving treatment anything at all presently having to do with their military duties."[58]

With characteristic bluntness, Simpson further explained that "veterans surely do not need an even stronger voice or more effective advocate than they already have. Congress itself is their greatest ally. . . . When they 'put out the word' about a veterans' bill in the halls of Congress, you'd better step back into the cloakroom, because the velocity of those of us rushing in to cast an 'aye' vote nearly sucks all the air out of the chamber."[59]

Simpson's desire to reduce entitlements was perhaps matched by a generational wariness about mental health care. Studies conducted in 1979 and 1992, for example, found, respectively, that "older adults hold the attitude that seeking mental health services is a sign of personal weakness" and "tend to associate mental disorder with personal failure or spiritual deficiency."[60] Simpson's opinion of therapy remains a mystery, but his sense that readjustment counseling for older veterans was medically unnecessary and financially irresponsible was prominent throughout the eighties and nineties. Three weeks prior to Cranston's speech, he sent a letter to his colleagues opposing the legislation, writing, "It is mind-boggling to suggest that veterans of World War I, World War II, and the Korean conflict now 'suddenly' need assistance in order to adjust to civilian life." He reminded his readers that VA psychological services remained available to veterans "to the extent that they qualify for them"; he concluded, however, by explaining that "to the extent that those veterans need help readjusting after all these years, perhaps that suggests more severe psychological problems."[61] Simpson's quotation marks hint at his disdain and assumption that older veterans simply wanted in on more programs.

Moments after Cranston's remarks, Simpson took the floor to deride his colleague's position. Claiming to be sympathetic to older veterans' psychic needs, he argued that existing VA Medical Centers were sufficient to treat them. Yet he remained skeptical of the need for readjustment counseling. "It boggles the mind to me that veterans of World War II, the hideous war that ended 45 years ago, are still having trouble readjusting to life after military service," he complained, before arguing that diagnosing those veterans with PTSD was anachronistic: "Let us not deal with the readjustment for World War II veterans under description of an ailment that was not even in existence at the time."[62]

Simpson's position was fully in line with that of the administration of President George H. W. Bush. In June 1990 Secretary of Veterans Affairs Edward J. Derwinski had written him, "We do not believe the long period of time that has elapsed since those conflicts would warrant the provision of special readjustment benefits now available to Vietnam era veterans."[63] Characteristically, Simpson toed this line with a bit more flair, scrawling on a set of talking points, "What are we up to now?" again claiming that "these fine vets made the transition" and averring that his colleagues had "work[ed the provision] in just to pick up more votes."[64]

In 1991, when the provision reappeared, he said it was "bizarre" and explained, "The VA fully treats those who have that distress from the Second World War and from Korea."[65] However, he seemed unwilling to accept that such problems actually endured: "It seems to me to be stretching things to the breaking point of absurdity to attribute problems of [*sic*] difficulties now for a war that ended 45 years ago. . . . I think we must honestly conjecture how many decades it takes to readjust to civilian life."[66] Clearly, Simpson's desire to shrink government aligned with his attitude about the Second World War and psychic trauma.[67]

Simpson's most vigorous exchange came in 1993 in a hearing on "VA Mental Health Programs" that again sought to expand Vet Center treatment. The senator summarily dismissed a witness who claimed that PTSD "does not relinquish itself with time and does not remit over the passage of time," a VA psychiatrist who protested that "PTSD is not just something that happens to Vietnam veterans . . . it's something that happens to older veterans from other wars," and the committee chairman Jay Rockefeller (D-WV), who suggested that "the whole understanding of this problem has been grossly underestimated."[68] "Surely somebody has to recognize," Simpson said, "that if somebody was in the service in 1943 or 1944 and it's 1993, that they've been through all the riveting, sandblasting processes of life. . . . Now, is whatever has happened to them at this point in life due to what happened in 1943? I don't believe that is so."[69] Simpson went on to couch his complaint in fiscal terms, but even this revealed his sense that psychological wounds were less significant than physical ones: "The cost of it is going to take from the very veterans that need it the most. The older veteran who doesn't have PTSD or anything else, who served in combat, had a piece of himself shot off, and he is now looking for the proper pensions and disability and so on, will not find that help available. Because the money is being diverted to a cadre of people who don't want to give up the great role of 'counselor.'"[70] Simpson's grievance was thus as much philosophical as financial. Vet Centers did not simply duplicate an existing VA medical service; implicit in contending that Vet Centers served a specialized purpose to which Second World War veterans had no claim was tantamount to saying that their experience could not be equated with that of Vietnam veterans.

The next week Simpson sent a note to a staffer admitting that he "was really stringing it out that day" and "really hopped in that tank and got wet all over."[71] But he also didn't "want to change one thing in substance."[72] He maintained this position even as the fiftieth anniversary of the end of the war refocused media attention on the veterans' psychological struggles. In 1994 and 1995 newspapers cautioned readers that veterans might develop PTSD or experience relapses as they watched commemorative celebrations, that veterans "still fight private battles with nightmares, depression, alcoholism, and rage," and that they were arriving at hospitals "stunned and disturbed, weeping and guilt-ridden, as commemorative tales of 50-year-old battles sweep the nation with nostalgia but rake their peace of mind."[73]

Unsurprisingly, Vietnam emerged as a touchstone, as coverage equated the two experiences—noting, for example, "We are used to seeing these symptoms in Vietnam veterans. The issues for these men are no different" and that "if post-traumatic stress is an invention of the Vietnam War, it's only because by then people had given it a name."[74] Such comments furthered the discourse in which PTSD in older veterans was simultaneously surprising and evidence of their having been insufficiently cared for. Vietnam veterans at least had a condition "with a name."

Other articles similarly portrayed older veterans as being more deeply afflicted than Vietnam veterans because they had silently suffered for so long. Calling veterans men "of that good and victorious war for humanity's future" who "never dreamt, until nightmares struck in retirement, that they might suffer, decades delayed, from the post-traumatic stress disorder more familiarly associated with veterans of Vietnam, that war of muddled guilt," the *New York Times* construed PTSD as unexpectedly tainting the supposed good war.[75] The Associated Press made a similar gesture, reporting that "to the extent that World War II veterans even thought about [PTSD], it was often to draw a distinction between themselves and the Vietnam vets. But now psychologists are finding that PTSD is ambushing many World War II veterans."[76] Here, Second World War veterans were *more* victimized, "struck," and "ambush[ed]," either long suffering or facing "unexpected" PTSD. One Indiana newspaper opined, "Today's better understanding of [PTSD] is part of the legacy of the Vietnam War. But even Vietnam didn't tell us it could last so long."[77]

The renewed media attention to Second World War veterans' struggles with PTSD did little to move the Vet Center debate along, and Simpson was apparently equally unmoved; Vietnam remained unique and providing similar counseling to older veterans was inconceivable. In a 1995 hearing on the matter, he continued to avow that the facilities "were created to serve combat veterans of Vietnam—that's who they were for—with unique readjustment problems and needs. . . . And to go back and look at World War I, World War II, or Korean War veterans and think we need vet centers to deal with their needs—that's beyond my comprehension. Those wars ended some time ago."[78]

In 1996, however, the provision finally passed in the Veterans' Health Care Eligibility Reform Act, which provided that "upon the request of any veteran . . . who served in the active military, naval, or air service in a theater of combat operations . . . during a period in which hostilities (as defined in subparagraph (B)) occurred . . . the Secretary may furnish counseling to the veteran to assist the veteran in readjusting to civilian life."[79] Bringing the bill to the floor, Sen. Daniel Akaka (D-HI) declared himself "especially pleased with sections of the bill that make improvements in the Readjustment Counseling Service [RCS] program," particularly those "making World War II and Korea theater veterans eligible for vet center services for the first time."[80] Two days earlier Senator Simpson had similarly risen to support what he termed "one of the most significant veterans' bills of the last few years" and one that "changes the nature of our Nation's health care commitment to veterans that are more far-reaching than any decision since the end of World War II."[81] Surprisingly, he made little mention of the provision, mentioning only, "Mandatory counseling eligibility would be limited to combat theater veterans."[82] His apparent acceptance, whether in contentment or resignation, of this compromise perhaps emerged from a political calculation; having not sought reelection in 1996 and "in the last days of [his] chairmanship of the [Veterans' Affairs] committee" as well as of his Senate career, Simpson was perhaps mindful of his legacy and eager to see such major legislation become law.[83] Whatever the case, advocates of expanding readjustment counseling to older veterans had finally succeeded.

During the decade and a half after PTSD entered the American lexicon, a growing body of psychological research demonstrated that veterans of both Vietnam and the Second World War endured similar trauma because of similar encounters with war's violence and brutality. As these discoveries challenged dominant remembrances that differentiated the two wars, veterans' organizations and liberal legislators, as we have seen, clashed with conservative opponents over whether older veterans deserved the treatment options offered to Vietnam veterans. Amid these debates, Americans encountered memoirs of the Second World War that portrayed combat as traumatic in much the same way Vietnam had been, and did so in terms familiar—if not borrowed—from the memoirs of Vietnam.

"No One Had Heard of Post-Traumatic Stress Disorder, But . . . I Experienced Something Close to It"

Paul Fussell, unlike Alan Simpson, was only too happy to retroactively apply a term coined for Vietnam veterans. In 1989 Fussell published *Wartime: Understanding and Behavior in the Second World War,* which complained that "for the past fifty years the Allied war has been sanitized and romanticized almost beyond recognition by the sentimental, the loony patriotic, the ignorant, and the bloodthirsty."[84] In a *Washington Post* interview, Fussell remarked that Vietnam veterans "have a lot to say about post-traumatic stress," but "their experience is nothing compared to those who have lived with it for 40 years."[85] That his strong words bordered on the dismissive is somewhat ironic, given that his own memoir, *Doing Battle: The Making of a Skeptic,* which appeared in 1996, borrowed heavily from the tropes and language of the Vietnam memoir as it explained "how a young person was damaged . . . and what happened as a result."[86] He was not alone in doing so. He had, in fact, been preceded by two luminaries whose memoirs comprise the canon of post-Vietnam memoirs of the Second World War: William Manchester's *Goodbye, Darkness* and E. B. Sledge's *With the Old Breed.* Both of these works also challenge familiar remembrances of the Second World War by crafting story lines that comported with and borrowed from the dominant discourse of Vietnam memory.[87]

As John Bodnar has noted, these memoirs mark a departure from the prevailing recollection of the good war, a point he demonstrates by adverting to many of the passages I analyze below.[88] What has gone unstudied, however, is that that departure relies on recalling and redeploying the expressions and motifs central to Vietnam memoirs. By 1980 the notion that particular experiences precipitated trauma among American servicemen was central to Vietnam's legacy, and a vocabulary had been created to describe those experiences and that impact. In crucial scenes, Fussell, Sledge, and Manchester appropriate and adapt the discourses, tropes, and language of Vietnam memory, and above all of the most important Vietnam memoirs—those by Philip Caputo, Ron Kovic, and Tim O'Brien—to emphasize that in encountering wounded bodies, witnessing American atrocities, and experiencing disillusionment one undergoes enduring psychological damage. These memoirs thereby contributed to the broader claims that the wars were similarly traumatic.

In presenting their experience in ways that resonate with contemporary remembrances of Vietnam, these texts are notably different from memoirs of the early Cold War era, advancing and bringing into sharper focus notions of wartime experience that were absent or occluded in those earlier texts. Cold War texts themselves revise memoirs written in the Second World War's aftermath (a moment when Americans were anxious about the psychology of returning veterans), accounts which are relentless in their portrayal of the war as horrifically brutal.[89] In the earliest memoirs, death is omnipresent and graphically rendered. Men are run over by their own tanks, the air is filled with the smell of charred corpses, limbs are severed, and flesh is peeled from bones. People die slowly as they scream, breathe haltingly, and suffer bloody wounds. German prisoners are executed, American soldiers despair, commanding officers are incompetent careerists, and returning veterans have difficulty adapting to postwar life.[90]

By the 1950s, however, memoirists had begun rendering combat in ways that contributed to and accorded with the growing national veneration of the Second World War.[91] A reader of the most popular memoirs of the war, that is, the prize-winning, best-selling, and widely reviewed works published between 1950 and 1968—including Ross Carter's *Those Devils in Baggy Pants* (1951), Howard Randall's *Dirt and Doughfeet: Combat Experiences of a Rifle Platoon Leader* (1955), Lester Atwell's *Private* (1958), Robert Leckie's *Helmet for My Pillow: From Parris Island to the Pacific* (1958), and James C. Fry's *Combat Soldier* (1968)—did not frequently encounter graphic descriptions of wartime violence, and indeed, would have found that such violence was often obscured. Even as such works paint the war as a trying and dangerous enterprise, they barely acknowledge combat's dehumanizing effects and its enduring physiological and psychological damage and hardly find fault with its modes of conduct and political imperatives.

This is not to say the texts neglect the oppressive conditions under which the men fought.[92] Leckie's and Carter's early pages sound more like a vacation postcard than a war story: "We lived a rollicking, boisterous life for about a week, until the liquor ran out" and "There was plenty of wine. Cantaloupes, tomatoes, and grapes abounded." By the end, however, Carter describes his platoon as "refugees from the law of averages" and "miserable pawns on the checkerboard of battle," and Leckie is "emaciated and weakened beyond measure."[93]

Whatever difficulty these soldiers might face, though, is mitigated by both the courage of the men they fight with and their larger commitment to the cause. When Americans must fight, they do so bravely and take risks willingly. The composite American soldier is strong, decent, and dedicated; if they fear death, they also fear that their nerve might fail.[94] While unsoldierly behavior such as self-inflicted wounds or the mistreatment of prisoners is occasionally mentioned, it is dismissed casually, condemned quickly, and juxtaposed against more egregious atrocities committed by the enemy.[95] When, in Atwell's memoir, an American soldier's court-martial for killing German soldiers becomes an opportunity for American troops to embarrass an unpopular general, "the justice or injustice of killing the German prisoners had dwindled far to the back of the picture."[96]

Moreover, these memoirs are unquestioning as to the wisdom and necessity of the war. Carter writes in the preface that he "belonged to a Legion of doomed men, but death is less bitter when the alternative is slavery"; Leckie writes, "I did not know what I had gotten out of it, or even that I was supposed to profit. Now I know. For myself, a memory and the strength of ordeal sustained; for my son, a priceless heritage; for my country, sacrifice"; Randall prefaces *Dirt and Doughfeet* by declaring, "The author emerged from the war with a deepened love for America" and ends it by touring Buchenwald, with one of his buddies getting the last word: "You know—I can see why we fought this damned war."[97] Passages like these establish the war as a patriotic defense of democracy and contribute to the veneration of the Second World War as a noble and necessary pursuit fought with bravery and dignity.

This vision of the war is buttressed by the memoirs' representations of combat. Certainly, these texts do not shy away from the reality that in war men are injured and die or that the deaths of close friends are tragic. Carter grieves for his lost platoon-mates, and Atwell describes one man's death as a "terrible, careless waste."[98] And yet the injured body rarely receives sustained attention. In these books, representations of war as gory and inhumane are frequently and insistently replaced by images of painless deaths and insignificant wounds, and violent death never becomes an occasion for denouncing the war or its policies.

When injuries are described, they are quickly passed over.[99] Fry's description of a decapitated soldier and Atwell's description of a hospital are the two most graphic scenes in these works. Leckie's most vivid scene is of a crocodile eating a Japanese corpse, and his meditation that to see a severed hand "was to see the especially brutal savagery of our own technique of rending, and it was to see men at their eternal worst" stands alone within these texts as a moment of critical reflection on the war's moral valences.[100]

Wounds that are described are often rendered in the language that Elaine Scarry notes is central to obfuscating the reality that "the main purpose and outcome of war is injuring."[101] According to Scarry, the body and the trauma it suffers can be "actively escorted out of view," described in a "vocabulary . . . of cost"; "*redescribed* and hence be as invisible as if omitted," especially when it is redescribed as "inanimate"; or, finally, simply "omitted."[102] In these texts, Germans and Japanese die instantly with neither apparent pain nor deadly wounds. A German soldier "dropped his chow, grabbed his chest, and fell off the tank to the ground"; others simply "did not rise" after battle.[103] Leckie's shooting of Japanese soldiers doesn't even produce bodies. He "fired and he wasn't there anymore," and he describes bodies "rolling over and over, down the hill, to disappear from sight forever."[104] In Randall, bodies are "faint dark blobs" and "olive drab forms."[105]

When the dead or wounded body must be confronted, the vocabulary of redescription renders the sight not overly traumatic. In Atwell's *Private*, bodies are "no more convincing than the figures in a wax museum."[106] In other memoirs they are "like irregular pieces of driftwood on a rocky beach," "stacked like cordwood," or "like a log," and injured men look "like gray marble."[107] In what might otherwise be an exceptionally gruesome scene, Fry writes that a "dead German's brains lay on the grass . . . with scarcely a speck of dust or blood to mar their appearance. It reminded me of calves brains in the glass case at a butcher shop"; Fry calls this a memorable and "gory sight," but his language elides the violence: the brains are not mutilated, dirty, or even human.[108]

When bodies are not redescribed, they are quickly obscured by handkerchiefs, tarps, or tents or by the author's simply looking away.[109] Lacking the option to push the reality of bodily trauma from their vision, narrators instead push it from their consciousness. One of Atwell's men describes finding a dismembered head on the battlefield and being only momentarily shocked before "a split-second later the whole thing had left his mind;" Atwell himself recalls that when tasked with carrying a corpse, the man he was carrying "was anonymous. My mind did not go out to him, scarcely wondered about him. He was heavy to carry, that's all."[110] These lines perhaps represent what Gerald Linderman has called soldiers' "working to advance their own desensitization," but my point is that the trauma to the body and its impact on those who witness it are absent; men become accustomed to or even indifferent to death, but they are not shocked by it.[111] Indeed, these memoirists downplay the extent and nature of soldiers' physical and mental suffering. Atwell describes a military hospital as being less gruesome than he had expected: "There was seldom a great deal of blood. . . . There were few tears, few big scenes, seldom any cries even when the pain must have been outrageous."[112] Unlike those in both earlier and later war memoirs, this narrator is not horrified by combat; rather, it fails to meet his expectations.

In the rare instances in which memoirists fully note the trauma that war produces, such mindfulness quickly gives way to a vocabulary of emotional distance. When Fry encounters a dead German whose personal effects reveal that he was a husband and father, the recognition of the man's "grievability" is only momentary: "My thoughts turned for a brief second to that family which would get a report equivalent to our 'Missing in Action' and of a little girl who would never again see her daddy. Then I turned to the affairs of the moment. My job was to kill as many of these boys as possible with minimum cost to our side."[113] Fry certainly discerns his opponent's humanity and the likely tragedy of his death, but that awareness is quickly reintegrated, to use Scarry's term, "within a vocabulary of cost," something to be dealt with rather than mourned.

Perhaps the most vigorous elision of trauma, however, comes in the use in these memoirs of the word "peaceful" to describe the appearance of dead and wounded soldiers. Fry writes of an expression of "relaxed peace" on the faces of dead Germans, of another German who "looked as peaceful as if he were merely resting," and of German and American dead as "appear[ing] more relaxed and peaceful than we who were living."[114] Randall, too, describes a dead American as having "his eyes closed in peaceful sleep," and Atwell portrays injured men as "looking surprisingly peaceful—even relaxed."[115] The term is a staggering redescription of individuals who have endured tremendous violence; imaging dead soldiers as "resting," "sleeping," and "relaxed," erases the violence visited upon them.

Such elision extends to descriptions of soldiers who survive gruesome wounds and become the model veterans of Simpson's later speeches. One of Carter's platoon mates loses a leg in battle but "lived, made the states, has a cork leg, and sells insurance for a living."[116] One of Fry's men, found "unconscious and bleeding profusely from a dozen different wounds," is by 1968 "fully recovered and, as a regular Army colonel, is serving on active duty."[117] Psychological maladies are similarly often dismissed; one memoir makes a passing reference to postwar nightmares, and two engage the psychiatric ward for comic relief.[118] The war thus seems hardly to impinge on the combatants' ability to readjust to civilian society and achieve the idealized life available in 1950s America.

Leckie forcefully denies that the encounter with mutilated bodies is traumatic by denying that it fundamentally challenges his worldview. In a passage that anticipates the most psychologically wrenching scenes in Philip Caputo's *A Rumor of War*, Leckie describes bodies whose "vital force [had] fled" but declares, "It is blasphemy to say a bit of metal has destroyed life, just as it is presumptuous to say that because life has disappeared it has been destroyed. . . . death is only a sound we make to signify the Thing we do not know."[119] This encounter occasions not a loss but a reaffirmation of faith, and this reflection both obscures the reality that metal *does* end lives and upholds, rather than subverts, the principles according to which Leckie understood the world.

By prohibiting sustained interrogation of the war's brutality and its psychological effects, these memoirs contributed to the construction of the Second World War as not exactly sanitized or without struggle but necessary and noble. Manchester, Sledge, and Fussell depart from this discourse, embracing instead the narrative promulgated by Lipton, Cranston, and others who viewed Second World War veterans as having much in common with those who fought in Vietnam. The works of these three writers contributed to that narrative by presenting their experience in ways that resonated with and were indebted to the most substantial Vietnam memoirs of their moment. They do so by embracing both the structure and the language of these Vietnam memoirs, depicting the memoirists' childhood and their fascination with their father's experience in the First World War; detailing their decision to join the military and their progress through basic training and the war itself, in passages that focus on the physical violence, dehumanizing brutality, and atrocity they experience, witness, and perpetrate; and presenting their struggles on returning to civilian life.[120]

The linguistic indebtedness is apparent in the first five pages of Sledge's work, which echo Caputo, Kovic, and O'Brien. Like Caputo, who "was not really ambitious to become an officer" and "would have dropped out of school and gone in immediately as an enlisted man had it not been for my parents," Sledge writes that he "wanted to enlist in the Marine Corps as soon as possible," but because "Mother and Father were mildly distraught at the thought of me in the Marines as an enlisted man . . . I compromised and signed up for one of the Corps' new officer training programs."[121] Like Kovic, who is impressed by marine recruiters "with their dress blue uniforms and their magnificently shined shoes," Sledge notes that his recruiter "wore dress blue trousers. . . . His shoes had a shine the likes of which I'd never seen."[122] And once he gets to basic training, he, like O'Brien, relates an experience in which a recruit is made to hold both his penis and his rifle while chanting, "This is my rifle . . . and this is my gun."[123]

Whether Sledge read Caputo, Kovic, or O'Brien is immaterial. For readers familiar with them, his experience would immediately appear to parallel theirs. Moreover, he is hardly alone. Manchester, writing that he was "transported by dreams of leathernecks sweeping all before them, and the glint of moonlight on the sabers of the French cavalry" and that he "yearned for valor," sounds much like the young Caputo, who "would dream of that savage, heroic time and wish I had lived then" and "wanted to find in a commonplace world a chance to live heroically."[124] Fussell's opening pages tell of him and his friends "play[ing] trench warfare, bombarding one another's positions with dirt clods, blowing whistles to signal attacks, and coming as close as possible to miming the actualities of the Western Front as we'd seen them depicted in books." These terms echo Kovic's, down to the dirt bombs: "The army had a show on Channel 2 called 'The Big Picture,' and after it was over Castiglia and I crawled all over the backyard playing guns and army . . . blasting away at the imaginary enemy we had created right before our eyes, throwing dirt bombs and rocks into the windows."[125] These instances of literary debt perhaps deal with minor details, but through them post-Vietnam memoirs of the Second World War establish the Vietnam War, not earlier memoirs of their own war—which discuss none of these matters, let alone in the same language—as their literary antecedents and establish the broader contours of the good war's combat experience as similar to the one in Vietnam.

That the two wars mirrored each other in many ways is most evident in the memoirists' adoption of the tropes central to Vietnam memoirs' portrayal of trauma in ways that affirm psychologists' findings that the mental impact felt by combatants in both wars was similar. Seeing the mutilated body, scholars note, is a defining experience for Vietnam memoirists; in Scarry's phrase, they "place the injured body several inches in front of our eyes, hold the light up to the injured flesh, and keep steady the reader's head so that he cannot turn away."[126] Caputo's description of bodies, for example, is a far cry from the dead of 1950s memoirs. "The dead looked so much alike," he writes. "Black men, white men, yellow men, they all looked remarkably the same. Their skin had a tallowlike texture, making them appear like wax dummies of themselves; the pupils of their eyes were a washed-out gray, and their mouths were opened wide, as if death had caught them in the middle of a scream."[127]

Inverting Atwell's description of the dead as figures in an unconvincing "wax museum," these deaths are not painless, and the dead are not "peaceful." Caputo's awareness of the enemy's suffering and humanity is likewise apparent in his description of his first encounter with the enemy dead:

> He had been hit in the worst, most painful place a man can be hit, in the place that is the center of so many aches, the ache of fear, the ache of hunger, sometimes even of love. We feel so many things in our guts, and that is where two 7.62-mm bullets had caught him. Judging by the distance he had crawled, a good thirty yards, he had had ample time to feel pain and perhaps to realize that death was not decades, but moments, away. It was surprising he had lasted that long. A modern, high-velocity bullet strikes with tremendous impact. No tidy holes as in the movies. The two in his belly were small—each about the size of a dime—but I could have put my fist into the exit wounds in his back. An enormous amount of blood had poured out of him and he was lying in it, a crimson puddle in which floated bits of skin and white cartilage.[128]

This length of the passage alone disavows the body's earlier obfuscation. And Caputo emphatically denies metaphor, moving from the abstractions of feelings to the actual pain of injury, from sanitized movie images to anatomical descriptions. He appreciated this man's "precarity" by recognizing the extent of his wounds and his suffering as well as his awareness of it, and his "grievability," when he comes to see him and other dead as "men whose deaths would afflict other people with irrevocable loss."[129]

Similar descriptions occur in O'Brien and Kovic. In an extended account, O'Brien and his platoon mates gather around a female Vietnamese nurse who has been shot in the stomach; as "blood gushed out of the holes, front and back," they watched her die.[130] Here again, death is neither sudden nor painless. Flies land on the woman; she shakes and moans.[131] And, like Caputo, these men recognize the wounded body's precarity as they comment on her suffering and her humanity, as they note her beauty and seek to comfort her. Likewise,

Kovic, after opening his memoir with an account of the wounding that left him paralyzed, describes the military hospital as a repository for mangled bodies, "twenty-year-old blind men and amputees, men without intestines, men who limped, men who were in wheelchairs, men in pain," and what Kovic *sees* is a source of his increasing traumatic disillusionment. In the hospital he "lay back in his bed and watched everything happen"; he "watch[es]" the other men in the enema room, "see[s]" the scars on his friend's head at the parade, and "watche[s] his once strong twenty-one year old body become crippled and disfigured."[132] Ultimately, Kovic realizes that publicizing his opposition to the war depends on making public the spectacle of his wounded body.[133]

The witnessing of the wounded body is thus a defining traumatic experience. This is nowhere more apparent than in *A Rumor of War,* in which Caputo repeatedly insists that seeing maimed bodies ungrounded his identity as a Catholic. In a passage that directly contradicts Leckie, he writes, "The sight of mutilation did more than cause me physical revulsion; it burst the religious myths of my Catholic childhood. I could not look at those men and still believe their souls had 'passed on' to another existence, or that they had had souls in the first place. I could not believe those bloody messes would be capable of a resurrection on the Last Day."[134] Commenting on this passage, Thomas Myers writes that "Caputo can only record the death of some old personal truths" and suffers "the loss of [his] deepest philosophical and spiritual beliefs."[135] This assessment is accurate but somewhat understates the trauma; the collapse of a belief system that had been central to the soldier's understanding of his relationship to his culture engenders a loss of *identity.*[136]

Kovic, as many scholars have noted, is similarly traumatized when he loses his national subjectivity.[137] Seeing the wounded body is "a nightmare," and he complains, "This isn't like the poster down by the post office where the guy stood with the shiny shoes."[138] Kovic's trauma lies precisely in his inability to reconcile the idealized image of the soldier body with the mutilated bodies of the war's victims, and it prompts Kovic's transition from "all-American boy" to "a cheap small nothing to make mincemeat out of."[139]

Similar scenes recur throughout post-Vietnam Second World War memoirs, which offer similarly lengthy descriptions of mutilated bodies and document the psychological impact of the memoirist's witnessing. The resonance between Vietnam memoirs and the Second World War memoirs that followed them is evident in the extent to which Manchester and Fussell recall Caputo in their own description of dead bodies. Peering into a pit of Japanese bodies,

Manchester remarks, "Most of the bodies looked alike. There is little variety in the postures of violent death. When the end comes instantaneously, the rag doll effect is common. If there are a few moments of awareness between the wounding and the dying, muscular spasms draw up the legs and arms in the fetal position and hands are clenched like boxers' fists."[140] Fussell, encountering an African American soldier's corpse, has a similar revelation: "I knew he was dead because his skin was no longer dark brown but blue-black, or rather, dark brown with a dark blue, almost fluorescent, tinge. As I contemplated this sight, it came to me that Negroes were not at all what I'd thought of them before. In important things, they were like us. In fact, they were us. The lucky among us, black or white, survived; the unlucky, black and white together, died."[141] In language that recalls the parallel passage in Caputo's memoir, Manchester and Fussell insist on an unsettling acknowledgement of the war's production of maimed bodies by holding that death is not pleasant, peaceful, or painless but universally and unmistakably gruesome.

These writers' embrace of the narrative techniques of the Vietnam memoir continues in their descriptions of encounters with war's violence and its psychological impact. Manchester, for example, opens *Goodbye, Darkness* by graphically describing his killing of a Japanese soldier:

> My first shot had missed him, embedding itself in the straw wall, but the second caught him dead-on in the femoral artery. His left thigh blossomed, swiftly turning to mush. A wave of blood gushed from the wound; then another boiled out, sheeting across his legs, pooling on the earthen floor. Mutely he looked down at it. He dipped a hand in it and listlessly smeared his cheek red. His shoulders gave a little spasmodic jerk, as though someone had whacked him on the back; then he emitted a tremendous, raspy fart, slumped down, and died. . . .
>
> Already I thought I detected the dark brown effluvium of the freshly slain, a sour, pervasive emanation which is different from anything else you have known. . . . He continued to sink until he reached the earthen floor. His eyes glazed over. Almost immediately a fly landed on his left eyeball. It was joined by another. . . . I knew from previous combat what lay ahead for the corpse. It would swell, then bloat, bursting out of the uniform. Then the face would turn from yellow to red, to purple, to green, to black.[142]

In tone, style, and level of detail, this passage exceeds any in earlier Second World War memoirs and recalls Vietnam writers' representations of death. Manchester nearly paraphrases Caputo's assertion, "The stench of death is unique, probably the most offensive on earth."[143] The passage also recalls Caputo's description of dead Vietnamese soldiers and particularly O'Brien's dying Vietnamese nurse, establishing the enemy body as a spectacle that simultaneously fascinates, compels, and disgusts. Moreover, Manchester focuses the reader's attention on the severity of the wound and the dying body's changes by noting identical details in similar language. Like the nurse's wounds, the Japanese soldier's "gush," and here as well flies readily alight on a person likewise aware of impending death. Manchester, like O'Brien's platoon mates, who declare "I wish I could help her" and call the shooting "a crime," finds himself repelled by his actions: "My father's account of the Argonne had omitted certain vital facts. A feeling of disgust and self-hatred clotted darkly in my throat, gagging me," he writes, and "I began to tremble, and next to shake, all over. I sobbed, in a voice still grainy with fear, 'I'm sorry.' Then I threw up all over myself. . . . I knew I had become a thing of tears and twitchings and dirtied pants. I remember wondering dumbly: *Is this what they mean by 'conspicuous gallantry'?*"[144]

Manchester's response is not simply shame and regret but trauma.[145] Referring to his father's First World War service, which recalls Vietnam veterans' frequent embrace of the mythology of the Second World War, establishes this as a moment of traumatic disillusionment.[146] His act, in fact, precipitates a social death, and his response parallels the Japanese soldier's death, replete with "jerking," bodily excretions, and repellant odor.

His response thus parallels Caputo's in its recognition of the enemy's suffering and humanity and in a reimagining of the fundamental attitudes that had guided the soldier's service or life. Sledge's reaction to killing Japanese soldiers, which is also marked by appreciation for the enemy's precarity and his own sense of guilt and shame, is nearly identical to Manchester's: "As the first bullet hit him, his face contorted in agony. . . . Even in the midst of these fast-moving events, I looked down at my carbine with sober reflection. I had just killed a man at close range. That I had seen clearly the pain on his face when my bullets hit him came as a jolt. It suddenly made the war a very personal affair. The expression on that man's face filled me with shame and then disgust for the war and all the misery it was causing."[147] Here again, the Second World War shares the Vietnam War's emotional valence. Like the Vietnam memoirists, Sledge emphasizes looking and seeing, and, like Caputo, Sledge is uncomfortable with this moment because it forces him to take notice of the enemy's humanity and challenges his attitude toward the war.

Fussell's is the most explicit appropriation of *A Rumor of War* in his account of his first encounter with the enemy dead. Waking up among German corpses, Fussell finds that the upper-middle-class values of his childhood that had defined his worldview are immediately destroyed:

> If darkness had mercifully hidden them from us, dawn disclosed them with staring open eyes and greenish white faces and hands like marble. . . . Michelangelo could have made something beautiful out of these forms, in the tradition of the *Dying Gaul,* and I was astonished to find that in a way I couldn't understand, at first they struck me as awful but beautiful. But after a moment, no feeling but horror. My boyish illusions, largely intact to that moment of awakening, fell away all at once, and suddenly I knew that I was not and would never be in a world that was reasonable or just.[148]

Fussell initially retreats to benign redescription, describing the bodies as marble sculptures in a manner that accesses the refined values of his upbringing and recalls earlier Second World War memoirs. But his belief system cannot withstand seeing mutilated bodies, and the "horror" that attends his revelation is a secular analogue to the violent rupturing of Caputo's theological worldview.

In addition to embracing the Vietnam memoirists' emphasis on the physicality of the wounded body, the precarity of enemy lives, and the capacity of that encounter to violently rend the soldier's worldview, post-Vietnam Second World War memoirists' accounts of the brutality of combat recall and rely on the language of the Vietnam memoir. Manchester, for example, confesses to his enduring guilt at having participated in combat actions that took their greatest toll on civilians: "I remember the corpse of the girl [who had been murdered by American servicemen] on the beach. . . [and] the homes our 105-millimeter and 155-millimeter guns leveled; the callousness with which we destroyed a people who had never harmed us"; ultimately he decides that "no one comes out of a fight like that with clean hands."[149] Manchester's dismay at and shame over the civilian death toll, which he lists for each island he visits, is a motif familiar from Vietnam memoirs, which likewise frequently describe dead civilians and destroyed villages. His references thereby challenge the dominant remembrance of the Second World War by aligning it with a troubling aspect of Vietnam's legacy.

Sledge's contention that the marines who fought in the Pacific became increasingly brutal and amoral borrows more explicitly from Vietnam memoirs' logic and language. His accounts of this brutality—most notably his widely quoted account of a marine extracting gold teeth from a live Japanese soldier, an episode which renders the violence in far more explicit terms than a parallel account by Leckie, who compares the atrocity to dental work—far exceed those offered in earlier memoirs.[150] To forthrightly describe this violence at all affirms that atrocity could be more frankly acknowledged and more vividly discussed in Vietnam's aftermath. More important, Sledge draws on Caputo's and O'Brien's structure and language in a scene that Linderman argues reveals "the apprehension of at least some fighting men that combat was degrading them."[151] Sledge describes a friend who "told me he had a unique souvenir to show me. We sat on a rock as he . . . unwrapped layers of wax paper . . . and proudly held out his prize for me to see . . . as I stared in horror at the shriveled human hand he had unwrapped."[152]

Severed body parts are a staple of Vietnam memoirs. Michael Herr and Caputo note the pride with which soldiers displayed severed body parts and referred to severed ears as souvenirs, but Sledge's description most forcefully recalls O'Brien's platoon leader, Mad Mark, who "sat cross-legged and unwrapped a bundle cloth and dangled a hunk of brown, fresh human ear."[153] And when Caputo describes a parallel encounter as illustrating "the kind of things men are capable of in war if they stay in long enough," he foreshadows Sledge's horror "that I might do the same thing if the war went on and on."[154] Like so many of his descriptions of the Pacific War, Sledge's claim that "the fierce struggle for survival in the abyss of Peleliu eroded the veneer of civilization and made savages of us all. We existed in an environment totally incomprehensible to men behind the lines" finds its literary antecedent in Caputo's description of Vietnam as a place where "our humanity rubbed off of us as the protective bluing rubbed off the barrels of our rifles. . . . It was no orderly campaign, as in Europe, but a war for survival waged in a wilderness without rules or laws; a war in which each soldier fought for his own life and the lives of the men beside him, not caring who he killed in that personal cause or how many or in what manner and feeling only contempt for those who sought to impose on his savage struggle the mincing distinctions of civilized warfare."[155] These passages share many signifiers: morality defined as a coating, the war as a descent into "savagery" and a "struggle for survival," and its "incomprehensibility" to noncombatants among them; and Sledge's ruminations craft a picture of the Second World War that aligns with familiar recollections of Vietnam. But again, Fussell is most explicit, going so far as to quote Caputo in recording what he calls "The Great Turkey Shoot":

> In a deep crater in a forest, someone had come upon a squad or two of Germans, perhaps fifteen or twenty in all. Their visible wish to surrender—most were in tears of terror and despair—was ignored by our men lining the rim. . . . Laughing and howling, hoo-ha-ing and cowboy and good-old-boy yelling, our men exultantly shot into the crater until every single man down there was dead. A few tried to scale the sides, but there was no escape. If a body twitched or moved at all, it was shot again. The result was deep satisfaction. . . . If it made you sick, you were not supposed to indicate it.[156]

The execution of German POWs is not central to the dominant remembrance of the Second World War, nor was the victims' terror and the Americans' barbarity so graphically rendered in earlier memoirs. But such acts do recall incidents of wanton destructiveness familiar from the Vietnam War's remembrance, especially Paul Meadlo's account of Lt. William Calley's behavior in the My Lai massacre: "pushing" Vietnamese civilians "off into a ravine. It was a ditch. . . . And we started shooting them" as they were "waving their arms and begging."[157]

If these similarities are subtle, Fussell makes the shared depravity of men who fought in Vietnam and the Second World War explicit. "I was beginning to understand," he writes, "what a marine sergeant told Philip Caputo during the Vietnam War: 'Before you leave here, Sir, you're going to learn that one of the most brutal things in the world is your average nineteen-year-old American boy.' "[158] The chronological conundrum of exactly how Fussell could have understood in 1944 a comment made in 1966 and published in 1977 reveals the extent to which Vietnam memoirs became a key source for writing about the Second World War. Fussell's quoting of Caputo is a literary analogue not only to research that repeatedly concluded that Second World War veterans were traumatized by witnessing atrocity in proportions that approached those of Vietnam veterans but also to political testimony about Vietnam veterans bringing older veterans to Vet Centers.

These writers likewise mobilize the tropes of the Vietnam combat memoir to document their growing disillusionment and psychological trauma. Fussell, for example, writes, "It wasn't long before I could articulate for myself the message the war was sending the infantry soldier: '*You* are expendable. . . . You are just another body to be used. Since *all* can't be damaged or destroyed as they are fed into the machinery, some may survive, but that's not my fault. Most will be chewed up, and you'll probably be one of them.' "[159] While an awareness of expendability occasionally appears in earlier memoirs, his language is again indebted to the Vietnam memoirist, this time relying on the same metaphors as Kovic, who famously wrote that "he had never been anything but a thing to them . . . a young thing to run through the meat-grinder, a cheap small nothing to make mincemeat out of."[160] When Fussell describes "the murder of the former 'nice' Boy Fussell" and combat as "requir[ing] a severe closing-off of normal human sympathy. . . . For the naturally compassionate, this is profoundly painful, and it changes your life," he again paraphrases Kovic, who complains that "somewhere along the way he had forgotten to be polite anymore, and how to be a nice person. . . . he would give almost anything to be kind to people again, but the big machine, the one that had given him the number and the rifle, had sucked it out of him forever."[161] Like Kovic, who referred to himself as "their all-American boy," Fussell, who initially describes himself as "radiat[ing] college-boy optimism," realizes that he is nothing more that "another body to be used," a revelation that traumatizes him by undermining his earlier assumptions about his privileged place in American culture.[162]

As in Vietnam memoirs, the realization of personal insignificance is matched by the failure of patriotism. Like Caputo, who writes that he "was finished with governments and their abstract causes, and I would never again allow myself to fall under the charms and spells of political witch doctors like John F. Kennedy," post-Vietnam Second World War memoirists trouble the idealized language of unity and dedication that continues to define the Second World War's legacy.[163] Both Sledge and Manchester describe the war as precipitating their disenchantment with the jingoism that surrounded the war effort. Sledge, who ultimately reaffirms a hawkish patriotism and continues to justify the war, nonetheless repeatedly condemns politicians' sanitized rhetoric, writing, "As I looked at the [blood] stains on the coral, I recalled some of the eloquent phrases of politicians and newsmen about how 'gallant' it was for a man to 'shed his blood for his country,' and 'to give his life's blood as a sacrifice,' and so on. The words seemed so ridiculous. Only the flies benefited."[164] This language evokes a sentiment more familiar from the cultural memory of Vietnam than from that of the Second World War. As Tobey C. Herzog explains, "Caputo loses his remaining romantic illusions about 'good ways to die in war,' 'noble sacrifices,' and a war fought with order, rules of engagement, and battlefield ethics."[165]

Ten pages later, Sledge is more explicit: "But something in me died at Peleliu. Perhaps it was a childish innocence that accepted as faith the claim that man is basically good. Possibly I lost faith that politicians in high places who do not have to endure war's savagery will ever stop blundering and sending others to endure it."[166] The evident disgust for the policymakers shielded from war's violence recalls Caputo's condemnation of Kennedy as well as Kovic's vitriolic assault on "men who wore suits . . . and sat behind big desks sticking pins in maps in rooms he had never seen" but who "had never seen blood and guts and heads and arms. . . and watched the blood drip into the sand below."[167] Sledge's loss of faith in humanity and declaration that the war was a "blunder" made by men who don't bear its costs are sentiments drawn from Vietnam's legacy more than from the Second World War's, and through them Sledge defines dehumanization and alienation as the chief legacies of that celebrated war.

A similar revelation is the source of the larger traumatic rupture that dominates *Goodbye, Darkness.* Like Kovic, Manchester describes a childhood spent waiting for the opportunity to go to war and defined by myths that are destroyed by the war's brutality and the nation's postwar failures.[168] Manchester's most painful trauma, expressed in language that again recalls the Vietnam memoir, is the realization that the causes that spurred him to battle were empty: "Half the evil in the world, I thought, is done in the name of honor. . . . I saw through the Corps' swagger, the ruthless exploitation of the loyalty I guilelessly pledged in that Springfield recruiting station after Pearl Harbor. . . . [B]anners and swords, ruffles and flourishes, bugles and drums, the whole rigmarole, eventually ended in squalor. . . . I, to my shame, had been among the enchanted fighters. My dream of war had been colorful but puerile. It had been so evanescent, so ethereal, so wholly unrealistic that it deserved to be demolished."[169]

Like Kovic, Manchester juxtaposes the recruiting office and the combat zone; like the "charmed" Caputo, he derides the "enchanting" jingoism that enabled the war. One of Manchester's central themes—and in this his memoir diverges from orthodox cultural memory of the war—is that the Second World War may not have delivered on its promises, an anxiety evident in the memoir's central conceit: Manchester is haunted by nightmares in which his 1945 self accosts his 1977 self, "angrily demand[ing] an accounting of what had happened in the third of a century since he had laid down his arms. Promises had been made to him; he had expected a nobler America. . . . He hadn't anticipated that his country would be transformed into what it has become."[170]

Manchester's most profound moment of disillusion, however, comes not, as he claims, after the war but when he witnesses the death of Lefty Zepp, a Harvard intellectual whose innocence is symbolized by a voice that "had been arrested in midpuberty."[171] Zepp's death, caused by a bullet that entered his groin, is Manchester's first exposure to the traumatized body and the moment of his disillusionment. The gory wound is graphically described, but Manchester's response is most important. Zepp appears not as a soldier but as a youth whose promise is truncated by the war, a sentiment furthered by Zepp's emasculating wound. Manchester subverts the notion that the death was a patriotic sacrifice: "I thought: *Dulce nec decorum est pro patria mori.* If anyone had hummed the 'Marines' Hymn' then I would have pistoled him."[172] Manchester's reaction to his friend's death parallels Herzog's analysis of Caputo "los[ing] his remaining romantic illusions about 'good ways to die in war' [and] 'noble sacrifices.' "[173] And while Manchester's remarks surely show his artistic license—it's hard to imagine that in that moment he had the wherewithal to revise Horace—the replacement of the affirmative *et* ("and") with the negative *nec* ("neither") reflects his rejection of the myths that had heretofore defined his service. Most important, it recalls O'Brien's own critique that "Horace's old do-or-die aphorism—'Dulce et decorum est pro patria mori'—was just an epitaph for the insane" and, more explicitly, Caputo's thoughts about a Quantico classmate's death: "It was not altogether sweet and fitting, your death, but I'm sure you died believing it was *pro patria.*"[174]

Casey Clabough contends that "Manchester's speculation upon his responsibility" amid his final nightmare is the moment in which he "would have the reader believe that he has consciously made peace with his past."[175] Perhaps. But in doing so, Manchester's critique of the postwar United States echoes Kovic, who writes in his final pages,

> *It was all sort of easy, it had all come and gone. . . . Getting nailed at home plate, studying the cub scout handbook, tying knots, playing Ping-Pong, reading* National Geographic, *Mickey Mantle was my hero and Joan Marfe was the girl I liked best. It all ended with a bang and it was lovely.*
>
> There was a song playing called "Runaway" by a guy named Del Shannon.. . . I really got into it and was hitting baseballs and feeling like I could live forever.
>
> It was all sort of easy.
>
> *It had all come and gone.*[176]

This is the idealized imagery of Cold War suburban citizenship—Scouting, baseball, and a virginal heterosexuality—long understood as having motivated a generation's service in and having been shattered by Vietnam.[177]

If, as Bodnar suggests, Manchester "makes a plea for the restitution of faith in the traditional values he felt had shaped his life as a boy before 1941," he does so in language that mirrors that of Kovic:

> You had to remember your father's stories about the Argonne, and saying your prayers, and Memorial Day, and Scouting, and what Barbara Frietchie said to Stonewall Jackson. And you had to have heard Lionel Barrymore as Scrooge and to have seen Gary Cooper as Sergeant York. . . .
>
> You also needed nationalism, the absolute conviction that the United States was the envy of all other nations, a country which had never done anything infamous. . . .
>
> You needed a precise relationship between the sexes. . . . [Girls] you knew were still pure because they had let you touch them here but not there, explaining that they were saving themselves for marriage. All these and 'God Bless America' and Christmas or Hanukkah and the certitude that victory in war would assure their continuance into perpetuity. . . .
>
> Later the rules would change. But we didn't know that then. We didn't *know.*[178]

Sentiments familiar from Vietnam memoirs describe the Second World War veteran's profound disappointment. Like Kovic, Manchester implies that an idealized culture that spurred young men to fight did not survive the war and what came after. Like the representation of the brutality of the war, such language appropriates Vietnam's remembrance to establish the two wars as equally traumatic.

Critically, these memoirists embrace the rhetoric of the Vietnam memoir to describe combat's enduring psychological impact. There are both surface similarities—for example, like Caputo, Fussell and Sledge now look for tactical advantages in the landscape—and highly consonant descriptions of more troubling psychological ailments.[179] Like Kovic, who confesses to having "terrible nightmares about the war" and "wak[ing] up scared in my room in the middle of the night," Manchester builds his memoir around recurring nightmares while Sledge confesses to having "ghastly war nightmares that have haunted me for many, many years." In his sequel, *China Marine*, he admitted what psychologists had by that point been reporting for two decades: "For the first twenty-odd years after my return, nightmares occurred frequently, waking me either crying or yelling, always sweating, and with a pounding heart. Some nights I dreaded going to bed, dreaded the inevitable nightmares."[180] At least one referent is more direct. A nightmare in which Sledge imagines that "the dead got up slowly out of their waterlogged craters or off the mud and, with stooped shoulders and dragging feet, wandered around aimlessly" recalls Caputo's dream of a "platoon of crippled corpses, hopping along on the stumps of their legs, swinging the stumps of their arms, keeping perfect time while I counted cadence."[181]

As some politicians and medical professionals were questioning whether Second World War veterans suffered from the same symptoms of PTSD as Vietnam veterans, these memoirists mobilized language very much in the vein of Caputo's to bluntly admit to the symptomatology. Caputo opens *A Rumor of War* by conceding that he "had all the symptoms of *combat veteranitis:* an inability to concentrate, a child-like fear of darkness, a tendency to tire easily, chronic nightmares, an intolerance of loud noises—especially doors slamming and cars backfiring—and alternating moods of depression and rage that came over me for no apparent reason. Recovery has been less than total."[182] Manchester makes a similar confession, writing, "The fear continued after the war; the sudden zip of a heavy zipper made me jump for a year after I discarded my uniform, and it was late in the 1940s before I could walk near New York's old Third Avenue El without trembling."[183] Fussell, always more explicit in linking his experience in the Second World War to the experience of soldiers who fought in Vietnam, claims, "No one had heard yet of post-traumatic stress disorder, but for the first couple of years after the war I experienced something close to it. Emotionally, I was very shaky, given to tears at late-night parties... [and] lying under the furniture crying my eyes out." He states that even in the 1990s "I still jump at loud noises in the street, and at the machine-gun sound of a compressed-air hammer, I want to throw myself prone regardless of who might think it funny."[184] Manchester's and Fussell's postwar experience, in short, is indistinguishable from that of Vietnam veterans.

Even as they remain confident that the war was necessary, Sledge, Manchester, and Fussell counter the Second World War's dominant legacy by appropriating the language and discourses of Vietnam memoirs to recount their witnessing of grotesque violence and to emphatically identify in themselves symptoms of psychological suffering that are the equivalent of those associated with Vietnam veterans. In doing so, they recalled the Second World War in ways that validated psychologists' and politicians' contentions that the experience of veterans of the Second World War differed little from that of Vietnam veterans.

Fussell's claim to have suffered "something close to" PTSD and his closing admission that the war had left him "angry for a long time" firmly situate his memoir within its cultural moment.[185] Between 1979 and 1996 clinicians increasingly encountered older veterans who complained of the same symptoms that plagued Vietnam veterans and discovered that many had witnessed similar incidents of violence and atrocity. On Capitol Hill this awareness prompted vigorous debate about whether older veterans deserved to have access to readjustment counseling created for Vietnam veterans. Implicit in both this research and these debates was the question of whether the Second World War was, in fact, more like Vietnam than Americans had previously admitted.

The most noteworthy Second World War memoirs of this period declared that it was. Writing at a moment when Americans had become able to think about war as traumatic and seizing the language in which they had been able to do so, Sledge, Manchester, and Fussell appropriated and redeployed the conventions and tropes of Vietnam memoirs to present fighting in Europe and the Pacific as very similar to combat in Indochina. Challenging earlier representations of the war, they contributed to Americans' reassessment of the Second World War's legacy. This discourse, however, never gained much purchase. The Second World War remained a paragon of righteous militarism, and Americans continued to appropriate Vietnam's remembrance in order to recuperate from, rather than expand the reach of, the trauma of Vietnam.

Figure 3.1. Vice President George H. W. Bush, accompanied by the mayor of San Antonio, Henry Cisneros, rides a covered wagon into Alamo Plaza to open the Texas Sesquicentennial celebration on March 2, 1986. Bush's speech that day embraced the logic of neoconservative Vietnam revisionism to construct the Alamo as a model for overcoming the Vietnam syndrome. Item L-7218-11-1, San Antonio Light Photograph Collection, MS 359, University of Texas at San Antonio Libraries Special Collections from the Institute of Texan Cultures.

CHAPTER 3

"WE SEE A LOT OF PARALLELS BETWEEN THE MEN AT THE ALAMO AND OURSELVES"

Recovering from Vietnam at the Alamo

ON MARCH 2, 1986, AFTER RIDING A COVERED WAGON INTO SAN ANTONIO'S Alamo Plaza to officially open the Texas Sesquicentennial celebration, Vice President George H. W. Bush stepped to a podium in front of the shrine at which 187 men died during the Texas revolution of 1836 and told the gathered crowd, "What a great day to be a Texan" (fig. 3.1).[1] "Texan" was a self-professed identity because Bush had in fact been born in Massachusetts.[2] His remarks, however, were consistent with the notion that one's identity was a matter of choice. As Bush went on to explain, being Texan had less to do with birthplace than with being willing to risk American lives to assist fledgling democracies through interventionist foreign policies. Texans, that is, embraced the political posture that many conservatives argued the nation had lost after Vietnam.

Bush's arrival differed substantially from one that had taken place just five months earlier. On November 7, 1985, about a hundred Vietnam veterans calling themselves the Last Patrol marched down the breakdown lane of Interstate 35 and into San Antonio (fig. 3.2). The march had begun in Dallas when Michael J. Martin, a descendent of an Alamo defender, had symbolically drawn a line on the ground and challenged other veterans to walk with him to raise awareness of the plight of Vietnam veterans and the government's failure to address the POW/MIA issue. Six hundred miles later, the march

FIGURE 3.2. The Last Patrol arrives in San Antonio, November 7, 1985. The march had begun days earlier when Michael J. Martin, a descendent of an Alamo defender, symbolically drew a line on the ground—a reference to William Barrett Travis's celebrated "line in the sand" at the Alamo—and challenged Vietnam veterans to walk to the Alamo. The Last Patrol drew on its own narratives of Vietnam to remember the Alamo defenders as men fighting for each other in a futile conflict. L-7247-37-30, San Antonio Light Photograph Collection, MS 359, University of Texas at San Antonio Libraries Special Collections from the Institute of Texan Cultures.

ended at the Alamo, where the Daughters of the Republic of Texas had raised the POW/MIA flag in welcome.[3] The marchers set up a twenty-four-hour vigil, and Henry Cisneros, the mayor of San Antonio, reenacted the annual recitation of the Alamo defenders' names by reading aloud the names of San Antonians unaccounted for in Vietnam. He prayed that "they are well and that some time in the future on a Veterans Day, they will be back in our midst."[4]

In diverse ways conservative interventionists and Vietnam veterans revised the Alamo's remembrance to articulate how the nation could recover from the defeat in Vietnam. Both groups saw the Alamo as a historical example of the so-called noble cause that they likewise increasingly asserted the Vietnam War had been. Yet while the Alamo was already an honored site in narratives of American patriotism, its relevance to Vietnam was not self-evident. Rather, both conservatives who embraced revisionist narratives of Vietnam and Vietnam veterans seeking recognition used the tropes and language central to their respective Vietnam remembrances to describe the Battle of the Alamo in ways that countered the perceived crises that followed defeat in Vietnam—namely, the Vietnam syndrome and the failure to appropriately honor Vietnam veterans—by contending that American militarism was righteous and benevolent even when deployed unwisely and unsuccessfully. That is, the Alamo became useful as a space in which the nation could heal *from* Vietnam because it was remembered *as* Vietnam.

Each group's recuperative revision of Alamo memory stemmed from its anxiety over the defeat experienced in Vietnam. Defeat, Wolfgang Schivelbusch has argued, is nearly inconceivable and thus culturally debilitating, giving rise "to disillusionment, moral outrage, and retreat into the bastion of nationalism."[5] Cultures are left struggling to explain the defeat and reassert their strength and integrity.[6] Recovery, Schivelbusch explains, is often marked by the culture's adoption of the posture of the "heroic loser," who can claim "the satisfaction of having fought bravely and honorably, if hopelessly, to the bitter end."[7] Writing about the Confederacy, he observes that "like every other defeated nation, it drew a distinction between military defeat and moral victory . . . and transformed the distinction between failure on the battlefield and moral superiority into the central dogma of its new identity."[8] This distinction facilitates the culture's redemption in problematic ways: a society that imagines itself as having been justified in its choices and having acted valiantly in the face of an insurmountable or even unwise struggle is one able to return to its prior posture without critically interrogating the factors that led to the conflict and defeat.

Such was the case in the post-Vietnam United States. Efforts to recover turned on two issues in particular: first, overcoming a Vietnam syndrome, which conservatives believed had left the United States enervated and unable to fulfill its global responsibilities; and, second, rectifying the damage done when the nation was, as Ronald Reagan put it in 1980, "shabby in [its] treatment of those who returned."[9] Throughout the 1980s, efforts to resolve these crises turned on a redefinition of the war as, in Reagan's famous phrase, "a noble cause."[10] However, veterans and interventionist conservatives meant slightly different things when they characterized the war as a noble one. For foreign policy hawks seeking to overcome the Vietnam syndrome, the military and political righteousness of the intervention outweighed the defeat; for disenfranchised veterans, the solidarity they had shown in combat trumped their failure to prevail in a meaningless, unwinnable war.

As perhaps the most famous defeat in American culture, the Alamo was profoundly useful because it could be reimagined as a historical antecedent that legitimated these revisionist narratives. A chapter nearly as central in American culture as the Civil War and the Second World War, the Alamo and the veneration surrounding it have been complicated, and arguments that cultural memory of the site has often had more to do with the present than the past are not new.[11] In particular, narratives of patriotic self-sacrifice have historically dominated Alamo remembrance, marginalizing other histories, especially the site's meaning for Latinos; likewise, the honoring of the men who died there has demanded that some of their motivations and actions—including the fact that many were attracted there by the prospect of gaining wealth through landownership, that the cotton-growing economy in which many hoped to participate would have depended on slave labor, and that they may not have died as heroically as has been imagined—be downplayed or ignored.[12] "The essence of the symbol of the Alamo," Edward Linenthal explains, is ". . . that sacrifice in war is a product of human choice made by courageous and principled individuals."[13] This was particularly true in the early Cold War, when, Linenthal explains, "Alamo rhetoric also present[ed] communism as a spiritual challenge to the resources of America," and, as Randy Roberts and James Olsson put it, "Davy [Crockett] was a visible expression of the Truman Doctrine, and his mission in Texas was to fight the encroachment of an evil empire."[14]

In the later Cold War, as scholars have noted, the Alamo was invoked in debates over interventionist foreign policy and visited by Vietnam veterans.[15] In his comprehensive study of the Alamo's contested memory in the years surrounding the Alamo Sesquicentennial, Linenthal convincingly shows that in 1986 the Alamo became central to foreign policy debates, especially in the Reagan administration's support of the contras in Nicaragua.[16] Using language that implicitly positions the Alamo within the post-Vietnam historical moment, he writes that for some who discussed the Alamo, "there are still ideals worth dying for," but that "modern America's insidious loss of the will to sacrifice makes the historical analogy all the more important."[17] Linenthal further explains that in response to anxieties about nuclear war, "Alamo celebrants have intensified their insistence that the nation must look to the heroes of 1836 as patriotic archetypes who set forth the ideal to which every future age must aspire."[18]

If, as Linenthal points out, celebration of the Alamo "reminds us of the care we take to cultivate symbols that link us to events perceived as crucial . . . to our understanding of contemporary dilemmas," it is important to interrogate the terms through which Americans accomplish that cultivation.[19] I build on Linenthal's analysis by arguing that while the Alamo has persistently been used symbolically to justify wartime sacrifice, its legibility and relevance within efforts to recover from the defeat in Vietnam depended on the incorporation within Alamo remembrance of signifiers and narratives explicitly drawn from Americans' remembrances of Vietnam. Drawing on the language and ideas that dominated discussions of Vietnam in the popular press, in conservative political rhetoric, and in veterans' culture, interventionist conservatives and Vietnam veterans told the Alamo story in a manner that resonated with their understandings of Vietnam and its legacy.

I examine how proponents of an interventionist, militarized foreign policy, though they continued Cold War–era narratives of the Alamo, adapted the shrine's remembrance by including elements central to revisionist narratives of the Vietnam War.[20] In the 1980s, Richard Nixon, the leading neoconservative Norman Podhoretz, and others argued that the United States had intervened with good intentions and had been morally justified—Nixon, in fact, maintained that the United States had won the war—and that the Vietnam syndrome had weakened the United States. Appropriating their ideas and language, Bush and others recalled the battle of 1836 as an early instance of Americans intervening to help a developing country cast off a despotic regime. Reimagining the defenders as altruistic Americans come to assist the Texans, their ideological commitment as parallel to neoconservative visions of post-Vietnam citizenship, and the battle as either the defeat of a benevolent, well-meaning nation or a tactical military victory, they recast the Alamo as a historical precedent that retroactively justified American involvement in Vietnam and validated interventionist policy in the 1980s.

During the same period, the veterans in the Last Patrol remembered the Alamo defenders as ordinary men unconcerned with political causes who had knowingly fought a losing battle for the sake of their friends. This interpretation likewise depended on the veterans' describing the Alamo defenders in the language in which they defined their own service. They too made the Alamo a historical precedent, in their case for the national veneration of vanquished heroes even while establishing Vietnam veterans as uniquely positioned to help the nation recapture the patriotism it had lost after Vietnam.

In the 1980s, celebrating the Alamo often meant embracing revisionist narratives that justified the Vietnam War. The revision of the Alamo according to the logic of Vietnam remembrance and the way in which the Alamo became a site at which revisionist and redemptive narratives of Vietnam could be validated had political consequences. In constructing Vietnam as a morally just, well-intentioned intervention of the sort that Americans should embrace in the future and in arguing that soldiers' service should be honored despite the political realities of the wars they fought, revisionist scripts prohibit critiques of the Vietnam War and of the reliance on military power to sustain American empire more generally.[21]

"They Heard the Call for Help . . . and They Came Running"

On March 3, 1986, readers of the *San Antonio Express-News* were greeted by a front-page picture of Vice President Bush waving to the crowds as he arrived in San Antonio. Turning the page, they would have learned that President Reagan was about to "embark on an aggressive campaign in [his] uphill battle to win congressional approval for $100 million in aid to anti-government rebels in Nicaragua."[22] The Reagan administration had been supporting the right-wing contra rebels, who were battling the ruling leftist Sandinista regime that had overthrown the dictator Anastasio Somoza in 1979. To Reagan, this conflict represented a crucial front in the Cold War.[23] Inside the front section, beneath further coverage of Bush's visit, the paper profiled an anti-Sandinista activist who claimed the "government is trying to exterminate his people" and told of "burned villages" and "concentration camps."[24] The placement of articles about the Alamo close to articles about the Reagan administration's efforts to support the contras helps explain why, as Linenthal notes, many people celebrating the Alamo Sesquicentennial linked it to contemporary U.S. policy toward Central America.[25]

But Americans were also comparing Nicaragua to another conflict. Two days after Bush's visit, 167 religious leaders released a letter declaring, "A scaffold of deception is being constructed around Nicaragua . . . to prepare the American people for further U.S. military action" and invoking "the official deception that undergirded the war in Vietnam."[26] At the end of the week, the *New York Times* averred that "if the $100 million is voted, it will be poured down the most noisome sinkhole since Vietnam."[27] These comments reflected a national sentiment, as that same day two congressional committees rejected Reagan's proposal.[28]

The comparison between Nicaragua and Vietnam was hardly new. In 1985 the *New York Times* reported that Reagan "came to office determined to overcome what conservatives call the Vietnam syndrome" and that "Nicaragua is the chosen place."[29] Two years earlier Reagan had made this apparent in an address that, despite dismissing the comparison, concluded with a plea that evoked the Vietnam syndrome and offered a prescription for renewal. If the United States turned away from aiding resistance movements in Central America, Reagan explained, "our credibility would collapse, our alliances would crumble, and the safety of our homeland would be put in jeopardy. We have a vital interest, a moral duty, and a solemn responsibility. . . . It is a question of our meeting our moral responsibility to ourselves, our friends, and our posterity."[30]

To the left, intervention in Nicaragua seemed like Vietnam all over again.[31] A columnist in *Defense and Foreign Affairs* opined that "the likelihood of a Contra defeat brings out the lingering Vietnam Syndrome in almost everyone: Americans off and dying in some godforsaken land for a cause but poorly understood."[32] Vietnam veterans were highly critical. *VVA Veteran*, the magazine of the Vietnam Veterans of America, worried about "too many alarming similarities in the way the Reagan Administration approaches the Central

American issue and the way previous administrations approached Vietnam."[33] In Washington, veterans fasted in front of the Capitol and, replaying Vietnam-era protests, returned their medals.[34] The former Catholic chaplain Charles Liteky, who famously returned his Medal of Honor in protest, told the *VVA Veteran*, "I'm happy to say that I'm a Vietnam veteran who went there to fight communism. . . . But I'm asking veterans to ask themselves: look at Central America—would you want your son to go there and do what you did in Vietnam?"[35]

These remarks highlight the reality that if the Alamo, in Linenthal's words, has long "set forth the ideal to which every future age must aspire," its relevance within debates about U.S. policy in Central America must be read in terms of continuing efforts to overcome the Vietnam War's traumatic legacy.[36] Throughout the eighties and especially around the Sesquicentennial celebration in 1986, the Alamo defenders were regularly identified as men who, like the idealized volunteers of the Vietnam era, had met a moral obligation by helping a foreign country cast off a tyrannical regime, willingly risked casualties to achieve a tactical victory, and boldly assured the world of their willingness to do so. Those constructions relied on language that explicitly echoed the rhetoric and ideas of notable conservatives from Reagan and Nixon to Podhoretz and his writers at *Commentary*, and they made the Alamo not simply a story of patriotism but a site that explicitly validated conservative interpretations of the Vietnam War and prescriptions for national healing in its aftermath.

WITH THE CONSERVATIVE ASCENDANCY OF THE 1980S CAME A REFRAMING of the Vietnam War as a well-intentioned, morally justified cause, and, for some, it was a victory before it became a defeat. Such rethinking was part of a larger effort to overcome the Vietnam syndrome, the sense that the United States had succumbed to a national public scourging that left it unwilling to use military force abroad.[37] To many conservatives, overcoming the syndrome demanded that the nation realize that the intervention was nothing to be ashamed of and that embracing interventionist policies was vital to regaining American hegemony.

Reagan's frequently analyzed speech to the VFW in 1980 exemplifies this reimagining. In his defense of the war, Reagan maintained that it had begun when "a small country newly free from colonial rule sought our help in establishing self-rule and the means of self-defense against a totalitarian neighbor bent on conquest."[38] He further decried any "feelings of guilt," any sense that "we were doing something shameful."[39] This revisionary view of the Vietnam War, however inaccurate—South Vietnam, after all, had never been an independent country, and the National Liberation Front was bent on reunification, not "conquest"—was, Patrick Hagopian notes, emblematic of Reagan's reassertion of pre-Vietnam ideas of U.S. foreign policy; it was also the most public assertion of Schivelbusch's "heroic loser" narrative in which the war had been justified and morally principled.[40]

Reagan's claim that the war had been the moral act of a benevolent nation's bravest youth modeled the vocabulary that defined Vietnam revisionism and, subsequently, Alamo commemoration. Five months later, Podhoretz echoed Reagan's statements in *Commentary* magazine, chiding Vietnam-era radicalism that "attacked the use of American power to contain Communism as politically ill-advised and morally wrong"; in the same issue Jeane Kirkpatrick, who would become Reagan's ambassador to the United Nations, dismissed "the famous 'lessons of Vietnam'—that . . . forceful intervention in the affairs of another nation is impractical and immoral.' "[41] Soon thereafter Podhoretz reiterated in another article that the Vietnam War had been a morally just enterprise to rescue the Vietnamese. He lamented that "one of the 'Lessons of Vietnam' that is rarely mentioned is that public support became impossible to maintain in the absence of a convincing moral rationale for our effort there," despite, he contended, the reality that "what we were actually trying to do was save the South Vietnamese from the horrors of Communist rule."[42] Claims of ethical righteousness and assistance were central to the revisionist narrative, appearing as well, for example, in Reagan's speech calling for support of the contras. By the time Podhoretz published his book *Why We Were in Vietnam*, he seemed almost frustrated at his continued need to make them. Dismissing what he termed the antiwar movement's "desperate need to find or invent selfish or self-interested motives for the American presence in Vietnam, the better to discredit it morally," he protested. "Why, then, were we in Vietnam? To say it once again: because we were trying to save the Southern half of that country from the evils of Communism."[43] Fully embracing the heroic loser logic, Podhoretz ended the book by calling the war "an act of imprudent idealism whose moral soundness has been so overwhelmingly vindicated by the hideous consequences of our defeat."[44] To Podhoretz, the fact that the United

States had lost the war was immaterial, and the painful defeat could be salved by focusing on the righteousness of the cause.

The need to justify the war in these terms persisted. In April 1984 Podhoretz fumed that conservatives had "conceded" antiwar liberals' definition of Vietnam as morally unjust.[45] In October of that year, a diatribe in *Commentary* railed that the Vietnam Veterans Memorial demonstrated that "America had come to the profoundly wrong belief that war has little or nothing to do with politics or morality."[46] At least one Vietnam veteran agreed. In the *VVA Veteran* for April 1984, Stan Carrier published his poem "The Unknown Soldier," which likewise defined the war as an intervention aimed at ensuring Vietnamese self-determination. It not only had not been a defeat but also had publicly demonstrated the stalwart commitment of the United States to preserving democracy:

> In Southeast Asia I trudged through rice fields,
> And there was no doubt in my mind that we were there to
> liberate the oppressed.
> We didn't lose but rather showed the world
> That wherever men live under tyrants and exist
> In fear—We will come to their aid.[47]

Carrier's poem, while a minor text, exemplifies the widely proffered narrative of the Vietnam War as a worthy endeavor the nation could take pride in.

Carrier even took the somewhat more controversial position that the United States had not lost the war, an assessment with which Podhoretz would have disagreed but that Nixon would have embraced. In 1985, over a decade after he had resigned in disgrace, Nixon published *No More Vietnams*, a polemical memoir aimed at redeeming his image by defining himself as an elder statesman with sound foreign policy prescriptions. Many reviewers agreed with the *New York Times*'s criticism that "as history, it is second-rate"—*VVA Veteran* even less charitably called it "perhaps the most sloppy and intellectually lazy effort at revisionist history of the US war in Indochina to date"—but others viewed his policy prescriptions favorably.[48]

Nixon's book fit squarely within Reagan's and Podhoretz's narrative, professing that "the United States intervened in the Vietnam War to prevent North Vietnam from imposing its totalitarian government on South Vietnam through military conquest" and that "South Vietnam simply wanted the chance to fight for its survival as an independent country."[49] It had been a war fought by "the most idealistic young Americans of an idealistic generation," men "from modest backgrounds. . . 'common men'" who "when each was confronted with the ultimate challenge—risking his life to save the lives of others—he demonstrated that he only had to be tested to display uncommon qualities of extraordinary courage and patriotism."[50] This was the definition of Reagan's noble cause, a war in which ordinary but extraordinary men "fought because our idealism was at stake" and to help a "friend."[51] It was also, in Nixon's view, a victory in 1973 before it became a defeat in 1975.[52]

Americans' failure to realize the nobleness of the cause and of the soldiers' conduct and the ultimate triumph, he proclaimed, had left "Americans ashamed of their power, guilty about being strong, and forgetful about the need to be willing to use their power to protect their freedom and the freedom of others." The upshot was a loss of American credibility: "Every leader and diplomat we encounter in Washington and abroad wonders whether we can be counted upon in a crisis or if we will cut and run when the going gets tough."[53] This thesis, too, was familiar: in 1980 Reagan had lamented, "Our allies are losing confidence in us, and our adversaries no longer respect us."[54]

The United States was a country that must "be unmistakable in our will." In fact, Nixon professed that "a lesson that our adversaries should learn from our intervention in Vietnam is that the United States, under resolute and strong leadership, will go to great lengths and endure great sacrifices to defend its allies and interests."[55] He avowed that Americans needed to adopt a more modest vision of success, like the one that allowed Nixon to claim a victory in 1973 despite the eventual loss of the war: "Everyone agrees that we should never commit our forces to a losing cause. But *win* must be properly defined. . . . We *win* if we prevent the enemy from winning."[56] To Nixon as well as to his fellow believers, Vietnam could not be what it had actually been—a defeat; it had to be rewritten as something more palatable, a demonstration of national will and a tactical success of which Americans could be proud.

Such claims allowed Nixon to argue that Americans must again become willing to intervene in uncertain situations: "We must recognize that where our interests are clearly involved, we must take risks to protect them. Every military operation cannot be a sure thing. The United States is a great power with worldwide responsibilities. We will not prevail against an enemy willing to take any risk to achieve victory if we are unwilling to take some risks to prevent defeat."[57] This passage is Nixon's most strident call for the nation to recover from the Vietnam syndrome by understanding that being a "responsib[le]" world power means assuming risk, a word that appears three times in three sentences.

This word became an important signifier in the debate. Nixon had earlier used it to describe Medal of Honor winners who had been killed—and hence not only risked but also in fact lost their lives—and he described draft dodgers as people "afraid of risking their lives."[58] Others also emphasized risk. A year earlier Tod Lindberg had observed in *Commentary* that, after Vietnam, Americans had forgotten that "many soldiers *like* being soldiers very much . . . because they are eager to serve their country, believe there is something worth fighting for, and even relish an opportunity to risk their lives in that cause."[59] The week of the Alamo Sesquicentennial, the former Nixon adviser and neoconservative commentator Pat Buchanan complained in the *Washington Post* of a nation that had "voted to abandon Southeast Asia" and had been unwilling "to risk war" in Eastern Europe in the 1950s. And he was convinced that in Central America risk meant accepting American casualties. "Who wants Central America more . . . ," he asked, "Fidel Castro, who has sent in 3,500 combat advisers to keep Nicaragua communist, or the United States, which restricts to 55 the number of advisers it sends to keep Salvador free?"[60] Buchanan was certain that the experience of Vietnam had left the United States unwilling to take the risks necessary to aid small countries that needed its help.

The concept of risk, if not the term, appeared elsewhere as well. Podhoretz wrote that his prescriptions should be adopted even though there was no "guarantee that an anti-Communist strategy of containment would be applied in the future with greater prudence," that is, that there would not be another Vietnam.[61] In 1985, in an article admonishing those opposed to funding the contras, Maggie Gallagher and Charles Bork chided the people who selectively supported foreign aid to "safer," more distant countries "because it is unlikely that U.S. troops would ever be sent to that distant corner of the world, at least in the post-Vietnam era" but feared that in Central America "military aid might escalate into direct U.S. action."[62] Like Nixon, Lindberg, and Buchanan, they criticized those who had become risk averse and disinclined to place American lives in danger after Vietnam.

Gallagher and Bork made their point most forcefully in their conclusion, in which they discussed Americans' attitudes toward resistance movements: "The same intelligentsia which maintained that the United States could not win in Vietnam now can be heard asserting with equal confidence that the Soviets cannot lose the war in Afghanistan. Fighting to the death is all very gallant, they reason, but the end result will be the same whether partisans fight or acquiesce." Such an attitude, the authors bemoaned, "suggests that many in the West no longer believe that political liberty is worth dying for."[63] In many ways, these remarks echoed familiar post-Vietnam condemnations of antiwar liberals as being overly intellectual, insufficiently patriotic, and critical of the use of military force.[64]

In the early 1980s Americans were regularly entreated in *Commentary* and elsewhere not only to think of Vietnam as a morally courageous intervention by a nation willing to risk its young people for another country's liberty but also to embrace that view as central to recouping American strength and security. The lesson of Vietnam was not that defeat should lead to a more circumspect use of military force; it was that Americans should first realize that an interventionist foreign policy was moral, benevolent, and a source of pride and then renew their commitment to militarism. Celebration of the Alamo in the 1980s helped legitimize this narrative, though not simply because it was always already a defining moment of American militarism and patriotism. Rather, Americans remembering the battle of 1836 consistently mobilized terms and ideas familiar from the revisionist thinking of Reagan, Podhoretz, Nixon, and others to make the Alamo speak on behalf of that narrative.

Vice President Bush was undoubtedly the most notable speaker at the Alamo Sesquicentennial celebration. His remarks were brief (a page and half), but they reference nearly every tenet of Vietnam revisionism. He situated the Alamo in the context of global geopolitical problem areas that troubled conservative thinkers, who regarded them as places where it was thought the Vietnam syndrome had sapped American will. "All over the world," he announced, "I've found that—whether you're in China or Europe, Africa or the Soviet Union—people understand what it means to be a Texan."[65] China and the Soviet Union had totalitarian, communistic forms of government, and conservatives worried that the USSR had become emboldened after the Vietnam War. In parts of Africa, the United States had lately sought to support resistance movements.[66] Less than a month earlier, for example, Reagan had called the Soviet Union "a closed dictatorship in which democratic freedoms are denied," and in celebrating the Polish Solidarity movement and Jonas Savimbi's anticommunist insurgency in Angola, he said that "serving the cause of freedom also serves the cause of peace. It is for this reason that Americans have always supported the struggle of freedom fighters."[67]

Bush carefully articulated the Alamo defenders' motivations in terms that resonated with conservatives' rethinking of Vietnam: "The defenders of the Alamo wanted the world to know that they fought not against Mexico itself... that they fought against tyranny and for a democratic republic.... They fought for principle. They fought for freedom. They fought for democracy. They fought for all the rights and privileges that we as Texans and we as Americans enjoy today."[68] Bush's remarks, eliding other principles for which the Alamo defenders fought, for example, acquiring land and preventing abolition, highlight the defenders' ethical decision, their democratic goals, and their opposition to a country falling under despotism. Having "fought against tyranny and for a democratic republic," they mirrored Reagan's vision of the United States as helping "a small country newly free from totalitarian rule" and fearful of its "totalitarian neighbor" and Nixon's articulation of America as assisting a country that "simply wanted a chance to fight for its survival as an independent country"; having "fought for principle," they evinced the moral rectitude that the *Commentary* writers ascribed to those who supported the war in Vietnam. In sum, they embodied the ethos of Podhoretz's frustrated exclamation that the United States had fought the Vietnam War "because we were trying to save the Southern half of that country from the evils of Communism." In so describing the fighters at the Alamo, Bush offered a historical antecedent that validated conservative revision of the Vietnam War.

The vice president was not alone in evoking such rhetoric. The revisionist discourse of moral rectitude had been apparent five years earlier in *Discovery*, the newspaper published at Brooks Air Force Base in San Antonio. Sgt. David Lyons, a member of the air force, argued in the newspaper that the Alamo defenders "died because they believed that at this time and place they should take a stand for what they believed to be right" and that "they stood for the rights of people to have the basic human freedoms."[69] Articles in other parts of the country echoed such descriptions. William Travis, a hero of the Alamo who would become the central figure of the commemoration, was described as having "an absolute code of honor and duty" and "a sense of mission"; the Alamo defenders were said to be "men willing to subordinate lives to ideas."[70]

If Sergeant Lyons's rhetoric fit called the broader, historical language of Alamo commemoration even as it evoked contemporary conservative arguments about Vietnam, articles published closer to the Sesquicentennial studiously overlooked the defenders' economic and personal stakes in Texas and subtly revised the Alamo story as they aligned the defenders with revisionist justification of Vietnam. In *Texas, Our Texas: 150 Moments That Made Us the Way We Are*, a commemorative book that *Texas Monthly* magazine produced for the Sesquicentennial, the editor, Gregory Curtis, included some words from a letter written by the Alamo defender Micajah Autry: "I go whole hog in the cause of Texas. I expect to help them gain their independence and also to form their civil government, for it is worth risking many lives for."[71]

Notably, Autry positions himself as an outsider (he had, in fact, come from Tennessee), as he describes independence and the civil government not as "ours" but "theirs." Omitting the fact that Autry was a slave owner and that the rest of the letter details Autry's plan to eventually settle in Texas on land acquired through his service, Curtis excerpts the words that define him as having come solely to aid the Texan cause.[72] Bush made this point as well, asking Americans to "remember that those who fought and died here were from all over America and from other places as well."[73] In subtly challenging the received narrative of the Alamo volunteers as defending their home state, Bush's comment confirms that *Texan* is an ideological rather than a geographical designation. Crucially, he asserts that the men who "fought against tyranny and for a democratic republic" were outsiders who had come to aid the beleaguered state. *Southern Living* magazine made a similar argument in March 1986:

> The war for Texas' independence was, in some ways, an extension of the American Revolution. That same spark of freedom burned in those volunteer soldiers who joined the fight.
>
> Here and there they heard the call for help—on farms in Tennessee and Georgia, in rallies in Mobile and New Orleans.
>
> And they came running. . . . More than a few came because they thought Texas was land worth fighting for. And among them, a fire was burning.[74]

Texans in 1836 did indeed invoke the American Revolution.[75] Yet here again was a recollection in which the men who fought and died at the Alamo had come to Texas not for land, wealth, or a new start and subsequently been frustrated by the Mexican government. They came solely to help unspecified others who sought freedom. As in Reagan's recollection of a Vietnam that "sought our help," Americans had received a "call for help" from Texas; the Alamo exemplified the posture that Nixon proposed in Vietnam's aftermath: "Being willing to provide military aid to friends who need it." The portrayal of those who went to Texas also paralleled Nixon's claim that "the most idealistic young Americans of an idealistic generation" had fought in Vietnam. Here again, the mobilization of the language of conservative remembrances of Vietnam to tell the Alamo story invoked the celebrated shrine to legitimize those revisionist accounts.

Other articles revised Alamo memory as well, casting the battle in terms familiar from Vietnam's remembrance. During the 1980s, one issue that emerged was whether the battle had been militarily significant within the larger revolutionary effort. That the Alamo defenders had slowed the Mexican army long enough for the Texan army to organize remained the most popular argument; alternative scenarios, however, held either that Santa Anna had made a tactical error in laying siege to the garrison and even that the Alamo defenders could have left San Antonio, with little ill effect, long before the Mexican army's arrival.[76]

In 1986 both the traditional narrative and one that held that the Alamo defenders' deaths could have been avoided were revised in ways that recalled post-Vietnam conservative rhetoric. The *Houston Post*'s weekly magazine wrote, "History proved that the defenders of the Alamo did not die in vain. They had held up [Gen. Antonio López de] Santa Anna's advance for two weeks, badly mauled his army and bought time needed for their fellow Texans to set up an independent government."[77] This was nearly the standard narrative, but with one critical difference. Traditional Alamo memory almost universally emphasized that the siege had enabled the Texan *army* to organize, but here it is the entire *government* that the Alamo defenders had midwifed. This version recalled Nixon's claim that the Vietnam War had been a series of battlefield victories that had ensured that "the South Vietnamese people would have the right to determine their own political future."[78]

Even the contention that the Alamo defenders had died in vain was cast in language that recalled conservative rhetoric about Vietnam. The day before Bush spoke, a column in the *San Antonio Light* remarked that "those who died were brave men, to be sure, but in a sense foolhardy as well" because "holding [the Alamo] would have accomplished nothing of military significance" and "they shouldn't have been wasted on a lost cause."[79] This was a rebuke to dominant Alamo memory. And yet, the article ends its critique with a familiar assertion of traditional patriotism: "The Alamo . . . represents our independence, our commitment to principle, our willingness to die in the cause of freedom. Never mind that it shouldn't have happened."[80] This view is anathema to Texan cultural memory, but the declaration that the Alamo deaths were unnecessary yet that they evince an enduring moral integrity echoes Podhoretz's idea that the Vietnam War had been "an act of imprudent idealism whose very soundness has been so overwhelmingly vindicated."[81]

Evoking and at times directly borrowing from these politicians' and pundits' language, media coverage and commemorative materials constructed the Alamo as an object of patriotic veneration that vindicated prominent conservatives' arguments about Vietnam's location within the pantheon of American wars and America's proper posture in its aftermath. Together, these representations painted the Alamo defenders as morally principled men who had aided in a fledgling democracy's opposition to a tyrannical government and as the predecessors of the soldiers who had fought in Vietnam. They validate the notion that defeat in Vietnam had been noble because the commitment to the war had been morally appropriate.

Indeed, some descriptions of the defenders very much evoked that comparison. The comment by the historian Joe B. Frantz that at the Alamo men "died gallantly for a cause, unclear though they were as to what the cause was all about" rebuked the anxiety of *Defense and Foreign Affairs* mentioned above, in which the columnist worries about "Americans off and dying in some godforsaken land for a cause but poorly understood" by holding that such deaths were nonetheless honorable.[82] Similarly, in *Parade* magazine the poet Diane Ackerman took *Southern Living*'s suggestion that the Texas revolution was the American Revolution's successor a step further, making the Alamo defenders the idealistic sons of the men who had fought in it: "Driven west in search of land and opportunity, they were restless and often troubled men, drifters, people looking for a fresh start. . . . Too young to have fought in the Revolutionary War 60 years before, they had fathers who told vivid stories about it. Liberty was still a tang in the air. In many ways, Santa Anna reminded them of the fight they had missed."[83] Ackerman's language recalls the dominant representation of Vietnam-era volunteers as reared on family stories and popular culture that celebrated the last great war—Tim O'Brien being taught by "flushed veterans of the war," and "young boys growing up in the 1950s and early 1960s [who] were captivated by fantasies of warfare."[84] The Alamo defenders here become Vietnam veterans' forerunners, men eager to engage in "the fight they had missed."

Ackerman's sketch of the Alamo volunteers as decidedly working-class men looking for a better life echoes Nixon's assessment of those who fought in Vietnam as "idealistic young Americans" coming "from modest backgrounds" but who, "when each was confronted with the ultimate challenge—risking his life to save the lives of others—he demonstrated that he only had to be tested to display uncommon qualities."[85] Curtis made this point three years earlier and somewhat less charitably, calling the battle in San Antonio "an act of courage by brave men. I also believe the men who fought at the Alamo were bums, liars, runaway fathers, land swindlers, drunkards, and Yankees. But they redeemed themselves by deciding to stay and fight for a noble cause."[86] Calling the Alamo noble was hardly new, but in the 1980s that term's deployment could hardly be separated from Vietnam revisionism. Curtis likewise defined the Alamo defenders as antecedents of the men who fought in Vietnam.

The historian T. R. Fehrenbach's description of the Alamo defenders—"men who rode to the sound of the guns, who never backed down from a fight, who placed a sense of personal honor above personal extinction. They did not want to die, had not intended to die. But still they were the happiest of men who found, as few do, their time and place upon these walls"—recalls Lindberg's description that I quoted earlier: men who "*like* being soldiers very much . . . because they are eager to serve their country, believe there is something worth fighting for, and even relish an opportunity to risk their lives in that cause."[87] Repeatedly, the language used to describe the Alamo defenders recalled language of the sort used by Reagan, Nixon, Podhoretz, and others to portray those who fought in Vietnam and to equate Vietnam with its indisputably patriotic predecessor in ways that justified the Vietnam War itself, made the American defeat there acceptable, and legitimated interventionist foreign policy prescriptions.

Central to the alignment of Alamo memory with this discourse was an emphasis on the defenders' acceptance of risk and their willingness to make public, global statements about their commitment to fighting for democracy. Sacrifice, both as a concept and as a signifier, had by the 1980s long been central to orthodox Alamo memory.[88] And while this idea remained meaningful during the Sesquicentennial, the concept of being willing to accept risk was at key moments identified as the Alamo defenders' defining quality. Not quite a synonym of *sacrifice*, the word *risk* and its frequent use in the eighties brought Alamo memory squarely into line with revisionist narratives of Vietnam.[89]

Micajah Autry's letter, for example, describes Texas as "worth risking many lives for." This letter can perhaps be dismissed—Autry, after all, hadn't arrived in San Antonio at the time he wrote it and didn't know he would die at the Alamo—but that an excerpt from it was chosen for inclusion in a commemorative book hints at the sentiment's significance. And the letter is not the only example. When Bush spoke on March 3, he explained that "being a Texan means . . . daring to take chances."[90] Three days later, Fehrenbach, the keynote speaker at the Sesquicentennial celebration, said, "There are times in which people who are sophisticated without being wise can say, no war is a good war if one is killed in it. . . . The Alamo is a fearful symbol for any age that hopes to eradicate risk, or proclaims the avoidance of risk as an ideal."[91] Two years later, he marked the 152nd commemoration of the battle in nearly identical language, calling it "a frightening symbol to those who seek the eradication of risk, to any age that fears war more than servitude."[92]

These complaints about the timidity of the 1980s image those of Nixon, Podhoretz, and others. Thus, while the concepts central to Alamo memory in the 1980s were consistent with those of earlier moments, they were expressed in terms that resonated explicitly with revisionist narratives of Vietnam. Fehrenbach's repeated invocation of the term *risk* mirrors Nixon's statement, "We must recognize that where our interests are clearly involved we must take risks to protect them" as well as the assertions by *Commentary*'s writers that service members "relish an opportunity to risk their lives."

Other elements of Fehrenbach's speeches recall this narrative. His insistence that the Alamo reveals that wars can be good despite their high death tolls echoes Reagan's insistence that "we dishonor the memory of 50,000 young Americans who died in that cause when we give way to feelings of guilt as if we were doing something shameful." Fehrenbach's mention of "people who are sophisticated without being wise" echoes critiques of antiwar liberals in Nixon's contempt for the "political and intellectual leaders who belonged to the so-called leadership elite [and who] remain in the darkness, muttering to one another the tired old verities of the 1960s." More emphatically, Gallagher's and Bork's dismissal of an anti-Vietnam "intelligentsia" that believes, as I quoted earlier, that "fighting to the death is all very gallant . . . but the end result will be the same whether partisans fight or acquiesce" and their complaint that "many in the West no longer believe that political liberty is worth dying for, an attitude which, if widely accepted, would signal the ultimate triumph of Marxist materialism in the west" can also be heard in Fehrenbach.[93] For Americans reading these accounts, the commemoration of the Alamo worked to affirm revisionist narratives about Vietnam not because the shrine was a stable symbol of American patriotism but because those who remembered it publicly did so in terms that explicitly recalled Vietnam's memory. Through such rhetoric, Vietnam could be more easily be imagined as a noble cause coherent with the nation's finest military traditions.

Alamo memory also embraced the precepts of Vietnam revisionism by stressing the fact that the defenders made public their willingness to fight. Bush alluded to this in his address, remarking, "Being a Texan means what it feels like to stand up any place in the world and say, 'I'm proud to be a Texan.' "[94] Here again, *Texan* is ideological, marked by the willingness to issue global proclamations about one's "courage" and "determination."[95] Throughout the eighties and particularly around the Sesquicentennial, a letter Travis had written from the Alamo proclaiming his courage and determination received more attention than the more traditionally celebrated elements of the story—for example, Travis's line in the sand, when Travis challenged his men to stay and fight by asking them to step over a line he had drawn on the ground inside the Alamo, or the battle itself. The letter was read into the *Congressional Record* twice during the 1980s. *Alamo: The Price of Freedom,* an IMAX film produced in 1988, prominently features a dramatic reenactment of Travis writing the letter, and it was reprinted in both *Texas, Our Texas* and the *Texas 150th Celebration Program and Guide.*[96] In 1985, when the *North San Antonio Times* reported that Fehrenbach's book *Lone Star* was being filmed, it noted that the "battle was not reconstructed. Instead, that segment focuses on a narration of William B. Travis's letter pledging victory or death to the cause."[97]

Travis's letter contains many elements of the orthodox narrative, and yet for Curtis, the editor of *Texas, Our Texas,* and for Suzanne Carter and Larry

Hodge in their article in the *Program and Guide,* what is most important is the act of having written it. What makes Travis "the first Texan" is not simply his willingness to die for a patriotic cause but his having publicly embraced militarism. Curtis as well as Carter and Hodge notes that he began the letter with a phrase that explicitly positions the letter as a global statement: "To the People of Texas & All Americans in the World."[98] To Curtis, Travis's letter is a centerpiece of Alamo memory because it was the first worldwide public proclamation that refusing to surrender, aiding those in need, and willingly risking death were central attributes of the American character.[99]

Curtis repeatedly conflates heroism with publicly assuming a militant posture. His essay opens with the sentence "1836—'Victory or death,' Travis writes from the Alamo, transforming himself into a hero."[100] He subsequently writes, "[Travis] wanted to be a hero and a patriot, and he became a hero and a patriot. He wrote his famous letter from the Alamo proclaiming his new role, and the world listened. . . . Travis . . . was the first Texan because he made the world accept his vision of himself."[101] He explains that "Travis had found his stage at the Alamo and his destiny. . . . Now he needed to present his vision of himself to the world. He sat down to write his letter."[102] Here, patriotism and heroism are achieved not by valor in battle nor even by the personal decision to sacrifice oneself but by "ma[king] the world accept his vision of himself."

Curtis's argument constructs Travis as a model of the militarized citizenship that Nixon and others averred had motivated American intervention in Vietnam and that they lamented had failed afterward, from Carrier's declaration in his poem about Vietnam that the United States had "shown the world" to Nixon's warning that "leader[s] and diplomat[s]" were unsure about "whether we can be counted upon." Here again, Alamo remembrance was a historical antidote to conservatives' post-Vietnam anxieties because it was constructed in the rhetoric and tropes of revisionist narratives of the Vietnam War.

To be sure, the ascendant strand of Alamo remembrance affirmed that the battle had made possible the organization of the Texan army. However, one piece of writing echoed Nixon's claim that the United States had won the Vietnam War in asserting that the Alamo battle, despite its extraordinary carnage and its *appearing* to be a defeat, had actually been a Texan victory. This argument marks a major shift in the underpinning of the Alamo myth, making it no longer a sacrifice that had galvanized the Texans or enabled the formation of the Texan army but a success. The statement resonated with Nixon's sophistic reasoning that "*win* must be properly defined. . . . We *win* if we prevent the enemy from winning."

This explicit reimagining of the Alamo occurred in "The Battle for the Alamo," an article in *Infantry: A Professional Journal for the Combined Arms Team* (May–June 1983), a specialized military magazine. Dismissing the notion that the Alamo defenders were fighting a symbolic battle by stating that James Bowie, another hero of the Alamo, and Travis were "both no-nonsense men who would not have asked their men to die for a mere symbol," the author of the article, Bob Boyd, instead posits that beyond simply delaying Santa Anna's advance, the Battle of the Alamo was a model of military planning that made the Mexican army's continued campaign through Texas nearly impossible.[103]

The upshot of the Alamo, Boyd argues, was that "in a five-hour battle, Santa Anna [threw] away the best bargaining chip the Mexican nation had—the elite of its army."[104] Boyd goes to great lengths, however, to point out that that elite was not overly impressive, that the Mexicans were afraid of combat, and that Santa Anna idolized Napoleon but didn't understand his tactics.[105] The Alamo fighters, on the other hand, were skillful soldiers who "dived under the awkwardly thrust bayonets and gutted their opponents or deftly stood aside from the thrust to cut a jugular vein"; their "battle plan worked to perfection" despite "all of the defenders having been killed."[106] In the battle's wake, Boyd warrants, the Mexican army realized they had been damaged beyond repair:

> Only when their battalions were reformed did the senior Mexican officers realize what the Texans had done. Carefully picking their targets, they had killed every noncommissioned officer they spotted. . . . Not that the Texans didn't also kill more than a few officers, but their aim was to clearly gut the army. And the best way to gut an infantry unit is to eliminate almost every corporal and sergeant in sight. There was no way of replacing those experienced men and no time to rebuild the shattered formations. . . . When next the main Mexican army faced a force of Texans with their blood up, the Mexicans stood for only 18 minutes despite a numerical superiority of two to one.[107]

Boyd's analysis unmistakably favors the Texans, whom he sees as model soldiers. Most critical, though, is that Boyd views the battle as a victory because it created not the spiritual but the actual possibility of the larger Texan victory. The Texan army did not become better organized because of the Alamo battle; to Boyd, the Texans won because the Battle of the Alamo had *already* defeated the Mexican army. Paying little attention to the lives lost, he defines victory solely in terms of tactical advantage gained and political outcome achieved, a definition that accords with that of Nixon: "We win if we prevent the enemy from winning."

Boyd's assertion that the Alamo was a victory in Nixonian terms stands alone, but it is not far outside the mainstream of Alamo remembrance in the eighties. Even as the shrine maintained its long-standing position as an inspiring patriotic symbol, it became a place at which the nation sought to take solace from the Vietnam syndrome. This was not simply because the Alamo was a long-venerated patriotic site. Rather, throughout the 1980s the battle was explained in terms that recalled and resonated with conservative revision of the Vietnam War. Through these descriptions, the shrine, long privileged as symbolizing American patriotism's highest ideals, helped legitimize revisionist narratives that celebrated, rather than denounced, the Vietnam War and prescribed continued adherence to, rather than a reassessment of, an interventionist foreign policy.

"We Have Marched . . . to Remember the Alamo and Not to Forget Vietnam"

May 6, 1985, was a day of celebration. After a week's worth of media coverage of the tenth anniversary of the fall of Saigon, New York City turned its attention to the war's veterans. Mayor Ed Koch dedicated the city's Vietnam Veterans Memorial, residents admired a fireworks display set to 1960s music, and police closed the Brooklyn Bridge to allow eight thousand veterans to march across it.[108] About half that many ended the day aboard the U.S.S. *Intrepid*, an aircraft carrier that had been deployed during the Vietnam War but was by the 1980s a struggling museum. There they held what one veteran described as a gathering "like a college reunion, only not as romantic," complete with hamburgers, hotdogs, and live music.[109] Among those present were the Vietnam veteran singers and songwriters Michael Martin and Tim Holiday. Martin, who served with the Americal division in 1968 and 1969, and Holiday, who served multiple tours as a navy corpsman, had carved out a niche performing at veterans' gatherings after meeting in a Texas roadhouse in 1979.[110] In the audience was Bill Callahan, a Floridian who had walked the twelve hundred miles from Fort Myers to Manhattan, distributing POW/MIA flags along the way.[111]

It was a day full of good feelings, Martin recalled, of veterans feeling they were finally getting some long-overdue attention.[112] The celebration continued late into the night in someone's smoky hotel room, among a group of veterans swapping war stories and having more than a few drinks. It was there, Martin recalls, that "it just flashed before me," the image of not one man marching but dozens, hundreds: "I said, 'Tell you what, Callahan. If you march to the Alamo, we'll put it together.'"[113]

The Alamo had long been important to Martin. When he was a child, his grandmother had taken him to San Antonio and told him about his ancestor Isaac Milsaps, who had died there. By the 1950s, he said, the Alamo "had already shaded [his] thinking."[114] That thinking had shifted, though, by the time he came home from Vietnam. There was still, he felt, "a natural correlation" between the men who had died on the dusty Texas prairie and the men he had led through Vietnam's Central Coast, but that correlation was based on his realization that "by the time we got [to Vietnam], we all knew that it was a lost cause."[115] Martin returned to Dallas a few days after the celebration in New York and, at the local Vet Center, started getting organized. His goal was to fill Alamo Plaza on Veterans' Day, 1985, with fifty-eight thousand people, one for every American killed in Vietnam.[116]

Martin and Holliday christened the group the Last Patrol, a name meant to evoke those who they believed had been literally or figuratively left behind after Vietnam, and the purpose of the march was twofold: they intended to raise awareness of POW/MIA issues and honor Vietnam veterans. Repeatedly, Martin and Holiday decried Vietnam veterans' marginalization. "We'd like to get the respect now that we didn't get when we came back from Vietnam," Martin told the *San Antonio Light;* he told the *Dallas Morning News* that "the Vietnam vet is long overdue recognition of their valor. Our mission isn't completed. The Last Patrol hasn't come home yet."[117] Holiday made a similar point: "The government and the people have been negative about Vietnam for two decades. . . . Well, we're aware the politicians got us into the mess in Vietnam, and we're just now able to march out of it. People have got to realize there's a lot of positive things the Vietnam veteran can offer."[118]

These comments placed Martin and Holiday squarely within the larger culture of "national 'healing' and societal acknowledgment of Vietnam veterans" that, Patrick Hagopian argues, was premised on the assumption that "American citizens who had taken different positions on the war could come together in bestowing this overdue recognition on the veterans."[119] As Hagopian and others explain, the building of the Vietnam Veterans Memorial, a series of parades across the nation, growing activism around PTSD and the defoliant Agent Orange that was used in Vietnam, and the POW/MIA movement were part of a larger response to many veterans' sense of disillusionment and displacement, a disconnect between what their remembrance of earlier wars had taught them to expect as veterans and what many actually experienced.[120]

These shattered expectations were hardly helped by media coverage and popular culture, which frequently portrayed veterans as alternately pathetic and dangerous figures living on society's margins. Some stories were simply bizarre, like those of a marine veteran sent to prison for "conspiring to murder a lawyer by putting a rattlesnake in his mailbox" and of a veteran who stole "a self-propelled 155mm howitzer . . . and knocked down fences and ripped up lawns as he drove it through a residential neighborhood . . . [before he] turned the huge cannon around and began pursuing the police."[121] Other reports seemed to confirm the representation of troubled, dangerous veterans popularized in films, television programs, and novels.[122] The *Washington Post* of June 21, 1980, for example, profiled two Vietnam veterans, one an African American who "feared a frontal attack, and as in the past, herded his three children into the living room for the night, barricading the hallway with furniture and placing his wife Bettye on guard at the dining room table," and the other the white police officer who shot him to death.[123] A *Post* story five months later described a veteran who fired a rifle out the window of his apartment building before being found "sitting in a dark corner, a rifle across his lap. . . . [shouting] 'Kill the gooks! Kill the foreigners!' [and] screaming his name, rank and serial number."[124]

Veterans lamented their position as outsiders. Philip Caputo complains in the opening pages of *A Rumor of War* that he left the marines "almost completely ignorant about the stuff of ordinary life, about marriage, mortgages, and building a career."[125] Robert Mason, whose memoir *Chickenhawk* (1983) divulges his post-Vietnam struggles with PTSD, alcoholism, and readjustment, similarly laments that he "tried to learn a new career and rejoin society. I could not sleep without having nightmares. I arrived at my eight o'clock morning classes only after at least two stiff drinks. If I drank all day, I could sleep at night"; in the epilogue, he admits that he has been convicted of drug smuggling.[126] The agony of being perceived as pariahs was evident in Stuart Smyth's poem "Back Home," which appeared in the second issue of the *VVA Veteran.* Smyth's speaker wonders what would have happened "had [he] not enlisted" and whether he would have "[fallen] in love, married, bought a house / and entered the urban establishment," only to determine that such imaginings are futile: "It is too late to speculate; I am infected with Asia / and can never lie down with the dwarfs / of my hometown in quiet middle-age."[127] Here, Vietnam is a contagion, an idea that the editors of *VVA Veteran* likewise evoked when they proclaimed that "for all its reality, [Agent Orange] is nothing if not a physical symptom of much deeper things that have yet to be faced, yet to be questioned and yet to be resolved."[128]

Many veterans blamed not just the war but a society that had turned its back on them.[129] Caputo condemns a country that "wishes to forget and it has forgotten," while Mason ruefully mentions a letter he received rejecting him for a government job, which arrived "in an envelope stamped with the slogan 'Don't forget, hire the vet.' "[130] These long-standing grievances were amplified as veterans condemned the Reagan administration's efforts to cut Vet Center funding and its insufficient attention to the perceived incapacitating aftereffects of Agent Orange. The *VVA Veteran* wrote, "The President and his stalwarts have absolutely no idea what the needs of veterans, particularly Vietnam veterans, actually are."[131] Seven months later, the *VVA Veteran* published a cartoon titled "A Memorial to the Last Ten Years" that showed a disabled veteran before a brick wall spray painted with the words "hypocrisy," "reduced benefits," and "VA Doubletalk."[132]

One way in which veterans demanded recognition was through repeated assertions of their similarities to earlier soldiers.[133] Reagan made this point in 1980 in a speech before the Veterans of Foreign Wars, remarking that Vietnam veterans "fought as well and as bravely as any Americans have ever fought in any war."[134] Similar logic marked his speeches at the dedication of Frederick Hart's sculpture *Three Soldiers* at the Vietnam Veterans Memorial and during the entombment of the Unknown Soldier from Vietnam. At the entombment he offered a play on the tomb's inscription, "Known But to God":

"The individual who finds his last resting place at Arlington on this occasion will remain nameless to the entire world. . . . But to generations of Americans who left their homes and families to fight and defend the freedom and independence of our nation, he will be known well."[135]

Reagan was not alone in making such claims. At the first convention of the Vietnam Veterans of America, Rep. David Bonior (D-MI), a staunch supporter of Vietnam veterans' issues, said, "The veterans of [past] conflicts . . . all received the most valuable yet most intangible of benefits: the almost unanimous gratitude and adulation of their countrymen. . . . Both the Congress and the country have since been considerably less enthusiastic in their support for those they committed to the Vietnam War."[136] This lack of acknowledgment, he went on to argue, resulted from the nation's having failed to recognize that Vietnam veterans "were equal, or superior, to soldiers of past conflicts."[137] In *VVA Veteran*, the retired general Albin F. Irzyk, who commanded troops in Vietnam, expressed his irritation as well: "It is time for America to wake up, to recognize that the Vietnam veteran . . . stand[s] every bit as tall, [is] every bit as great a group of heroes, and should be honored every bit as much as any group of men who fought and died for this country since that first War for Independence."[138]

Martin and Holiday were active in efforts to assuage Vietnam veterans' suffering by incorporating them within the larger, celebratory history of the American soldier. The Alamo was a highly useful setting in which to force these reparations. As the Texas state historian Bill Green observed in an interview in 1980, veterans "were drawing from the Alamo to meet their needs. The parallel is pretty impressive—the feeling that we lost the Vietnamese War and the defenders of the Alamo lost. They lost but we have a lot of respect for them—that we lost, and we're worthy of respect, too."[139] Green's observation is insightful, but it takes into account neither the extent to which such claims emerged from the larger discourse of the veterans' movement nor that "drawing from the Alamo" required at once embracing, adapting, and reconfiguring the shrine's legacy according to veterans' own remembrance of Vietnam. Martin and Holiday repeatedly did this over the course of Veterans Day weekend in 1985, making direct comparisons between the two groups while also shifting Alamo memory by isolating defeat at the Alamo from the larger Texas revolution, depoliticizing the defenders' motives by casting them as having fought for their friends, and reenacting fundamental scenes in Alamo mythology in ways that addressed contemporary veterans' concerns.

FIGURE 3.3. Members of the Last Patrol: Tim "Doc" Holiday, Mike Standerfer, Michael J. Martin, and Bill Callahan at the Alamo on October 3, 1985, following Callahan's and Standerfer's march from Crystal River, Florida. Ostensibly an effort to raise awareness of POW/MIA issues, the Last Patrol marches revised Alamo memory to establish the Vietnam veteran's place within the pantheon of American military heroism. Image E1985-10-2-24a, San Antonio Express-News Photograph Collection, MS 360, University of Texas at San Antonio Libraries Special Collections from the Institute of Texan Cultures.

In doing so, they validated calls to honor Vietnam veterans by establishing a historical precedent for honoring heroic soldiers without consideration of the political contours of the conflict in which they fought.

THE MARCH TO THE ALAMO ACTUALLY HAD TWO PHASES. CALLAHAN AND Mike Standerfer, another veteran, left Crystal River, Florida, on August 3 for a preliminary march, arriving in San Antonio on October 3, where Martin and Holiday met them and performed in Alamo Plaza (fig. 3.3). Callahan and Standerfer were ostensibly walking to raise awareness of POWs and MIAs. They followed an earlier activist, Ron Villarealle, who was not connected with the Last Patrol but who arrived two months earlier on horseback and appeared at a City Council meeting where he "recited a poem . . . regarding the plight of Vietnam's Prisoners of War" and "spoke to the evidence indicating that these men are still alive and are still being held captive in Vietnam." Then he "ask[ed] for a letter of support from the Mayor" and for the city to fly the POW/MIA flag.[140] Callahan and Standerfer likewise appeared before the City Council after their journey to the Alamo, explaining that they "decided to stage this symbolic 1,300 mile walk to call the public's attention to the plight of the POWs and MIAs in Southeastern Asia."[141] Callahan did Villareale one better by giving the city a POW/MIA flag; in return, Mayor Cisneros presented each man with a belt buckle and an Alcalde, a ceremonial certificate naming Callahan the honorary mayor of San Antonio.[142]

Awareness of POW/MIA issues was central to these veterans' use of the Alamo. Yet this issue was only part of their larger effort to earn respect from the broader public. As Bruce Franklin writes, "For every missing man . . . there are now probably at least one thousand homeless on the streets of the United States, whom some people refer to as 'M.I.A.: Missing in America." Kristin Hass has pointed out, veterans' participation in this movement often has much to do with redeeming their own image and citizenship.[143] There's no reason to doubt the sincerity of the Last Patrol's concern about those unaccounted for in Indochina. However, those "Missing in America" were as much, if not more, important. Martin made clear his view that Vietnam veterans had become the country's most noticeable pariahs when he told reporters, "We have POWs here in America who have not come home from Vietnam" and claimed that "there are more Vietnam vets dying from suicide than people dying from AIDS."[144]

Martin and Holiday sought to raise awareness of veterans' problems by being as inclusive as possible. They invited Gold Star Mothers, an organization of women whose sons had been killed in combat, and African Americans to join them on the march. Holiday noted that African Americans "were overrepresented in the Vietnam War, and we are aware and sensitive of that fact." The fact that on their way to the Alamo they marched with—not behind, as veterans had two years earlier in Washington, D.C.—Gen. William Westmoreland and Lady Bird Johnson demonstrated an egalitarianism that extended even to those whom many veterans blamed for the war.[145] "We were looking for the guy who never had a chance to be proud of serving in 'Nam," Holiday explained. "And, by God, we found 'em."[146]

They actually found more than one hundred. When that group marched into Alamo Plaza on November 7, the Daughters of the Republic of Texas had already raised the POW/MIA flag on the Alamo's guest flagpole.[147] The Last Patrol established a four-day encampment over the Veterans Day weekend that featured a "vigil fire," a symbolic beacon to veterans trying to find their way home, and concerts by Martin and Holiday that "ranged from the atmosphere of a country and western show to a spiritual revival." Newspapers reported that Vietnam veterans had come from across the country and speculated that the crowd might reach ten thousand (fig. 3.4).[148] The weekend culminated in what amounted to an insurgent takeover of San Antonio's Veterans Day parade, when the group to whom organizers had given "a reluctant invitation to participate" and relegated to the back of the parade offered to include members of the Vietnam Veterans Against the War, who had been banned. Martin and Holiday even pulled Vietnam veterans out of the crowd, swelling their numbers to six hundred, and "urged some of the Generals in the reviewing stands to join their group."[149]

Almost every element of the weekend, however, revolved around the veterans' use and rescripting of Alamo memory. When Martin described the purpose of the march as being to "remember the Alamo, remember we can't forget the Vietnam veteran, remember the POWs, remember the MIAs," he continued the rhetorical assertion of the POW/MIA as a meta-identity for all Vietnam veterans.[150] At the same time he highlighted an equivalency between those veterans and the Alamo defenders and implicitly demanded on behalf of the former the heroism that had indisputably been afforded the latter.

Martin told reporters from the *Express-News* that "the valor there [in Vietnam] was equal to the valor at the Alamo. We equaled the fighting for our country that Davy Crockett, Jim Bowie and the boys did here." The *Dallas Morning News* quoted him as saying, "A lot of people have branded us cowards because we lost a war. We're just as tough as Davy Crockett."[151] These statements reflected much earlier ones about twentieth-century soldiers meeting the Alamo's standard, and it repeated the rhetoric of the larger Vietnam veterans' movement.[152] It was not, however, a comparison that immediately made sense. The Alamo defenders were unquestionable members of the pantheon of American military heroism, whereas the image that Vietnam veterans were fighting against was nearly the opposite of this.

To make the comparison work, veterans challenged customary Alamo remembrance by reimagining the Alamo defenders as having shared the motivations and combat experiences of the men who fought in Vietnam. In doing so, they established Schivelbusch's "heroic loser" who had "fought bravely and honorably, if hopelessly, to the bitter end" as a valid, patriotic identity. Like the conservatives who spoke and wrote about the Alamo Sesquicentennial a few

FIGURE 3.4. Members of the Last Patrol standing vigil outside the Alamo, Veterans Day Weekend, 1985. By revising Alamo memory, these veterans asserted both their own patriotism and their national belonging. Image L-7247-48-10, San Antonio Light Photograph Collection, MS 359, University of Texas at San Antonio Libraries Special Collections from the Institute of Texan Cultures.

months later, their reimagining of the Alamo aimed to heal them from the failure in Vietnam by making the defeat itself the least important aspect of the war and by incorporating the conflict within broader discourses of patriotic orthodoxy.

One way in which they did so was to craft the Alamo battle as politically and militarily insignificant. Callahan and Standerfer began this project in October, when they "said they chose the Alamo to symbolize that Vietnam soldiers were fighting a losing cause but continued to fight out of a sense of duty."[153] In the broadest strokes, this is congruent with the traditional narrative of men who, knowing they would be killed, stayed to fight the Mexican army. However, unlike the traditional narrative's contention that the Alamo defenders' willing sacrifice enabled the Texan army's ultimate victory, Callahan and Standerfer implied that the Alamo defenders died for no larger cause. Martin made this revision himself a month later, explaining, "We see a lot of parallels between the men at the Alamo and ourselves" in that both were " 'raiders of the lost cause' who gave all their energy to fighting battles they knew they could not win."[154] A more complete version of this quote illustrates Martin's sense that both conflicts were marked by futility: "We were all sent to fight a war that couldn't be fought, and we fought it anyway."[155]

Like those that surrounded the Sesquicentennial, these comments adapted the traditional narrative. The Alamo defenders had died nobly, but the veterans extracted their deaths from the larger context of the Texas revolution, thereby making the Alamo independent and politically neutral.[156] At the same time, they construed the defenders as having ultimately been wholly *defeated,* a signifier uncommon within the dominant memorial discourse. Instead, previous acts of memory had celebrated the Alamo defenders for *sacrificing* their lives—a term that signifies death in order to protect a greater ideal—to ultimately ensure the Texans' victory.

This is not a shallow distinction. The concept of meaningful sacrifice is so central to the Alamo myth that Mark Lane, then the director of San Antonio's Witte Museum, included the proviso "Have furthered 'the cause' with their lives" among the "five major points that must be present in a historical event for it to become a prime candidate for legendary status" and that are "present in some fashion in the 'Alamo sacrifice.' "[157] As Tom Engelhardt writes about events like the Alamo and Pearl Harbor, "The only acceptable defeats or last stands would be those that were the end of the beginning for us and the beginning of the end for them."[158] Veterans, however, eschewed this remembrance, instead constructing a more narrow view in which the Alamo defenders had, like Vietnam veterans, been tasked with fighting a futile, meaningless conflict.[159] These assertions made Vietnam unexceptional and made possible its celebration in traditional patriotic terms.

Perhaps more important, the Last Patrol reimagined the Alamo defenders' motivations in ways that accorded with veterans' own understanding of Vietnam. If the traditional story viewed those inside the Alamo as engaged in a spirited defense of freedom and liberty—whether their own or those of less fortunate others—or, more cynically, of an attempt to secure their economic interests, Martin and others cast them as having fought solely for each other. In other words, they crafted a tale of homosocial bonding that adapted the notion of the Alamo as "the nation's most famous site of male sacrifice" to create a historical precedent for the narrative they had created about their own valor.[160]

That soldiers fighting in Vietnam ignored politics and simply struggled to keep themselves and their friends alive is central to many soldiers' remembrances. As Christian Appy writes, "In one account after another, veterans insist that . . . they felt a profound comradeship" and that "soldiers drew together around the shared assumption the war itself had no meaningful purpose, that the only meaning was located in the collective unity necessary to survive."[161] So it was among members of the Last Patrol. "In Vietnam," Martin told a *San Antonio Light* columnist, "we had to find a reason to fight. We had to motivate ourselves. And we ended up fighting for our brothers."[162]

"Brotherhood" was a frequent rejoinder to the question of what the fighting meant, and the Last Patrol clearly imagined a fraternal bond tying Vietnam veterans together. Holiday congratulated a fellow veteran at the end of the parade by declaring, "Welcome home, brother. Welcome home." In a moving moment "Holiday asked the patrol to keep the memory of Vietnam alive. 'For our brothers dead and missing, for those brothers here among us, let's keep the fire alive.' "[163] Another veteran pointed to veterans' ordinariness to refute the stereotype of them as being mentally disturbed: "We're not the crazies they think we are.' . . . 'We're just regular guys."[164] Martin, for his part, rejected the iconic image of the recuperated Vietnam hero: "We're not into that Rambo stuff. . . . We're talking about real flesh-and-blood people who gave everything they had and then were spit on by their own country for doing it."[165] Two years later, when the Last Patrol marched from the Alamo to the Vietnam Veterans Memorial in Washington, he made a similar point by shunning the heroic imagery of both Vietnam and the Alamo: "We understand the reality of war, and it ain't John Wayne and Sylvester Stallone."[166]

The veterans' understanding of their experience in fraternal, working-class terms shaped their remembrance of the Alamo. Their viewpoint that the defenders were similarly ordinary is evident in Martin's pointed dismissal of Wayne's famous performance as Davy Crockett and his description of the defenders not as deserving of veneration but simply as "Davy Crockett, Jim Bowie, and the boys." The idea that veterans were regular guys was most evident, though, in Martin's and Holiday's performance of Martin's song "I Am with My Friends," a song "based on a letter Crockett had written to his daughter."[167] Unlike "The Ballad of Davy Crockett," the hit song written and marketed by the Disney Company in the 1950s, which declares that "freedom was fightin' another foe / An' they needed him at the Alamo," Martin's title alone portends a shift in the memory of the Alamo that reflected many Vietnam veterans' remembrances.[168]

Martin's song embraces elements of the orthodox narrative, declaring, for example, that "We are the Alamo's defenders / We'll pay the price to buy some time." He explains how he came to be at the Alamo in a way that mixes foreign policy adventurism with uncertainty about his cause:

> Well we rode down to Texas
> From our homes in Tennessee
> Looking for a reason worth fighting for
> Some call it liberty.[169]

Whether that mission was fulfilled and who considered it liberty go unanswered and quickly become immaterial as Martin constructs a Crockett who seems more like a Vietnam veteran than a Texan hero. Finding himself in "the most desperate situation / I ever have been in," Crockett urges, "Don't you worry about me, dear daughter. / I am with my friends."[170] This refrain dominates the song, becoming "the reason to remember / It's in the hearts of all good men," and the lyrics establish the Alamo as an idealized homosocial setting: "There's never a need to explain yourself / When you're a man among men."[171] Here, the Alamo's larger politics are simply unimportant; the speaker sees no "need to explain" himself, as the brotherly camaraderie offers sufficient rationale for not fleeing the battle.

Through these rewritings of the Alamo in the terms through which Vietnam veterans understood their own experience, the Last Patrol underscored that their valor stemmed from their having fulfilled the same fraternal commitments as the venerated Alamo heroes. This rhetorical parallel was reinforced by the appearance of that ethos in another song played that weekend, "I Ain't Here Alone." The lyric tells the story of a barstool encounter between veterans, one of whom had "been through hell in the jungles and the jails" and had "just lost another job and another wife," and goes on to condemn a culture intent on "bury[ing them] while [they're] still living." The song ends with one vet saying, "I don't need no parades, I don't need no forgivin'. / I just need to know is that I ain't here alone."[172]

Moreover, Holiday's invitation to veterans to join the Last Patrol outside the Alamo in 1985 evokes Martin's lyrical vision of what transpired inside in 1836, as he encouraged veterans to "sit around the vigil fire and share brotherhood together. There's always somebody they can relate to, no matter what branch of service."[173] This sentiment was echoed in the *Dallas Morning News*, which discovered veterans who had only recently met each other but who "talked with easy familiarity about where they had spent their youth."[174] The gathering, it seems, was "men among men" who didn't need to "explain themselves." The constructing of these similarities was yet another way in which the Last Patrol recreated themselves effectively as descendants of the Alamo defenders and therefore as deserving of the same recognition. Here, then, was another example of Alamo memory being seen through the lens of Vietnam remembrance in ways that made its already sacrosanct status speak on behalf of redemptive narratives about Vietnam.

But the Last Patrol also adapted Alamo memory in other ways, using its legacy to affirm veterans' place in a culture that they felt had abandoned them. For instance, the Last Patrol invoked the Alamo's position *as* a site of memory to criticize a society that they believed had not met its obligation to remember Vietnam veterans and POW/MIAs. In 2012 Martin told me that when he spoke to the press his message was, "Hell yes, remember the Alamo, and quit telling us to forget about Vietnam."[175] This colorful quote never made it into the press, but others did: "The reason we have marched 300 miles is to remember the Alamo and not to forget Vietnam," and they were there to "remember the Alamo, remember we can't forget the Vietnam veteran, remember the POWs, remember the MIAs."[176] Similarly, when Callahan and Standerfer arrived in October, they told reporters, "People are always saying, 'Remember the Alamo,' but we say, 'Remember the POWs and MIAs.'"[177] They then touched the Alamo building itself, "vowing never to forget the 2,400 servicemen still listed as missing in action in Southeast Asia."[178]

The veterans' use of the Alamo thus had the dual intent of demonstrating their patriotism, reflected in their appropriate veneration of the Alamo, and of reminding Americans of their obligation to remember all war heroes.[179] Veterans elsewhere had been urged to play this role as well. In *VVA Veteran*, Joseph M. Puggelli wrote, "We must again make it fashionable for Americans to love their country openly."[180] Refuting the veterans' position as that of a social outlier, he explained that "in this circumstance Viet Nam veterans can provide some help. We loved America enough to fight for her, we were intimately involved with this great country's worst moments and we still love her. We should stand up and speak about this love."[181] In Puggelli's logic, the veteran becomes the agent of social renewal, one who demonstrates that patriotism is possible even in difficult times.

The Last Patrol embraced this notion that veterans were the custodians of appropriate citizenship and encouraged others to meet the Alamo's commemorative demands. The march, after all, was called "A Journey to Remember," and Holiday told the Associated Press that "the group hopes to focus attention on 'the valor of the people who served in Vietnam. They haven't had a chance to be thanked for what they did.' "[182] In other interviews, he remarked, "What we hoped to do was give the message that the Vietnam veterans—the living, the dead, and the missing—will not be forgotten," and he "hope[d] all American veterans will get caught up in the feeling of accountability" for POWs and MIAs.[183] The march in 1987 from the Alamo to Washington was characterized by similar rhetoric. The Last Patrol walked over the Memorial Bridge in the capital chanting, "Don't you tell me not to care. It's my brother over there." One marcher said, "Our country forgot. We're going to make them remember."[184] If the Alamo remained "the ideal to which every future age must aspire," it became one that contemporary Americans could achieve by replicating the commemoration, rather than the combat, that had occurred there by recognizing Vietnam veterans.[185]

The most deeply symbolic revision, however, was of the Alamo myth's defining event, the crossing of Travis's line in the sand.[186] According to Linenthal, "The Travis legend is often used to express a model of patriotic conversion required of each generation of Americans."[187] Martin and Holiday appropriated this myth to suit the Last Patrol's purposes, asking the veterans to commit not to combat but to recovery. The result was a truly powerful scene in which Martin drew a line in front of the Alamo.[188] He told the crowd, "Travis said that anyone who wanted to die for freedom should step over the line.... We proved we were willing to die for our country. We went to Vietnam. We're asking you to cross that line and pledge to live for freedom. We don't want any more suicides of Vietnam veterans."[189] Martin recalls that the crowd "turned into a big bear hug, and a chant broke out, 'I will live.' "[190] This act marked the apex of the veterans' efforts to stand with the Alamo defenders while reconfiguring the site's memory. They had not only exhibited similar bravery and camaraderie but also transformed the site's central ritual of military commitment into a gesture of rehabilitation.

The Last Patrol's appropriation of the Alamo defined Veterans Day in Texas that weekend in 1985. The *Dallas Morning News* lionized the patrol, noting that "as they marched... their numbers grew. And the applause increased like ocean waves through downtown streets."[191] Because of this "ragtag army," its front-page article declared, "Monday did indeed become Veterans Day."[192] Jay Odom, a veteran who joined the vigil, was equally celebratory. "I learned I'm not alone," he told the *Austin American-Statesman.* "We've rekindled the spirit of American patriotism. We got a second chance to be heroes to the people we've met."[193] The next morning the *San Antonio Light* editorialized, "As the Last Patrol raised its POW flag and the Stars and Stripes at the Alamo Monday... there were signs that the healing is proceeding nicely" before going on the suggest, "Though it has taken a long time, we have them to thank, not only for the sacrifices they made, but for forcing this nation to recognize the bitter experience and the enduring legacy that is war—any war."[194] The appropriation of the Alamo accomplished precisely what Martin and Holiday had intended it should: it made the Vietnam veteran a welcomed patriot and an agent of national renewal.

This "second chance to be heroes," however, relied on the Last Patrol's appropriation and adaptation of Alamo memory. Against a persistent narrative of Vietnam veterans' marginalization and in light of their insistence that the culture had failed to adequately serve them, Martin, Holiday, and others revised the Alamo's dominant remembrance to craft a recuperative narrative that accorded with their remembrance of the Vietnam War.

The Last Patrol undoubtedly helped veterans—Martin says that several veterans who later contemplated suicide did not take their lives because of promises made that weekend—but the terms in which they discussed the war nonetheless limited discussion of the political and strategic factors that led to the war.[195] Establishing themselves as counterparts to the Alamo defenders and as the catalysts of a larger patriotic renewal, they emphasized that the moral imperative the Alamo portended to future generations included the depoliticized commemoration of Vietnam veterans. Their endeavor, while commendable, reveals the difficulty of combining veterans' recuperation with meaningful political censure of that war.

In the mid-1980s, Americans persistently met the demand to Remember the Alamo by imagining the shrine's significance in the language of revisionist and recuperative narratives of the Vietnam War. In different ways, conservatives who viewed the war as having caused the American retreat from interventionist foreign policies and veterans who felt forgotten appropriated the Alamo as a site at which amends could be made, healing could be accomplished, and defeat in Vietnam could be reimagined as noble. George H. W. Bush, T. R. Fehrenbach, and others who celebrated the Alamo's one hundred and fiftieth anniversary echoed the rewriting of Vietnam that portrayed the war as righteous, necessary, and even successful and recalled the Texan heroes as models of a long history of intervention to help struggling democracies cast off repressive regimes. Vietnam veterans, on the other hand, responded to their feelings of cultural marginalization by recasting the Alamo defenders as men who, like themselves, had knowingly fought a losing battle solely because of their dedication to each other. Both groups' use of the Alamo reveals that Americans drew upon the logics of their understanding of Vietnam and its aftermath to remake notable sites of cultural memory into sites of national healing. And in both cases, the revision of the Alamo to promote healing had political consequences, as it made the defeat in Vietnam not an occasion to rethink U.S. empire, the interventionist foreign policies that sustain it, and the militarism it requires. Rather, by paralleling the defeat with a sacrosanct moment in American patriotic discourse, the use of Vietnam's remembrance to shape Alamo memory facilitated the continued uncritical acceptance of—and continued lack of attention to—troubling policies of the sort that had led to the Vietnam War. Healing from the Vietnam War was too long a process, however, to be accomplished over a weekend in November 1985 or a few weeks in March 1986. Even after the supposed catharsis of the Gulf War, Vietnam remained the primary lens through which Americans viewed the role of military intervention in the aftermath of the Cold War.

CHAPTER 4

"WE SHOULD HAVE SAID NO"

The Legacy of Vietnam, the Remembrance of Somalia, and Debates over Humanitarian Intervention in the 1990s

ON MARCH 24, 1999, PRESIDENT BILL CLINTON TOLD AMERICANS THAT the United States had bombed Kosovo. "Ending this tragedy is a moral imperative," he said, referring to the ethnic cleansing that had followed the collapse of Yugoslavia in the early 1990s, during which, in its 1998–99 incarnation, Kosovo's Serbian-led military killed thousands of ethnic Albanians. "It is also important to America's national interest."[1] Clinton's determination that the maintaining of "peace, freedom, and stability in Europe" was necessary came after months of contentious debate over whether a potential American intervention in the former Yugoslav Republic constituted a national interest, could be militarily successful, and was worth risking American lives. Clinton answered all three questions affirmatively.

His opponents, meanwhile, identified a different moral imperative: protecting U.S. troops from dying in unnecessary, unwinnable conflicts.[2] "America risks a debacle," Pat Buchanan opined in the *Washington Post* three weeks after Clinton's address, portending that "U.S. troops may have to go marching into the Big Muddy." "Such," he dismissively complained, "are the fruits of Utopian crusades for global democracy."[3] Six months later Clinton said the mission had enabled the century to close "with a ringing affirmation of the inherent human dignity of every individual," but Oklahoma City's *Daily Oklahoman* editorialized, "Clinton's zeal for peacekeeping [is] stretching the U.S. military beyond reasonable limits," and "the more it is used in far-flung peacekeeping operations, the less it will be able to look after America's vital defense interests."[4] Such opposition was rooted in an anxiety about what endangered troops might be able to accomplish and at what cost, and Buchanan pointedly alludes to another conflict that loomed over these worries: the original "Big Muddy," Vietnam.

Clinton's speeches and these editorial rejoinders are reminders that between the end of the Cold War and the terrorist attacks of September 11, 2001, the central debate in U.S. foreign policy was not about whether the nation could win a long-term ideological struggle but whether it had a moral and political obligation to intervene in humanitarian crises. That it did have such an obligation was not a universally embraced position. If, as Peter Beinart writes, "Clinton-era liberals were more confident than their Cold War predecessors that human rights were achievable everywhere, soon . . . [and] militarily, they were more confident that America could defend those rights at the point of a gun," realists and isolationists held that such missions were fool's errands. They counseled instead adherence to the narrow boundaries of the Powell doctrine, the strict criteria for military action that Colin Powell and Caspar Wineberger had prescribed in the 1980s. Those criteria recommended "an all-or-nothing approach to warfare, with the ideal war being one in which the U.S. wins with overwhelming force, suffers few casualties, and leaves immediately."[5] The Powell doctrine was the key to not repeating the errors of Vietnam.

This debate continued even after 9/11 precipitated a shift in U.S. foreign policy. Interventionist liberals like John Shattuck, who had been the Clinton administration's assistant secretary of state for democracy, human rights, and labor, encouraged Americans "to recognize that the costs of *not* engaging can be greater than the benefits of remaining on the sidelines"; Samantha Power, who would become a proponent of human rights interventions in the Obama administration, avowed that "the United States has consistently refused to take risks in order to suppress genocide."[6] By contrast, realists have condemned such missions as examples of American overconfidence that are unlikely to succeed. Andrew Bacevich wrote that in the 1990s humanitarian interventions "fritter[ed] away most of what the [post-Vietnam] reform project had wrought" and exemplified the problematic "marriage of a militaristic cast of mind with utopian ends."[7]

The debate over whether and how the United States ought to respond to humanitarian crises in the post–Cold War world began in 1992, when President George H. W. Bush told Americans that meeting the nation's interests and obligations required sending troops to end a famine on the Horn of Africa. This deployment ended with the most infamous military disaster of the post-Vietnam era. In the fall of 1993, Bush's successor, Bill Clinton, ordered the U.S. military to capture the Somali warlord Mohamed Farrah Aidid. A U.S. special forces raid in Mogadishu, Somalia, on October 3, 1993, resulted in the deaths of nineteen American soldiers, and American television showed Somali civilians mutilating American bodies. Within days, newspapers around the country and politicians from both parties were bringing up Vietnam.[8] In a cartoon in the *Los Angeles Times*, Clinton is shown tiptoeing into a quagmire; in the *Chicago Tribune*, the father of Casey Joyce, a Vietnam veteran who had been killed in the war, wondered, "What are we doing there? This is how we got into Vietnam, isn't it?" Two days later Anna Quindlen marveled, "We were as naïve about Aidid as we were about his ancestor, Ho Chi Minh. We learned a quarter-century ago that people can be inspired to fight tooth and nail for the sovereignty of their own small country, where they know the turf and we do not." She concluded that "just as we were flummoxed . . . [when] faced with that ignominious war in which we were to destroy Vietnam in order to save it, we are flummoxed by how to be humanitarian in tanks."[9]

As Quindlen makes clear, opponents of humanitarian intervention invoked the Powell doctrine somewhat differently than they had a few years earlier. To her, Vietnam was not a war the United States could have won had the troops not, as Bush famously put it when he announced the start of the Persian Gulf War in 1991, been "asked to fight with one hand tied behind their back"; rather, it was one by which it had been "flummoxed."[10] If for Bush in 1991 the imperative to support the troops and have a speedy, low-casualty war was crucial, for Quindlen and others, the doctrine's demand that "the relationship between ends and means 'must be continually reassessed and adjusted if necessary'" predominated.[11] Vietnam was no longer a noble cause poorly fought; it was the wrong war fought for the wrong reasons.

Quindlen was joined in her opinion by the retired three-star general Harold Moore, who as a lieutenant colonel had commanded the Seventh Cavalry regiment of the First Cavalry Division in the battle of the Ia Drang Valley, which in 1965 was the Americans' first major confrontation with the North

Vietnamese Army. In 1992 Moore, together with Joseph Galloway, a reporter who had been embedded with Moore's unit at the battle, had written *We Were Soldiers Once . . . and Young: Ia Drang—The Battle That Changed the War in Vietnam.* Interviewed two months after the Mogadishu battle, Moore remarked, "We all know that it was a stupid war, we never should have gotten involved in Vietnam in 1954. . . . We would hope that, if we do get involved, there would be a clear military strategy and a good objective. . . . That's why we think both Somalia and Serbia are swamps; we hope this book would help prevent such capricious military adventures."[12]

This fused remembrance of Vietnam and Somalia as well-intentioned interventions marred by unrealizable goals that had caused unnecessary deaths of Americans drove opposition to humanitarian interventions for the rest of the decade. And as Americans considered intervening in the Balkans and elsewhere, they encountered the popular literature of Somalia, which included Mark Bowden's wildly popular *Black Hawk Down: A Story of Modern War* (1999), the best-selling memoir *In the Company of Heroes* (2003) by Michael J. Durant, *Somalia on Five Dollars a Day: A Soldier's Story* (2001) by Martin Stanton, and *The Battle of Mogadishu: Firsthand Accounts from the Men of Task Force Ranger* (2004) by Matt Eversmann and Dan Schilling. These books drew on the tropes central to Vietnam's remembrance during the 1990s, particularly those of *We Were Soldiers Once* but also those of Robert McNamara's *In Retrospect: The Tragedies and Lessons of Vietnam* (1995), in which the vilified former secretary of defense admitted that policymakers had erred in escalating the Vietnam War. These major reassessments of Vietnam presented American soldiers in Vietnam as consummate professionals but explicitly criticized the war as misguided, unnecessary, and unwinnable. They did so through portrayals of soldiers as exceptional but sent to fight a savage enemy in a wrongheaded war; multivalent representation of the traumatized bodies to simultaneously confirm American professionalism and tenacity, Vietnamese brutality, and American suffering; and explicit condemnation of policymakers who pursued the war despite knowing it was a doomed enterprise. At least one reviewer acknowledged these parallels, noting that *Black Hawk Down* "recalls the epic Vietnam narrative 'We Were Soldiers once . . . and Young'" before suggesting that "[Bowden's] book may join [Moore's and Galloway's] as required reading for military officers. For the rest of us, hungering to understand the world of one superpower and the forces swirling around it, it might also be required."[13]

In language with which American audiences were already familiar, the Somalia literature reached conclusions parallel to Moore's and McNamara's as it found fault with the Somalia intervention in particular and humanitarian missions in general. Bowden and other authors persistently recalled and redeployed language and imagery drawn from *We Were Soldiers Once* and *In Retrospect* to show that the American troops sent to Africa were of equal quality and suffered as grievously as the combatants in Vietnam, that the Somalis and the Vietnamese were similarly barbaric, and that policymakers had repeated the Johnson administration's failures.

These are more than aesthetic parallels. In borrowing from Vietnam's remembrance to reprehend the first humanitarian intervention undertaken by the United States, this literature helped sustain narratives in which humanitarian commitments replicated America's errors in Vietnam and contributed to Americans' willingness to allow their enduring shame over that war to inhibit consideration of the potential for military force to help ensure human rights.

"We Were Wrong, Terribly Wrong": Vietnam in the 1990s

The reviews of McNamara's *In Retrospect,* a memoir that broke his three-decade silence over the Vietnam War, were scathing. It wasn't the quality of the writing that was attacked but the author's admission that poor planning and arrogance had caused U.S. soldiers to die unnecessarily. The planners were "bumblers of the worst sort," one reviewer fumed, men "contemptuous and ignorant of the land and people they sought to save, preoccupied in the most irrational of ways with global games, using the cloak of national security to mask a paucity of logical thought."[14] Another, only slightly more sympathetically, credited the author's admission that officials "never re-examined the faulty premises from which they operated and thus were unable to understand that no compelling national interest was at stake."[15]

Such was the outcry when *In Retrospect* appeared, thirty months after the American deaths in the failed mission in Somalia. Veterans derided McNamara for not speaking up sooner. Reviewers called the book an admission that the author's opponents had been right all along and that their decades-long mistrust of the government had been well founded.[16] The memoir, *USA Today* argued, "confirms what critics have long held: that " 'McNamara's War' was plotted by reckless, uninformed civilians who didn't know what they were doing."[17] An editorial in the *Providence Journal* seethed, "How we hate him for telling us now what he should have told us then."[18]

The outcry revealed that Bush's poetic protestation that Vietnam had been "buried forever in the desert sands of the Arabian peninsula" was something of an overstatement.[19] Critically acclaimed texts about the war appeared throughout the nineties. Some, like Tim O'Brien's *In the Lake of the Woods* (1994) and Tobias Wolff's *In Pharaoh's Army* (1994), continued well-established discourses of the war's absurdity and atrocity. In 1996 James Carroll's *An American Requiem*, the memoir of a former priest who had protested the war, told of his father, an air force general, weeping because "the War was wrong. He knew it."[20] Carroll's memoir won the National Book Award, beating out Paul Hendrickson's *The Living and the Dead: Robert McNamara and Five Lives of a Lost War*.

But *In Retrospect* and Moore's and Galloway's *We Were Soldiers Once* introduced a remembrance of Vietnam that emphatically denounced the intervention as an unnecessary disaster rooted in a failed political vision. In arguing that Vietnam had been an avoidable disaster, they drew on and revised earlier remembrances. Popular culture of the early 1980s, most explicitly the *Rambo* franchise, presented idealized soldiers fighting a savagely inhumane enemy and a dysfunctional bureaucracy that famously refused to let them win.[21] By contrast, later films and books like *Platoon* and *The Things They Carried* construe the war as a chaotic theater in which soldiers must endure and ultimately triumph.[22] Although these works acknowledge the soldier's capacity to commit atrocities, they do so primarily in order to emphasize, as Marita Sturken has shown, "the rift in morality among Americans and their own victimization."[23] Even O'Brien's short story "The Man I Killed," which concedes the war's brutality and impact on Vietnamese bodies, does so to emphasize American ambivalence.[24] Most significantly, scholars have shown, these texts make few political claims, instead "show[ing] boldly that we . . . don't know why we were in Vietnam and are no longer afraid to admit it. Nor are we interested in finding out, in a political sense."[25]

Informed by the celebration of both the soldier and the Powell doctrine that dominated the Persian Gulf War, the Vietnam literature of the 1990s builds on but in a major way adapts these discourses. During the Gulf War, media coverage and political rhetoric sought to recuperate from Vietnam, a conflict that Bush declared would not be repeated. Soldiers were particularly celebrated, Michelle Kendrick notes, for their "education, training . . . willingness to subordinate themselves to their country's good, and the absolute nature of their commitment."[26] These images made the war nearly immune to criticism; even its opponents claimed to "Support the Troops."[27]

As the popularity of Moore's and McNamara's texts reveal, however, Vietnam endured. Yet its remembrance did not continue unaltered. As the reviews of *In Retrospect* reveal, it was no longer Bush's or Reagan's Vietnam War. A war fought by men "preoccupied . . . with global games" was not a noble cause that could have been won had bureaucrats not hamstrung soldiers, nor was it one about which political questions were inconsequential.

In the 1990s Vietnam remembrance combined elements of both earlier narratives to articulate a more complex vision. The soldiers were simultaneously the exceptionally competent, dedicated figures of the early 1980s and the Gulf War and the vulnerable victims of the later 1980s. The Vietnamese once more became uncomplicated bestial villains, and explicit political critiques returned while soldiers remained victims of their government. However, the fault was no longer policymakers' refusal to let the soldiers win; it was having sent them to fight a war that had always been a mistake.

This narrative is most clearly articulated in *We Were Soldiers Once,* one of the first noteworthy Vietnam texts of the 1990s. The book was read as a provocative reassessment of the war's early years, one in which American bravery was squandered by ignorant, venal politicians and military leaders. Reviewers foreshadowed the claims they would make three years later about McNamara's memoir. A *USA Today* review lamented, "Perhaps the saddest significance of Ia Drang, beyond the actual deaths on both sides, was the way the leaders on each side read those deaths" and then concluded that "courage of the sort the rest of us can barely imagine was the currency of Ia Drang. The tragedy, of course, is how easily our political leaders spent it." The *Seattle Post-Intelligencer* called the book "a testament to both the courage of those soldiers and the folly of that war" and warned readers that "this is a Vietnam War story, perhaps the definitive Vietnam War story, so do not expect its authors to conclude that all that heroism and sacrifice served some worthy purpose."[28] The *Christian Science Monitor* declared, "The lesson Americans should derive . . . pivots on a terrible word: ignorance—overestimation of American power and underestimation of the enemy's skill, tenacity, and dedication."[29]

Moore's and Galloway's ability to simultaneously valorize and celebrate the

American soldier, vilify Vietnamese brutality and sadism, and chastise American political and military leaders depends largely on the historical moment about which they write. In the fall of 1965, when the battle of Ia Drang took place, the violence of the war's later years as well as the ambivalence that surrounded America's involvement lay in the future. These later years have historically dominated the war's remembrance, a distance that enables Moore and Galloway to emphasize the volunteer soldier's exceptionalism while criticizing the Johnson administration's early failures.[30]

We Were Soldiers Once repudiates earlier descriptors of the Vietnam-era soldier as ambivalent about the war and merely enduring it. Members of the First Cavalry (Airmobile), quite unlike the draftee army that followed, seem more like the mythic Special Forces of the early 1960s: "The 1st Cavalry Division (Airmobile) was born of President John F. Kennedy's determination that the U.S. Army . . . prepare to fight a series of small, dirty wars on the world's frontiers," Moore and Galloway write. "Something new and totally different had to be created to meet the challenge of the jungles of Indochina."[31]

The account of the battle itself further redeems the Vietnam-era soldier. Throughout, competence, commitment, and patriotism replace frustration, fear, and ambivalence. Moore's officers are "simply superb" and "exceptionally competent," not inept careerists; the enlisted men's courage and commitment explicitly belie remembrances of fearful, insubordinate draftees.[32] Even after a battle in which nearly three dozen Americans are killed, Moore finds that "morale among the men was high" and "[I] heard weary soldiers say things like: 'We'll get 'em, sir' and 'They won't get through us, sir.' Their fighting spirit had not dimmed."[33]

In spite of Moore's occasional praise of the enemy's bravery and his efforts to look at the situation from a North Vietnamese perspective, enemy soldiers appear as near savages. They describe a captured North Vietnamese soldier who reports that his colleagues "very much 'wanted to kill Americans.' "[34] This line is a nearly verbatim quote from Moore's after-action report, but in the context of a memoir it becomes an explicit indicator of Vietnamese barbarity, a quality later reinforced by Moore's statement that the Vietnamese "were eager to kill us [and] hungered for our deaths."[35] Over a dozen portrayals of Vietnamese soldiers executing Americans substantiate these claims, including one description of "at least a couple of hundred of them walking around for three or four minutes . . . shooting and machine gunning our wounded and laughing and giggling."[36] The vaguely feminized glee of the Vietnamese executioners undermines accounts elsewhere of Vietnamese professionalism, instead making them seem depraved.[37]

American soldiers, by contrast, never commit such acts. The Vietnamese body is almost entirely absent, and American killing is described as though Vietnamese soldiers were vegetation or refuse—American soldiers "mow down," "clean up," and "get rid of" them.[38] Elsewhere, killing is a display of steely courage and military skill, as when a soldier "calmly dropped to one knee and methodically shot fifteen enemy before help finally arrived."[39] Another soldier's description of shooting a Vietnamese soldier hidden behind a tree combines these means of marginalizing Vietnamese precarity: "I am a good shot and this was close. I took a shooting-range stance and . . . kept shooting this pop-up target. I fired ten more times, methodical single shots until the pop-up target range closed down."[40] Here, the enemy body is merely a prop that puts the soldier's professionalism on display; the body and the violence visited on it are absent.

American bodies receive more complicated treatment. At times, Americans appear unfazed by injuries, while at others they are devastated. The contrast between painstaking accounts of American precariousness and descriptions of wounds that hardly matter reflects the text's simultaneous embrace of tropes from heretofore competing remembrances of Vietnam, namely, the spectacle of gruesome injury that dominates texts critical of the war and the image of impervious bodies central to recuperative texts.[41] This dichotomy allows American bodies to function simultaneously on behalf of Moore's intersecting conclusions: that the soldiers are honorable and heroic and that the war was a disaster that should never have been fought.

American soldiers frequently suffer what appear to be serious wounds that hardly impinge on their fighting ability. In one skirmish, "Specialist Clarence Jackson took a round clean through his left hand, shifted his rifle to his right, and continued firing until he was hit a second time"; "Sergeant Ruben Thompson was struck by a bullet above his heart that exited under his left arm; bleeding heavily, he grabbed a rifle and fought on."[42] Psychological trauma receives similar glossing over. Having rescued soldiers trapped overnight in vicious fighting, one of Moore's men, Dennis Deal, represents them as being "still in a state of shock because of what they'd been through."[43] Deal elsewhere describes them as being "so traumatized by what happened to them that they preferred to lay down and be as safe as possible."[44] Beyond the sparse attention given to this trauma—there are, for example, no reports of PTSD in Moore's afterword—the difference in language matters. To be "still in a state of shock" suggests an impermanent, milder wound than one suffered by men "so traumatized" that they wouldn't stand up. Men's bodies and minds are thus not impermeable, but their ability to suffer grievous wounds and carry on fighting reveals their tenacity and commitment.

Moore's description of the wounded American body does not, however, turn solely on accounts of improbable resilience. Just as frequently he presents massive suffering. "Lefebvre's right arm and dangling hand were both mangled and shattered, with bones protruding," he recalls. "One of Taboada's legs was a gaping, raw, bloody mess from hip to foot; he was screaming in agony."[45] But especially striking are the authors' nearly clinical descriptions of American wounds. One death occurred when a lieutenant "was shot in the throat and the round had ricocheted down and came out his left side."[46] Another soldier describes a bullet that "went in my leg above the ankle, traveled up, came back out, then went into my groin and ended up in my back close to my spine."[47] Such detailed accounts of bullets' paths force the reader to be aware of, to use Michel Foucault's description of the autopsy, "the evolution of a whole morbid series" of events related to wounds that are neither neat nor painless.[48] Such accounts, which demand that readers sympathetically imagine similar wounds on their own bodies, further emphasize American precarity.[49]

The stark juxtaposition of bodily trauma with earlier accounts of soldiers' endurance enables American bodies to simultaneously convey American commitment and vulnerability. These concerns lie at the heart of Moore's broader critiques; soldiers who acquit themselves well but suffer grievously are precious commodities, and while they prove their martial skill and patriotic fervor on the battlefield, the war remains a tragedy in which they suffer unnecessarily. Implicitly invoking the Powell doctrine's command to reevaluate "the relationship between ends and means," Moore writes that McNamara "now knew that the Vietnam War had just exploded into . . . a cause that he was beginning to suspect would be difficult to win" and notes that, in his view, increased troop levels "will not guarantee success."[50] The secretary hardly gets a free pass, however; Moore recounts a White House meeting in 1965 in which "McNamara's option number one—get the hell out of Vietnam now, while the getting is good—was never seriously considered, nor was it pressed by

McNamara. Option number two—the huge buildup of American combat and support troops—was readily approved by all, including McNamara."[51] Moore condemns the policymakers and military leaders who escalated the war and expended American lives despite fully recognizing the likelihood of failure.

McNamara's skepticism about the war, starting at least in 1962, and the degree to which American escalation was, by 1965, a foregone conclusion are well documented.[52] After Ia Drang, military leaders did not suggest that the United States withdraw: "At MACV, General Westmoreland and his aides gushed about the success." The historian John Prados notes Moore's skepticism but writes that Moore's commander, "General [Harry] Kinnard also considered Ia Drang a success, validating the air assault tactics that now became a mainstay."[53] The documentary record makes Prados's claim a virtual understatement. The First Cavalry's Presidential Unit Citation, the war's first, declares that after the battle "what we now know to be a certain truth could be seen: The enemy can never win Vietnam by armed conquest."[54] Six months later the luster hadn't worn off. The *Washington Star* declared, "Since last July, Pentagon officials have been looking for a battle which proves to the enemy in Viet Nam that he cannot win. . . . Ia Drang may have been that battle."[55] Kinnard's after-action report of the Pleiku campaign declares, "Defeat must have brought some measure of despair and pessimism to the enemy," and as late as June 1968 Westmoreland himself wrote, "The performance of the 1st Cavalry Division was magnificent. . . . [Their] timely victory produced a sharp upturn in the morale of the South Vietnamese government and its armed forces."[56] Moore seems to have kept his own council if he was unconvinced after the battle. In a *Chicago Sun* profile that gloated, "When it comes to destroying the enemy, Moore has a record unmatched by any other U.S. battalion or brigade commander in Viet Nam," Moore did not suggest that victory wasn't at hand. Instead, he only remarked, "I hope they don't send me home before the fight is over."[57]

Although Moore doesn't account for his own silence, he concludes that American soldiers suffered from that of others while reiterating Kinnard's and Westmoreland's vision of a tactical victory:

> What, then, had we learned with our sacrifices in the Ia Drang Valley? We had learned something about fighting the North Vietnamese regulars—and something important about ourselves. We could stand against the finest light infantry troops in the world and

> hold our ground. General Westmoreland thought he had found the answer to the question of how to win this war: He would trade one American life for ten or eleven or twelve North Vietnamese lives, day after day, until Ho Chi Minh cried uncle. Westmoreland would learn, too late, that he was wrong; that the American people didn't see a kill ratio of 10–1 or even 20–1 as any kind of bargain. But we had validated . . . the principle of airmobile warfare. . . .
>
> Finally—even though it took ten years [and] cost the lives of 58,000 young Americans and inflicted a humiliating defeat on a nation that had never before lost a war—some of us learned that [Carl von] Clausewitz had it right 150 years earlier when he wrote these words:
>
> "No one starts a war—or rather no one in his senses ought to do so—without first being clear in his mind what he intends to achieve by that war and how he intends to conduct it."[58]

Eliding references to Vietnam's destruction, Moore elaborates on the complimentary assessments of the NVA and the praise of airmobility common in 1965 to amplify soldiers' tactical successes while condemning policymakers' strategic failures.[59] Vietnam's tragedy thus lies in McNamara's silence, Westmoreland's miscalculations, and policymakers' ignorance regarding a fundamental principle of warfare, one consistent with Powell's dictum on achievable goals.

The most profound affirmation that such condemnation was deserved came from Moore's central target. McNamara's memoir, published to coincide with the twentieth anniversary of the war's end, repeatedly implies that the United States was well intentioned but made faulty assumptions about both Vietnam's strategic importance and the Americans' chances of effectively prosecuting the conflict. In what became an infamous line, he writes that he and his colleagues "acted according to what we thought were the principles and traditions of this nation. . . . Yet we were wrong, terribly wrong."[60] His chief lesson, one that reviewers applied to contemporary politics, cautions against overestimating the potential of the United States to influence another nation's affairs: "Military force—especially when wielded by an outside power—just cannot bring order in a country that cannot govern itself."[61]

Moreover, McNamara, like Moore, defines the men he sent to Vietnam as being above reproach: "Does the unwisdom of our intervention nullify their effort and their loss? I think not. They did not make the decisions. They answered their nation's call to service. They went in harm's way on its behalf. And they gave their lives for their country and its ideals. That our effort in Vietnam proved unwise does not make their sacrifice less noble."[62] Here again the soldier is a victim not of a bureaucracy reluctant to let him win but of one foolish enough to send him to fight.

The soldiers whom McNamara celebrates are implicitly Moore's patriotic volunteers. It seems unlikely that many of the draftees and reluctant volunteers whom McNamara sent to war, including those drafted through programs like Project 100,000—which so lowered enlistment standards that men who lacked basic skills and who even met the criteria for mental retardation were sent to Vietnam—were inspired by the Kennedyesque rhetoric that McNamara invokes or saw themselves as "giving their lives for their country and its ideals."[63] Remaining silent about many soldiers' motivations and the inequalities of Vietnam-era service, McNamara, too, valorizes soldiers by stressing their exceptionalism.[64]

This forgetting was central to Vietnam remembrance that combined celebrations of American soldiers' professionalism and patriotism with explicit condemnation, including self-condemnation, of the war's planners. This discourse appropriated aspects of earlier remembrances of betrayal, combining images of soldiers' physical toughness and their vulnerability with strident critiques of the war's escalation. The war remained the fault of its planners, not because they prosecuted it ineffectively but because they prosecuted it at all, leaving capable and willing soldiers to win tactical victories but to suffer unnecessarily. Together, these texts craft a legacy of Vietnam that validates calls to adhere to the Powell doctrine. This logic and the representational strategies it relied on would come to dominate how Americans debated whether humanitarian interventions could be successful and above all how they remembered the Somalia intervention within that debate.

"We Saw It . . . in Vietnam. We Saw It in Somalia"

Shortly after *In Retrospect* appeared in 1995, the *Washington Post* wrote, "As for the Bosnia hawks, they ought to read this book, too. Here, once again, is a treatise about . . . what happens when you underestimate an enemy and the ideology that animates him."[65] A few days after the *Post* editorial, A. M. Rosenthal of the *New York Times* took the Senate majority leader Bob Dole (R-KS) to task: "He calls [Vietnam] incrementalism and is critical. He also talks about Bosnia and what he intends to do about that." He then entreated Dole to "turn to page 29 of Robert McNamara's book 'In Retrospect' for the questions that the Kennedy administration failed to ask itself." Dole should do so, Rosenthal concluded, because "what America needs least is another memoir of dereliction."[66]

Dole's position on Bosnia was complicated. He was convinced that the United States should work to end the genocide, but he was equally committed to ruling out American boots on the ground in the Balkans. Shortly after becoming majority leader in January 1995, Dole introduced legislation to allow the United States to arm the Bosnian Muslims but prohibited committing U.S. troops to the United Nations peacekeeping mission.[67] Two months after Rosenthal's editorial appeared in April, Dole marked the fiftieth anniversary of the UN Charter by reminding his colleagues that "the tragic record of Somalia and Bosnia make [*sic*] one fact very clear—the United Nations is not capable of mounting serious military operations." "In Somalia," he noted, "the United Nations changed the mission and began a vendetta against one Somali faction. Many brave Americans died in the ensuing disaster . . . and the United Nations finally left Somalia little better than when the humanitarian mission began."[68] The complaints here, notably, were akin to Moore's: Americans had died unnecessarily in an unwise intervention in which the United States had little chance of success.

Vietnam may well have been on Dole's mind. A few hours after Dole spoke, Sen. Trent Lott (R-MS) introduced a bill that the majority leader had cosponsored, the Ia Drang Valley Military Awards Act. Inspired by Moore's book, the bill recognized the "numerous acts of bravery, sacrifice and dignified service to the flag of the United States [that have] largely gone unrecognized."[69] Coincidence, perhaps. Yet these events reveal that *We Were Soldiers Once* and *In Retrospect* shaped Americans' thinking at precisely the moment they were questioning the wisdom of humanitarian interventions, often by recalling the Somalia intervention of 1993 as a Vietnam-like debacle.

Whether the United States should undertake humanitarian missions became a matter of public debate on a gray December afternoon in 1992. Speaking from the Oval Office at the White House, President George H. W. Bush announced he was sending U.S. troops to famine-stricken Somalia. The announcement followed months of internal debate. In June, Bush had ordered a National Security Review, noting that the Cold War's aftermath "requires a new look at U.S. policy in sub-Saharan Africa" and asking, "Should we be selective in the conflicts we attempt to resolve, and if so, what criteria should be applied?"[70] Eleven days before Bush addressed the nation, the answer arrived in the form of National Security Directive 74, which concluded that "U.S. forces will emphasize training of its combat, engineering and logistical units for the full range of peacekeeping and humanitarian relief."[71]

Military intervention, Bush declared, was the only way to resolve a crisis that had claimed the lives of "as many people as live in Buffalo, New York."[72] Yet he cast the mission as conforming to the Powell doctrine. Reprising the language of speeches he had made in advance of the Persian Gulf War, he said three times that the intervention would end quickly. He assured Somalis that "we do not plan to dictate political outcomes" and U.S. troops that "you will have our full support to get the job done." Simultaneously, he appealed to a national sense of empathy and exceptionalism, assuring Americans, "When we see Somalia's children starving, all of America hurts," while declaring, "Some crises in the world cannot be resolved without American involvement. . . . Only the United States has the global reach to . . . save thousands of innocents from death."[73] Somalia, Bush warranted, was a matter of national interest that could be resolved quickly and easily. The deployment met another of the Powell doctrine's requirements, as reports of horrific conditions produced widespread calls for American intervention. As the *Atlanta Journal and Constitution* bluntly explained, "There could hardly be a more justified use of arms. . . . To fail to act in cases where mass starvation is being applied as a military tactic would be the worst form of indifference, especially from a nation as richly blessed as America."[74]

This positive attitude persisted as troops landed. On *Nightline,* the historian Said Samatar told Ted Koppel that "I have been around town for some time and I have never seen anything so popular and so enthusiastically expected as the arrival of the Americans."[75] Two days later *Good Morning America*'s Denise Richardson reported, "People's lives got turned around automatically. . . . People who would normally shoot at each other all of a sudden had something to say on a different level."[76] Marines on the ground likewise suggested that the mission was an appropriate use of American power; one remarked, "I think they wanted the help, and now they're getting it, and I'm glad to be here."[77]

The optimism didn't last. When the marines left Somalia in the spring, the recognition that many Somalis had been saved from starving did not stop the Associated Press from painting U.S. troops as "disillusioned with the animosity that remains"; one Marine reflected that the mission "wasted the soldiers, wasted the money, we did nothing."[78] The *Washington Post* reported on efforts to make the subsequent UN mission in Somalia, UNOSOM II, more successful than its predecessor (UNOSOM I), "which had become a symbol for all that has been judged wrong with U.N. operations around the world."[79] Others matched acknowledgments of success with wariness regarding a still-tenuous mission. A *New York Times* article—whose title, "Declare Victory, Hand Off, Slip Out, Cross Fingers," echoed Sen. George Aiken's (R-VT) now-aphoristic advice on Vietnam (Aiken is often remembered as having suggested that the United States should "declare victory and go home")—cautioned, "So simple from afar, Somalia demonstrates how intractable the problems that demand the rescue by foreign armies can be."[80] Two weeks before Bill Clinton told troops returning from Somalia that "the world is ready to mobilize its resources in new ways to face the challenges of a new age," the former congressman Otis Pike complained, "It is time we grew up. . . . [W]e can't stop starvation or impose our will on all bad people or make them act the way we think they should."[81]

Had UNOSOM I been the end of American involvement in Somalia, its ambiguous outcome would hardly have quelled debate over America's participation in humanitarian missions. The United States did not, however, declare victory and go home. In June 1993, newspaper headlines declared, "Hundreds hungry as violence returns [to Somalia]," and the UN special envoy to Somalia, the retired U.S. admiral Jonathan Howe, persuaded the United States to send Special Forces to capture the warlord Mohamed Farrah Aidid. The Quick Reaction Force's most infamous mission, on October 3, left two Blackhawk helicopters shot down, one American soldier captive, and nineteen others dead.

The next morning Americans watched Somalis drag American bodies through the streets of Mogadishu, and newspapers brimmed with Vietnam comparisons, calling Somalia a quagmire and a morass and noting Clinton's opposition to Vietnam as well as the fact that Secretary of Defense Les Aspin had been a protégé of McNamara. The *New Orleans Times-Picayune* invoked the Powell doctrine on consecutive days. "The overriding lessons of Vietnam, tragically missed by a series of American presidents," it argued, "is that limited missions have a way of expanding into impossible missions without precise, realistic objectives and the support of the American people." The next day it inveighed that "if American lives are ever put in harm's way, the objective should be clear and attainable, the public must support the operation and sufficient numbers of military personnel must be committed at the beginning to overwhelm any resistance and to ensure victory."[82] Although the editorial nods to the doctrine of overwhelming force, Vietnam's most important lesson became divining the "realistic" and "attainable" from the "impossible."

Lawmakers levied similar complaints. Rep. Porter Goss (R-FL) offered a typical grievance, fuming that "our troops have no clear mission, the chain of command is blurred, the rules of engagement are unclear."[83] But a second narrative, one of good intentions gone awry, also emerged. Sen. Frank Lautenberg (D-NJ) opined, "We went over there to be of help, not to sacrifice our youngsters. . . . This evokes all kinds of recollections of what Vietnam looks like"; on the House side, Rep. Rick Lazio (R-NY) said, "We find American troops in a quagmire all too reminiscent of another American tragedy—Vietnam. . . . If we had withdrawn from Vietnam in 1962, over 50,000 young Americans would have been spared."[84] Vietnam was again not the war that could have been won if fought appropriately, but the war that should never have been escalated.

Clinton failed to turn the tide. His suggestion in a speech of October 7 that "if we were to leave today . . . [o]ur leadership in world affairs would be undermined at the very time when people are looking to America" sounded like nothing so much as Nixon justifying the invasion of Cambodia.[85] Somalia became a key factor in debates over subsequent humanitarian interventions. A week after his speech Clinton refused to land forces in Haiti, and he quickly signed Presidential Directive 25, which limited American involvement in UN peacekeeping missions.[86] The reluctance of the United States to embark on peacekeeping operations soon earned a name indebted to Vietnam—the Somalia syndrome—and prevented American intervention to stop the Rwanda genocide of 1994.[87]

To opponents of such missions, Somalia and Vietnam remained fused for the rest of the nineties as missions the United States pursued in spite of their acknowledged futility. This was evident in the debate over troop deployments to the Balkans. In early December 1995 Clinton, visiting troops stationed in Germany who would shortly begin enforcing the Dayton Accords, which ended the war in Bosnia, recorded a radio address that echoed his predecessor's 1992 announcement of the U.S. deployment to Somalia. He spoke of the hundreds of thousands of deaths that had occurred in the Balkans, of concentration camps, and of mass rapes, declaring, "We have a responsibility to act."[88] Clinton, too, carefully assured listeners that he was applying the most important tenets of the Powell doctrine to his liberal interventionist model: "Our military commanders have done all they can to minimize the risks to our troops while maximizing their ability to carry out a clearly defined mission with a clear endpoint."[89] Bosnia, Clinton implied, would be neither another Somalia nor another Vietnam.

His opponents disagreed. Even before Clinton announced the deployment, McNamara's shadow loomed over Bosnia. Sen. Judd Gregg (R-NH) referenced *In Retrospect* on the Senate floor, coining a neologism: "McNamaranism," he said, "is when you pursue a policy which you know is substantively wrong but you pursue it because of the political need." He added, "Let us hope that McNamaranism does not strike us in Bosnia."[90] In the House, Rep. Bob Dornan (R-CA) quoted an article calling the Clinton administration's claims "the same guff that McNamara tossed off during Vietnam."[91]

This rhetoric reached its apogee ten days after Clinton's announcement, when Senate Republicans engaged in a lengthy debate that featured intertwined allusions to Somalia and Vietnam. For two Vietnam veterans, Sen. Hank Brown (R-CO) and Bob Smith (R-NH), Vietnam emerged not as a righteous cause that had been poorly prosecuted but a debacle entered into without sufficient forethought. Brown declared, "I volunteered to serve in Vietnam because . . . I believed we were there to defend freedom worldwide, and . . . blood could be proudly spilled to save their freedom. Mr. President, our political leaders did not believe that."[92] Conspicuously absent is the familiar proclamation that Vietnam was a cause the country *should* have supported; instead, Brown reiterated the sentiment of the 1960s and 1970s that had met McNamara's memoir earlier that year, an assertion that an untrustworthy government had taken advantage of naïve, patriotic Americans. Sounding more like John Kerry, who in 1971 denounced the war, than like a conservative

Republican in the 1980s, Brown positioned Vietnam as a war that the United States should never have fought. He queried, "How could you ask people to give their lives when their political leaders did not believe in the cause?"[93] But Vietnam was not the only example Brown invoked. "The line is drawn when you ask Americans to give their lives for nothing," he thundered before pivoting: "I believe it is morally wrong, to have Americans give their lives in Somalia when you do not have a clear military mission and you will not stand behind them. . . . It is wrong to ask them to do it for nothing in Vietnam, when our very leaders would not stand behind the men and women who risked their lives."[94] To Brown, Vietnam and Somalia were identical failures.

Smith likewise remembered Vietnam as a war that should have been avoided but went a step further, casting Vietnam as a peacekeeping mission: "I remember the charts, the McNamara charts and the pointers, how, if we could just . . . secure the peace, everything would be allright. Mr. President, 58,000-plus lives later, we gave it back to the North Vietnamese."[95] Like Brown, Smith revises earlier conservative remembrances. Vietnam, futile from the outset, was not a worthy cause that Americans abandoned. It was one that they shouldn't have pursued. "I am asking a lot of interrogatories here, but there are a lot of lives at stake" Smith continued, echoing the instructions of the *New York Times* to Dole. "If we had asked them in the Vietnam War," he concluded, "we would not have lost 58,000 people."[96] He, too, pivoted to a contemporary example: "We saw it in Somalia, if you do not like the Vietnamese example. . . . It is easy to get the troops in. It is a little tough to get them out, though."[97]

The most powerful conflation of Somalia and Vietnam came from Sen. Jim Inhofe (R-OK) and Sen. Kay Bailey Hutchison (R-TX), the cosponsors of the resolution condemning the deployment. Both recounted their conversations with Vietnam-veteran fathers of soldiers killed in Somalia, constructions that cast Somalia as a continuation of the Vietnam veteran's suffering and positioned veterans as recognizing the government's continued errors. Inhofe called Jim Smith, Jamie Smith's father, "an American hero. He was a career military officer. He lost his leg in Vietnam. He lost his son in Mogadishu."[98] Inhofe's rhetoric is important. Smith was not disillusioned by his service and in fact continued it despite his grave injury, to which Inhofe equated the loss of his son in Somalia. Inhofe, listing critiques that recall those made of Vietnam, called on Congress not to equip the troops better but to "stop the appropriations so they cannot be sent there in the first place."[99]

Such privileging of Vietnam likewise informs Hutchison's speech, which transfers earlier discourses of veterans' uncertainty about the wisdom of Vietnam to Somalia. Demanding an explanation, the Vietnam veteran Larry Joyce purportedly told Hutchison, "I went to Vietnam twice. I am a military man. And now my only son, on his very first mission as a Ranger, is not coming home."[100] Like Smith, Joyce is hardly a disillusioned, antiwar veteran; he is a man doubly wronged by political leaders who cavalierly send men into battle, one who felt he was owed a justification not for the mission's failure but for the fact it was undertaken.

Hutchison carefully celebrates the soldier as she disparages the mission. "I do not think our troops should have been doing what they were doing in Somalia," she said, quickly adding, "[Joyce's] son did not die in vain because he was doing what he had signed up to do, and he was doing it with honor."[101] Yet she insisted on what she called "the Larry Joyce Test": "I would never vote to send our troops into harm's way if I could not give the mother or father a good answer about why. Mr. President, sending our troops into Bosnia under these circumstances is not meeting the test."[102] To Hutchison, sending troops to Bosnia would repeat the wrongs done to patriotic Vietnam veterans.

But the troops did go. And if the American public was similarly wary of troop deployments and remained skeptical throughout the deployment, the Bosnia intervention was widely seen as a success.[103] By 1998 Secretary of Defense William Cohen, who as a senator had opposed the mission, declared that "two years after IFOR [Implementation Force] deployment, there's been a dramatic transformation"; Sen. Joe Lieberman (D-CT) felt that "things had really changed as a result of continued U.S. presence and active engagement."[104] Even as ardent a conservative as Rep. Newt Gingrich (R-GA) "speculated that the current mission in Bosnia may define the post-cold war mission of the nation and its military—nation building." "Your mission and activities here," Gingrich remarked when his delegation visited Bosnia, "represent the forward edge of where we, as a nation, are going."[105]

The army, eager, as Beth Bailey has shown, "to 'sell' Congress and the American people on its continued importance" after the Cold War and preparing to transition to a Full-Spectrum Force, presented itself as welcoming and capable of meeting such challenges.[106] In 1997 a memo vividly celebrated the Bosnia mission, foreshadowing the army's future: "U.S. Army Europe (USAREUR) entered the 21st Century on 31 December 1995. . . . Against a backdrop of mud and rain, soldiers from the 65,000-strong USAREUR showcased their versatility by shifting from high-intensity-conflict focus to one of peacekeeping."[107] Military leaders as well embraced the need to develop doctrine to meet these challenges. A memo to Gen. Eric Shinseki, the U.S. commander in Bosnia, recognized that soldiers deployed on peacekeeping missions might lose their combat readiness, but, rather than disparage such deployments, sought ways to best prepare soldiers for both.[108] At the Command and General Staff College at Fort Leavenworth, Kansas, one student analyzed the battle of Ia Drang not as a harbinger of disaster but as an example of the military successfully meeting the needs of the moment's foreign policy. "A lesson from the 1965 experience that is directly transferable to 1994 is the need to develop a doctrine . . . for whatever type of warfare the political leaders believe is necessary," Peter Schifferle wrote, going on to suggest that "if America's political leaders are serious about peace operations, the military should develop force structure and training to support our political superiors."[109]

And while students at the Army War College during the late 1990s and early 2000s found fault with the Somalia deployment in their "Personal Experience Monographs"—essays written by graduate students that draw on their experiences during deployments to evaluate doctrine—the after-action report, completed in 1994 but not published until 2004, hardly rejected peacekeeping.[110] Initially asserting that "the U.S. should limit its participation in Chapter VII [i.e., peacekeeping] operations to U.S. led coalitions . . . or to participation with competent regional organizations such as NATO [North Atlantic Treaty Organization]," the report realistically appraises humanitarian missions.[111] "The United States in its world leadership role may not be able or desire to avoid participation in [similar] operations," the authors concluded, adding, "Properly constituted, peace operations can be a useful tool to advance United States national interests and pursue our security objectives."[112] Moreover, they troubled the emphasis on force protection, arguing, "Nations participating in peace enforcement operations must be committed to stay the course, deal with the inherent potential for violence, and accept the fact that casualties may result from combat operations."[113]

Military leaders considered peacekeeping missions inevitable and strategically necessary and didn't dwell on comparisons to Vietnam or Somalia. Their confidence, in addition to congressional leaders' apparent satisfaction with the Bosnia mission, however, did not carry over into public support of future missions. Although Peter Beinart maintains that "by 1999 Somalia's cautionary tale had been forgotten amid the broader narrative of Clinton-era military success," the debate reignited when Clinton threatened military action against Slobodan Milosevic's regime in Kosovo.[114]

Interventionist editorials reminded Americans that "thanks to the efforts of the United States, many places in the world have new hope for harmony" and chastised NATO and the United Nations for "stand[ing] like deer in the headlights" and not "deploying a sufficient force at the outset."[115] Politicians with ideologies as varied as Sen. Tom Daschle (D-SD), Dole, and Lott argued that diplomacy was insufficient, and Lieberman, who had lauded the Bosnia mission, remained optimistic.[116] "In the future," he told an audience at the Fletcher School of Law and Diplomacy at Tufts University in the fall of 1999, "we will also ask our military to project power not just to defend national interests but also to promote American principles as well. This means acting not just to defeat an opposing military force but also to prevent or reverse humanitarian catastrophes." Like military leaders, he rejected the Powell doctrine's utility in such scenarios, holding that "the current doctrine of overwhelming force is not desirable politically nor necessary militarily in all cases."[117]

The military, unsurprisingly, agreed. By 1999 Shinseki had been nominated to become army chief of staff. Ahead of a May meeting with the chair and ranking members of the Senate Armed Services Committee, his staff encouraged him to acknowledge the "need to be realistic about the duration and scope of our commitment" in Kosovo but insist that "the Army can support whatever policy option it is called upon to execute, from a peacekeeping force in a permissive environment to ground force operations in a hostile environment."[118] His office repeated this sentiment six months later: "We must have inherent in all forces the ability to shift intensity of operations. . . . Our forces will frequently be called upon to transition within or between operations from non-combat disaster relief to low intensity contingencies to high intensity warfighting."[119]

Dwarfing those voices, however, were opponents still rooted in the Powell doctrine. Richard Parker wrote that a plan in which American troops could be left in the Balkans "perhaps for years . . . received a chilly reception" in Congress.[120] "Any clash with Serbians," the *St. Louis Post-Dispatch* opined, "would be the sort of foreign campaign that Americans dread most—an infantry war, one that would kill and wound a lot of 19-year-old Americans."[121]

Rhetoric that invoked Vietnam and Somalia returned as well. Senator Smith recycled elements of his Bosnia speech: "When presidents use force in a way that they do not or cannot explain to the American people, and for a cause the American people do not in their gut support, that policy collapses. We saw it by the end of the war in Vietnam. We saw it in Somalia, in 1994."[122] Sen. John Ashcroft (R-MO) said, "As we consider a possible deployment to Kosovo, the lessons learned 6 years ago in Somalia should not be forgotten. The American people will not support a Kosovo deployment that costs American lives when America's vital security interests are not at stake."[123] Sen. Larry Craig (R-ID), meanwhile, insisted—strangely, given that he had not served in Vietnam—that "putting American troops in a quagmire is something I know a little bit about" and called Vietnam "a quagmire that we finally simply had to drop . . . because we could no longer sustain it politically."[124] Continuing the rhetoric of 1995, senators remembered Vietnam not as a war that could and should have been won, but as one that was intractable even before American intervention, could never be sufficiently "explained," and unnecessarily killed U.S. troops. Such rhetoric apparently gained traction among the American public. Three weeks after Clinton announced the bombing campaign, a Gallup Poll reported, "When the air strikes began at the end of March, just 31% of the public supported the idea of using ground troops if the air mission failed to achieve NATO's objectives in Kosovo," but went on to say that while the percentage was substantially higher three weeks into the campaign, there remained "a deep division among Americans on the issue."[125]

Whether the United States had an interest in or an obligation to stop famine and genocide was thus hardly settled by decade's end. Throughout the 1990s and into the 2000s military leaders and interventionist liberals persistently proclaimed that the United States could and should meet these challenges. Realists, however, voiced their opposition by invoking and conflating Somalia and Vietnam. To these adversaries, Vietnam was not simply an all-purpose referent for disaster; rather, it signified something different than it had previously. Vietnam was now an ill-conceived misadventure, a moment marked by deceit on the part of ignorant, prideful politicians who overestimated America's capabilities. Editorial rants and legislative remarks linked Vietnam and Somalia in language that echoed the critiques of *We Were Soldiers Once* and the confessions of *In Retrospect.* As these discussions played out on Capitol Hill and in the Pentagon, Americans began encountering popular literature that contributed to a current of realist skepticism about humanitarian intervention by remembering the Somalia intervention through the tropes and discourses that dominated Vietnam's memory.

"We Should Have Said No"

If editorials and congressional speeches identified danger to the soldier, the mission's futility, the lack of a compelling national interest, and the potential repetition of the Vietnam era's prideful mistakes as the primary reasons to oppose humanitarian interventions, they did so largely in abstractions. It was in the realm of popular culture that Americans became able to contemplate how the soldier and the nation would experience humanitarian missions. Mark Bowden's *Black Hawk Down* (1999) reintroduced Americans to the events of October 3, 1993. Over the next four years, Bowden's best-seller would be joined by additional works, ranging from another best-seller, *In the Company of Heroes* by the captured pilot Mike Durant, to less celebrated works like Martin Stanton's *Somalia on Five Dollars a Day* and Dan Schilling's and Matt Eversmann's *The Battle of Mogadishu.* These texts, the only body of popular American war literature dealing with humanitarian intervention, are also, because the cultural memory of the Gulf War was so slow to emerge, the only popular books that at the turn of the twenty-first century described the post-Vietnam military in combat.

This corpus has gone largely unstudied. A few scholars have interrogated Ridley Scott's film version of *Black Hawk Down* (2001), which Stephen A. Klein calls a "pro-soldier, anti-war" film, one that emphasizes and defends soldiers' character even amid "poorly executed" wars and "marginalize[s] ethical assessment of policymaking on the part of American audiences."[126] While Klein hints that the film ultimately enables acquiescence to war, Mark Lacy notes, "We achieve proximity only to the deaths of Americans" but "do not get to see the deaths of Somalis with any moral proximity. . . . [They] just fall to the ground, and . . . the film taps into a far broader historical discourse about the irrational and immature 'nature' of Africans." He posits further that "the movie suggests that it is best to leave the irrational savages to themselves" and avoid humanitarian interventions.[127]

Several of these points are, as I demonstrate, true of the book as well. However, these observations do not recognize *Black Hawk Down*'s reliance on the tropes of contemporaneous Vietnam remembrance as it constructs these narratives and contributes to a discourse opposed to humanitarian interventions. One of Klein's and Lacy's points about the film, however, does not hold true for the book. Although the film may absolve readers from questioning policy decisions, the book assuredly does not.[128] *Black Hawk Down* and other literary texts about Somalia, in fact, directly and stridently challenge U.S. policy in language that borrows from and evokes contemporary Vietnam remembrance.

These texts' remembrance of the Somalia intervention does not rely on direct comparisons to Vietnam—in fact, the works hardly mention it. However, the relationship between this literature and Vietnam's legacy was not lost on some reviewers. Yet even this observation fails to recognize that nearly every trope in these books recalls its analogue in *We Were Soldiers Once* and *In Retrospect.* Bowden, Stanton, and other chroniclers of Somalia adopt and redeploy the language and strategies through which Moore and McNamara imagine Vietnam, especially their highlighting of American soldiers' exceptionalism, the enemy's savage bestiality, and the shifting import of the wounded American body. The texts criticize policymakers' flawed logic as well intentioned but misguided. In the texts' appropriation of this language, Somalia in effect becomes akin to the Ia Drang, that is, the first intervention in a transitional moment in which the U.S. military sought to redefine its capabilities and the scope of its missions. The episode represented one in which policymakers erred in becoming unnecessarily involved in a conflict in which the country's interests were few and its chances for success were slight and in which soldiers met the challenge with courageous professionalism only to suffer grievously. As humanitarian interventions became insistently compared to Vietnam and in similar terms, the texts' adoption of these tropes legitimated broader assertions that such interventions replicated Vietnam's errors.

LIKE MOORE, WHO DESCRIBES THE AIRMOBILE CAVALRY AS UNIQUELY suited to realizing the Cold War's political objectives, those who wrote about Somalia consistently emphasized the exceptionalism of the men who fought there and their membership in special units created to address contemporary foreign policy problems. Bowden's central characters, the Army Rangers and Delta Force operators sent to capture Mohamed Farah Aidid, belong to units whose exceptionalism lies in their political relevance. The Delta operators are the foot soldiers of what Beinart calls the "new liberalism" of the 1990s, one "idealistic about ends, but somewhat brutal about means . . . and confident that vanquishing evil and extending American dominance were usually one and the same."[129] Bowden writes, "If the good-hearted ideals of humankind were to prevail, then they needed men who could make it happen. Delta made it happen. . . . It allowed the dreamers and the politicians to have it both ways. They could stay on the high road while the dirty work happened offstage. . . . They were noble, silent and invisible. They did America's most important work, yet they shunned recognition, fame, and fortune."[130] Taking for granted that American foreign policy and "the good-hearted ideals of humankind" are synonymous, Bowden portrays Delta's soldiers as professionals uniquely suited to the moment's needs and as enabling the United States to maintain a facade of diplomacy while exercising its military force. More purely heroic than the soldiers who populate the Vietnam films of the 1980s and disdainful of the gratitude that veterans sought after Vietnam, they instead recall Moore's idealistic, heroic First Cavalry.

Durant and Stanton echo Moore's description of airmobile warfare in the 1960s, presenting their units as, like Moore's, specifically designed to fight modern warfare in the developing world. Recalling Moore's contention that airmobility derived from the conviction that "something new and totally different had to be created to meet the challenge" of "small and dirty wars," Durant writes, "America was entering an era of unconventional warfare, yet we did not have dedicated unconventional capabilities. As always, there were fine groups of highly trained commandos and special forces who could do the job on the ground, but if we couldn't insert them, support their combat missions, and extract them, they were limited in what they could do."[131] The 160th Special Operations Aviation Regiment, developed after the failure of the mission President Jimmy Carter ordered in 1980 to rescue American hostages in Iran, addressed this problem by establishing a corps of highly trained helicopter pilots dedicated to transporting and supplying special operations missions.

Stanton, the only Somalia memoirist not a member of the Special Forces, nonetheless rhetorically separates his Tenth Mountain Division from the regular army by describing it as tailored to the peculiarities of post–Cold War foreign policy. More than the others, Stanton seems to have based the opening section of his *Somalia on Five Dollars a Day* on *We Were Soldiers*

Once. Consider his description of the formation of his unit and its relevance: "We, of course, had to maintain heavy forces to face our potential adversaries in Europe and Korea. But we also had to have forces ready to deploy swiftly to conduct operations on the lower end of the spectrum of conflict. . . . The 10th Mountain was indeed a rapidly deployable outfit. We could be anywhere in the world in a matter of days."[132]

Soldiers are similarly celebrated. And while laudatory remarks about American soldiers are a fixture in post–Gulf War culture, the language in these texts explicitly resonates with Moore's lionization of the cavalry troopers. The Rangers, Bowden writes, "were the cream, the most highly motivated young soldiers of their generation." They are, he continues, "achingly earnest, patriotic, and idealistic" and "held themselves to a higher standard than normal soldiers. . . . [T]hey saw themselves as the army at its gung ho best."[133] A far cry from Vietnam-era draftees, these soldiers represent an idealized vision of militarized American citizenship akin to Moore's troopers. The intellectually and physically formidable Delta Force operators are even more glamorous. "Allowed a degree of personal freedom and initiative unheard of in the military," they "were trained to think and act for themselves. Nothing was done by the book for its own sake; they were guided by their own experience."[134] One had "so little body fat and was so buff that he looked like a walking atlas of male musculature"; another "had the massive frame of a serious body builder, and a fine, if impatient, analytical mind."[135]

Bowden's borrowing of Moore's exceptionalist rhetoric isn't unique. The Rangers "were certainly a different breed of men, a different caliber of soldier," Eversmann writes. "They were *expected* to perform difficult and dangerous things. . . . Young men were given a lot of responsibility and taught to be problem solvers."[136] Durant, too, offers a nearly hyperbolic account of his fellow pilots' tenacity and professionalism: "If you didn't have patience, perseverance, determination, and nerve, the 160th SOAR (A) was not for you. You would be constantly honing your skills, improving, improvising, developing new techniques." Pilots "had to be cool under fire, take harsh criticism, and offer it constructively," and "every member of the team had to have the skills of a quarterback, the grit of a linebacker, and the brains of a coach."[137] Stanton, in a twenty-eight-page introduction of his unit, once again explicitly reflects Moore. His men, like Moore's, are skilled, efficient, and effective. He portrays his unit in near idyllic terms: "The soldiers were motivated. The NCOs [noncommissioned officers] and officers were competent and professional. . . . [E]veryone had a common sense of mission."[138] The battalion's leaders are "absolutely competent," the NCOs "pure gold."[139] Adopting the dominant discourse of Vietnam memory, these texts deny associations between the contemporary military and troubling memories of Vietnam's disillusioned draftees and post-Vietnam questions about the army's quality.[140] Cool professionalism is the contemporary soldier's defining attribute.

These comparisons continue when the soldiers enter combat. Like their predecessors at the Ia Drang whose "fighting spirit had not dimmed," the soldiers trapped in Mogadishu remain undiscouraged by the battle's violence and continually risk their lives to achieve a tactical victory.[141] One soldier recalls that "if he was afraid, he simply filed the emotion away."[142] Another Ranger, contemplating returning to the city to rescue the trapped Rangers, is said to reflect that "if he was going to die today, so be it. The pull of loyalty felt stronger in him than the will to survive."[143] Eversmann is somewhat more elegiac: "Each man felt the same regardless of rank: fear, pain, anger, and unbelievable dedication to his duty."[144] Tim Wilkinson, meanwhile, demurs that he was "only holding up my end of the deal, like everyone else."[145] Even when faced with combat's gruesome realities and their friends' deaths, these men remain undeterred and their commitment is undiminished.

These sentiments, presented in language tinged with melodrama, recall one of Moore's soldiers telling another, "If I have to die, I'm glad to give my life for my country."[146] This quote and the analogous ones in the Somalia literature obscure the reality that men in battle—above all those who are dying—rarely act out of an "unbelievable dedication to his duty." Rather, they amplify the exceptional dedication of both Moore's men and the Rangers fighting in Mogadishu and thereby make the deaths they incurred more tragic.[147]

The Somalis, in spite of Bowden's efforts to include a Somali perspective—like Moore in discussing the experiences of Vietnamese soldiers—share none of these traits, just as the enemy depicted by Moore does not. They are, throughout this literature, dehumanized racial others whose destruction is appropriate.[148] These tropes reach their apogee in Somalis' perverse, orgiastic pleasure in killing people, particularly injured Americans. Though mutilation is occasionally acknowledged to be a political tactic, it seems most often to be the Somalis' natural tendency, and it is described in terms that parallel the descriptions in *We Were Soldiers Once* of Vietnamese sadism.[149] Paralleling

Moore's observation that "if the air bridge failed," the Americans in the Ia Drang "would be . . . butchered to the last man," Bowden quotes a Somali militiaman who "believed if the Rangers didn't have the helicopters helping them from above, he and his men would surround and kill them with ease, with their bare hands."[150] Somalis, it seems, can't help but do precisely that to their victims.[151] Stanton describes encountering "with depressing frequency" scenes in which "the victim had his or her abdomen split open, then the intestines yanked out and dropped in the dirt."[152] Durant, unable to move after his helicopter has crashed, was certain that "as soon as they came around the nose of that helicopter and saw me, they were going to chop me to pieces. . . . That's what they did to *everybody.*"[153] If Bowden's accounts of Somali brutality are extreme versions of the "laughing and giggling" North Vietnamese executing wounded Americans, he comes close to quoting Moore's accounts of the North Vietnamese soldiers' eagerness to kill: "It was as if 'Kill-an-American Day' had been declared in Mog[adishu]," he writes, later adding, "Everybody in the city wanted suddenly to help kill Americans."[154]

Just as Somalis share North Vietnamese troops' bloodlust, American bodies receive the multifaceted treatment central to *We Were Soldiers Once.*[155] Like Moore's First Cavalry, Bowden's Rangers and Delta operators are alternately brutally victimized and strangely unaffected by their combat wounds. These juxtapositions simultaneously establish the soldier's heroism and vulnerability and preserve his integrity while second-guessing the wisdom of a deployment that causes such suffering.

Throughout *Black Hawk Down,* Bowden renders American wounds through the signifiers of skinning, disembowelment, and dismemberment already established as characteristic of Somali brutality. Head wounds reveal soldiers' brains, and men in combat hear "the awful slap of bullets into flesh and heard the screams and saw the insides of men's bodies spill out."[156] Other soldiers' combat wounds reprise the descriptions of Somali mob violence, as they are portrayed "holding his entrails in his hands" with "the whole back of his pelvis . . . gone" or as "torn in half" with "his insides . . . lying next to him on a gurney" and a limb "twisted off the side of the stretcher, swinging, attached to the trunk by a hunk of meat."[157] Like Moore's Lefebvre and Taboada, these men are gruesomely wounded, if not killed, by a brutal enemy, one whose actions are eerily related to those of the North Vietnamese.

Bowden more explicitly follows Moore by focusing the reader's attention on such wounds through explicit delineations of the paths bullets take through Americans' bodies. Describing Jamie Smith's death, Bowden writes that the bullet "had entered Smith's thigh and traveled up into his pelvis. A gunshot wound to the pelvis is one of the worst. The aorta splits low in the abdomen, forming the left and right iliac arteries. As the iliac artery emerges from the pelvis it branches into the exterior and deep femoral arteries, the primary avenues for blood to the lower half of the body. The bullet had clearly pierced one of the femoral vessels."[158] Bowden offers equally wrenching descriptions of other injuries. One "bullet had exploded [a soldier's] shinbone and traveled on down his leg and exited at his ankle, shredding the foot"; another soldier is "hit by a round that entered his buttock and bored straight through his pelvis, blowing off one testicle as it exited through his upper thigh."[159] As in *We Were Soldiers Once,* this trope demands empathetic recognition of soldiers' precarious bodies.

However, the wounded body functions in an opposite manner as well, signifying, as it often did in *We Were Soldiers Once,* the soldier's tenacity. After a rocket-propelled grenade hit his vehicle, a soldier "felt no pain, just some numbness in his hand. . . . The shrapnel had fractured a bone in his forearm, severed a tendon, and broken a bone in his hand. It wasn't bleeding much and he could still shoot."[160] Here, the pathological description renders the soldier's body a marvel; despite sustaining seemingly immobilizing injuries, he is neither in pain nor incapacitated. A later account is even more inconceivable:

> He had a trickle of blood running down his face and a neat hole, a small one, in the middle of his forehead. . . . Doctors would later determine that a piece of shrapnel had lodged between the frontal lobes of his brain, missing vital tissues by fractions of an inch in either direction. He was all right. It felt like he had just banged his head. It hurt a lot worse minutes later when he took a bullet to his right pinkie, which left the tip of it hanging off by a piece of skin. . . . Lamb just swore and stuck the fingertip back on, wrapped it with a piece of duct tape, and continued working his radio.[161]

Here, what seems like a fatal wound is merely a nuisance. As in Moore, the merging of antithetical representations of wounded bodies allows the soldier to simultaneously occupy two opposing roles: the invincible hero and the vulnerable victim of trauma that could have been avoided had political leaders made better decisions. *Black Hawk Down*'s appropriations of these discourses enable Bowden to reach conclusions not unlike those of Moore: although American soldiers fight valiantly, the gruesome suffering they endure makes untenable their deployment in wars fought to secure human rights.

The soldiers' professionalism and quality are further established through the incorporation of Moore's contrasting of the enemy's brutality with the trauma-free precision with which he kills. The Somali body rarely receives sustained attention in this literature. Somali deaths are instantaneous and painless, and the writers' language consistently denies that their injuries are traumatic.[162] Like North Vietnamese soldiers at the Ia Drang, Somalis simply die, as when "the Somali just fell forward... without getting off a shot" or "just fell over sideways."[163] Like Moore, Bowden relies on metaphors of inanimateness and refuse. One woman, shot by an American, "fell face forward, dropping like a sack"; other Somalis are "dropped" and "flattened" by American bullets or, after being shot, "lay in a rumpled heap."[164] Sometimes they simply disappear. "One moment the Somali's head was there, and the next moment he was gone," Durant writes of a man he shoots. "I can't say for certain, but I think I killed that man."[165] One soldier, conjuring up Moore's account of the "pop-up target range," regarded killing Somalis as being "just like target practice, only cooler."[166]

Black Hawk Down and the other texts about the Somalia intervention contributed to a discourse fearful that humanitarian interventions would reprise policymakers' failures to avoid escalating the Vietnam War by using the strategies through which *We Were Soldiers Once* represents Americans' experience in that earlier war. These texts likewise repeat Moore's and McNamara's careful distinction between tactical success and strategic failure and their critiques of the policies that underlay the Vietnam War.[167]

Recalling Moore's conclusion that the validation of airmobility was a satisfactory outcome, nearly every writer on the subject of the Somalia intervention underscores tactical success over strategic failure. "The Battle of the Black Sea was perceived outside the special operations community as a failure," Bowden writes. "It was not, at least in strictly military terms.... [A] gainst overwhelming odds, the mission was accomplished."[168] Stanton makes a comparable estimation, going so far as to declare strategy immaterial: "The whole Somalia mission was a disorganized mess," he argues, but "no matter what happened or what task we were given, we would do it well. This in and of itself was all that mattered."[169] Schilling, sounding very much like Moore professing that his men had learned they "could stand against the finest light infantry troops in the world and hold [their] ground," writes, "We'd accomplished our mission. . . . No matter how bloodied we were, we knew we were still militarily far superior to anyone there and had dished out more than we took against people who liked to dish it out."[170]

Such rhetoric is most pronounced in these writers' echoing of McNamara's contention, namely, that "our effort in Vietnam proved unwise does not make [soldiers'] sacrifice less noble." Both Stanton and Bowden nearly quote this passage. "Though the operation was a failure . . . [t]he soldiers, sailors, Marines, and airmen did all that was asked of them," Stanton writes on the first page of his memoir; "More's the pity the policymakers were not asking for the right things."[171] Nearly identically, Bowden writes, "No matter how critically history records the policy decisions that led up to this fight, nothing can diminish the professionalism and dedication of the Rangers and Special Forces units who fought there that day."[172] Bowden pointedly doesn't question *whether* the political calculations warrant critique, instead indicating that they do and that such criticism will be severe.

The criticism is, in fact, blistering, and, as in the Vietnam literature of the moment, the policymakers responsible for sending soldiers on a fool's errand are strongly condemned. One Ranger's complaint about "the politicians in Washington who'd gotten so many of his friends killed and hurt chasing a stupid warlord in Mogadishu" puts American blood on the hands of American political leaders, not on Somali militiamen, and he indicts them not for refusing to let him win but for sending him on the senseless mission of chasing down a "stupid warlord."[173] Other writers more forcefully echo McNamara's sentiments and language, insisting that the Somalia mission stemmed from the faulty conviction that the United States could and should right the world's wrongs. "Bush believed that going to Somalia to end the suffering there was the moral thing to do," Stanton explains, before paraphrasing McNamara's most infamous passage: "It was a noble decision—motivated by thoroughly decent impulses—but the wrong one."[174]

Bowden as well paraphrases one of McNamara's widely quoted lines, writing that Somalia has come to "represent the futility of trying to resolve local animosity with international muscle."[175] This is a concept to which he returns: "The foreign policy lesson I take from this story is like the old prayer, 'Lord, grant me the strength to change the things I can, accept the things I can't, and the wisdom to know the difference.' Learning what America's power can and can't accomplish is a major challenge in the post-cold war world."[176] Ultimately, he reaches a conclusion about Somalia similar to McNamara's admission that the United States had been wrong to continue the war in Vietnam: "It would have been hard for the United States not to go after Aidid, but it would have been better not to try. . . . We should have said no."[177] Bowden's judgment that the confidence of the United States in its ability to shape world affairs was misplaced rearticulates McNamara's foreign policy lessons of 1995, and Bowden, like Stanton, shares McNamara's conclusion that moral commitments should not lead to military ones. Most important, he and others who wrote about Somalia marshaled in their works the language and imagery of contemporary Vietnam literature.

In the late 1990s Americans repeatedly confronted the questions of whether stopping genocide and ending famine were in the national interest and of whether missions to accomplish those goals were appropriate ones for the U.S. military to undertake. Many internationalist interventionists—Presidents Bush and Clinton chief among them—viewed such missions as enterprises which the United States could hardly abstain from without surrendering its claim to global leadership and meeting its moral obligations. The military presented itself as ready and willing to tackle such missions. Others, however, argued that such campaigns met no national security goals and were likely to succeed only in killing American soldiers. For these opponents, Vietnam, remembered in the decade's most influential books as a policy debacle that could and should have been avoided and that led to a disastrous loss of American lives, remained a potent comparison.

The legibility of that political rhetoric depended on its making sense on a cultural level. The popular literature of Somalia played a central role in legitimating cultural anxieties about humanitarian interventions. Appropriating the language, tropes, and images of contemporaneous Vietnam remembrance—and at times paraphrasing and in effect quoting it—works of nonfiction and memoirs about the Somalia intervention of 1993 presented contemporary American soldiers as sharing the valor and suffering of Americans who had fought in the earliest battles of the Vietnam War and as having been the victims of similarly brutal enemies and equally ignorant policymakers. In this literature, the Somalia mission in fact appeared parallel to the war in Vietnam: a well-intentioned but disastrous effort to resolve an intractable problem.

How deeply indebted American popular culture with regard to Somalia is to Vietnam's remembrance reveals how deeply that war's legacy shaped Americans' thinking about post–Cold War military interventions, about U.S. foreign policy, and about the nation's global responsibilities. The inability to consider the merits of humanitarian interventions outside the shadow of Vietnam—however imperfect the comparisons were—was more than academic. The fear of another Vietnam, and the subsequent failure of the United States to intervene in Africa and Europe in robust ways, shaped the lives of millions of people throughout the world. It also furthered a narrative that viewed military action as appropriate only when it served the narrowly defined goal of preserving America's hegemony. The appropriation of Vietnam's memory to support such visions of the global roles and responsibilities of the United States, and of the military's role in fulfilling them, would only increase after the terrorist attacks of September 11, 2001.

CHAPTER 5

"IT'S ALMOST LIKE THE VIETNAM WALL"

The Legacy of Vietnam and Remembrance of Flight 93

MEMBERS OF RESERVE NAVAL CONSTRUCTION BATTALION 14, A SEABEE unit based at Jacksonville Naval Air Station in Florida but deployed to Camp Junction City, a marine base in Ramadi, Iraq, were most likely in a somber mood on May 2, 2004. As they prepared to be reviewed by Rear Adm. Charles Kubic, the division commander, their thoughts and conversations must have turned to Jason Dwelley and Christopher Dickerson, comrades who had been killed two days earlier when their truck hit a roadside bomb.[1] Seabees are not, by training, combat soldiers. They build things—roads and airfields in previous wars, sewage treatment facilities and electrical grids in this one. But the war in Iraq made no distinctions between combat and support personnel, between the front and the rear. This lesson would be reinforced moments later, when two insurgent mortars landed inside Camp Junction City. The first missed. The second did not. Three men died instantly, and two more within hours: Charles Anderson, Trace Dossett, Scott McHugh, Robert Jenkins, and Ronnie Ginther. Nearly three dozen other men were injured.[2]

Amid the families' grief and assurances that the five men had believed in their mission came complaints about the circumstances of their deaths and the wisdom and management of the Iraq war itself. McHugh's father said the men had been "fish in a barrel," while Anderson's mother wondered why her son was deployed to a combat zone in the first place.[3] The hostess at a bar near the Jacksonville Naval Air Station condemned the war, but the bartender at another was simply frustrated: "I think we need to get it over with and get out of it."[4]

Chris Bianchi, also present at Camp Junction City that day, did not speak to any reporters about these deaths. Although he served with the "Pride of Dixie," as the 14th NMCB, or naval mobile construction battalion, is nicknamed, it's not clear if he was wounded in that shelling or even if he was on the parade ground. His public statement about the war came more than six years later, thousands of miles from Ramadi, and a two-day drive from Jacksonville. On October 8, 2008, Bianchi appeared at the temporary memorial to Flight 93, a fenced-in gravel lot in the countryside near Shanksville, Somerset County, Pennsylvania. The simple memorial, which overlooked the site where the hijacked airliner had crashed on September 11, 2001, housed only a small shed for volunteers, wooden benches, and a length of chain-link fencing to which visitors had attached thousands of items.

Bianchi had brought with him a pair of khaki desert combat boots, filthy with the accumulated grime of his deployment (fig. 5.1). If he had tried to clean them, it didn't show. What was evident, however, was the care he had taken in transforming them into a memorial to his seven fallen comrades. The men's names were listed on the left boot's leather upper; around the perimeter of the right sole, he wrote, "To all those who paid the ultimate price for freedom, it is not forgotten, ever." On the right toe, he had written, "Let Freedom Reign." The inscription on the left instep was more troubling: "These boots stood up to the enemy and lost." Bianchi told one of the volunteer ambassadors who staff the site that "he wanted to leave the boots here in memory of the heroes of Flight 93 'who knew when to stand and fight.'"[5]

The Flight 93 National Memorial is one of hundreds of sites in the United States marked by practices of "temporary memorialization," a practice deeply indebted to the Vietnam Veterans Memorial, where, as Kristin Hass has argued, "objects . . . articulate a struggle on the part of ordinary Americans to be part of a conversation about how the war should be remembered and, therefore, part of a conversation about the shape of the nation."[6] Yet something different is going on in Shanksville. Bianchi is neither replicating familiar practices nor rejecting them. He is instead adapting them as he crafts a public memory of his war and his friends, appropriating the Flight 93 Memorial on behalf of his own experience.

FIGURE 5.1. Seabee boots left at the Flight 93 Memorial by Chris Bianchi on October 8, 2008. Like similar items left at the Vietnam Veterans Memorial, the boots are a memorial to Bianchi's fallen comrades. However, Bianchi is also drawing on the heroic narrative that surrounds Flight 93 to affirm the value of his own service and the significance of his friends' deaths. National Park Service, Flight 93 National Memorial. Photograph by the author.

It is not self-evident that the Flight 93 Memorial would serve as a space for such remembrances. The memorial is more than eight hundred miles from the Jacksonville Naval Air Station; none of the Seabees who died at Camp Junction City are memorialized there or even have an obvious connection to the area. But by choosing it, Bianchi is engaging in a multifaceted political discourse. In a moment of widespread disapproval of and weariness over the war in Iraq, the boots locate his friends' deaths in the best traditions of American patriotism and service while reaffirming the appropriateness of the war itself. His inscription "Let Freedom Reign!" repeats that of President George W. Bush, scrawled on a note from Secretary of State Condoleezza Rice informing him that a provisional government had taken control of Iraq, and his reference to terrorism maintains the long-discredited link between the war in Iraq and the attacks of September 11.[7] The boots don't simply remember Flight 93 or even the Seabees; they appropriate the space of the Flight 93 Memorial in an attempt to resolve the Iraq war's troubled place in American culture, and they do so by explicitly reconfiguring practices familiar from the Vietnam Veterans Memorial.

In this chapter I argue that remembrance of Flight 93 has relied on the evocation and revision of discourses central to Vietnam's legacy. In popular accounts, through visitors' interactions with the temporary memorial, and in the competition to select a permanent memorial design, the discourses and practices through which Americans have grappled with Vietnam's legacy have persistently been employed to mobilize Flight 93's legacy to recuperate a citizenship defined by support for interventionist foreign policy and aggressive militarism that many conservatives maintain faltered after Vietnam.

My analysis does not question whether the passengers and crew acted to retake the plane, saved lives, or deserve lasting respect. Surely they did, and still do.[8] But heroism emerges in many instances and from many motives, and it serves many purposes. It is not synonymous with or produced by patriotism. We would do well to keep in mind David Simpson's caution against ascribing patriotic motives to any of the dead of September 11 and his reminder that "the dead have become patriots and heroes by default or by the interpellation of others."[9] In the context of Flight 93 this means that the passengers' and crew's heroic actions do not inherently indicate their embrace of particular ideas about patriotic citizenship or of distinct political positions. That Flight 93 has been invoked on behalf of certain narratives of patriotism and foreign policy is a product of the culture in which it has been remembered, not of the passengers' and crew's inherent qualities.[10] My interest, then, lies in examining how ways of remembering Vietnam have been central to linking the actions that occurred aboard the plane to the subsequent privileging of preemptive military intervention.

I explore a range of formal and informal remembrances of Flight 93. I first examine how the well-known narrative of heroism and patriotic sacrifice which has defined the crash and positions the passengers and crew as models of the Bush administration's policy of preemption relies on representations of them as quite literally embodying certain qualities that conservatives still frequently claim the nation lost in the aftermath of Vietnam and amid the resultant Vietnam syndrome and that dominate recuperative post-Vietnam films. I then turn to an analysis of how veterans of the wars in Iraq and Afghanistan, their families, and Vietnam veterans have, as Bianchi did, engaged with the temporary memorial by revising the practice of leaving objects at memorials so that it nearly univocally validates their service by aligning it with the actions of the people on Flight 93. Finally, I discuss how the design and popularity of the Vietnam Veterans Memorial, known also as the Wall, informed the competition to select a permanent Flight 93 Memorial. I maintain that designers reconfigured the popular elements of Maya Lin's design in ways that enable an interactive visitor experience that does not challenge the dominant discourse of aggressive patriotism that surrounds Flight 93. Taken together, these acts of recollection reveal neither the embrace nor the rejection of the memory of Vietnam but a complicated nexus of revision that makes Flight 93's remembrance a site at which the nation continues to grapple with Vietnam's legacy.

"He Would Cause a Conflict Just to Make Sure You Understood His Viewpoint."

In the summer of 2002 the Bush administration rolled out a new foreign policy to a nation still reeling from the previous fall's terrorist attacks in New York City, Washington, D.C., and Shanksville, Pennsylvania. The articulation of what would come to be called the Bush doctrine, which provided the rationale for the invasion of Iraq in 2003, coincided with the construction of Flight 93's remembrance in popular culture. The story of the passengers' and crew's actions had been celebrated almost immediately. One of the most poignant moments in the president's address to the nation on September 20, 2001, was his introduction of Lisa Beamer, the pregnant wife of the flight's most renowned passenger, Todd Beamer, who, uttering "Let's roll," was one of the leaders of the attack on the hijackers. Within a year, editorials, popular music, Jere Longman's best-selling *Among the Heroes: United Flight 93 and the Passengers and Crew Who Fought Back*, and ceremonies marking the anniversary of the crash idealized its victims as patriotic citizens committed to traditional values and an aggressive response to injustice and danger. Insistently describing the passengers' and crew's physical strength, mental tenacity, impeccable morality, and willingness to fight, these texts enlisted motifs long central to conservatives' attempts to recuperate from Vietnam's trauma as they imagined the people aboard the plane as personifications of the Bush doctrine. In a moment in which Americans were asked to support preemptive war, the cultural representation of Flight 93 reaffirmed the idea that appropriate citizenship meant being fully recovered from the Vietnam syndrome.

President Bush first articulated the doctrine on June 1, 2002, when he told the graduating cadets at West Point that "if we wait for threats to fully materialize, we will have waited too long" and that "the war on terror will not be won on the defensive. We must take the battle to the enemy, disrupt his plans, and confront the worst threats before they emerge. In the world we have entered, the only path to safety is the path of action, and America will act."[11] These comments announced a policy shift that had begun as early as November 2001 amid Vice President Dick Cheney's assertions that the United States should preempt potential threats.[12] Adherents posited the doctrine as recuperative, a statement that, as the political scientist Robert Singh puts it, "distilled the best of American traditions together."[13] The effort to locate the doctrine within the nation's larger trajectory was evident in then-National Security Adviser Condoleezza Rice's remarks of April 2002: "There are right and wrong choices and right and wrong acts. . . . We can never let the intricacies of cloistered debate—with many hues of gray and nuance—obscure the need to speak and act with moral clarity. We must recognize that some states or leaders will choose wrongly. . . . And we must recognize that such regimes must be confronted, not coddled."[14]

Rice portrays moral clarity and an appetite for confrontation as standard American attributes: "September 11th reintroduced America to a part of itself that some had forgotten, or that some thought we no longer had. We have been reminded that defending freedom was not just the work of the greatest generation, it is the work of every generation."[15] Rice's claim that somewhere between the end of the Second World War and the 9/11 attacks the nation had lost its way reveals how central Vietnam remained to conservative foreign policy. The midpoint between Victory in Europe Day and September 11, 2001, after all, was the summer of 1973, when the United States was coming to terms with its withdrawal from Vietnam.

Supporters of the Bush doctrine did not have to look far for citizens who exemplified these qualities. Almost immediately after the attacks and escalating through 2002, Flight 93's dead were idealized as at once quotidian and exceptional.[16] Bush's own rhetoric defined the passengers and crew as exemplifying post-Vietnam militarized citizenship and as embodiments of a nation defined by moral clarity and accepting of intervention. Two months after the attacks he ended an address in which he told the nation that "our Government has a responsibility to hunt down our enemies, and we will" by referencing Todd Beamer: "We will always remember the words of that brave man, expressing the spirit of that great country. . . . We've defeated freedom['s] enemies before, and we will defeat them again. We cannot know every turn that this battle will take. Yet we know our cause is just and our ultimate victory is assured. We will no doubt, face new challenges. But we have our marching orders. My fellow Americans, 'Let's roll.' "[17]

The actions taken on Flight 93 were thus quickly incorporated into rhetoric that endorsed military intervention. Both directly and subtly, this construction relied on juxtapositions with perceived post-Vietnam failures. In a *National Review* editorial of 2002, for example, James Edwards wrote, "The terrorists apparently took the wrong war as their example of what to expect from Americans. They seemed to have latched onto the Vietnam War."[18] He argues, however, that the global war on terror does not risk repeating the tragedy of Vietnam because Vietnam was an aberration: "Americans are not a warring people, but we always are willing to finish what we start—assuming we have a clear goal and it's evident that our leaders are fighting to win."[19] Against the shopworn claims that Vietnam had been lost because of a weak intelligentsia and policymakers who refused to let the U.S. military complete its mission, Edwards offers Flight 93 as a model of patriotic citizenship: "Do we have the stomach to see this war through past the Afghanistan phase? Perhaps the best answer is found in the conduct of the average Americans who found themselves on hijacked flights. . . . [Todd] Beamer and the others gave their own lives in order to save innocent lives. How typically American."[20]

Nine months later the *Chicago Sun Times* columnist Mark Steyn made this point explicitly, promoting the Iraq war by contrasting Flight 93 to the imagined acquiescence of the sort of leftist intellectuals blamed for the defeat in Vietnam: "The Flight 93 hijackers might have got lucky. They might have found themselves on a plane with . . . an Ivy League professor immersed in a long *Harper's* article about the iniquities of U.S. foreign policy. . . . But, granted those exceptions, chances are that any flight full of reasonably typical Americans would have found a group of people to do the right thing, to act as those on Flight 93 did."[21] Paraphrasing Rice's dismissal of "cloistered debate," he explained that the passengers and crew "did not have the luxury of amused faculty-room detachment" and instead "effectively inaugurated the new Bush Doctrine: When you know your enemies have got something big up their sleeves, you take 'em out before they can do it."[22] Steyn's cynical, reductionist thinking—that people concerned about the impact of U.S. foreign policy in the developing world would willingly acquiesce to their own deaths at the hands of terrorist hijackers and that everyone aboard the plane uncritically endorsed American imperialism—is striking. Yet it demonstrates how deeply entrenched post-Vietnam anti-intellectualism remains; and it reveals that to many conservatives Flight 93's passengers and crew symbolized the sort of a militarized citizenship that embraced the Bush doctrine, which they believed must be embraced in order to prevent the war on terror from faltering by repeating the imagined failures of the antiwar left in the Vietnam era.

The discourse of patriotic, interventionist citizenship that dominates Bush's rhetoric and editorials like this one is visible as well in Longman's *Among the Heroes.* Published on the one-year anniversary of 9/11 and a few months after Bush's speech, it reached number fifteen on the *New York Times* best-seller list the day after newspapers reported that the administration had formalized preemption in the National Security Strategy.[23] The book, much like the *New York Times*'s "Portraits of Grief," constructs the dead as "civilians who could be and were readily identified with a national cause, victims of an attack on America and on democracy itself."[24] However, Flight 93's dead are decidedly not solely victims but also embodiments of strength, courage, moral certainty, and patriotism, people who link the Bush doctrine with the post-Vietnam recuperation of American militarism. As Susan Jeffords has argued, post-Vietnam films of the 1980s revive an enervated America by fetishizing the male body and its capacity for violence; they posit the "hard-body hero [who] masters his surroundings, most often by defeating enemies through violent physical action," as a signifier of an ideology that the nation must recover if it is to regain global dominance.[25] By the 1990s, Jeffords shows, these traits had evolved in such a way that William Munny, the main character of the film *Unforgiven,* modeled the new ideal. "[Munny] may still have the hard-bodied character that America needs, but he remains a family man," Jeffords explains, and he is "both warrior and father, both defender and provider, both killer and nurturer" and "motivated by a desire for justice."[26] Longman depicts Flight 93's passengers and crew within this post-Vietnam logic, emphasizing their physical vigor, their combat prowess, and the clarity of purpose in their quotidian lives.

Among the Heroes emphasizes the passengers' physicality repeatedly. Richard Guadagno, an agent in the Fish and Wildlife Service, "could bench-press three hundred fifty pounds, double his body weight."[27] Jeremy Glick, a "former collegiate judo champion," was "six foot one, two hundred twenty pounds, so broad-chested and slim-hipped that he had to have his suits custom-tailored," and Louis Nacke "was five foot nine and weighed two hundred pounds, with a weight-lifter's physique."[28] A college friend describes Donald Greene, a former wrestler, as "the strongest man I ever met." He recalls that "his body was like a piece of iron, all muscle bundled up in his medium height and strong girth" and that "he was a gentle man, with bursting capabilities at the ready, if needed."[29] While such descriptions are primarily afforded the men, one female passenger is described as being "small, but her muscular definition was pronounced from rigorous workouts."[30]

As the references to law enforcement, judo, and wrestling suggest, though, these idealized physiques are only one component of the passengers' and crew's construction as idealized post-Vietnam citizens. Their capacity to use that body in combat echoes post-Vietnam films' reliance on the hero's "violent physical action" and the viewer's enjoyment in the application of these bodies to combat.[31] Relating a confrontation about which few specific details are known, *Among the Heroes* encourages similar fantasies.[32] Longman imagines Mark Bingham's rubgy playing, for example, as him "running, headlong, his huge body amped on unpadded adrenaline, craving clean, hard, disruptive contact . . . nothing but the grunting slap of muscle and bone, the great satisfactory jab of a shoulder into an opponent's chest, that one crystalline instant of domination."[33] The judo champion Glick had learned techniques for "putting [opponents] into submission with a stranglehold, chokehold, or lock applied against the elbow," while the flight attendant Cee Cee Lyles, a former police officer, "had taken a course in handling herself in close-quarter physical confrontation. She knew how to stun someone with a chop to the neck . . . how to gouge at someone with a fingernail file, how to find weak points in an attackers knee and groin." Guadagno had "received the same training in hand-to-hand fighting as drug enforcement agents, alcohol, tobacco and firearm agents, and the border patrol" and had carried aboard "a small pickax."[34] By marshaling the tropes through which post-Vietnam film reinvented American masculinity, these graphic references furnish a script for readers' fantasies of the superior Flight 93 body's violent retribution against the inferior terrorist body.

The book matches physical tenacity and competence with ideological and moral commitments that link the discourse of masculinity to the Bush doctrine. Longman describes Tom Burnett as "a political conservative [who] valued qualities like sacrifice, valor, courage, patriotism, honor, dignity and citizenship, and longed for a time when these words carried weight and were not hollow platitudes." Burnett adorned his office with statues of "strong leaders who had acted decisively . . . in times of crisis, even in the face of public opposition."[35] Reenacting Rice's tone about right and wrong choices and Bush's contention at West Point that "moral truth is the same in every culture, in every time, in every place," Burnett's wife recalled that "moral values, [Tom] believed, were not debatable. . . . [T]here was right and wrong, and no in-between."[36] A lengthy quote from one of Burnett's speeches describes his business philosophy in terms nearly identical to Bush's version of foreign policy: "Identify what needs to be done before your competitors . . . then execute with speed. . . . Pick the battlefield and engage."[37]

Longman describes other passengers in much the same vein: Toshiya Kuge "had a very strong sense of what the right course in life was," Christine Snyder "had such a keen sense of what was right. . . . It was black or white. There was no gray," and Guadagno, who saw "the world was black-and-white. . . . Either you were right or you were wrong. There wasn't a lot of gray."[38] Nacke "would cause a conflict just to make sure you understood his viewpoint."[39] Appearing in the same moment that Rice, Bush, and others celebrated moral conviction and aggressive preemption as the central precepts of U.S. foreign policy, *Among the Heroes* defined idealized American citizenship as fully supportive of the Bush doctrine and imagined a culture recovered from the moral ambiguity remembered as tainting Vietnam's aftermath.

Speakers at the first anniversary ceremony of the crash continued this rhetoric. "This is where Americans hit back, and spoilt their plans," the Reverend Russell Kessler, a Baptist minister, told a reporter, establishing the dead as models of preemption. "That's what America is all about."[40] This sentiment was repeated by the former Pennsylvania governor and Secretary of Homeland Security Tom Ridge, who told the audience gathered at the site that those aboard the plane "met the challenge like citizen-soldiers, like Americans."[41] Collapsing "citizen" and "soldier" into a third identity, "American," Ridge reduces the meaning of *American* to being willing to fight, a rhetorical maneuver that conflates citizenship, patriotism, and militarism and excludes dissent.

The popular representation of Flight 93 adapted Vietnam's remembrance as it contributed to legitimizing the Bush doctrine. In the same moment that the political rhetoric defined the flight's victims as idealized citizens who embodied traits parallel to the Bush administration's foreign policy imperatives, Longman's best-seller mobilized language familiar from the post-Vietnam era to portray the passengers and crew as idealized, heroic Americans whose traits saved the nation. Together, these representations defined the global war on terror as both necessary and winnable by constructing the nation's contemporary heroism as antithetical to its previous failures. This discourse would also define how soldiers and veterans would engage with the temporary memorial at Shanksville.

"You Were in My Mind as Anti-Terror Warrior Also"

Visitors to the Flight 93 Temporary Memorial were often surprised by the weather. Sitting on one of the twenty park benches that overlooked the crash site or examining the hundreds of tributes left by previous visitors, they found it impossible not to notice how forcefully the wind came up from the crash site, how it was always twenty degrees cooler here than in nearby Somerset or Johnstown, where they had left the turnpike twenty minutes earlier.[42] In the winter it was so cold that the ink in the pens used for writing in the visitors' book froze.

On November 24, 2004, the day before Thanksgiving, the weather was typical. It was raining, and the volunteer ambassador expected few visitors.[43] She watched as Torrey Vap and Howard Flynn, both army recruiters, took their reenlistment oaths in front of the memorial fence (fig. 5.2). "We wanted to have the ceremony at the Flight 93 site as a way of expressing our personal respect and appreciation for what those passengers did for our country that day," Vap remarked.[44] November 17, 2005, almost exactly a year later, was even colder. That day an ambassador recorded her reaction to some other visitors: "[It was] truly an amazing and emotional sight to see these eight army men. They stood by the flags while 1 young man with his wife beside him on crutches took the oath to reenlist. Just wearing their camouflage uniform shivering as snow flurries brushed against their faces standing at attention. Nevin + I stayed with them to support them. It was hard to do, What lay ahead for these fine men + wife. My emotions were high. We really need to support + keep them all in our prayers."[45]

These enlistees are not alone in having visited the site. Service members, their families, veterans of Iraq, Afghanistan, and Vietnam, and POW/MIA activists are frequent visitors to the temporary memorial. At least twice, soldiers departing for Iraq have taken photographs of the memorial to carry with them on their deployment.[46] Returning soldiers, including some who have been wounded, are also frequent visitors. That these men and women routinely make these trips demonstrates their respect for the dead. Yet as

FIGURE 5.2. The recruiters Torrey Vap and Howard Flynn take their reenlistment oaths at the Flight 93 Temporary Memorial on November 24, 2004. The Flight 93 Temporary Memorial was popular among military personnel, their families, and veterans, who often linked their own service to the heroic actions of Flight 93's passengers and crew. Courtesy *Somerset County Daily American.*

Bianchi's boots reveal, in visiting the memorial they are making claims about their own service as well. During its nearly ten-year existence, the temporary memorial functioned like the Vietnam Veterans Memorial, as a meaningful space in which veterans worked through their wartime experiences.

The Flight 93 Memorial is quite different from the Vietnam Veterans Memorial. While the former initially emerged organically as a temporary memorial to those who had lost their lives and was quickly taken over by the National Park Service (NPS), the latter was conceived and enabled by the work of Vietnam veterans themselves, a site for their own healing.[47] Yet veterans of Iraq and Afghanistan have appropriated the Flight 93 Memorial in ways that replicate Vietnam veterans' use of the Wall as "a place of contemplation, a place that specifically marks their identities."[48] However, as the accounts given above demonstrate, to veterans this place is not, as the Wall is, a place of "healing" or of "uncontainable grief, ambivalence that refuses easy resolution, and political protest."[49] It has instead become nearly universally a place where soldiers reaffirm the appropriateness both of their service and of the wars in which they fought.

The memorial's frequent role as a place where, as Erika Doss puts it, "tragic death is remembered in terms of patriotic vengeance," is especially apparent in the diversity of ways in which soldiers, veterans, and their families have appropriated practices familiar from the Vietnam Veterans Memorial to justify their service.[50] Against an enduring remembrance of Vietnam as a war in which the nation failed to support both deployed troops and returned veterans, contemporary service members and their families have insistently used the Flight 93 Memorial to define service in the Iraq and Afghanistan wars as appropriate and worthy of recognition because it replicates the passengers' celebrated heroism. Vietnam veterans as well have persistently used the site as a space to heal from their perceived social marginalization and suspect patriotism by claiming for themselves the honors and heroism that have been afforded Flight 93's dead and defining themselves as the guardians of patriotic orthodoxy. POW/MIA activists also have used the site to foster attention to their cause.

These uses of the Flight 93 Memorial perhaps reflect a broader cultural shift that has taken place since the Vietnam Veterans Memorial opened in 1982, a moment when the United States was deeply engaged in working through the impact and legacies of the Vietnam War. In the intervening decades, particularly after the Persian Gulf War of 1991, the celebration of American soldiers has become a de facto element of patriotic citizenship. As Hass explains, in the memorial culture of contemporary America "the soldier is used to overcome the problems of war and military service raised by the Vietnam War, enabling and encouraging an unfettered celebration of military service." At many war memorials, she goes on, "military service becomes the ultimate expression of national belonging, regardless of the terms of that service or what that military service does in the world."[51]

Yet if overcoming Vietnam is the key project of war memorials, what is important at the Flight 93 Memorial—which is emphatically *not* a war memorial—is that a memorial practice that initially enabled multiple and ambivalent expressions about war, the military, and the role of the soldier has not been rejected but instead revised into one that is more uniformly celebratory. Hass observes that objects left at the Wall articulate multiple, competing positions within "a conversation about the . . . problem of patriotism in the wake of the war."[52] The nearly decade-long process through which highly visible constituencies appropriated the Flight 93 Memorial, however, was decidedly more univocal in its portrayal of a nation fully recuperated from the Vietnam syndrome and willing to embrace military interventions and those who participate in them. If service members' and their families' acts of remembrance at the Flight 93 Memorial are celebratory, though, they also reveal that this project of celebration is incomplete and unstable. The items and notes left by visitors not only are laced with anxiety that the soldier's lauded position might be precarious but also reveal an effort to shore up the narrative of a heroic, self-sacrificing military amid increasingly unpopular wars.

It was impossible to visit the Flight 93 Memorial without noticing how many military items hung from the fence. These conspicuous items, which range from patches, pins, and dog tags to carefully folded uniforms, a Kevlar helmet, and dress medals, directly link Flight 93, contemporary militarism, and Vietnam's legacy. Although some of the items are left for specific passengers—for example, the collection includes several items related to the air force career of the copilot, LeRoy Homer, and a patch from the 101st Airborne frequently decorated the slate angel bearing Joseph Driscoll's name—most serve a twofold function: they are both tributes to the dead and self-referential. Such duality revises the logic of the Wall by conferring on the giver the incontestable idealized citizenship, heroism, and patriotism already unquestionably associated with the recipient. Here, these items, rather than illuminating diverse attitudes about the recent wars, link those remembered as having fought "the first battle on terrorism," as Gen. Tommy Franks remarked at the ceremony marking the fifth anniversary of the crash.[53] These objects link Flight 93's remembrance to all American soldiers, who are imagined as in effect performing the same action and deserving the same honor.

The most public assertion of this narrative came in March 2006, when Secretary of Defense Donald Rumsfeld, like Franks, evoked the site as "the place where America really started to fight back" and left a challenge coin, a small medallion that military commanders present as accolades. The *New York Times* noted that Rumsfeld "hands out [these coins] to troops he meets in combat zones."[54] "His gesture," the article continued, "was intended to link that event, through the attacks on the World Trade Center and the Pentagon, to the wars started by the Bush administration in Iraq and Afghanistan." Yet Rumsfeld is not simply "link[ing]" the events by asserting that the wars are the appropriate response to the attacks. Honoring two distinct groups with an identical item equates their actions.[55] Leaving this coin just after the third anniversary of the Iraq invasion, when most Americans had already become frustrated with the war, Rumsfeld appropriates the widely accepted narrative of Flight 93's heroism on behalf of soldiers fighting in that unpopular war.[56]

The *Times* did not acknowledge that Rumsfeld was replicating a common activity. Hundreds of challenge coins appeared at the temporary memorial during its existence, and they represent but one conflation of Flight 93's remembrance and the Iraq and Afghanistan wars. In one instance an air force general "spoke to the crowd here + was very interesting. Telling us what a just + right war this is + it would take time. Asking for us to support our military."[57] On September 11, 2006, the fifth-anniversary celebration included the Pennsylvania National Guard raising flags that had flown in Iraq and the presentation of "a captured Iraq flag" to the NPS.[58] And like the Vietnam Veterans Memorial, the Flight 93 Memorial has become a therapeutic site for wounded veterans. In 2005 a volunteer ambassador recorded that she "started [her] shift off with tears, met a young soldier who lost his leg in Iraq, also his best friend was killed there, was headed to Walter Reed Hospital for rehab"; another wounded Iraq veteran "indicated that he comes to the memorial frequently."[59] In June 2008 an NPS employee wrote that he "had a group of Iraq vets (wounded in action) stop to hear the story of Flight 93 and why they served."[60] As these log entries indicate, veterans' uses of the memorial have nearly universally supported the Iraq and Afghanistan interventions.

These official uses represent but one way in which service members have adapted the Vietnam Veterans Memorial's defining memorial practice to establish their service as fundamentally like the lauded heroism of the passengers and crew and therefore deserving of the same recognition. Such uses arise from the larger framing of Flight 93's victims "as *war dead*," which Elle Kwok-Tin Ying explains has been "of central importance to the myth of Flight 93."[61] In notes to the dead, service members and their families have with some frequency expressed, as one Iraq veteran did, that "this was the reason for my service."[62] These statements are somewhat ambivalent and may connote revenge, as revealed by one veteran's note that he "hope[d he'd] killed enuf of them for you guys."[63]

Yet as exemplified by another veteran's gratefulness to the dead "for sacrificing your lives so that I may *begin* to live mine," many other notes regard the passengers and crew as inspirations or expressed the notion that soldiers are performing tasks identical to theirs.[64] In 2004, for example, a marine wrote, "I hope I can follow your lead when it's my turn to defend our great nation," and in 2007 a navy recruit wrote "I will support and defend this nation and wish I could be a hero like these people who die [*sic*] here."[65] A female Iraq veteran called the dead "my inspiration [who] gave me the courage to fight," while another, associating his service to the memory of male passengers who left behind wives and children, declared, "If every one could be as brave as these heroes. I just got back from a year in Afghanistan being away from my family, and after being here would GLADLY go again."[66] Another veteran, writing on an Operation Iraqi Freedom T-shirt, thanked the dead for "heroism [that] changed my attitude towards my country" and assured them, "I embarked on a journey to face that evil just as you did."[67]

Comments like these ignore the crucial divergences between the passengers and crew and deployed U.S. forces, chief among them that civilians are not soldiers, unsuspecting victims who fought back are not willing troops who volunteered, and a rebellion against a terrorist attack is not a preemptive invasion. The elision of these differences has enabled veterans to define their service as "continuing" or "finishing" the work of the crash victims, imagining the Iraq and Afghanistan wars as analogous to their resistance and hence acceptable. "We'll take the fight from here," wrote a member of the Eighty-second Airborne, while others say they will "continue to fight for what you have preserved" or they have "just returned from Iraq continuing the good fight [of] which your loved ones were also a part."[68] A military chaplain's card addressed to Todd Beamer reads, "I go to Iraq in a few weeks to continue the resistance movement you started."[69]

Some notes address the dead as "my fellow heroes" and declare, "I'm proud to have been part of your heroism as well" or claim, "It is because of brave men + women like those on Flight 93 and our men + women in uniform (including myself) that America endures." Others repeat the event's signature phrase by ending, "Well, time to roll" or saying, the "Sp[ecial] Operations Group—keeps it rolling" or, more vividly, explaining, "I was called back to active duty to serve with the Anti-Terrorist Task Force. We actively went to the Middle East to gather up known and suspected terrorists. This we did in your honor. You are in my mind as anti-terror warrior also. My team took '*Let's Roll*' to the limit."[70] Although this last writer suggests his military service was in "honor" of the dead, he also casts his service as not simply identical to theirs—both he and the passengers are "anti-terror warriors"—but, in claiming to have taken "'Let's Roll' to the limit," makes the war the culmination of what occurred aboard the plane. More than conflating the Flight 93 hero and the soldier, this note constructs the soldier as the embodiment of even greater heroism. Amid the public's growing anxieties about the wisdom and conduct of the wars in Iraq and Afghanistan and countering remembrances of Vietnam-era antiwar—and anti-soldier—sentiment, the items left at the Fight 93 Memorial revise the Wall's defining practice in order to sanction U.S. militarism.

Perhaps the most bizarre item in the collection is a yellow brick, now broken into two pieces, with an attached note reading, "This brick is from the compound of Taliban leader Mullah Mohammed Omar in Kandahar, Afghanistan. On October 20th, 2001 US Special Forces attacked and seized the compound. It is now used as a US base from which attacks are launched against the Taliban and Al Qaeda. Placed here in tribute to the first warriors of the Global War on Terror by members of the 19th Special Forces."[71] The brick demonstrates how deeply the Flight 93 Memorial has been militarized.[72] Unlike the quotidian objects frequently left at the memorial, the brick reveals the explicit effort to connect the 9/11 attacks and the wars and to equate the passengers and crew and the military.[73] As Marita Sturken contends, the Wall is "a place where veterans can speak to their dead friends."[74] The veterans who left the brick are also speaking to the dead. Yet these dead are civilians who died, however bravely, in a terrorist attack; they emphatically are *not* fellow soldiers, but these veterans nevertheless identify them as "warriors" whom they have succeeded. In leaving the brick, they imply that support of their actions is equivalent to and the logical extension of honoring Flight 93. Such objects indicate that practices that at the Vietnam Veterans Memorial attempt to articulate a complex response to unpopular wars have been remade to define contemporary military service as lacking Vietnam's complexities and controversies.

Such adaptation of the memorial practices central to the Wall in the service of militarized patriotism is most evident in the military awards that are left at the memorial, including Global War on Terror Expeditionary Medals, Purple Hearts, and Good Conduct medals.[75] They have been left both in their original packaging, as a National Defense Service Medal was, or as the full "salad" of ribbons taken from—and in at least one case still attached to—a service member's uniform.[76] This practice, too, revises one familiar from the Vietnam

Veterans Memorial. While Hass writes that a medal left at the Wall "might be left as a high honor for a fallen friend or as a demonstration of how little value the honor has," the most public instances in which veterans have returned medals—for example, the plan of the Vietnam Veterans Against the War to deliver a body bag filled with medals to Congress and Charles Liteky's act of placing his Medal of Honor at the Vietnam Veterans Memorial to protest Reagan's policies in Central America—have been explicitly antiwar.[77]

Given the discourse that has surrounded Flight 93, however, it would be impossible for such acts to be interpreted as signs of protest at this memorial; the veneration of the dead and their construction as patriotic heroes simply override any ambivalence about the wars. At a memorial to an event whose meaning is not contested and which has not been the site of a visible antiwar protest, that is, the medals retain their original meaning. The few notes that accompany medals bear this out. The clearest example comes from Oscar R. Garrett, a Desert Storm veteran who in September 2006 left his Kuwait Liberation Medal in its original box with this note: "To the Crew of Flight 93: Please accept this medal for your heroism and fighting back against all odds. Your actions were above and beyond your calling of which you executed with great strength and pride. You did not die in vain."[78] Garrett's note paraphrases the official citations that accompany military honors. In leaving this missive with the medal, he establishes himself as a person capable of discerning the heroism of others. The medal thus becomes an honor to the crew even as it validates the medal's original meaning.

Recent veterans have followed suit. On January 14, 2004, for example, an Afghanistan veteran named Russell Hoffman left his Combat Infantry Badge—one of at least six that have been left at the memorial—with a note reading, "This patch is the covitted [*sic*] US Armies Combat Infantry Badge (CIB). It was awarded to me for combat infantry ground operations during Operation Enduring Freedom. I hope it is a strong representation of the least I could do to honor your memory."[79] Hoffman values his medal, and his leaving of it does not reject its value. On the contrary, it is a re-presentation that confirms that value and the validity of the action for which it was originally awarded.

The literary critic Kyle Grimes has written that the awarding of the Medal of Honor to soldiers who fought in Vietnam was in part an effort "to make American involvement in Vietnam a replica of the myth of America as liberator" because it reproduces the "myth of heroism inherent in the Medal of Honor itself."[80] In that "there is a relatively fixed pattern of events to which all Medal of Honor winners will conform and thereby become replicas of the hero," Grimes explains, "the familiar cultural image of the war hero embodied in the medal is perpetuated through replication."[81] When Hoffman and others leave their awards at the Flight 93 Memorial, something similar, though perhaps in reverse, occurs. If placing an object at a memorial assumes that the object has some capacity to explain the event's cultural meaning, leaving a military medal at a civilian memorial equates those individuals' actions with soldiers' actions.[82] For the medal to do so for *these* civilians, already understood as patriotic heroes, the medal must not be meaningless or tainted; it must signify patriotism, self-sacrifice on behalf of the nation, and citizenship.[83] Yet if the medal is so understood, then it must also signify that the original conferee, despite serving in controversial conflicts, embodied those traits. Leaving the medal, then, simultaneously reaffirms Flight 93's patriotism and heroism and shores up those of the veteran.

This reaffirmation is true even in cases in which veterans defer to the passengers and crew, as one marine did when leaving his Global War on Terror Expeditionary Ribbon. He told the volunteer that it "belonged more to the Flight 93 crew and passengers than to him."[84] Such actions again confirm the veteran's honorable place in the nation. Like Hoffman, this marine is not denying the medal's value but stressing it's appropriateness as a reward for heroic behavior; in making this determination, he effectively affirms the righteousness of the conflict in which the medal connotes service. Moreover, by positioning themselves as capable of recognizing the qualities of heroism and making determinations about who deserves to be rewarded for it, these veterans declare their own membership in that group. Here again, a practice that at the Vietnam Veterans Memorial was ambiguous and multivalent has been reconfigured as emphatically militaristic.

The interactions of veterans' families with the Flight 93 Memorial establish a similar affinity. Like the Wall, the memorial has become a space at which military families seek to understand their loved ones' experience and grieve for their losses. At Shanksville this has taken the form of ascribing to contemporary veterans the self-sacrificing masculinity that defines Flight 93's passengers and crew, and families' uses of the memorial recall the logic of male passengers' phone calls to their wives and mothers. As late as 2007 one soldier bound for Iraq "brought his girlfriend—to show her why he was going."[85] In 2008 an air force technical sergeant left a card reading, "Today my son learned why daddy has to keep going away to war."[86] Another woman came to the memorial because her husband "wanted her to come here so she wouldn't forget why he was in Iraq."[87] Like the women who received calls from the plane, these women and children need to "learn," to be "shown," and must come to "understand" the necessity of male action. Like the veterans' notes, these visits warrant the service member's deployment by equating it with the remembrance of Flight 93's passengers and crew as suitably heteronormative and masculine and willing to sacrifice themselves for the nation.[88]

Women have been active agents in noting the parallels between Flight 93's dead and contemporary soldiers. The mother of two men deployed to Iraq—one for the fourth time—wrote, " 'Heroes' that is what the passengers & crews will always be. 'Heroes' is what my 2 sons are to me. . . . These Heroes stand up to terrorism & say NO More."[89] Another woman left a small crystal in a velvet bag with a note reading, "This rock blessed my boys and kept them safe in Cuba + Iraq. May it bless each and everyone of you and your families and may they always 'stay-safe.' "[90] Pamela Ryan, whose daughter and son-in-law were serving in Iraq and whose son had recently finished marine boot camp, left a Bible in which she wrote, "I had to witness why they had to be there. I know now and I leave this in peace."[91] For these mothers, leaving highly personal objects at the memorial was a public testimony not only to the anxiety they felt over their children's deployment but also to their ultimate acceptance of it. They were able to conceptualize support for the Iraq war as an act of peace, to disregard the troubling realities of multiple deployments, and to overlook the reality that, given the experiences of detainees at Guantánamo Bay, it is not U.S. personnel whose safety is most at risk in Cuba.[92]

Yet wives and mothers have also used the site to claim that military families share in the Flight 93 families' sacrifices. One woman wrote, "I was scared to death to have my only 2 sons in Iraq. I would think of the Sept. 11 and all of the other families and somehow draw strength from that."[93] More movingly, Denise Pannell designated the memorial a site at which her family could heal from the war: "In April 2003 [my husband] volunteered for duty in Afghanistan and spent a year away from us. He needed to. And we understood why. . . . We've come here today so my husband can have closure—come full circle, so to speak. I didn't realize I needed it too."[94] Portraying themselves as accepting the reality that men go to war but suffering from those deployments nonetheless, these women locate themselves in a place much like that of Flight 93's widows. They ratify soldiers' innocence by casting them in domestic terms that eschew critiques of the Iraq and Afghanistan wars and by defining them as replicating the decisive—and, in popular culture, decisively male—action aboard Flight 93. Visits to the Flight 93 Memorial are, like visits to the Vietnam Veterans Memorial, efforts to come to terms with the wars' impact on families; however, the therapeutic practices are rescripted to certify those wars as valid and demand recognition of contemporary (male) soldiers.

Visitors have also used practices familiar from the Vietnam Veterans Memorial to shore up support for the Iraq and Afghanistan wars by claiming the Flight 93 Memorial as a de facto memorial to soldiers killed in those wars. The collection contains a funeral program, a prayer card, several photographs of soldiers who have been killed, metal bracelets and magnetic ribbons impressed with soldiers' names, and at least one newspaper clipping from a marine's funeral. The discourse of mothers, wives, and children left behind is prevalent here as well. In October 2005 Sharon Klinger, whose son was killed in Fallujah that summer, makes this equation, asking, "How could we know that our lives would be so *directly* impacted on that fateful day, 9-11-01" and closing with the benediction "God Bless All Who Sacrifice" and the signature "Proud Mom of Our Fallen Hero."[95] This note explicitly establishes her son as a "hero," but she also implicitly links her son to Flight 93's "sacrifice." Similarly, a note reading "Never Forget 9/11 Tsgt. John A. Chapman, USAF-CCT, KIA Afghanistan, March 4, 2002," with a photograph of Chapman's wedding and the handprints of his two daughters recalls the young families of several of the Flight 93 dead and constructs soldiers' deaths as equally devastating.[96]

Such items are, effectively, memorials within a memorial. Remembrances that occur in a location that has, on the most literal level, nothing to do with the deaths of people who died thousands of miles away and probably never visited Shanksville are efforts to make the deaths meaningful by connecting them to Flight 93's legacy as both a tragedy and a moment of heroic intervention.[97] Yet Klinger and others—the parents of a soldier killed in Iraq taking a picture of the item they had brought to send to the soldier's deployed uncle, the father hanging his dead son's unit patch on the memorial fence, the veteran leaving behind a memorial bracelet with his friends' names on it, the military honor guard that held a flag-folding ceremony while on the way home from the funeral of a soldier killed in Iraq, and Chris Bianchi, who left the boots inscribed with his dead friends' names—all demand that the potentially troubling deaths of soldiers in unpopular wars be read as sacrifices equivalent to the always-certain heroic deaths of the Flight 93 passengers and crew.[98] They do so by revising the diverse ways in which visitors to the Wall have remembered the deaths of their loved ones. By making Flight 93's remembrance the context in which combat deaths in Iraq and Afghanistan must be understood and remembered, these objects endeavor to forestall antiwar sentiment, particularly comparisons to Vietnam, by constructing a nation recovered from Vietnam's traumatic failure of patriotism and military tenacity.

Vietnam veterans have themselves been frequent visitors, and, like more recent veterans, they have used the memorial space to assert the sincerity of their patriotism and the nobility of their service. Although Vietnam veterans have been publicly venerated at least since the dedication of the Vietnam Veterans Memorial in 1982, some persist in seeing themselves as being marginalized and outcasts in a society unappreciative of their service and skeptical of their place in the nation. At the dedication of the memorial in 2011, a veteran alluded to such isolation by wearing a T-shirt with the slogan "Never Again Will One Generation of Veterans Abandon Another."[99] The public and defiant declaration of their pride in their service, enduring patriotism, and role as the guardians and arbiters of patriotic orthodoxy remains an ongoing project. The members of the Last Patrol may have made their final march in 1987, but their successors continue their work in new memorial spaces.

The Flight 93 Memorial was a site where Vietnam veterans emphatically undertook this project. Like more recent veterans, they have no direct relation to Flight 93. No one on board the plane served there. And yet Vietnam veterans, above all, it seems, those who are motorcycle enthusiasts, are frequent, conspicuous visitors. They have been active fundraisers as well; a Vietnam veteran who presented a check to the NPS in May 2006 left behind his Purple Heart.[100] The memorial is a regular stop for Rolling Thunder groups—motorcycle enthusiasts active in POW/MIA and veterans' issues—headed to the National Mall each Memorial Day weekend, and at anniversary ceremonies self-identified Vietnam veterans are commonly in attendance (fig. 5.3).[101]

Vietnam veterans have left behind numerous items. One of the first items to arrive after the crash was a funeral bouquet from the Vietnam Veterans of Somerset County.[102] Before the temporary memorial was moved across the

FIGURE 5.3. A Vietnam veteran participates in ceremonies marking the eighth anniversary of the crash of Flight 93 at the Flight 93 National Memorial, Shanksville, Pennsylvania. Vietnam veterans have been frequent visitors to the site and have often asserted that their service paralleled the passengers' and crew's actions. © 2009, Landon Nordeman

street in 2008, a bumper sticker in the form of a Vietnam campaign ribbon adorned the guardrail overlooking the crash site. During a visit I made in August 2007 at least four Vietnam veteran hats, several flags, and other items adorned the memorial fence; some of them remained on Memorial Day weekend in 2010, when I counted nearly three dozen Vietnam and POW/MIA items.

Vietnam veterans at the Flight 93 Memorial have replicated but adapted their engagement with the Wall. While their visits no doubt attest to a sincere desire to honor the dead, they are simultaneously public performances of the veterans' patriotic citizenship and reminders of as well as calls for recognition of their own suffering and sacrifice. Like the Wall, the Flight 93 Memorial in this respect functions as a place of healing; yet these veterans, like their more recent counterparts, have eschewed political debate and deeply personal reflection in favor of a more emphatic embrace of the nation and profession of the nobility of their service. Like recent veterans, those from Vietnam position themselves as observing others' patriotic sacrifices while demanding commensurate acknowledgment for themselves.

These dual efforts are visible in the degree to which the objects left by Vietnam veterans signify on behalf of Flight 93's dead and the veteran alike. A set of Air Medals left in their original box from 1967, for example, is not an ambiguous symbol, nor does it reject the Vietnam veteran's service. That a veteran would choose to leave an award for airborne heroism makes sense, and perhaps, like the man who brought his War on Terrorism medals and a Vietnam veteran who left his Purple Heart, he felt that those aboard Flight 93 were more deserving.[103] Like terrorism medals, however, this medal must denote its intended honor; a meaningless or tainted medal would hardly honor Flight 93's dead. Leaving it enables the veteran to pay his respects while accrediting his own service.

Veterans of Vietnam have occasionally been quite explicit in their efforts to confer on themselves the heroism, patriotism, and citizenship that dominate Flight 93's remembrance. In the spring of 2004 a volunteer ambassador collected a faded blue baseball cap commemorating the attack on Pleiku air base in February 1965, a moment marking the escalation of the war.[104] A hat commemorating Pleiku makes a more precise, more profound statement than, for example, hats that simply declare the wearer to be a Vietnam veteran; it publicly declares one's presence at the war's onset. Moreover, the owner had written on the brim, "God Bless our Brothers and Sisters of Flight 93." Among the many honorifics that visitors accord the dead, "Brothers and Sisters" is rare, and this language speaks not simply of affinity but of shared experience. The hat thereby connects the two events, honoring the dead while demanding some notice of the wearer's analogous experience in "fighting the first battle."

Such a reading might seem strained if other items did not make similar assertions. A note addressed "To those who gave there [*sic*] all" is signed in nearly identical language: "A Viet Nam Brother who also gave as did all my other Brothers of Nam," and a card left in 2003 reads, "For My brother Dick who died in Vietnam. . . . Dick took a bullet in the head for our country. He was a very brave Marine. Thank God for 3 American heroes who stopped the hijacked plane."[105] Like the veterans themselves, the author characterizes Dick as being heroic and his death as patriotic and, by mentioning other accepted heroes, establishes his sacrifice as equivalent to theirs. To Dick's sister, Vietnam was hardly a lost cause. Years later a veteran sent a donation to the memorial campaign along with a note reading, "I wish I could send more, but I am 100% disabled vet from the Vietnam war. So I truly know what kind of guts it took for those people of Flight 93 to do what they did."[106] Through such notes veterans cast Vietnam as being like Flight 93: a noble endeavor defined by patriotic sacrifice.

These notes were likely not seen by many visitors. But other, more visible items have made similar statements. From at least the summer of 2007 on, a license plate that represented a Vietnam service ribbon and read "Flight 93 Firebase" hung from the memorial fence; it was deemed sufficiently distinctive that the NPS reattached it to the fence when the memorial was moved across the road. The license plate, clearly constructed for the memorial, merges a term that alludes to Vietnam's troubling violence and brutality with a location symbolic of undaunted heroism. Like the Last Firebase, a souvenir stand on the National Mall run by Vietnam veteran activists, it defines Vietnam veterans as vigilant patriots who safeguard the nation's treasured memories.[107]

The most visible example of efforts to verify Vietnam veterans' patriotism, however, was a large, red sign that the Vietnam Veterans of America attached to the temporary memorial fence sometime before September 11, 2006. By the time the memorial was dismantled in the summer of 2010, the sign had been seen by more than five hundred thousand visitors.[108] It declares, "Somerset County Chapter 587 Honors the Heroes of Flight 93. 'We Understand,'" a suggestion of shared experience or knowledge that constructs Vietnam veterans and Flight 93's dead as part of an exclusive group (fig. 5.4).

Yet the import of the sign lies precisely in its silence regarding exactly *what* is understood. As Jay Winter has explained, silence is "focused, directed and purposeful" and "always part of the framing of public understandings of war and violence."[109] This particular silence compels the visitor to complete the statement. However, the dominant discourse surrounding Flight 93 limits how it may be completed.[110] That is, a visitor can complete the sentence only in terms already available within Flight 93's remembrance—heroism, honor, service, bravery, sacrifice, and so on. Veterans may be stating that they understand serving their country; perhaps, as draftees, they understand being unexpectedly called on to fight for the nation; perhaps, like the Last Patrol argued at the Alamo, they understand fighting honorably in the face of certain defeat. Regardless, this object, like the others, replicates but alters veterans' interactions with the Wall in order to produce a public statement that affirms Vietnam veterans' heroic patriotism.

FIGURE 5.4. Sign placed on the memorial fence by the Vietnam Veterans of America. One of many items left by Vietnam veterans in honor of Flight 93, the sign asserts an affinity between Vietnam veterans and the passengers and crew that confers on the former the heroism and patriotism afforded the latter. Photograph by the author.

Veterans with more specific activist goals have similarly engaged with the memorial. On July 6, 2003, a visitor asked why the site did not fly the POW/MIA flag, offered to send one to the site, and left a sticker on the memorial's flagpole.[111] The request to fly the flag at the memorial is perhaps not surprising; it is, after all, nearly ubiquitous.[112] This person's request, however, was one of dozens of uses of the memorial by POW/MIA activists. On May, 28, 2010, a T-shirt, three baseball caps, a flag, a wooden plaque from Rolling Thunder Pennsylvania Chapter 7, two challenge coins, and three pins bearing the POW/MIA logo were visible there. The archive holds similar items: flags, pins, caps, bandanas, a coffee mug, T-shirts, name tags, coins, bracelets, silver POW/MIA bracelets, and a poster. At the dedication of the official memorial in 2011, a Rolling Thunder chapter led a flag folding and displayed a painting entitled "The Left Behind," which featured a woman and child grieving over a missing father and husband represented by a silhouette inspired by the POW/MIA flag.

Like other military-themed items, these quite simply cannot refer to the people who died aboard the plane. Being deceased, they are no longer captives; their remains having been identified and returned to their families, they are no longer missing. If they are tributes to the dead, then, these items also transform Flight 93's bodies into signifiers that warrant activists' repeated claims that the government has not fulfilled its obligation to locate and recover the remains of American soldiers missing in Vietnam.[113]

The recovery and identification of fragmented remains are immensely challenging undertakings, combining intense fieldwork with archival research. They must take into account the political difficulties of negotiating with foreign governments, the rugged terrain on which expeditions take place, and the reality that remains are often so fragmented that they are nearly impossible to find and identify.[114] These difficulties, however, have not discouraged activists from maintaining that the government's unwillingness to make the necessary effort accounts for the failure to repatriate veterans' remains.[115] The chief piece of evidence for this failure, Thomas Hawley demonstrates, is "the identification of one body," which "implies that despite the circumstances of loss and the extreme fragmentation of remains, such identifications can be—and will be—made."[116]

The significance of Flight 93 to POW/MIA activists rests partly on this logic; that is, these items identify the painstaking identification of Flight 93's dead as indicative of the possibility of recovering the remains of another group of Americans, those missing in Indochina, and of the government's unstinting failure to do so. Media coverage of the recovery operation after the crash fully documented official attempts to recover, identify, and properly inter bodies that were consistently presented as being absent.[117] A week after the crash, the principal figure in the recovery, the Somerset County coroner Wally Miller, told the *New York Times* that "there was no blood. You couldn't see any human remains. You almost thought the passengers had been dropped off somewhere." Miller later told the *Washington Post* that "about 92 percent of the potential remains were cremated on the impact. The rest was very fragmented."[118]

Recovering these missing bodies nonetheless appeared possible and, more important, essential. The *New York Times* reported that Miller's "heart breaks for families who will not have bodies to bury," and news reports prominently featured both his commitment to finding identifiable remains and his meeting with each family in order to prepare them for viewing them.[119] The unidentifiable remains were interred at the crash site in three caskets during a private ceremony on September 12, 2011.[120] Geographic and political differences aside, a "self-described hick coroner" accomplished in eight months something for which the families of men missing in Indochina have waited decades.[121]

That Shanksville's accounted-for dead have been juxtaposed with the still-missing soldiers of the Vietnam War might be dismissed as a stretch were it not for how extensively POW/MIA activism has been folded into the remembrance of 9/11 in general and Flight 93 in particular. The Veterans of Foreign Wars of Attleboro, Massachusetts, for example, annually holds "POW-MIA 9/11 Remembrance" day. At the ceremony in 2007 the local commander explained that the purpose of the gathering was "to remember the POWs and MIAs and also the 9/11 victims"; another member explained that "between the POWs and 9/11, we should do this all the time. They fought and lost their lives for us. We should be real grateful to them."[122] Quite literally, this ceremony marks not just a conflation of 9/11 remembrance and POW/MIA activism but a nearly complete cooptation of September 11 remembrance; like others who have sought to align veterans with Flight 93's dead, these activists position unrecovered soldiers as akin to those who died in the 9/11 attacks and as deserving of the same recognition. Tellingly, sometime in 2006 a visitor left a POW/MIA Christmas tree ornament from the 2005 ceremonies at the Flight 93 Memorial.[123]

Items like this establish the MIA issue as vital to remembrance at the Flight 93 Memorial. One could not visit the temporary memorial without seeing numerous POW/MIA items, attend an anniversary ceremony without seeing Rolling Thunder activists, or leave the dedication ceremony without passing the flag folding or the painting. Juxtaposing Flight 93's honored and accounted-for bodies with the MIAs' unaccounted-for and forgotten bodies, these items compel visitors to acknowledge the perpetual failure to resolve the MIA issue. Like other veterans, these activists appropriate the memorial on behalf of Vietnam's unresolved trauma while announcing their own patriotism.

This demand for recognition and action can be seen in the phrasing of some of the items left at the memorial. While a good many contain the standard motto, "You Are Not Forgotten," others do not. A T-shirt left in 2006 reads, "I wasn't there but I still care."[124] A hat on the fence in 2010 contained the statement, "Help Bring Them Home." A poster from the National POW/

MIA Remembrance Day, which occurs each September 15, demands that viewers "Honor Their Service" and "Fulfill Their Trust."[125] Until the temporary memorial was moved, visitors viewed the crash site over guardrails adorned with stickers reading, "They Still Wait," "Never Forget," and "If We Don't Care, Who Will?" At the anniversary celebration in 2010, a trio of activists pointedly wore POW/MIA shirts emblazoned with the logo "Let's Never Forget," a slogan that seems to revamp Flight 93's famous slogan, "Let's roll."

The significance of these items lies in their grammatical object. In the most common slogan, "You Are Not Forgotten," *you* refers to the missing; at the memorial, it refers to a public that has apparently forgotten those missing in Indochina while remembering Flight 93's dead. Whereas the person leaving the T-shirt declares the wearer's fulfillment of patriotic obligation, the other items remind visitors of the POW/MIA's continuing absence ("They Still Wait") and command ("Let's Never Forget") or cajole ("If We Don't Care, Who Will?") one into realizing the stark contrast between the POW/MIAs and the passengers and crew, who no longer "wait," who are not "forgotten," and who, it seems, everyone "cares" about. Such items make viewing the site an exercise in remembering the MIAs. In this scenario a strand of Vietnam's cultural memory has been reconfigured and redeployed in ways that co-opt Flight 93's remembrance and apply it to establish the veteran's dignity and the nation's continuing obligation after the trauma of Vietnam.

At the Flight 93 Memorial, contemporary service members and their families, Vietnam veterans, and POW/MIA activists have persistently left items and notes that simultaneously assert their patriotism and legitimate their service or political positions by aligning themselves with Flight 93's dead. More explicitly and directly than at other sites, this process reveals that practices which at the Vietnam Veterans Memorial have been essential to producing diverse, contested public memories have been redrafted and redeployed to produce a narrative that reinstates orthodox patriotism, supports American militarism, defends the Iraq and Afghanistan wars, and seeks to heal Vietnam's ongoing trauma. A similar process of appropriation and reconfiguration would play out in the selection of a design for the permanent memorial.

"It Reminds Me of the Vietnam Veterans Memorial"

The attacks on the winning design for the Flight 93 Memorial began in earnest just a few months after the selection committee made its announcement. The design manifested a culture incapable of giving its heroes their due, critics alleged, and of liberal elitism trampling on customary patriotism. The *American Spectator* railed, "Monuments are not neutral. They take a stand. They recognize virtue and heroism and point out the good guys."[126] In the *Weekly Standard,* Jonathan Last complained, "To those who prefer their monuments to be monumental, this may come as something of a disappointment, if not an outright betrayal. . . . The problem isn't that we've run out of heroes in America. We just don't know how to honor them anymore."[127] An op-ed in the *National Review* echoed Last, grumbling that "we breed heroes, not artists for them."[128]

These statements recall the debate over Maya Lin's design for the Vietnam Veterans Memorial, but they are more recent, emerging after September 2005. That was when the Flight 93 Advisory Commission selected Paul Murdoch's *Crescent of Embrace* from among the more than one thousand entries submitted to the Flight 93 Memorial Design Competition. Murdoch's design features a ninety-three-foot tower filled with forty wind chimes, one for each passenger and crew member, forty groves of red maple trees, and a curved path that follows the plane's final descent along the impact site, now called the sacred ground. The path is bordered by a waist-high black-granite wall into which slots are carved to hold items brought by visitors. The field itself is to be planted with flowers that bloom over the course of the year in shades of red, white, and blue. The path ends in a memorial plaza dominated by a highly polished, twelve-foot-high white marble wall of forty panels, each inscribed with the name of one of the dead.[129]

The most sinister attacks on Murdoch's design came from the conspiracy theorist and conservative blogger Alec Rawls, who claimed the memorial was an "Islamofascist shrine" that paid tribute to the terrorists and their religion by, among other things, secretly being a mosque. Thomas Burnett Sr., whose son died aboard the plane and who served on the design jury, later said the memorial was "riddled with Islamic symbols" and that his son "should not have his name bastardized."[130] The controversy ultimately forced Murdoch to modify his design, but the conspiracy theory has been remarkably resilient.[131]

The Flight 93 Memorial is neither a mosque nor a shrine to Al Qaeda, and Rawls's and Burnett's invective reflect nothing more than an offensive conflation of Islam with terrorism and the racist paranoia that are among the 9/11 attacks' most unfortunate legacies. Murdoch's design, however, had other critics who condemned the design as being too modern and insufficiently patriotic. As Doss notes, "Some Americans expect[ed] its commemoration as a war memorial."[132] If the *National Review* and the *Weekly Standard* recall the timbre of the debate over Lin's design for the Wall, the *American Spectator* was more explicit. In her editorial lambasting *Crescent of Embrace,* Lisa Fabrizio compared it to the Vietnam Veterans Memorial and disinterred the critiques that emerged after Lin's design was announced: "While feelings of pride and patriotism are no less due the brave men and women who served [in Vietnam], the Wall's effect is more sadness or even regret; precisely the emotions the left projects towards our military."[133] Clinton Taylor was even more direct, claiming that beyond insufficiently specific criteria,

> the second antecedent for the furor caused by the Flight 93 Memorial was Maya Lin and her Vietnam War Memorial.
>
> . . . Lin's design might have been a fitting monument for a tragedy—a national disaster or an accident where thousands died without a discernable reason. But the dead of Vietnam were not *victims.* They were *heroes.*
>
> As were the passengers of Flight 93.[134]

These editorials question Sturken's claim that "after Lin's memorial had actually been constructed, the debate about aesthetics and remembrance surrounding its design simply disappeared."[135] Her words may have been true in the eighties and nineties, but not in 2005. To Fabrizio and Taylor, the selection of Murdoch's design confirmed the nation's ongoing failure to appropriately honor its heroes with celebratory monuments, a failure specifically symptomatic of the deeper post-Vietnam loss of the patriotism that the Wall still represented.

Murdoch's design is no more a replica of the Vietnam Veterans Memorial than it is an "Islamofascist shrine," and the process of its creation and selection does not evince an unremitting betrayal of the American spirit by embracing Lin's design. For that matter, Lin's design was hardly a betrayal either. Rather, the Flight 93 National Memorial and the competition in which it was selected reveal a more complex effort to negotiate the legacy of the Vietnam Veterans Memorial. As at the temporary memorial, a variety of stakeholders—memorial designers, the NPS, the committees tasked with evaluating the entries, and the broader public—persistently recalled and adapted the Wall's design elements and affective appeal as they approached the problem of memorializing Flight 93.

The Flight 93 Memorial design competition, then, reveals the continuing debate over the Vietnam Veterans Memorial's place in American culture. Public comments frequently referred to the Wall as a model to be either embraced or rejected, while many entries, including the winning one, sought to marry modern aesthetics and memorial practices with traditional patriotic symbols and memorial elements. They revised elements of Lin's design in ways that enabled visitors to have an analogous interactive experience but that forestalled challenges to the discourse of heroism and appropriate citizenship that dominates Flight 93's remembrance. The competition evinced efforts to overcome the rupture to traditional patriotic memorialization that Lin's design represented while encompassing the elements that made it so wildly popular.

REP. BARBARA CUBIN'S (R-WY) COMMENT THAT "THIS SITE IS SO CLEARLY nationally significant and important to contemporary America that recognition now is totally appropriate" met with nearly unanimous consent when the Flight 93 National Memorial Act came to the floor of the House on July 22, 2002.[136] The consensus ended there. Stakeholders who submitted and debated memorial designs found the choice of an appropriate memorial a daunting, politicized task. Yet these groups had a common touchstone from which their opinions about memorialization sprang: the Vietnam Veterans Memorial.

In 2004 the NPS conducted a survey of visitors at the temporary memorial, visitors to its website, local residents, and family members about their hopes for a permanent memorial.[137] Among the responses, the Vietnam Veterans Memorial is referred to more frequently than any other memorial as respondents' reference point with regard to what a memorial should or shouldn't look like and the experience it should or shouldn't provide. Some visitors reiterated one respondent's desire for "a similar experience as that of the Vietnam War Memorial in Wash. D.C. A silent, beautiful yet somber structure that states the names of the passengers and has an impact that is unforgettable—even if you are not directly connected to the people on the memorial."[138] Others hoped the permanent memorial would be simple, include only a list of names or perhaps photographs, and afford an opportunity to leave objects.[139]

If these comments speak to the Wall's lasting popularity, others revealed lingering misgivings about its design. Asked to name their "biggest fear or concern" about the permanent memorial, several respondents worried that it would look like the Wall.[140] Others argued that the memorial design should promote traditional, conservative values: "My biggest fear concerning the creation of this new memorial is that it will become something completely abstract or conceptual, devoid of anything human, angelic, or scriptural (reflecting the emptiness that seems to characterize this age) and this for fear of appearing unsophisticated, too narrow or traditional, or 'offensive' to small special interest groups . . . not those of the citizens of this country."[141] This respondent's sentiments recall arguments over the Wall and seek to erase them through a return to more representational art. Other respondents recited this view in calling on the NPS to not "let political correctness and liberal multi-culturalism ruin this memorial as it has so many other memorials" and by commenting that visitors "should not go away with a feeling of disappointment in the memorial and its meanings (As in other memorials)."[142] A visitor to the website specified that "no anti-American traitors [should be] allowed" and added, presumably for clarification, "(Jane Fonda)," a reference to the actor's controversial anti-Vietnam war activism[143] Together, these responses present a culture still struggling with the legacy of Lin's design, on the one hand desiring to replicate the Wall's celebrated capacity for visitors' personal response and on the other remaining anxious about the Wall's reputation as the product of a defeatist, valueless culture.

The competition entrants were not privy to these remarks. Nonetheless, many entries reflect the prevalence of this discourse and make a concerted attempt to negotiate the complicated space occupied by the Vietnam Veterans Memorial in American culture. The Flight 93 Memorial Task Force, composed of local representatives, government officials, family members, and professional historians and architects, announced the memorial design competition on September 11, 2004, and by January 11, 2005, as noted, over one thousand entries had been received.[144] Registrants had little guidance: a slender spiral-bound book of brief guidelines, a set of maps, and the memorial's mission statement. The guidelines are intentionally vague about what the "memorial expression" should look like, stipulating that it "may range from an individual piece of art to larger treatments of the landscape."[145]

Officially, the NPS has endeavored to avoid explicitly political rhetoric, crafting instead a mission statement that declared the memorial to be a space in which visitors can "reflect on the power of individuals who choose to make a difference."[146] That is not, however, a rejection of ideas of heroism; the NPS did require entries to provide a "seamless flow of perception and information that ultimately focuses on the crash site and the extraordinary acts of the passengers and crew of Flight 93," and the accompanying video encourages designs that evoke "a theme of courage, of sacrifice, and ultimately of heroism."[147] To its credit, the NPS has tried to convey that heroism is not linked to specific kinds of nationalist discourses.

Yet in spite of the regulations' openness and the NPS's efforts, many entries participate in the discourse I have referred to throughout this chapter, and many attempt to do so by negotiating the complicated history of the Vietnam Veterans Memorial. The sheer number and diversity of the entries make the design competition impossible to fully analyze here. The entries range from the traditional (cenotaphs and arches) to the modern (multicolored beams of light or jagged glass sculptures) and from the explicitly patriotic, for example, those that include eagles and American flags, to simple treatments that focus on the individual dead. Some are quite elegant, others are not.[148]

Many entries explicitly promote the language of interventionist citizenship in rhetoric familiar from Flight 93's broader discourse. One design "protects us with the freedom, patriotism, and sacrifice that each member of Flight 93 contributed in that first battle against terrorism."[149] Others claim that "a nation was reborn with patriotism and pride through the courageous loss of life," that the passengers and crew "acted as Americans should" and "remind us of the bravery and selflessness it is to be an American," or that "like those brave passengers on Flight 93, it is for each one of us to defend and protect the ideals our nation represents."[150]

I am most interested, however, in tracing how the designers have contributed to the popular discourse that surrounds Flight 93 by adapting the design elements of the Vietnam Veterans Memorial. Memorial designs often draw on, incorporate, and respond to the elements of other memorials, and the Wall perhaps more than any other memorial has defined the past three decades of American memorial practice.[151] Many entries in the Flight 93 competition, however, exhibit more than a bald acceptance or rejection of the Wall and instead both appropriate and redraft elements that, as many scholars have noted, are central to the memorial's ambiguity about the war and the dead and its demand that visitors perform such interpretive work individually.[152]

Designers repeatedly employed reflective surfaces, listing of names, and the historical narration of the event in ways that recall the Vietnam Veterans Memorial but that subvert the potential those elements have for challenging the blending of the passengers' and crew's heroism with a broader rhetoric of interventionism.[153] The entries allow visitors to personally engage with the event while at the same time circumscribing those interactions and remembrances within a narrative of orthodox patriotism and citizenship. Many entries thereby seek to resolve the profound rending of orthodox discourses of patriotic citizenship that the Vietnam War and the "counter-memorial" design of the Vietnam Veterans Memorial still represent.[154]

The entrants' ventures at rescripting the elements of the Vietnam Veterans Memorial are visible in their handling of its defining features. The most noted aspect of Lin's design, the chronological listing of names, is fundamental to the production of these diverse responses because, as Sturken has shown, they "could be seen as alternately subverting, rescripting, and contributing to the history of the Vietnam War as it is being written."[155] While the listing of the names may take on countless meanings, the one reality that the Wall assiduously enforces is that they are the names of people who have died; they are in fact, Sturken asserts, "surrogates for the bodies" themselves.[156]

The naming of the dead at the Flight 93 Memorial reflects but rewrites this logic. After "exhibits about the day's events," "the crash site" itself, and the "tributes that have been left at the temporary memorial," a "wall or plaque with a list of names" was the most frequently mentioned specific feature that respondents hoped would be included at the permanent memorial, although one respondent feared that "it will look like a big marble, cold tombstone"—that is, like the Vietnam Veterans Memorial.[157] Designers were similarly divided; a great many projected a wall inscribed with a list of names, but others apparently agreed with one entrant who specified, "The heroes of Flight 93 deserve better than anonymous names carved into cold stone."[158]

Among the designs that include name walls are several that dictate how those names should be interpreted, ranging from defining the space as a "wall of honor" or a "wall of courage" to more emphatic statements about the dead and the event.[159] Submissions propose that "the names of the forty heroes will be etched . . . along with a statement about how ordinary Americans looked death in the eye and did the right thing"; listing the names under "the powerful and now immortal words 'Let's Roll' "; and adding to a name wall a quote from George W. Bush about the September 11 attacks.[160] Such descriptions aim to circumscribe visitors' affective and ideological responses within the boundaries of established patriotism that at least implicitly endorses aggressive militarism in response to terrorism.

Naming is not the only way in which elements that, at the Wall, are ambiguous or potentially subversive are reclaimed as patriotic signifiers. While at the Wall, as Sturken argues, reflective surfaces are the key means through which visitors "are implicated in the listing of the dead," such elements in the Shanksville competition often propose to align visitors with the dead and, by extension, with the narrative of appropriate citizenship on behalf of which they have been invoked.[161] In a design called "Walking Among Heroes," a reflective surface "[allows] visitors to see themselves in the heroes."[162] In another entry, visitors looking at a reflective wall into which portraits of those who died on the plane are carved in relief would "see themselves in the visage of the passengers and crew."[163] Such designs do not "implicate" but indoctrinate, and accountability here does not mean responsibility *for* the dead but responsibility to *be like* the dead. Asking visitors to "see themselves in the heroes" is asking them to have an ideological experience as well as a visual one. Superimposing the visitor's body on the heroic body, these designs function as a didactic space in which visitors are encouraged to identify with the passengers and crew and imagine themselves as embodying the same traits.

Designs that create a narrative of the event are similarly didactic, exchanging what Sturken has called a "chronology of . . . bodies destroyed" for paths that follow the trajectory of the flight and thereby invite visitors to imagine themselves as having been aboard the plane.[164] Yet designers who specified the emotions they imagined for visitors did not name shared suffering and sometimes named political sentiments. Following one design's chronological path, visitors "realize that they are . . . citizens who could one day be called upon to choose a path of heroism and sacrifice."[165] *Disturbed Harmony*, one of the five finalists, reconstructed the flight path as a "bravery trail" that ends in a "circle of heroism."[166] Both memorials explicitly instruct the visitor in how to characterize the dead, and both, one somewhat more implicitly than the other, force the visitor to adopt the ideology that has been attributed to the passengers and crew.

These revisions of the defining elements of the Vietnam Veterans Memorial would shape the meanings that the practice for which the Wall is perhaps best known—the leaving of objects by visitors—would take on. Objects left at such memorials would either become tributes, to use the NPS's favored term, that would be subsumed into the ascendant narrative or lose their iterative power.[167] Although the designers were asked to consider how visitors might leave objects, several entries effectively delimit the meaning of items left at the memorial, once again neither fully enveloping nor rejecting an aspect of Vietnam's legacy. Many designs incorporate objects belonging to the deceased within the official memorial, a practice that creates a hierarchy of objects that would diminish those left by visitors; others restrict the portions of the memorial at which items may be left or specify that only family members and friends will be able to leave objects at the memorial itself. One such entry imagines an engraved portrait of each passenger with a "small tube to hold any flowers or flags that the families may like to leave" while "visitors will be allowed to attach items to the fence of remembrance."[168] This entry reveals an anxiety over the challenge that objects might pose to the dominant narratives, trusting family members to mourn in an appropriately patriotic manner and wary of other visitors' potentially subversive "other items." Like the reappropriation of memorial elements and strategies that dominates the Vietnam Veterans Memorial, designers' handling of the memorial's interactive potential demonstrates an attempt to revise practices of Vietnam's remembrance in order to bolster the dominant cultural memory that equates Flight 93's dead with patriotism, sacrifice, and militarism.

In February 2005 the Flight 93 Memorial Commission's Stage I jury announced the five finalists for the expanded Stage II competition. As they had done in Stage I, they invited the public to view the designs at a Somerset County shopping center. Among the finalists, Leor and Gilat Lovinger's *Disturbed Harmony* and the eventual winner, Murdoch's *Crescent of Embrace*, were clear favorites, and visitors' comments continued to show efforts to negotiate the Vietnam Veterans Memorial's complicated impact on American culture. The Lovingers' design, which featured a two-and-a-half-mile-long stone "bravery wall" into which a timeline of the events had been carved, was favorably and unfavorably compared with the Vietnam Veterans Memorial. When it had been initially displayed, visitors remarked, "I really enjoy the Bravery Wall, it's almost like the Vietnam Wall. Great idea!" and another said, "It reminds me of the Vietnam Wall in DC. The simplicity appeals to me."[169] That similarity was "too much" for another respondent, however, who felt that "this site deserves something more unique."[170] Another called the bravery wall not derivative but insufficient: "To me, a 'wall' was a great idea to honor those who served and perhaps died or were injured in Vietnam. However, as elaborate as the five finalists are, I fail to see a national conscience of grieving, thankfulness, honor, and vengeance appropriate for such a national loss."[171] Even in the competition's final stage, Americans read the choices through their view of the Vietnam Veterans Memorial, whether as a model memorial or one insufficient to the task of cultivating appropriate attitudes about the September 11 attacks.

Only one visitor compared Murdoch's design to the Wall, but she did so favorably, calling herself "an ardent admirer" of Lin's design and declaring herself "convinced that this plan will be both enormously respectful of the 'victims' while imparting a sense of reverence to any visitors."[172] In many ways, the Flight 93 Memorial Commission succeeded in choosing a design that enables an individuated response and resists the direct inclusion of the primary narrative and its attendant ideology. Yet the Flight 93 National Memorial should be analyzed within the discourse of appropriation and reconfiguration that I have discussed throughout this section. Far from demonstrating modernism's victory over the traditional and representational and thus over the patriotic and monumental, Murdoch's design models the wider competition's struggle to activate the popular elements and tropes of the Vietnam Veterans Memorial without challenging the dead's affirmation as heroic, patriotic citizens.[173]

The planned 93-foot "Tower of Voices," which Murdoch described as "heroically mark[ing] [his] entry," exemplifies this tension.[174] The symbolism of its height is obvious, yet the tower avoids the blatant patriotism of the 1,776-foot-tall One World Trade Center in New York.[175] The wind chimes, inspired by "the fact that for many of the families, the last memory they have of their loved ones is hearing their voices on cell phones just minutes before the plane crashed," restyle the design of the Vietnam Veterans Memorial by returning to a more traditional design and offering a more tangible synecdoche for the body.[176] And while each wind chime's unique pitch acknowledges individual loss, the memorial obscures traumatic death at the same moment it presents it, subsumes the individual into a collective just as he or she is acknowledged. Individuals can never be associated with particular chimes, and no chime will ever sound alone. As a result, the "Tower of Voices" memorializes not the individual lives lost but the paramount memory of collective action.

The tower is a return to symbolic memorialization, but Murdoch's treatment of the sacred ground itself also subtly enforces a narrative of patriotic heroism by revising elements of Lin's design. To approach the memorial plaza, a visitor follows the flight path along a granite walkway flanked on the left by a black, waist-high granite wall that separates the viewer from the impact site. Niches in the wall furnish spaces in which visitors may leave objects. Murdoch's intent was to create "a more elegant place for them to be left so that others could easily see them."[177] The spaces accomplish that, but they also locate "vernacular" memorial expressions some distance from the memorial wall.[178] That the field of honor "is planted . . . White Crocus, blooming white in Spring and Fall, Camassia, that blooms blue during Memorial Day, Resurrection Flower, that blooms white or red in late Summer and Fall; and the perennials Rudbeckia, which blooms yellow-orange in September, and Indian Blanket Flower, blooming red in Summer" means that the remains of the deceased will be perennially covered in patriotic hues that not only subtly evoke the flag-draped caskets of patriotic casualties but also reinforce the extant narrative of the deaths as patriotic sacrifices and the dead as "citizen-soldiers."[179]

The memorial plaza itself most significantly comprehends but revises the Vietnam Veterans Memorial. The memorial consists of forty twelve-foot-high, highly polished white marble slabs. Slightly offset from one another in an accordion-like design, each slab is engraved with the name of one of the dead, creating a memorial that is simultaneously individual and collective. As at the nadir of Lin's wall, the visitor is overwhelmed by the scale of the panels, and by coming close enough to read them, she sees her reflection.[180] Yet the visitor confronts not the mass of names but each name in turn, and the memorial's white granite walls emphatically reverse the logic of Lin's black one. Like the Wall, the plaza "asks for a personal, thoughtful response," but not one that can challenge Flight 93's fixed narrative.[181]

It is not surprising that the first visitors at the memorial plaza acted in ways familiar from the Vietnam Veterans Memorial; they took rubbings, they touched the wall, they left wreaths, flowers, notes, and photographs at its base. Many items were explicitly patriotic: a picture of wreaths adorning tombstones at Arlington National Cemetery was attached to a wreath at Tom Burnett's panel; a floral bouquet wrapped in star-spangled cellophane lay in front of Donald Greene's. Clutching an American flag, Mark Bingham's

FIGURE 5.5. Detail of the Flight 93 National Memorial, September 11, 2011. Paul Murdoch's design recalls but revises popular elements of Maya Lin's Vietnam Veterans Memorial, including the color, the use of reflective surfaces, the overwhelming size of the panels, and the naming of the dead. In so doing, the memorial encourages personal reflections, but, as the patriotic items left at its base indicate, visitors have continued to construct narratives of traditional patriotism at the site. Photograph by the author.

mother gave interviews to the local media in front of her son's panel. More diverse items were sequestered in the niches along the low wall—patches from military units, more flags, and a plaque from the Ninth Airlift Squadron among them, but also a jar festooned with peace signs and a pink stuffed bunny (figs. 5.5, 5.6).

The NPS's desire to build a memorial not denotative of a specific patriotic narrative was, at least initially, overwhelmed by visitors' articulation of that narrative through memorial practices adapted from the Vietnam Veterans Memorial. In part, though, these actions have been facilitated by a memorial design that negotiates the tensions between the popularity of the Vietnam Veterans Memorial and the disruptive narratives it has enabled in ways that subtly privilege that patriotic rhetoric. The Flight 93 Memorial, perhaps even more than the World War II Memorial, represents how Americans have responded to and altered the impact of the Wall on American memorial practice.[182] All of the elements that made Lin's design compelling, moving, and popular are reproduced in Murdoch's compelling, moving, and, one hopes, popular design; however, the design elements that enable difficult and diverse questions about the nation and the meaning of American deaths have been rewritten in a memorial design that, while solemn, preserves Flight 93's mobilization on behalf of received versions of patriotism.

For more than a decade the Flight 93 Temporary Memorial was a site at which visitors and memorial planners have arrogated and reconfigured the design elements and memorial practices that have defined the Vietnam Veterans Memorial to craft a story in which Flight 93's victims represent a nation defined by its support for resurgent patriotism and interventionist militarism. Popular culture and political rhetoric about the crash rallied post-Vietnam discourses of recuperated masculinity to define the passengers as idealized interventionist citizens, ordinary men and women physically and ideologically committed to carrying out the dictates of the Bush doctrine. This ethos, in turn, shaped visitors' engagement with the temporary memorial. Although it is one of countless sites at which objects left by visitors have been central to public remembrance, the Flight 93 Temporary Memorial took on special meaning for veterans of Iraq, Afghanistan, and Vietnam, all of whom revised the logic of public memory at the Vietnam Veterans Memorial to align themselves with the dead and, in so doing, asserted their patriotism and the

FIGURE 5.6. A visitor takes a rubbing of the passenger Lauren Catuzzi Grandcolas's panel at the opening of the Flight 93 National Memorial, September 11, 2011. Visitors immediately interacted with the memorial in ways that replicate practices familiar from the Vietnam Veterans Memorial. Photograph by the author.

nobility of their service. In the permanent memorial design competition, entrants frequently revised both the formal elements and the visitor opportunities of Lin's design in ways that enforce Flight 93's dominant narrative while encouraging visitors to embrace the ideology on behalf of which it has been invoked. Paul Murdoch's memorial, though highly measured, also reworks elements of the Vietnam Veterans Memorial in ways that facilitate Americans' embrace of the narrative that surrounds Flight 93.

These uses reveal neither the uncomplicated acceptance nor the unequivocal rejection of the Vietnam Veterans Memorial, which remains too popular to disown and too controversial to fully embrace. Rather, the range of ways in which Flight 93 has been remembered demonstrates the continuing negotiation of Vietnam's problematic location in American memory and, more crucially, the extent to which debate over that war's meaning and legacy during the global war on terror has been silenced in favor of discourses that conflate patriotism with interventionist adventurism. As the global war on terror continued, veterans of the wars in Iraq and Afghanistan would likewise adopt this practice as they told their stories.

CHAPTER 6

"THE LESSONS OF HISTORY"

Vietnam's Legacy during the Wars in Iraq and Afghanistan

ON SEPTEMBER 28, 2007, BRUCE SPRINGSTEEN AND HIS E-STREET BAND appeared on NBC's *Today* show to promote their latest album, *Magic.* Toward the end of his set Springsteen launched into "Last to Die," a symphonic, minor-chord critique of the Iraq war. Before a jubilant crowd seemingly unaware of the song's angry politics, Springsteen banged away on his Telecaster, snarling, "We don't measure the blood we've drawn anymore. / We just stack the bodies outside the door" before launching into the chorus: "Who'll be the last to die for a mistake?"[1]

Earlier in the song Springsteen attributes this question to a "familiar voice from long ago." That voice was John Kerry's, the Vietnam veteran and antiwar activist and the Democratic presidential nominee in 2004, who had famously asked this question about the Vietnam War in 1971. Senator Kerry (D-MA) himself had recited the phrase two months earlier during a Senate debate over the Bush administration's Iraq war policies, saying to his colleagues, "I never thought that I would be reliving the need to ask that question again."[2] Kerry's reference, and Springsteen's musical riff on it, came at a nadir of support for the war. Six weeks earlier nearly six in ten Americans had said they thought the war was a mistake.[3] Audience members perusing the *New York Times* as they waited for Springsteen's performance that day would have learned that another serviceman had died, that employees of the contracting firm

Blackwater had perpetrated dozens of shootings in the past nine months, and that members of an army sniper platoon being court-martialed for murdering civilians had testified that they had been "pushed beyond limits by battalion commanders eager to raise their kill ratio against a ruthless enemy," a logic that chillingly recalled that of the Vietnam War's body count.[4]

The wars waged by the United States in Afghanistan and Iraq represent the most significant events in post-Vietnam U.S. foreign policy. Americans increasingly compared the wars to the one in Vietnam as they deteriorated into seemingly intractable conflicts marred by poor decision making, unreliable allies, public corruption, and, in the case of Iraq, deceit.[5] But as we have seen throughout this book, Vietnam was not simply a convenient metaphor; rather, Americans have insistently looked to competing narratives of Vietnam's remembrance for the language and tropes through which they could voice opposition or support to the wars and the policies that enabled them.

I want to examine here Americans' competing uses of Vietnam during the period between the Bush administration's troop surge of 2007 in Iraq and the Obama administration's escalation of the Afghanistan war in 2009. I look at two sets of cultural products: the political rhetoric and media coverage that criticized the widening of the wars and memoirs by Iraq and Afghanistan veterans that appeared in their midst. I begin by exploring how, at a moment when public dissent was often seen as unpatriotic, pundits' and politicians' resistance to expanded wars in Afghanistan and Iraq relied on their invocation of deeply patriotic Americans who were critics of the Vietnam War, including Martin Luther King Jr., Robert F. Kennedy, and career military officers, as voices of principled opposition whose example contemporary legislators were morally and politically obligated to follow.

Memoirists of Iraq and Afghanistan, however, did not share in this critique. The three memoirs I analyze below—Nathaniel Fick's *One Bullet Away: The Making of a Marine Officer* (2005), Donovan Campbell's *Joker One: A Marine Platoon's Story of Courage, Leadership, and Brotherhood* (2009), and Craig Mullaney's *The Unforgiving Minute: A Soldier's Education* (2009)—have greatly influenced the emerging remembrance of the two conflicts. They have been widely reviewed and read, and their authors have emerged as public figures. Yet despite being deeply indebted to their predecessors from the Vietnam era, they do not draw on critical representations of Vietnam to censure the Iraq and Afghanistan wars.[6]

Instead, the memoirists recall but revise the tropes and language of Philip Caputo's *A Rumor of War* and Tim O'Brien's *If I Die in a Combat Zone* to describe the contemporary volunteer's motivations and experiences as determinedly unlike those that dominate Vietnam's legacy.[7] They buttress exceptionalist narratives about U.S. militarism threatened by increasing uncertainty about the wars' troubling violence by undermining comparisons between the recent wars and Vietnam. They obscure critical questions about the violence of the Iraq and Afghanistan wars, celebrate the soldier, and refuse to denounce the wars or the policies that enabled them. Together, these competing narratives reveal that if Vietnam was a frequent referent during the first decade of the twenty-first century, it was a contested one, and that Americans mobilized its remembrance in competing ways as they confronted two protracted wars.

"We Must Apply the Lessons of History"

By the time President Bush announced his decision to commit an additional thirty thousand U.S. troops to Iraq in what would become known as the troop surge, comparisons of that conflict to the Vietnam War, having gone beyond commonplace, were approaching common sense.[8] Comparisons between the wars had begun even before the United States invaded Iraq, and years of brutal combat combined with a growing realization that the justification for the war had been manufactured gave the comparison more credibility. Scandals like the one at Abu Ghraib prison, at which American troops had photographed their torture of Iraqi detainees, and the massacre of civilians at Haditha, both of which were likened to the My Lai massacre, furthered the similarities.[9] By 2007 left-leaning websites sold bumper stickers and other items that derisively asked, "Is It Vietnam Yet?"

But opponents of the war were not the only ones thinking about Vietnam's legacy. The surge itself, in fact, was largely the product of military thinkers whose embrace of a counterinsurgency strategy, David Fitzgerald has shown, stemmed from their "attempt to create a new narrative of Vietnam" as a war that "had something to say about Iraq, not only in terms of the decision to intervene and the mistakes made, but in terms of how to fight the War on the ground."[10] The thesis that the United States had failed in Vietnam because it had not practiced counterinsurgency was voiced in numerous ways. As Gian Gentile, an army colonel who was a prominent critic of the doctrine, put it, "The counterinsurgency narrative as it would later emerge in Iraq and Afghanistan was born with the if-only histories of the Vietnam War. Arguments of the hearts-and-minds, if-only school resonated deeply in the ranks of some American Army officers and would come to fruition in the writing of FM 3-24," the army's counterinsurgency handbook.[11] For example, Vietnam is frequently mentioned in the Field Manual on Counterinsurgency of 2006. A contributor to the manual, Lt. Col. John Nagl published a book titled *Learning to Eat Soup With a Knife: Counterinsurgency Lessons from Malaya and Vietnam*, which the *Christian Science Monitor* said in 2007 was "the counterinsurgency book that's on every war commander's desk in Baghdad." Nagl concluded that "the U.S. Army has failed to form a consensus on the lessons of Vietnam and has not accepted the idea that revolutionary war requires a qualitatively different response from the conventional warfare it knows so well how to fight."[12] The influence of thinking like this was also apparent in the speech Bush gave announcing the surge. Declaring that "this time, we will have the force levels we need to hold the areas that have been cleared," Bush alluded to the thinking of scholars and military planners who were convinced that Gen. Creighton Abrams's clear-and-hold strategy had won the war in Vietnam or could have won it had it been applied earlier.[13]

That Bush did not actually mention Vietnam in the speech hardly mattered. In the days that followed, the withering criticism of the surge referred to Vietnam repeatedly. An editorial in the *Washington Post* lamented, "It no longer seems possible to avoid the grim conclusion: For the United States, Iraq has become another Vietnam."[14] Another editorial opened with the suggestion "Iraq is not Vietnam" but went on to say it was in fact worse.[15] When Secretary of State Condoleezza Rice testified before the Senate Foreign Relations Committee that week, Sen. Chuck Hagel (R-NE) condemned the surge as "the most dangerous foreign policy blunder in this country since Vietnam."[16] To Hagel and the *Post*'s editorial board, withdrawal seemed the only viable path.

Such critiques continued the sort of broad invocation that had long marked antiwar sentiment. Other congressmen and editorialists, however, reached for more specific references, positing the surge as akin to Johnson's and Nixon's escalations of the war. As they spoke against it, threatened to block its funding, and introduced legislation calling for an immediate withdrawal, these legislators aligned themselves with liberals from lesser-known and potentially forgotten political figures such as Ernest Gruening, Mike Mansfield, and George McGovern to the still-venerated Robert F. Kennedy and Martin Luther King Jr. Such allusions were a hedge against charges that opposition to the war was unpatriotic. By invoking respected men who had either been consistently against the war or had finally voiced their opposition, antiwar legislators in 2007 replaced remembrances of a disruptive, anti-establishment anti-Vietnam movement with one composed of figures whose stature was beyond reproach and whose position on Vietnam had been vindicated. In identifying themselves with such predecessors, opponents asserted that in contesting the surge they were morally justified and in keeping with the nation's best traditions.

THE MORNING AFTER BUSH'S SPEECH, THE NEWLY ELECTED CONGRESSMAN Keith Ellison (D-MN) said in his very first floor speech, "We are going to stand up with courage, just like Martin Luther King did" and demand "withdraw[al] from Iraq."[17] Ellison's reference was to a sermon titled "A Time to Break the Silence" that King delivered in 1967 at Riverside Church in New York City, in which he said, "In order to atone for our sins and errors in Vietnam, we should take the initiative in bringing a halt to this tragic war."[18] The speech, though widely criticized at the time, has since been remembered as one of King's most important.[19] As Mitchell K. Hall explains, "Though not by itself responsible for turning around public opinion, [the Riverside sermon] added respectability to the movement and helped to legitimize dissent against the war."[20] Michael Eric Dyson adds that King's earlier opposition to the war came "before such criticism was fashionable among liberals and long before it was viewed as a reasonable position that a true patriot might adopt"; with the speech, his "exemplary bravery marked him as the most controversial and visible figure in America to oppose the Vietnam War."[21] By mentioning King, Ellison made his point clear: liberals who had long acquiesced to the war now had a moral obligation to speak out.

Ellison was heeding the instructions of the newly elected Speaker Nancy Pelosi (D-CA), who a day earlier had encouraged the new Democratic majority to embrace King's anti-Vietnam rhetoric in opposing the escalation.[22] It was, as Sheila Jackson-Lee (D-GA) put it a few minutes after Ellison spoke, "a Martin Luther King Moment."[23] References to King's opposition to Vietnam and particularly to his Riverside Church address, dominated the subsequent King holiday. The Democratic presidential candidate John Edwards paraphrased King in his own antiwar speech at Riverside.[24] Peace in Iraq was the theme of a King Day parade in Washington, and memorial services in Norfolk, Seattle, and Brunswick, Florida, included readings of the speech.[25]

The *Washington Post* exhorted its readers to "Remember King and the words: 'A time comes when silence is betrayal.'"[26] The *Minneapolis Star-Tribune* maintained that "it is fair to speculate that, were he alive today, King would be leading those opposing President Bush's plan . . . much in the same way that he spoke out against the Vietnam War."[27] Readers in New York, Atlanta, Chicago, and at least eleven other cities encountered similar words.[28]

If, as the historian Julian Zelizer has argued, "the Democratic takeover of Congress in 2006 changed the terms of public debate over Iraq, shifting discussion toward the need for an exit strategy," that debate turned in January 2007 as the antiwar sentiments of the most widely respected American of the twentieth century were expressed anew. King was a practically unassailable figure remembered for having encouraged Americans to aspire to the nation's highest ideals.[29] This was a critical strategic choice during a war in which patriotism had seemingly required unflinching support for the Iraq war and during which the president had dismissed comparisons to Vietnam as hurting the war effort.[30] Invoking King removed the stigma of opposition and defined the newly empowered Democrats' opposition as a courageous act with the force of history behind it; claiming that their opposition was moral rather than strictly political and that acquiescent silence had become inexcusable, Democrats insulated themselves from charges that they were insufficiently patriotic and established their dissent as reflecting the nation's best traditions.

MARTIN LUTHER KING DAY IN 2007 WAS THE MOST VISIBLE OPPORTUNITY the surge's critics had in which to highlight a history of moral opposition to misbegotten wars, but it was not the only one. In the succeeding months, references to anti-Vietnam legislators punctuated debates over defunding the surge and troop withdrawal. To members of Congress, these references served a purpose similar to the more public invocation of King; namely, they reminded legislators that some of Congress's finest moments, and the actions of some of its most venerated members, had been efforts to stop an unjust, failing war.

The references were as numerous as they were diverse. Days after Bush's speech, Sen. Dick Durbin (D-IL) referred to the famous advice given by a senator that the United States ought to "declare victory and start bringing our troops home" by announcing, "The only way to convince the Iraqis of their responsibility is for us to start bringing the American troops home, as Senator [George] Aiken called for in Vietnam in 1966."[31] A week later Sen. Robert Byrd (D-WV) opposed the surge by quoting Sen. Wayne Morse's (D-OR) prophecy in 1965 that the Senate would regret supporting the Tonkin Gulf Resolution, which authorized the president to employ military force in Indochina.[32] In the House, Rep. Jim McDermott (D-WA) said, "We must apply the lessons of history in this Congress," quoted Sen. George McGovern (D-SD), and announced plans to craft legislation similar to the McGovern-Hatfield amendment, an effort made in 1970 to legislate removal of U.S. troops from Vietnam.[33] A month later, he read the original amendment and McGovern's speech, introducing it into the *Congressional Record*.[34] The newly arrived senator Jon Tester (D-MT) quoted the 1972 assessment of Mike Mansfield, the former majority leader and a fellow Montanan and Democrat, that "admitting a mistake is the first step in correcting it."[35] In the House, Rep. Patrick Kennedy (D-RI) reminded the chamber that "my uncle [Robert Kennedy] said a generation ago: If we examine the history of the conflict. . . . Every time, we have been assured that this one last step would bring victory" but that the war continued for another five years.[36] Rep. Ike Skelton (R-MO) also adverted to Bobby Kennedy three days later, as did Sen. Robert Menendez (D-NJ) in July, mentioning Kennedy twice in six days.[37]

George Aiken, Wayne Morse, and Mike Mansfield were hardly household names in 2007. But they were names that mattered within the history- and tradition-conscious Senate, for they were among the men who, as Zelizer points out, "popularized antiwar arguments among middle-class Americans and the media, threatened and cajoled the president, and gradually circumscribed the political options that were available to Richard Nixon as he started his first term."[38] In referring to them, antiwar liberals embraced the Iraq-is-another-Vietnam comparison, but did so as a call to action. In 2007, amid the failing Iraq war, anti-Vietnam legislators' demands for withdrawal became a model of courage in the Congress.

"Drawing the Wrong Lesson from History"

Six months after the surge began, only one-third of Americans believed it was working, while two-thirds felt that the continued sacrifice of American lives was unwarranted.[39] But when President Bush stepped to the podium at the Veterans of Foreign Wars convention in Kansas City on August 22, 2007, and acknowledged potential similarities to Vietnam, he hardly caved into his critics. Rather, as John Prados aptly puts it, the president "began using analogy to Vietnam to explain why the Iraq War needed to be continued."[40] In a passage for which the speech would become infamous, Bush embraced the revisionist perspective of the sort long advanced by conservative and neoconservative scholars and pundits who condemn the withdrawal in 1973 and the subsequent failure to support the regime of the South Vietnamese president, Nguyen Van Thieu. Withdrawal by the United States, Bush claimed, had precipitated untold human suffering, and withdrawing from Iraq portended the same fate.[41]

Bush's comparison backfired. Within hours Senator Kerry called the comparison "as irresponsible as it is ignorant of the realities of both of those wars." He declared that the only valid comparisons were that "as in Vietnam, we engaged militarily in Iraq based on official deception" and that "more American soldiers are being sent to fight and die in a civil war we can't stop and an insurgency we can't bomb into submission."[42] Kerry's senior colleague from Massachusetts was slightly more patrician, though no less dismissive. "The President," Ted Kennedy (D-MA) opined, "is drawing the wrong lesson from history."[43]

Only four members of Congress rose to Bush's defense. That number matched the number of supportive editorials in major newspapers, and two of those, written by neoconservatives no less pedigreed than Max Boot, whose book *The Savage Wars of Peace: Small Wars and the Rise of American Power* (2002) argued for the use of military force to create a world sympathetic to American interests, and Norman Podhoretz, appeared in the *Wall Street Journal.*[44] The editorial pages of nearly every other major newspaper launched a two-week onslaught that questioned the president's historiography and intelligence. Editorials condemned Bush's "surreal take on the Vietnam War," saying that the speech was "history stood on its head," that "reason and subtlety [were] left at the door," and that Bush went "far beyond the boundaries of truth."[45] The *Philadelphia Inquirer* wondered whether Bush failed to "realize the contradiction and twisted interpretation of likening the war in Iraq to the war in Vietnam, or does he just not care?"; the *Washington Post*'s Eugene Robinson confessed to his fear that "Bush actually believes the nonsensical version of history he's peddling."[46]

Both the *Washington Post* and the *New York Times* sought to correct the president's comparisons. The *Post* judged that "there is at least one area in which the metaphor is instructive: When we failed to achieve our objectives in Indochina, we kept hoping that a new South Vietnamese government would solve our problems for us." The *Times* averred, "There is a chilling similarity between the two American foreign policy disasters": in each "American presidents and military leaders went to great lengths to pretend that victory was

FIGURE 6.1. This cartoon by Mike Lukovich was one of many cartoons, editorials, and letters critical of George W. Bush's speech to the Veterans of Foreign Wars in August 22, 2007. In the speech the president sought to build support for the Iraq war by declaring that the United States had erred in withdrawing from Vietnam. By permission of Mike Lukovich and Creators Syndicate, Inc.

at hand when nothing could be farther from the truth."[47] The *Boston Globe* declared that what the two conflicts shared most was their having been futile from the outset.[48]

The avalanche of criticism reveals that by 2007, after years of hearing comparisons between Iraq and Vietnam and witnessing incidents that seemed to give them credence, the notion that Vietnam had been a disaster perpetuated by ignorance and deception had become deeply entrenched; so much so that the notion that in Vietnam the United States had lost a war it could have won through perseverance and a better strategy—a long-abiding article of faith for some on the right—no longer held any real cultural capital. A widely reprinted cartoon by Mike Lukovich showed a historian gesturing toward a map labeled "Vietnam Quagmire" and explaining, "The real lesson is, we never should've gotten . . ." only to be interrupted by a diminutive Bush, who exclaims, "Out." The cartoon made it obvious that public sentiment in 2007 dubbed anyone who peddled that narrative a fool (fig. 6.1).[49]

The denunciation was not limited to Bush. Months later, in September, when David Petraeus, the nation's most popular general, appeared before Congress to testify to the progress of the surge, he faced a similarly hostile reception and an unflattering comparison to one of Vietnam's most loathed figures, Gen. William Westmoreland.[50] Even before Petraeus arrived on Capitol Hill, his testimony was billed as the appearance "most anticipated by an Army officer since April 29, 1967, when . . . William C. Westmoreland traveled from Vietnam to address a joint meeting of Congress at a time of deep public doubts about a faraway war." Media coverage of the hearing followed suit.[51] The *New York Times* described a hearing room so tense that comments "struck a tone not heard on Capitol Hill in 40 years, since Gen. William C. Westmoreland defended the American approach to defeating North Vietnam"; the *Washington Post* seemed to pity Petraeus, describing him as "more charismatic, to be sure, but he is exactly in the same position Westy was in in 1967 when he tried to make the case to Congress that victory was achievable in Vietnam."[52] An editorial cartoon in the *Columbia (Mo.) Daily Tribune* suggested that Westmoreland's misleading testimony was being replicated when a voice from within the Capitol promising "light at the end of the tunnel" turned out to be that of Westmoreland (fig. 6.2).[53]

The persistent rhetorical linkage of Petraeus to Westmoreland was more than an acknowledgment that it had been forty years since a general had addressed Congress during wartime. It drew on a primary recollection of Westmoreland as being disingenuous and incompetent in order to preemptively question Petraeus's account of the surge's success.[54] When Petraeus testified before the House and Senate on September 10 and 11, Rep. Robert Wexler (D-FL) and Senator Kerry, respectively, noted the comparison, Kerry pointing out that "almost half the names that found their way etched into the Vietnam Wall after Westmoreland's testimony found their way there when our leaders had acknowledged, in retrospect, that they knew the policy was not working, and would not work."[55]

Before an audience primed to make such comparisons, the general perhaps did little to help his cause. His assurance that "it is possible to achieve our objectives in Iraq over time" reprised Westmoreland's declaration in 1967 that the U.S. military was "unbeatable in carrying out [its] mission." Petraeus's explanation of how he had arrived at that conclusion, which, like Westmoreland's claim that "several indices clearly point to steady and encouraging success," derived from "considerable data collection and analysis to gauge

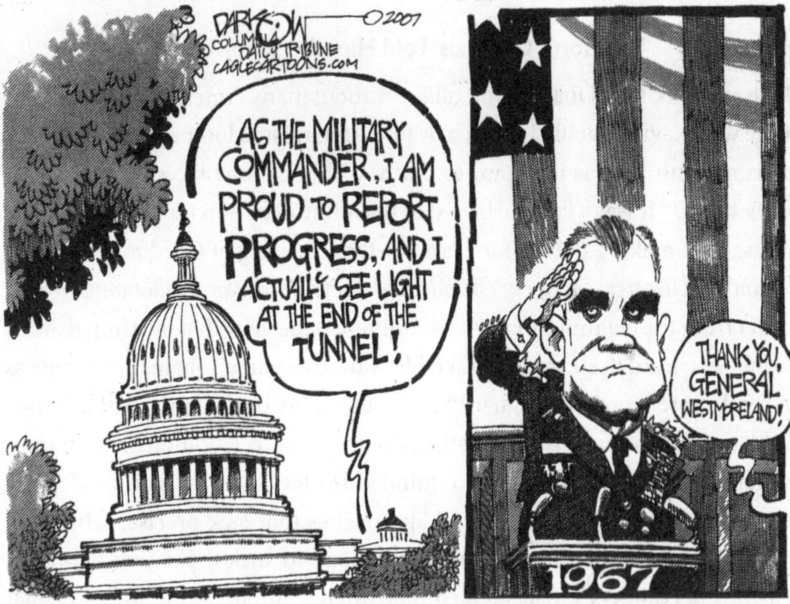

FIGURE 6.2. A cartoon by John Darkow titled "General Information" that appeared in the *Columbia (Mo.) Daily Tribune* on September 11, 2007. Several newspapers and at least two members of Congress unflatteringly compared Gen. David Petraeus's congressional testimony in 2007 on the progress of the Iraq surge to Gen. William Westmoreland's sanguine address about Vietnam to Congress in 1967. © Cagle Cartoons.

progress" that appeared in charts and graphs. One observer was reminded of the widely lampooned "Five O'Clock Folly" briefings given in Saigon throughout the war, while images of Petraeus explaining his data reminded another of McNamara.[56]

Thomas Ricks argues that Petraeus emerged victorious from these hearings because he became better known, deflected legislators' critiques of the surge, and held that the drawdown should occur according to his schedule.[57] But, as Ricks notes, Petraeus's one failure was that he "underestimated the depth of anti-war feeling in the United States."[58] However popular Petraeus was, he could not escape suspicion that he was sugarcoating bad news, and that suspicion was articulated through incessant comparisons to a man pitied, if not vilified, for Vietnam's failures. That for even a few days the most well-regarded general in the U.S. military was judged in such terms reveals how deeply the remembrance of Vietnam as a war marked by deception and incompetence shaped Americans' thinking about the Iraq war in 2007.

"Johnson's Generals Told Him the Same Thing"

By the time Barack Obama took office in 2009, many Americans credited the surge with having pacified much of Iraq.[59] Afghanistan loomed as the primary crisis now, and it was in regard to that war that Obama faced the metaphor of Vietnam.[60] It was a comparison that the administration resisted, the White House staff making public, for example, their reading of Gordon Goldstein's *Lessons in Disaster: McGeorge Bundy and the Path to War in Vietnam.*[61]

Yet from the beginning, critics committed to the view that the United States should extricate itself from intractable wars compared Obama's willingness to send more troops to Afghanistan, as they had Bush's surge, to Johnson's escalation in Vietnam. Rejecting the past few years' celebration of counterinsurgency, a *USA Today* editorial reminded readers that "as the United States learned earlier in Vietnam, logical approaches that lack precise, achievable objectives backed by overwhelming force tend to suck the nation into long, frustrating conflicts"; it speculated that "there's ample reason to worry that Obama's plan . . . could become another venture down that familiar, mine-laden path."[62] A month later the same paper wrote, "In the absence of a strategy, we're doubling our troop commitment. . . . Unable to describe our ultimate goals with any clarity, we're substituting means for ends" in a war in which, "echoing Vietnam, . . . we're fighting with restrictions against an enemy who enjoys sanctuaries across international borders."[63] These remarks, as they mirrored the realism of the 1990s, which held that the United States needed to set clear, manageable expectations and win wars quickly, also continued the discourse that had been central to Iraq opposition two years earlier: Obama, like Bush—and, more important, like Johnson and Nixon before them—was haplessly escalating a futile war without having a viable plan to end it.

Similar inclinations drove congressional anxiety about escalating the war, and again Vietnam-era congressional opposition proved to be a model for contemporary action. Rep. David Obey (D-WI) made his concerns known in a widely reported explanation: "I came here in 1969, 3 months after Richard Nixon became President. I was vehemently opposed to the Vietnam War. But Nixon correctly pointed out that he had inherited that war from his Democratic predecessor, Lyndon Johnson. And so I thought, well, it's reasonable for him to ask for some measure of time to see whether he could move the policy forward. So I decided to give him a year before I started speaking out against the war, and that's what I did. I'm pretty much in the same situation today."[64] The comparison of the newly arrived President Obama to Nixon hardly amounts to a ringing endorsement. Implicit was that Nixon had deviously expanded the war and thereby earned Obey's opprobrium, and the representative's comment portended a similar response to Obama.

Several legislators sided with the administration, reprising earlier claims that demanding a withdrawal date unnecessarily handicapped the military, reduced morale, and emboldened the enemy.[65] At least one conservative, however, crossed party lines to embrace his progressive colleagues' Vietnam comparisons. Four days after Obey spoke, Rep. Walter Jones (R-NC)—most notable for the somewhat bizarre habit of always repeating the sentence "God please continue to bless the United States" three times at the end of his remarks on the House floor, for having sponsored legislation in 2003 requiring the congressional dining room to call french fries Freedom Fries, and for having become so guilt-ridden over his support for the Iraq war that he had written thousands of letters to the family members of servicemen killed there—confessed that he was "concerned that the United States has not articulated a clear strategy for victory or an end point to our efforts"; he feared that "without focus and targeted objectives, adding more manpower to our efforts . . . leave[s] our troops in never-ending, no-win situations."[66] Jones went on to quote from Andrew Bacevich's article in the *American Conservative* "To Die for a Mystique: The Lessons Our Leaders Didn't Learn from the Vietnam War."[67]

Jones was evidently quite fond of the *American Conservative* article. A prominent conservative opponent of escalation, he quoted from it no fewer than five times. Bacevich's opposition was adamantly realist. He decried that Vietnam's lessons—"Finish the job quickly and go home"—had been "demolished" by the global war on terror, such that "now we are, in our own day and in our own way, repeating LBJ's errors." He asked Americans to honestly appraise what was achievable in Afghanistan and reject the impulse to "exaggerate the importance of places like Afghanistan" and to engage in nation building "with expectations of thereby winning Afghan hearts and minds."[68]

Bacevich's strident critique of counterinsurgency and his plea for a restrained foreign policy suited Jones, who told the House on May 21 that he'd "heard from many Vietnam veterans who are concerned that Afghanistan could become the next Vietnam."[69] Jones reiterated this point on June 23, when he submitted the entire article to the *Congressional Record,* telling his colleagues that Bacevich "was a Vietnam veteran. He, himself, was a veteran of Desert Storm. He, himself, taught at West Point. He lost a son in 2007, a young lieutenant who was killed in Iraq. So I think he brings great credibility to this article."[70]

Just as Democrats in 2007 invoked King, Kennedy, and others, Jones cited Bacevich and his "credibility" as the quality that made his invocation meaningful. This was an author who could hardly be caricatured as antimilitary or unpatriotic, but he was harshly critical of the war in Vietnam. By appealing to him, Jones helped legitimize the notion that opposing the Afghanistan war could be carried out within the nation's best traditions.

Jones returned to this theme in October, when many felt that Obama's review of the Afghanistan war had become protracted. He again read from the article and summarized Bacevich's biography before reporting a conversation with a marine general based at Camp Lejeune, in Jones's district, who likewise pleaded for caution in escalating the Afghan war and who, Jones carefully noted, "fought in Vietnam for this country."[71] Jones's repeated rooting of the authority to critique the Afghan war in his subjects' status as career military officers, Vietnam veterans, and patriots—his statement that the general had "fought . . . for this country" is not insignificant—it challenged dominant memories of the ragged, medal-throwing, potentially unpatriotic antiwar veterans that conservatives had caricatured Kerry as being during his presidential campaign. Like opponents of the surge, those wary of Obama's plan to expand the Afghanistan war recalled establishment opposition to the Vietnam War to warrant that dissent was patriotic and to establish that their critiques were in the nation's best traditions.

As Bush was in 2007, Obama, contemplating an escalation, was incessantly compared to Johnson. Despite Obama's protestations that the metaphor didn't hold, the notion that he was the new Johnson sounded throughout editorials and letters published prior to his announcement of the Afghan troop surge.[72] Reflecting on Gen. Stanley McChrystal's request for forty thousand more troops, a letter writer in the *New York Times* avowed that "Johnson's generals told him the same thing" and that "unfortunately, he believed them, and 58,000 American boys came home in boxes."[73] Two days later the *New York Times* columnist Bob Herbert similarly argued for restraint, praising Vice President Joe Biden's support for a counterterrorism strategy that focused more on killing Al Qaeda operatives than on securing Afghanistan. As he pointed out, "Lyndon Johnson made the mistake of not listening to the Joe

FIGURE 6.3. A cartoon by Jimmy Margulies titled "Afghanistan Exit Strategy" that appeared in the *(Hackensack, N.J.) Record* on November 25, 2009, recalls Hubert Van Es's famous photograph of an American helicopter on the roof of the American embassy during the fall of Saigon in 1975. Like his predecessor, President Barack Obama faced criticism that his foreign policy—particularly his plan to commit additional troops to Afghanistan—would replicate the failed policies of the war in Vietnam. © Cagle Cartoons.

Bidens of his day. There's a lesson in that for President Obama." The next day's *Pittsburgh Post-Gazette* warned, "If [Obama] accedes to Gen. McChrystal's request, he will own the war in Afghanistan in the same way Lyndon Johnson owned the war in Vietnam."[74] Meanwhile, the president found little support from more hawkish constituencies, who referred to Johnson in protesting that Obama was micromanaging the war.[75] At the end of September, the cartoonist Daryl Cagle drew Johnson's ghost chasing Obama from Vietnam to Afghanistan.[76] Two months later, Jim Margolies portrayed Obama's exit strategy as the fall of Saigon (fig. 6.3).

Given the climate, it is no wonder that Obama pointedly declared the comparison "a false reading of history" when he announced the deployment of twenty thousand additional troops to Afghanistan in December 2009.[77] This line was widely reported, and the speech was, the *New York Times* suggested, one that tried to appease both those who wanted to end the war and those who wanted to expand it.[78] It did neither, however, and critics on both sides reverted to Vietnam comparisons.[79] Even before the speech was given, Herbert, a longtime critic of the surge, quoted a conversation between Johnson and Sen. Richard Russell (D-LA) in which the president bemoaned his inability to extricate himself from Vietnam without losing face; Herbert protested that the war had "long since failed" and the surge "will prove to be a tragic mistake."[80] The next morning the *Philadelphia Daily News* suggested that Obama's plan "sounds like Vietnamization," and Rep. Ted Poe (R-TX) that in announcing an end date, Obama had "reintroduced the Vietnam syndrome of conditional commitment to America's cause. And that's just the way it is."[81]

Poe was not, however, the first to speak on the floor of the House, as was his custom.[82] He was beaten there by Rep. Dennis Kucinich (D-OH), who decried civilian deaths and the corruption of the Afghan government under the administration of President Hamid Karzai. Capturing the sense of the Democratic caucus, Kucinich asked, "What part of 'get out' do we not understand?"[83]

VIETNAM WAS, NOT SURPRISINGLY, A TOUCHSTONE IN DEBATES ABOUT America's involvement in Iraq and Afghanistan. How Vietnam was used, however, again reveals that its legacy is not simply an all-purpose signifier for a disastrous intervention. While some hawkish politicians and commentators argued that the United States should make a more complete commitment to both wars and that failing to do so left the nation in peril, the widespread opposition relied on the recollection of those who had opposed the Vietnam war, were respected for having done so, and remained celebrated and respected figures in American public life. To the war's opponents, the antiwar stances of King, Kennedy, and the antiwar senators of the 1960s in addition to the critical appraisal of Vietnam by career military officers modeled a form of dissent that was both patriotic and necessary in a moment when the prospect of escalating seemingly intractable conflicts appeared to be replicating Johnson's and Nixon's myopic, guileful failures. If these competing uses demonstrate the continuing instability of Vietnam's remembrance, the strength of the latter narrative during the most daunting foreign policy crises of the post-Vietnam era also reveals the critical possibilities of Vietnam remembrance: in recalling those who opposed an unjust war, Americans became better able to challenge the notion that patriotic citizenship demands uncritical support for an aggressive, expansive militarism.

"Whatever Acts We Committed in Iraq We Had to Carry Home with Us to America"

The frequent references to Vietnam by politicians and pundits were not the only way in which Vietnam's legacy shaped Americans' thinking about the wars in Iraq and Afghanistan. By the time Obama told West Point cadets he would be sending some of them to Afghanistan, Americans were reading memoirs of both wars. The most impressive of these texts are Fick's *One Bullet Away,* Mullaney's *The Unforgiving Minute,* and Campbell's *Joker One.* All three, as noted earlier, are deeply indebted to their Vietnam-era predecessors, but they encompass neither those texts' critical views of war nor their own moment's antiwar predilections. Instead, they appropriate the tropes of Caputo's *A Rumor of War* and O'Brien's *If I Die in a Combat Zone* to emphatically define the contemporary wars as "not Vietnam" and reestablish support for the military and the wars as components of contemporary patriotism.

These memoirs are part of a larger discourse that affirms the soldier's privileged place in contemporary American culture. This view has been central to the uncritically hagiographic Support Our Troops rhetoric that has both surrounded the military and facilitated military interventions since the attacks of September 11, 2001. In this rhetoric, as Kristin Hass explains, "The sacrifice made by the soldier is celebrated, and what the soldier did (or is doing) in the world is obscured . . . allowing a horror-free commemoration of war."[84] An uncritical perspective like this one has political consequences, both for those who suffer at the hands of American interventions and those sent to fight in them; this narrative, Hass contends, enables "still more soldiers to be sacrificed."[85] At a time when Vietnam's troubling legacy was central to Americans' anxieties about Iraq and Afghanistan, these memoirs revise central elements of Vietnam remembrance to reject such claims. Through their depiction of contemporary service members' motivations and combat experiences, their stipulation that they commit none of their predecessors' atrocities and experience none of their disillusionment, and their refusal to engage in political commentary, these texts certify contemporary soldiers' commitment and professionalism and establish that Vietnam has little to do with the global war on terror.

Campbell's *Joker One,* for example, counters the reigning image of both the reluctant draftee and those whose privilege enabled them to escape service in Vietnam by rendering his motivations in language that explicitly contrasts with O'Brien's ambivalence in *If I Die in a Combat Zone.* O'Brien, who "grew out of one war and into another," whose "father came from leaden ships of sea, from the Pacific theater," and who "learned to play Army games," identifies himself as opposed to the war but accepting of the draft because he fears "censure, embarrassment, [and] the end of everything that had happened in my life."[86] Once in the army, he hopes his privilege will protect him, that "they would use me for more than a pair of legs . . . that someone would see the value of my ass behind a typewriter."[87]

Campbell, by contrast, constructs his volunteerism in terms that recall but invert these beliefs. He writes, "I was neither born into the military nor bred for it . . . no one in my family had ever served in the armed forces. Indeed, the thought of joining the armed forces never really occurred to me until my junior year at college." But after graduation he "found [him]self casting about for a pursuit that would force me to assume responsibility for something greater than myself, something that would force me to give back."[88] Moreover, Campbell explicitly rejects the privilege that O'Brien hoped would protect him: "I also knew that in the infantry I'd be in a place where I could no longer hide behind potential, a place where past academic achievements and family connections were irrelevant."[89] Campbell moreover applies this refusal of privilege to his men, explaining, "Many . . . had either disenrolled from college or turned down college scholarships after 9/11 to serve in the armed forces. . . . [N]early all of my men were with us because they very much wanted to be with us. . . . [N]early to a man they gave me a variation of the same answer: *Sir, I love this country and I wanted to serve and I wanted to be the best, so I joined the Marine infantry, sir.*"[90]

Campbell's description repudiates both the inequity of the Vietnam-era military and the evasion of service by many who had the privilege necessary to gain educational deferments, attain a place in the National Guard or reserves, obtain a letter from a family physician attesting to a disqualifying medical condition, or find other ways to obtain deferments.[91] At the same time, this rhetoric allows Campbell to avoid acknowledging the racial and economic realities of recruitment during the global war on terror.[92] Here again, he does so through an uncannily explicit inversion of Caputo's delineation of his men in *A Rumor of War:* "With depressing frequency, the words *2 yrs. high school* appeared in the square labeled EDUCATION in their service record books. . . . They were volunteers, but I wondered for how many enlisting had been truly voluntary. The threat of the draft came with their eighteenth birthdays, and they had no hope of getting student deferments. . . . Others were driven by . . . something else, less tangible but just as valuable—self-respect."[93] Campbell's descriptions might verge on hyperbole, but what is most important is how he makes them.[94] Mobilizing and explicitly revising the narrative structures through which Caputo describes the Vietnam-era military, Campbell constitutes the contemporary force as inherently unlike that which dominates Vietnam's legacy and challenges the legibility of critiques based on comparisons of the wars.

Unlike Campbell, Nathaniel Fick, in *One Bullet Away*, presents his eagerness to join the Marine Corps as nearly identical to Caputo's, an opening that only strengthens his subsequent representation of combat as dramatically different from Caputo's and, thus, of Iraq as fundamentally unlike Vietnam. Writing that his decision to join the marines was born of his being "sick of the safe, suburban existence I had known most of my life," Caputo refers to a childhood in which he "would dream of that savage, heroic time and wish I had lived then. . . . That is what I wanted, to find in a commonplace world a chance to live heroically. Having known nothing but security, comfort, and peace, I hungered for danger, challenges, and violence. I had no clear idea how to fulfill this peculiar ambition until the day a Marine recruiting team set up a stand in the student union at Loyola University . . . [and] I had one of those rare flashes of insight: the heroic experience I sought was war."[95] The parallels in Fick's memoir, written three decades later in the midst of another unpopular war, are evident: "I wanted to do something so hard that no one could ever talk shit to me. . . . I felt as if I had been born too late. There was no longer a place in the world for a young man who wanted to wear armor and slay dragons." He describes becoming convinced, after listening to a talk at Dartmouth, that the marines were "the last bastion of honor in society" and that he "want[ed] to be a warrior."[96]

One Bullet Away posits the similarity between the high-minded volunteerism of contemporary soldiers and the first men sent to Vietnam before critically upending crucial moments in Caputo's memoir to present combat as being justified and nontraumatic and producing neither disillusionment nor political opposition to the war. If *A Rumor of War* is what Tobey Herzog has rightfully called "a story of an individual's loss of innocence as well as a country's loss of innocence and coming of age in a war that . . . left the country scarred," Fick eschews the applicability of such language to the Iraq war by redrafting Caputo's narration of critical moments in combat.[97]

This is most visible in Caputo's treatment of the initial encounter with an enemy body. In a passage I discussed above in greater detail (see chapter 2), Caputo acknowledges not only physical trauma but also the enemy's humanity:

> The enemy soldier appeared to be about eighteen or nineteen. . . . We feel so many things in our guts, and that is where two 7.62-mm bullets had caught him. . . . he had had ample time to feel pain and perhaps to realize that death was not decades, but only moments, away. . . . A modern, high-velocity bullet strikes with tremendous impact. No tidy holes as in the movies. . . . An enormous amount of blood had poured out of him and he was lying in it, a crimson puddle in which floated bits of skin and white cartilage.[98]

This passage, as I noted earlier, makes combat's violence graphic and sees the soldier's suffering. Caputo's discovery of enemy soldiers' personal effects "gave to the enemy the humanity I wished to deny him. . . . These were men we had helped to kill, men whose deaths would afflict other people with irrevocable loss."[99] His unsettling reaction results largely from his inability to maintain what Judith Butler has termed "a way of dividing lives into those that are worth defending, valuing, and grieving when they are lost, and those that are not quite lives, not quite valuable, recognizable, or, indeed, mournable."[100] Butler further argues that precisely in this recognition lie "the affective conditions for social critique"; this is, to recall Herzog's formulation, a moment that "raise[s] moral issues" related to the war.[101]

In Fick's memoir, by contrast, death is seen as necessary, appropriate, and psychologically insignificant: "I looked at the dead bodies sprawled in the trees. Six or seven of them, young men like us. . . . They looked more like computer programmers than Islamic fighters. AK-47s surrounded the bodies, along with RPG [rocket-propelled grenade] launchers and piles of grenades. Clutched in the death grip of one of the men were two hand grenades, seconds from being thrown."[102] As N. E. Anderson notes, this scene obfuscates physical injury, but equally important is that its cultural meaning relies on recalling and rewriting the equivalent scene in Caputo's memoir.[103] *A Rumor of War* emphasizes the destruction *of* the enemy body, but *One Bullet Away* hints at its potential *to destroy;* Fick ignores the wounds that Americans cause but vividly describes weapons poised to injure U.S. troops. Indeed, that these sentences follow his characterization of the fighters as being "young men like us"—a sentence that virtually repeats one of Caputo's men's comments in the same scene that "they're young men. . . . They're just like us"—defines them as not similarly grievable.[104] Indeed, although they might appear to be harmless "computer programmers," they are, in fact, "Islamic fighters," most assuredly not, as Caputo's dead were, husbands and boyfriends who would be grieved.

Further, when Fick finds documents that identify these men, they hardly humanize them: "Each man carried a Syrian passport, complete with official Iraqi entry visas. . . . Their written reasons [for entry] were all the same: Jihad."[105] The term *jihad* contributes to the moment's prowar rhetoric in two ways. First, it defines these men as dangerous others, what Butler calls "living figure[s] that [figure] the threat to life."[106] Second, the term identifies them as Islamic terrorists, which, together with the reference to "official Iraqi entry visas," helps sustain the discredited belief that Iraq was linked to terrorist networks targeting the United States. Precisely because of this framing of the encounter with the dead body, Fick, unlike Caputo, does not question his actions: "I found no joy in looking at the men we'd killed . . . But I wasn't disturbed, either."[107] By echoing and overturning the Vietnam memoir the representations of the current wars contribute to a discourse that constructs the violence of these wars as being necessary, appropriate, not requiring interrogation, and, correspondingly, unlike that of Vietnam.

In *The Unforgiving Minute* Mullaney similarly portrays his discovery of an Afghan insurgent's body in terms that evoke and reconfigure this passage from Caputo, whom he acknowledges having read: "Flies buzzed around the dried blood. . . . *This*—5.56 millimeters—was how a bullet plowed through a human torso."[108] In his precise reference to the measurements of American munitions and his focus on their impact on the body, he echoes Caputo's surprise. However, that recognition does not lead to consideration of this Afghan's life or the appropriateness of his death, and hence not to an indictment of the war. Rather, Mullaney quickly pivots to a contemplation of Americans' vulnerability, first writing, "These bodies weren't bouncing back. Neither would we" and then viewing the death of one of his own men as most powerful.[109] Mullaney, in other words, summons Caputo only to subvert him. His encounter prompts a consideration not of the American soldiers' morality, only their mortality; it reveals that American lives, those lives targeted by American violence, are precarious and can be grieved.[110] Like Fick, Mullaney alters a critical scene from Vietnam's legacy to define the contemporary soldier's experience and emotional response as being unlike that of his earlier counterpart and American suffering as the only tragedy of the war.

Contemporary war memoirists likewise revamp critical aspects of Vietnam's legacy in their dismissal of atrocity, which scholars have noted is central to Vietnam memoirs' raising of "moral issues."[111] Caputo, for example, acknowledges that "both we and the Viet Cong began to make a habit of atrocities" and that he felt "contempt for those who sought to impose on [our] savage struggle the mincing distinctions of civilized warfare."[112] In his description of a woman whose village his men have destroyed, he writes "You let the VC use your village for an ambush site, I think, and now you're paying the price." Elsewhere, he describes an interrogation in which "our interpreter . . . was yelling at [a Vietnamese woman] and waving a pistol in front of her face. . . . I did not have to be a linguist to guess that he was threatening to blow her head off."[113] O'Brien offers similar, though more vivid commentary: "Jet fighters were called in. The hamlet was leveled, and napalm was used. I heard screams. . . . There were Viet Cong in that hamlet. And there were babies and children and people who just didn't give a damn in there, too. But Chip and Tom were . . . dead, and it was hard to be filled with pity."[114]

Contemporary memoirists eschew such behavior, but, critically, they do so in language that directly contrasts with these portrayals. Campbell is again the most explicit, inverting Caputo as he recounts the orders he gave his men: "We never eschewed basic morality. No matter how much we despised our opponents . . . we could not, and would not, emulate them." He then enumerates a list of prohibited actions familiar from nearly any work of Vietnam literature but particularly resonant with O'Brien's description:

> We wouldn't fire artillery indiscriminately into the city . . . or use our tanks and jets to level buildings hiding suspected insurgents and civilians alike. . . . We wouldn't beat or torture our prisoners, or routinely threaten uncooperative local families. . . . There was undoubtedly quite a bit of altruism in our stance, but I believe that we were equally driven by hard practicality. From my first deployment, I knew that . . . whatever acts we committed in Iraq we had to carry home with us to America. . . . If we opened fire randomly, or out of hatred and a desire to kill those who refused to help us, then, quite frankly, we did not deserve the title of United States Marines.[115]

Campbell distances his experience from that of soldiers who fought in Vietnam by nearly directly rebutting the language of the Vietnam memoir. As Herzog notes, Vietnam memoirs "suggest how the special features of guerrilla warfare in Vietnam and how the emotional and psychological factors of combat contributed to such abhorrent acts." Milton Bates writes that Caputo "believes that the physical setting had released the horror within."[116] Campbell, on the other hand, posits that the avoidance of civilian casualties is simply a matter of personal discipline and that the trauma that followed the Vietnam War resulted from a failure to make appropriate choices. In saying his men are rather easily able to avoid those acts and that horror, Campbell separates both his soldiers and their war from familiar accounts of Vietnam. Moreover, in emphasizing that his men would lose the privilege of being called marines, Campbell attaches an unquestionable moral authority to the military, one that subverts the claims of those contemporaneously critiquing the military or opposing the war on moral grounds. He likewise erases any consideration of whether the atrocities central to Vietnam and, subsequently, Iraq were the result not of individual bad actors but of the war's systemic and structural violence and the policies that enabled it.

This construction contributes to an emerging remembrance that elides ample evidence that the Iraq war during Campbell's tour was as violent as the war Caputo and O'Brien describe, including a mounting American death toll, a growing insurgency, high civilian casualties, and numerous atrocities.[117] The day after Campbell issued this order in Ramadi, Cox News Service reported that in Fallujah a "Cobra helicopter fired a Hellfire missile at the base of a minaret and an F-16 fighter dropped a 500-pound laser-guided bomb. . . . Witnesses said as many as 40 people were killed and several others injured, a claim disputed by U.S. authorities."[118] Over the next two weeks, as the battle of Fallujah continued, one reporter noted, "Military action against his forces—which inevitably causes civilian casualties—has increased [Iraqi] support" for the Shiite cleric Muqtada al-Sadr's opposition to the U.S. occupation. The Associated Press reported that "many residents have reported civilian casualties they blame on U.S. fire," and the *New York Times* quoted an Iraqi civilian who commented, "Why do they kill children? Before, I liked the Americans, but now I hate them."[119]

I question neither the veracity with which Campbell reports his instructions to his men nor his desire not to "descend to the level of Abu Ghraib." Certainly, news coverage from the period in which he was in Iraq describes marine commanders taking pains to avoid killing noncombatants.[120] Nonetheless, in claiming that his men were not engaging in these behaviors and suggesting that the most egregious example of American atrocity is the benchmark to be avoided, Campbell obscures the true scope of American violence in Iraq. He simply fails to acknowledge the reality, one with which he surely would have been familiar, that such violence as he condemns occurred regularly.

Recent American combat memoirs likewise distance the behavior of troops fighting in Iraq and Afghanistan from the mistreatment of the dead body that is a familiar motif in popular culture about the Vietnam War. After the battle in which he encountered the dead Vietnamese, Caputo writes, "a photographer—I think he was with the *Stars and Stripes*—was taking pictures of [the bodies] from various angles."[121] This evidently officially sanctioned photography of corpses is part of a larger tradition in the literature of Vietnam. In *Dispatches,* for example, Michael Herr relates that such images were endemic: "There were hundreds of these albums in Vietnam, thousands, and they all seemed to contain the same pictures . . . the severed head shot, the head often resting on the chest of the dead man or being held up by a smiling Marine, or a lot of heads, arranged in a row, with a cigarette burning in each of the mouths."[122] Herr, like Caputo, presents such behavior as being at least implicitly sanctioned, telling of a soldier's confession to a chaplain who "had only told him that it was forgivable and put the pictures in his drawer and kept them."[123]

If Vietnam memoirists present such acts as being common and arousing neither outrage nor disgust, in their respective memoirs Fick and Mullaney reveal that if those impulses endure among some soldiers, they have become morally reprehensible and are easily mitigated by either public shaming or effective leadership. Faced with shutter-happy soldiers, Fick declares that these actions "make [him] sick," and Mullaney more gently reminds one of his men that "we don't photograph dead bodies."[124] If the offending soldiers are displeased by these rebukes, they nonetheless change their behavior.

These passages thus envision a contemporary military in which morality and discipline prevent the disagreeable behavior endemic to Vietnam or, alternately, perpetuate the notion that such actions are committed by a select few improperly supervised soldiers. Here again, the memoirs blur the reality that atrocities of the sort familiar from Vietnam regularly occurred in Iraq. That is, American troops assuredly *do* take gruesome photographs, most infamously at Abu Ghraib, but also in 2005, when soldiers exchanged pictures of Iraqi corpses for access to pornographic pictures, in 2010 when U.S. troops charged with killing civilians allegedly took photographs "holding up the heads of dead Afghans," and in 2011, when marines recorded themselves urinating on the corpses of Taliban fighters.[125] In reversing a dominant signifier of Vietnam's troubling history to dismiss such behavior as egregiously unacceptable within the current wars, these memoirs further define not only the contemporary soldier and the contemporary military as observing a morality fundamentally unlike that which dominates Vietnam's remembrance but also the Iraq and Afghanistan wars as unlike Vietnam.

In short, Fick, Mullaney, and Campbell rewrite critical moments in Vietnam memoirs in order to assert that the soldiers fighting in Iraq and Afghanistan, the military for which they fight, and the wars themselves share little of the trauma, atrocity, and ambiguity that dominate the Indochina war's remembrance. This assessment continues in their refusal to censure the wars themselves. As several critics have noted, condemnations of the war are central to the Vietnam memoir.[126] O'Brien writes early in his memoir, "The war was wrong. And since it was wrong and since people were dying as a result of it, it was evil"; at the end of the war, he has hardly changed his opinion, dismissing the conflict as "certain blood for uncertain reasons."[127] Similarly, after watching a friendly fire incident that he identifies as "a tableau of the madness of the war," Caputo writes, "We could never hope to win the war. To go on with the war would be folly—worse than folly: it would be a crime, murder on a mass scale. . . . I tried to do a bit of proselytizing among the clerks in the HqCo office. The war, I said, was unwinnable. It was being fought for a bunch of corrupt politicians in Saigon. Every American life lost was a life wasted. The United States should withdraw now, before more men died."[128]

Iraq and Afghanistan memoirists again explicitly obviate this language in their refusal to find fault with the wars they were fighting. Not surprisingly, it is Campbell who rebukes Caputo's disillusionment and political condemnation, writing that his men had "seen all the horrors of war firsthand, again and again, but somehow they retained their faith in each other and in their mission. They knew with unshakable certainty that . . . given enough time, we'd prevail no matter what the circumstances."[129] The contemporary soldier is seen yet again as constitutionally different from those who fought in Vietnam, and particularly as having a stronger commitment to the war, even after seeing its "horrors." Fick and Mullaney do not share Campbell's sheer optimism, but Elizabeth Bumiller, in an article from 2010 in the *New York Times* about the literature of the Iraq and Afghanistan wars, somewhat inaccurately noted that such memoirs are different from those of earlier wars in that they do not ask "questions about the conflicts themselves."[130] It is not that the memoirists don't engage in such interrogation; rather, they adamantly refute the notion that they should do so. Fick does reproach the managers of the war—though, notably, never their purpose—yet quickly and decisively refuses to debate the war's political stakes: "Pro-war. Anti-war. War for freedom. War for oil. Philosophical disputes were a luxury I could not enjoy. War was what I had. We didn't vote for it, authorize it, or declare it. We just had to fight it. And fighting it, for me, meant two things: winning, and getting my men home alive."[131] This feeling can be detected as well in Mullaney's dismissal, in words nearly identical to Fick's, of his judgment that "the best thing we could have done for Afghanistan was to get out of our Humvees and drink more green chai": "Getting the strategy right hadn't been my responsibility. My mission had been to fight well and bring my men home."[132]

Refusing to comment on the war is in itself a comment on the war, one that uncritically acquiesces to it and encourages others to do the same. As Jay Winter points out, "Silence is chosen in order to suspend or truncate open conflict over the meaning of or justification for violence."[133] In refusing to appraise the wars negatively, more recent memoirs embrace the logic of the Support Our Troops imperative. They establish that soldiering in Iraq and Afghanistan is carried out by apolitical professionals who not only bear no responsibility for the war but also do not think about it very much. For them, the notion of protest or even commentary of the sort carried out by Vietnam memoirists is inconceivable. Given the cultural capital accorded to soldiers and particularly to war memoirists, the refusal to make those evaluations effectively undermines critiques of the wars that rest on comparisons to Vietnam.[134]

Ultimately, however, Fick admits that "combat had nearly unhinged me" and that he experienced symptoms of PTSD.[135] Tellingly, his description of those symptoms seems taken directly from Caputo, who writes early in his memoir, "I came home from war with the curious feeling that I had grown older than my father, who was then fifty-one. . . . I had all the symptoms of *combat veteranitis:* an inability to concentrate, a childlike fear of darkness, a tendency to tire easily, chronic nightmares, an intolerance of loud noises—especially doors slamming and cars backfiring—and alternating moods of depression and rage that came over me for no apparent reason."[136]

Fick, too, describes a nightmare that recurred "often enough to make sleep an act of will." He said he "cried sometimes for no reason at all. When a driver cut me off in the merge lane, I visualized, without emotion, pulling his head back and cutting his throat with my car key. On the Fourth of July, a firecracker sent me diving behind a car door. . . . I felt older than my father."[137] Campbell relies on the same image, similarly confessing, "I felt nervous around crowds, and I avoided them. Loud noises scared me, and I jumped every time a door slammed or a car backfired. I still had trouble sleeping."[138] Mullaney has a more complicated relationship with post-traumatic stress, but his first meal upon surviving the war—"an entire chateaubriand steak by myself and . . . half a bottle of red wine"—is identical to Caputo's first meal while on leave from Vietnam: "chateaubriand and half the bottle of red wine."[139]

If these passages demonstrate the extent to which all three memoirists are indebted to Caputo, it is most important that Fick and Campbell direct attention away from the war's trauma to defend their participation in it. Although Fick acknowledges some mixed feelings about what he had done, that "the good didn't feel as good as the bad felt bad," he quickly dismisses these feelings.[140] Scoffing at civilians' gratitude, he writes, "Thanks for what, I wanted to ask—shooting kids, cowering in terror behind a berm, dropping artillery on people's homes? There wasn't any pride simply in being there. The pride was in our good decisions, in the things we did right. I hoped I'd done more right than wrong. . . . I was learning to accept that sometimes the only way to fight evil is with another evil, however good its aim."[141]

Here, Fick acknowledges atrocities of the sort that dominate the Vietnam War's legacy and seems initially troubled by some of his actions. These misgivings, however, are soon set aside, displaced first by the other "good decisions" and "the things we did right" and then by the notion that even "evil" acts are sometimes necessary. Ironically, the last sentence demonstrates a quite different way in which Fick's memoir intersects with Vietnam's legacy, as it very nearly echoes McNamara's ninth "lesson" in Errol Morris's documentary *The Fog of War* (2003), namely, "In order to do good, you may have to engage in evil."[142] Like McNamara, Fick concedes but rationalizes his complicity in violence, while at the same time implicitly justifying the intervention and once again prohibiting any critique of the rationale offered for it. In describing his actions as "fight[ing] evil," he echoes language familiar from the Bush administration's justification of the war.[143] In Fick's memoir, the veteran's reflection takes the form not of struggling, as Caputo does, with the recognition that "perhaps the war had awakened something evil in us" and that "the thing we had done was a result of what the war had done to us"; rather, he simply accepts "doing evil" as an excusable inevitability.[144]

In this way Fick undermines consideration of the larger political issues surrounding the war. In his final statement, which follows his attempt to weigh his good and bad feelings, Fick dismisses his anxieties with a striking historical obfuscation: "I hope life improves for the people of Afghanistan and Iraq, but that's not why we did it. We fought for each other. I am proud."[145] Improving the lives of Afghans and Iraqis was precisely how the Bush administration justified the war, as in the president's assertion in March 2003 that "we will be changing the regime of Iraq, for the good of the Iraqi people."[146] Claims that men fought for each other are preemptive separations of the soldier from the war and those who planned it, and they are reminiscent of claims made by Vietnam veterans—including, for example, the members of the Last Patrol—in that war's aftermath.[147] Yet they are also declarations that political concerns are not worthy of thought and debate. To question why these men fought and to challenge their depoliticized assertions would amount to a failure to meet the requirements of a patriotic citizenship premised on the unquestioning celebration of soldiers.

These memoirs were written and published at a time of increasing opposition to the wars in Iraq and Afghanistan, when comparisons to Vietnam were increasingly prevalent, and after a number of events had transpired that gave credence to those comparisons. They appeared in a moment when those who had opposed Vietnam were routinely invoked to legitimize contemporary antiwar sentiment. Given the historical moment, these texts might be expected to embrace those comparisons and to rely on extant discourses of Vietnam remembrance to criticize the interventions they describe.

Instead, the memoirs' rewriting of Vietnam remembrance facilitates these texts' larger valorization of the military as an exceptional element in American culture, a notion that increasingly dominated post-Vietnam society but during the Iraq and Afghanistan wars came under scrutiny amid reports of atrocities on the battlefields and lowered recruiting standards at home.[148] Fick and Mullaney joined the military before the terrorist attacks of 9/11, Fick taking his commission in 1998 and Mullaney entering West Point in 1996. These dates locate the decisions they made squarely within a period in which, as Beth Bailey has argued, the army, in particular, "presented itself as a force for good in civilian society. It was a provider of education, of training, of discipline. It was a creator of good citizens, of good employees, and of good leaders. It took America's youth and from them created strong, principled, and committed men and women who made America a better place."[149] Notably, the effort to cast the military in this light is decidedly distinct from the image of the post-Vietnam military. As Bailey writes, "By the end of [the 1960s], the army was in crisis. The flood of news articles about drug addiction and combat refusal, fragging and racial conflict, undermined the army's public image."[150]

It is against this image of the Vietnam-era military and in sympathy with the image of the military as "a provider of social good" that Fick, Campbell, and Mullaney write.[151] Each regards the military as having the capacity to improve society because it is far superior to what they perceive as the decadent culture of the turn-of-the-century United States. Fick, after reading Thomas Ricks's *Making the Corps* and hearing Ricks speak at Dartmouth, decides, "The Marine Corps was a last bastion of honor in society, a place where young Americans learned to work as a team, to trust one another and themselves, and to sacrifice for a principle. . . . Ricks used words such as 'duty' and 'honor' without cynicism, something I'd not often heard at Dartmouth."[152] In the term "last bastion" Fick fashions marines as an alternative to a society apparently bereft of morality.

Mullaney's assessment is almost identical. Rejecting the "beautiful old colleges of New England"—those, like Dartmouth, often imagined as enclaves of privilege and liberal elitism—because "they'd asked nothing of me" and "[he'd] been taught . . . that responsibility preceded privilege," he describes West Point as an antidote to the softness he saw in American society, "the only school I visited where a bookworm couldn't possibly graduate."[153] Indeed, Mullaney uses language nearly identical to Fick's: "Cadets discussed courage and duty without a note of irony. They spoke without slouching, oozing confidence. . . . West Point offered more than an academic education. It offered an almost religious quest for perfection. I wanted to graduate a better man."[154] The vision of the military as an alternative to a permissive, valueless society is unmistakable.

Campbell, the only one of the three who likely joined the military after September 11, 2001, writes in parallel terms.[155] As I noted above, Campbell joins the marines because he finds himself "casting about for a pursuit that would force me to assume responsibility for something greater than myself, something that would force me to give back, to serve others."[156] Yet that altruism contains an explicit rejection of wealth and privilege; it appears after "the Fortune 500 recruiters and the postgraduation salaries lost their luster."[157] The juxtaposition of the materialism of "postgraduation salaries" and "responsibility" and "service" points to a vision of the military as exceptional.

Notably, however, what Bailey presents as the military's socioeconomic benefits are conspicuously absent from these texts. Perhaps owing to each memoirist's racial and socioeconomic privilege, none implies that the value of military service lies in economic opportunity.[158] Nonetheless, both Campbell and Mullaney state their explicit purpose as that of valorizing the military in broad terms. Campbell writes, "For what they did and what they suffered, my men deserve to have their story told."[159] Such a comment might seem standard fare for the opening of a war memoir, might seem, in fact, ambiguous, as though it could be woven into a narrative critical of the war. And yet, by the end of the memoir it is clear that Campbell's view of his men and what they have done remains steadfastly idealistic:

> It has taken time and distance from it all for me to understand fully what my Marines had been telling me then, but now I think that I get it. Now I think I understand a bit more about what it means to truly love, because for my men, love was something much more than emotion. For them, love was expressed in the only currency that mattered in combat: action—a consistent pattern running throughout the large and the small, a pattern of sacrifice that reinforced the idea that we all cared more for the other than we did for ourselves.[160]

There is some measure of irony in referring to combat as an act of love, regardless of the well-documented reality that men do fight for each other.[161] Yet here Campbell echoes Fick, eschewing larger political questions about the war in favor of a celebration of camaraderie. This is not Caputo's angry elegy for his Quantico classmate Walter Levy, in which he castigates a country that "wishes to forget and it has forgotten" a war whose "very name is a curse."[162] Instead, Campbell is didactic: "I hope and I pray that whoever reads this story will know my men as I do, and that knowing them, they too might come to love them."[163] The message of these memoirs is not to evaluate the wars but to uncritically honor those who served.

Mullaney even more explicitly presents his book as a sort of jeremiad: "I recognized that this book might be helpful to readers. If I could tell the story well, it might help America better understand its military, might inspire some to serve, and might shed some light on operations in Afghanistan that seem to have been largely forgotten by the American public. I could either continue complaining that people lacked understanding about military service, or I could do something to bridge that gap."[164] For Mullaney as well, "understanding" the military equates to celebrating it, if not, in fact, joining it. Here again he is recalling but inverting Caputo, and the cultural work these memoirs do through their inversion of Vietnam's remembrance is perhaps nowhere more apparent than in the contrast between Mullaney's claim that his book "might inspire some to serve" and Caputo's dejected declaration that his memoir "might, perhaps, prevent the next generation from being crucified in the next war. But I don't think so."[165]

This passage reveals the extent to which Iraq and Afghanistan memoirists have revised the language and tropes of their post-Vietnam predecessors to craft a narrative that depoliticizes the Iraq and Afghanistan wars and valorizes the contemporary soldier and his service. That stance came at a time when the idealized vision of the soldier and the military was increasingly troubled by media coverage of American violence that resonated with popular remembrances of the Vietnam War. Furthermore, the opponents of the conflicts were regularly comparing the Afghan and Iraq wars to Vietnam and embracing Vietnam-era antiwar activism as a model for contemporary action.[166]

By appropriating and revising tropes familiar from Vietnam memoirs, these three works rhetorically distance the contemporary military from these troubling comparisons. Quite simply, a military and a war described as the antithesis of the Vietnam War and the military that fought it deserve none of the critiques that have followed in Vietnam's aftermath. In explicitly crafting that oppositional narrative by revising the remembrance of Vietnam, contemporary veterans help maintain an exceptionalist discourse that unapologetically, unwaveringly, and largely uncritically celebrates the military's prominent place in American culture.

As the wars in Iraq and Afghanistan grew increasingly protracted, critics unsurprisingly invoked Vietnam's troubling legacy. In addition to comparing the conflicts, however, critics of the Iraq and Afghanistan surges countered protestations that dissent was unpatriotic and established the moral and political credibility of their opposition by evoking specific memories of antiwar activism. Such principled, celebrated figures as Martin Luther King Jr. and liberal senators spoke out against the Vietnam War, and such men were remembered as representing the best attributes of American culture. These articulations represent a moment in which mobilizing Vietnam's remembrance created the capacity to define a patriotism skeptical of aggressive militarism and supportive of a restrained foreign policy.

Yet this antiwar posture was countered by best-selling memoirists whose work contributes to the Iraq and Afghanistan wars' emerging remembrance. Despite their deep debts to the most important Vietnam memoirists, Nathaniel Fick, Donovan Campbell, and Craig Mullaney revise the tropes central to Vietnam remembrance to establish the current wars as unlike that conflict, undermine critiques that rest on such claims, and affirm that the military is a morally upright and essential component of American public life. These memoirs reveal how contemporary veterans did not seize—and, in fact, rejected—the potential that Vietnam's remembrance held for legitimizing dissent that defined the moment.

The contrast between these two cultural sites—one the popular media and political discourse that invoked a marginalized element of Vietnam's legacy to counter unpopular wars and the other a set of popular texts that revised a key element of Vietnam's remembrance to shield the wars from critique—reveals the instability of Vietnam's legacies. Neither unified nor stable, they cannot simply be accessed, and they do not serve only one political purpose; rather, Americans have struggled to make Vietnam meaningful within their contemporary political debates. How they have done so matters, too. If this chapter shows that the maintaining of exceptionalist discourses of American militarism requires not simply a rejection of comparisons to Vietnam but also a revision of critical remembrances of that war to make them endorse current militarized narratives, it also reveals that a complete genealogy of Vietnam's history and legacy provides the grounds on which that dominance can be productively challenged.

AFTERWORD

"THE TASK OF TELLING YOUR STORY CONTINUES"

ALTHOUGH AS A PRESIDENTIAL CANDIDATE HE SAID THAT THE VIETNAM War "had drawn to a close when I was fairly young. And so, that wasn't formative for me in the way it was, I think, for an earlier generation," Barack Obama found his own foreign policy relentlessly compared to that war.[1] It is not surprising that when he traveled to the Vietnam Veterans Memorial on Memorial Day weekend 2012 to open commemorations of the war's fiftieth anniversary, he declared the occasion "another chance to set the record straight" and hewed to a familiar narrative.[2] He stated that the treatment of Vietnam veterans had been "a national shame," reminded the audience that those who had fought there had "won every major battle" before going on to lead lives of service and activism, and affirmed his "resolve to do everything in our power" to account for missing servicemen.[3] He offered assurances that Vietnam veterans were being appropriately remembered and that "because of Vietnam and our veterans, we now use American power smarter, we honor our military more, we take care of our veterans better."[4]

If Obama's speech repeats familiar claims about a war marked by resilient soldiers, an uncaring public, and unresolved trauma and does not acknowledge the flawed policy that led to Vietnam's devastation, the fact that he made them, and indeed delivered the speech at all, demonstrates that the war remains an enigma that must be explained, a trauma that must be healed, a disaster that must not be repeated. Efforts to "set the record straight" about Vietnam have been major projects in American public life for half a century. Over those decades Americans have debated what constitutes a compelling explanation, complete healing, and better decision making in its aftermath. These efforts have occurred in myriad venues: films and novels, memorials and media coverage, a president's speech at the Vietnam Veterans Memorial, and a veteran's decision to leave a medal there.

Yet efforts to resolve Vietnam's troubling legacy have not been limited to sites of memory that are explicitly about that war. As this book shows, Americans have persistently used Vietnam's remembrance to memorialize and contextualize other events. From nearly the moment the United States escalated its presence in Vietnam and continuing through the final years of the wars in Iraq and Afghanistan, Americans have appropriated and revised the tropes, the language, and the representational strategies through which they have remembered Vietnam to make those events' legacies into cultural spaces in which they could articulate positions about the Vietnam War and the troubling questions of foreign policy and militarism that followed.

Americans' use of practices and narratives central to Vietnam's legacy to remember other events is deeply political. I have shown in this book how these processes have both enabled and preempted broader debates about U.S. foreign policy and the place of the military within the larger culture. I also show, however, that those two potentials have not existed in equal measure. In a few instances, the redeployment of Vietnam's remembrance has enabled critiques of American militarism and the foreign policies it supports by challenging narratives that positioned Vietnam's brutality as a historical outlier. PBS's promotion of *The Andersonville Trial,* for example, explicitly linked the My Lai massacre to historical atrocities and called for communal accountability for the war's violence. Memoirists of the Second World War who wrote after Vietnam appropriated the tropes of and recalled significant moments in Vietnam memoirs to counter the dominant remembrance of the Good War as an example of the righteous use of military power in which veterans fought nobly and came home unscathed. And in 2007 opponents of the Iraq war recalled earlier antiwar activism as a model for patriotic dissent. These efforts enabled criticism of the exceptionalist narratives on which the nation's enduring embrace of and commitment to militarism rests; appropriating ways of thinking about Vietnam to locate My Lai within a historical pattern of

American atrocity, identify combat in the Second World War as equal to that in Vietnam in its amoral brutality and psychological devastation, and declare that the Iraq war deserves moral condemnation encourages more cautious uses of military force and demands recognition of veterans' struggles.

More often, though, Vietnam's remembrance has been deployed or rewritten to validate revisionist narratives of the war, justify a foreign policy narrowly aimed at preserving American empire, and endorse militarism. At Andersonville, the National Park Service's initial efforts to capitalize on the nation's war-weariness to promote critical perspectives on war steadily gave way to officially sanctioned revisionism that foregrounds American suffering and the mythology of the POW/MIA movement. Similarly, conservatives' remembrance of the Alamo echoed and thus validated revisionist narratives of the Vietnam War as a benevolent intervention, while Vietnam veterans rewrote the story of the famous siege as a historical precedent for celebrating veterans without contemplating the war's political realities.

Americans have also mobilized Vietnam's remembrance as they have considered how the legacies of more recent military interventions intersect with contemporary foreign policy debates. In the 1990s and early 2000s, the use of the tropes and language of Vietnam remembrance to narrate the Somalia intervention helped substantiate a vision of U.S. foreign policy that did not include commitments to ending famines and stopping genocides. After the terrorist attacks of September 11, 2001, the practices through which Americans debated and critiqued the Vietnam War were persistently remade to endorse the Iraq and Afghanistan wars, distance them from Vietnam's legacy, and shield service members from any censuring of their actions abroad.

Such uses of Vietnam's legacy serve narratives that sanction American empire and the military's role in perpetuating it while truncating debates about the crises that wars create. The use of other historical sites to proclaim the nobility of the Vietnam War contributes to the enduring silence on the policies and attitudes that enabled the war and the subsequent devastation of Southeast Asia. Explicitly remembering Somalia as being "just like Vietnam," by contrast, hamstrings meaningful debate over the viability of humanitarian interventions. Constructing Iraq and Afghanistan as "not Vietnam" obscures the devastation that more than a decade of war has wrought. In those countries, that devastation includes the deaths of approximately 120,000 Iraqi civilians since 2003 and approximately 17,000 Afghan civilians in the past five years, the lack of functioning infrastructure, and high civilian PTSD rates.[5] In the United States, veterans of these wars face similar crises. One in five suffers from PTSD, a quarter of a million have mild traumatic brain injury, a quarter abuse prescription drugs and alcohol, more than 200,000 are unemployed, and dozens commit suicide each year—all amid a paucity of veterans' services.[6] That Americans' cognizance of the recent wars is filtered through the lens of Vietnam has resulted in little attention being paid to these issues and counters Obama's claim that "because of Vietnam and our veterans, we now use American power smarter, we honor our military more, we take care of our veterans better." In practice, this has often meant that Americans have used Vietnam's legacy to remember other events in ways that foster their continued embrace of a foreign policy that endorses aggressive militarism to maintain American empire while remaining largely ignorant of or apathetic about the wars' costs.[7]

Scholars thus need to consider Vietnam's legacy more broadly. It is not enough to think about how the war itself has been remembered or to note the inevitable comparisons to it that every new crisis engenders. Instead, we must ask how understandings of Vietnam have shaped Americans' encounters with the nation's violent past and present and how those encounters in turn shape their support or condemnation of policies that impact the lives of people living in the United States and around the world.

This book, then, is also an argument about how we should study war and memory. Scholars must be more attuned to how one event's remembrance affords both possibilities and limitations for remembering others. Only when we do so can we fully grasp the event's significance to American culture. More important, by uncovering the cultural phenomena through which Americans embrace one event's remembrance as a means of explaining the meaning of another, we can illuminate the contours of contemporary imaginings of war, violence, empire, and justice; critique the uncritical acquiescence to the first three of these; and encourage the pursuit of the fourth. Only by dismantling the processes that obscure the troubling political realities and injustices that surround issues of war and militarism can we promote vigorous, meaningful debate about the actual costs of America's global military presence. And only then can we encourage a rethinking of the often willing acceptance of military interventions without consideration of their consequences at home and abroad. This task will become more vital as the United States emerges from more than a decade of sustained wars in Iraq and Afghanistan, begins a new process of recovery, and contemplates anew its global roles and responsibilities. As the Iraq war grinds to an indeterminate conclusion that is not quite a victory, scholars interested in that war's legacy would do well to contemplate the reach of its nascent remembrance.

A DECADE INTO THE TWENTY-FIRST CENTURY, IRAQ IS BECOMING THE new favored metaphor for those who are worried about the uses of American military power. Even before the presidential election of 2008, Café Press, which had for years been selling bumper stickers reading, "Is It Vietnam Yet?" to critics of the Iraq war, began offering a sticker in which the letters spelling "Iraq" appeared in an odometer, with the final letter rolling over to spell "Iran."[8] The sticker captured the moment's growing fear that the United States might soon launch another preemptive, intractable war to destroy Iran's nuclear weapon's program.[9]

And Iran was not the only potential intervention to which the Iraq war was compared. In July 2012 the *New York Times* columnist Thomas Friedman proclaimed that "Syria is Iraq" and that "the only reason Iraq has any chance for a decent outcome today is because America was on the ground with tens of thousands of troops to act as that well-armed midwife, reasonably trusted and certainly feared by all sides, to manage Iraq's transition to more consensual politics." Friedman concluded, "My gut tells me that Syria will require the same to have the same chance."[10] This was not, however, a call for intervention, but a rebuke to "those who have been advocating a more activist U.S. intervention in Syria" for "not being realistic about what it would take to create a decent outcome."[11] In the vice presidential debate of 2012, Joe Biden similarly described his opposition to intervention in Syria, proclaiming, "The last thing America needs is to get into another ground war in the Middle East requiring tens of thousands if not well over a hundred thousand American forces."[12] And in July 2013, the retired marine general James Mattis, who had commanded the First Marine Division in Iraq and led U.S. Central Command, told an audience in Colorado that the United States should be wary of intervening in Syria. According to Politico, "Mattis said the U.S. also needs to define what 'end state' it is seeking in Syria, if further action is to be taken. 'Otherwise, you invade a country and pull down a statue and then say: "Now, what do we do?" . . . Know what I mean?' "[13] His audience knew. It was, as the article points out, "an obvious reference to the chaotic aftermath of the U.S. toppling of Saddam Hussein in Iraq."[14]

Indeed, the United States did not intervene in Syria in the fall of 2013 largely because of public, political, and military weariness over the Iraq war. A *Los Angeles Times* editorial explained the "public opposition to [Obama's] call for military action against Syria" by pointing out that "Americans have additional reasons to be skeptical. There's the toll of wars in Iraq and Afghanistan. There's the fear that any war in the Middle East will inevitably become a quagmire."[15] The term so often used to evoke Vietnam had seemingly been fully transferred to new wars. A letter to the *Washington Post* defending the president's change of course regarding a military strike countered a critical editorial with the comment, "If only President George W. Bush had been capable of 'mind changing,' 'indecision,' and 'lurching' in the run-up to the Iraq War."[16]

As Americans debated the wisdom of a Syria intervention by citing Iraq, critically acclaimed texts about the Iraq war began to appear. Kathryn Bigelow's film *The Hurt Locker* (2008) was the first, but it has been joined by novels like Ben Fountain's *Billy Lynn's Long Halftime Walk* (2012), Kevin Powers's *The Yellow Birds* (2012)—both of which were nominated for the National Book Award in 2012—and Roxana Robinson's *Sparta* (2013).[17] Neither Fountain nor Powers won, but Quiara Alegría Hudes won the Pulitzer Prize for *Water by the Spoonful*, her play about a troubled veteran.[18] As we read these texts, we must ask what earlier remembrances inform their portrayal of the Iraq war, but we also ought to pay attention to whether Iraq's emerging legacy shapes the cultural representation of military interventions yet to occur and the commemorations of those long past—including the Vietnam War, particularly given that the fiftieth anniversary of the withdrawal of U.S. combat troops from Vietnam will coincide with the twentieth anniversary of the Iraq invasion. Indeed, that political and military leaders and pundits are already relying on Iraq in new debates over U.S. foreign policy and the application of military force abroad reveals one way in which Iraq has, in fact, become the next Vietnam.

ABBREVIATIONS USED IN THE NOTES

NEWSPAPERS AND NEWS AGENCIES

AJC	*Atlanta Journal-Constitution*
AP	*Associated Press*
BG	*Boston Globe*
CSM	*Christian Science Monitor*
CST	*Chicago Sun-Times*
LAT	*Los Angeles Times*
NYT	*New York Times*
PI	*Philadelphia Inquirer*
PPG	*Pittsburgh Post-Gazette*
SAL	*San Antonio Light*
UPI	*United Press International*
WP	*Washington Post*
WSJ	*Wall Street Journal*

ARCHIVAL COLLECTIONS

AKS	Alan K. Simpson Papers, American Heritage Center, University of Wyoming
ANDE	Andersonville National Historic Site, Andersonville, Georgia
ANDE VF	Andersonville National Historic Site Vertical File
CHC	Charles F. Hatcher Collection, Richard B. Russell Library for Political Research and Studies, University of Georgia Libraries, Athens, Georgia, 30602-1641.
CPB	Corporation for Public Broadcasting Archives, Special Collections in Mass Media and Culture, University of Maryland

DRTL VF	Daughters of the Republic of Texas Library Vertical File, San Antonio, Texas
EKS	The Eric K. Shinseki Collection, Box Number, the U.S. Army Military History Institute, Carlisle Barracks, Pennsylvania.
ELF	E. L. (Tic) Forrester Papers, Richard B. Russell Library for Political Research and Studies, University of Georgia Libraries, Athens, Georgia, 30602-1641.
FLNI	Flight 93 National Memorial Archives, Somerset, Pennsylvania
FLNI ALB	Flight 93 National Memorial Ambassador Log Book
FLNI VCC	Flight 93 National Memorial Visitor Comment Card
FLNI UCC	Flight 93 National Memorial Unnumbered Comment Card
FLNI VCB	Flight 93 National Memorial Visitor Comment Book
GHWBPL	George H. W. Bush Presidential Library, College Station, Texas
JBC	Representative Jack Brinkley Collection (MC 4), Columbus State University Archives, Columbus, Georgia
LBJ	LBJ Presidential Library, Austin, Texas
NAACP	Records of National Association for the Advancement of Colored People, Manuscript Division, Library of Congress, Washington, D.C.
NARA	National Archives and Records Administration, Washington, D.C.
NARA CP	National Archives and Records Administration, College Park, Maryland
NPS-DSC	National Park Service, Denver Service Center
RBR	Richard B. Russell Papers, Richard B. Russell Library for Political Research and Studies, University of Georgia Libraries, Athens, Georgia, 30602-1641.
USAHEC	United States Army Heritage and Education Center, Carlisle Barracks, Pennsylvania.
USAWC	United States Army War College, Carlisle Barracks, Pennsylvania.

GOVERNMENT DOCUMENTS

CR	*Congressional Record*
PPP:GHWB	*Public Papers of the Presidents: George H. W. Bush*
PPP:GWB	*Public Papers of the Presidents: George W. Bush*
PPP:WJC	*Public Papers of the Presidents: William J. Clinton*

Note: The *Public Papers of the Presidents* are compiled by the Government Printing Office, Washington, D.C., with multiple volumes for each year; rather than provide a full bibliographic entry with publication dates, I have given the volume and page numbers in each citation.

NOTES

INTRODUCTION

1. On the Twenty-Fifth Infantry Division's role in the Cambodia invasion, see John M. Shaw, "The U.S. Army in the 1970 Cambodian Incursion" (Ph.D. diss., University of Kentucky, 1995), 168–204, and Melvin C. Walthall, *Lightening Forward: A History of the Twenty-Fifth Infantry Division (Tropic Lightning), 1941–1978* (25th Inf. Div. Assoc., 1978), 156–57. On responses to the Cambodia invasion, see John Prados, *Vietnam: The Unwinnable War* (Lawrence: University Press of Kansas, 2010), 367–74.
2. The contours of this narrative have been adequately treated by others. See, for example, Edwin A. Martini, *Invisible Enemies: The American War on Vietnam, 1975–2000* (Amherst: University of Massachusetts Press, 2007), 7; H. Bruce Franklin, *M.I.A., or Mythmaking in America: How and Why Belief in Live POWs Has Possessed a Nation* (New Brunswick: Rutgers University Press, 1993), 34–35; Michael Allen, *Until the Last Man Comes Home: POWs, MIAs, and the Unending Vietnam War* (Chapel Hill: University of North Carolina Press, 2009), 6.
3. On the mythology surrounding Vietnam veterans' homecoming, see Jerry Lembke, *The Spitting Image: Myth, Memory, and the Legacy of Vietnam* (New York: New York University Press, 1998), esp. 71–100.
4. H. Bruce Franklin provides an excellent, concise overview of the competing schools of thought on Vietnam's legacy. *Vietnam and Other American Fantasies* (Amherst: University of Massachusetts Press, 2000), 41–42.
5. John Hellman, *American Myth and the Legacy of Vietnam* (New York: Columbia University Press, 1986), 221.
6. Kristin Ann Hass, *Sacrificing Soldiers on the National Mall* (Berkeley: University of California Press, 2013), 3; Katherine Kinney, *Friendly Fire: American Images of the Vietnam War* (Oxford: Oxford University Press, 2000), 135.
7. On atrocities committed during the Vietnam War, see Nick Turse, *Kill Anything That Moves: The Real American War in Vietnam* (New York: Metropolitan Books, 2013).
8. See, for example, Wilbur J. Scott, *Vietnam Veterans since the War: The Politics of PTSD, Agent Orange, and the National Memorial* (Norman: University of Oklahoma Press, 1993);

Allen, *Until the Last Man Comes Home*, 2; Edwin A. Martini, *Agent Orange: History, Science, and the Politics of Uncertainty* (Amherst: University of Massachusetts Press, 2012).

9. Hass, *Sacrificing Soldiers on the National Mall*, 3; Andrew Bacevich, *The New American Militarism: How Americans Are Seduced by War* (New York: Oxford University Press, 2005), 2; Patrick Hagopian, *The Vietnam War in American Memory: Veterans, Memorials, and the Politics of Healing* (Amherst: University of Massachusetts Press, 2009), 19.
10. Among others who have commented on this, see Peter Beinart, *The Icarus Syndrome: A History of American Hubris* (New York: Harper Collins, 2010), 171; Bacevich, *The New American Militarism*, 70, and Andrew Bacevich, *Washington Rules: America's Path to Permanent War* (New York: Metropolitan Books, 2010), 115. The most famous articulation of this was the Powell doctrine, which specifically sought to lay out the criteria under which an intervention could be successful by avoiding the errors of Vietnam. Bacevich, *The New American Militarism*, 48.
11. Bacevich, *The New American Militarism*, 2.
12. Kristin Ann Hass, *Carried to the Wall: American Memory and the Vietnam Veterans Memorial* (Berkeley: University of California Press, 1996), 2–3; Marita Sturken, *Tangled Memories: The Vietnam War, the Aids Epidemic, and the Politics of Remembering* (Berkeley: University of California Press, 1998), 50; Thomas Myers, *Walking Point: American Narratives of Vietnam* (New York: Oxford University Press, 1988), 72.
13. Hass, *Sacrificing Soldiers on the National Mall*, 3.
14. I take the term "sites of memory" from Pierre Nora's concept of the *Site of Memory*. Nora explains that such places are the "consecrate[d] sites embodying" memory. *Realms of Memory: The Construction of the French Past*, vol. 1, trans. Arthur Goldhammer (New York: Columbia University Press, 1996), 2.
15. This body of scholarship is indeed extensive. I cite the texts that have been most useful to me throughout in the pages that follow. However, the best histories of the war itself are Marilyn Young's indispensable *The Vietnam Wars: 1945–1990* (New York: Harper, 1991) and Prados, *Vietnam: The History of an Unwinnable War*. Any study of the Vietnam War's legacy should begin with Hagopian, *Vietnam War in American Memory*, and Sturken, *Tangled Memories*.
16. Andreas Huyssen, *Present Pasts: Urban Palimpsests and the Politics of Memory* (Palo Alto: Stanford University Press, 2003), 95, 98.
17. Jay Winter, *Remembering War: The Great War Between Memory and History in the Twentieth Century* (New Haven: Yale University Press, 2006), 1.
18. My sense of Americans using remembrance to tell stories is indebted to Jay Mechling's suggestion that we should "think of American culture simply as those stories that Americans tell one another in order to make sense of their lives." "An American Culture Grid, with Texts," *American Studies International* 27.1 (1989), 3.
19. Bacevich notes that to policymakers, "Vietnam became enshrined as a one-off event." *Washington Rules*, 134.
20. As Hass explains, this has been a larger trend within recent American memorial practice. *Sacrificing Soldiers on the National Mall*, 19, 198–99.
21. On these issues, see Herman Graham III, *The Brothers' Vietnam War: Black Power, Manhood, and the Military Experience* (Gainesville: University Press of Florida, 2003); James E. Westheider, *Fighting on Two Fronts: African-Americans and the Vietnam War* (New York: New York University Press, 1997); Lorena Oropeza, *Raza Sí! Guerra No! Chicano Protest and Patriotism during the Viet Nam War Era* (Berkeley: University of

California Press, 2005); Sturken, *Tangled Memories*, 109–16; Hagopian, *Vietnam War in American Memory*, 23–48; Christian G. Appy, *Working-Class War: American Combat Soldiers in Vietnam* (Chapel Hill: University of North Carolina Press, 1993); Natasha Zaretsky, *No Direction Home: The American Family and Fear of National Decline, 1968–1980* (Chapel Hill: University of North Carolina Press, 2007), 25–70; and Susan Jeffords, *The Remasculinization of America: Gender and the Vietnam War* (Bloomington: Indiana University Press, 1989).

22. Fitzhugh Brundage, ed., *Where These Memories Grow: History, Memory, and Southern Identity* (Chapel Hill: University of North Carolina Press, 2000), 4.
23. Ibid., 5.
24. Winter, *Remembering War*, 3, 5. Hass takes a similar approach, and is similarly indebted to Winter. *Sacrificing Soldiers on the National Mall*, 6.

1. "HOW FAR IS ANDERSONVILLE FROM VIETNAM?"

1. Jim Medlin, "Ex-Prisoners of War Gather in Andersonville for National POW Museum Dedication," *Macon County Citizen/Montezuma Georgian*, April 15, 1998, 2, Binder April 9, 1998, ANDE.
2. Ibid.
3. Ibid.
4. Sherri Martin, "Where Heroes Walked," *Macon County News Leader*, April 16, 1998, Binder April 9, 1998, ANDE.
5. On the significance of POWs and MIAs within the war's legacy, see H. Bruce Franklin, *M.I.A., or Mythmaking in America: How and Why Belief in Live POWs Has Possessed a Nation* (New Brunswick: Rutgers University Press, 1993); Michael Allen, *Until the Last Man Comes Home: POWs, MIAs, and the Unending Vietnam War* (Chapel Hill: University of North Carolina Press, 2009); and Edwin A. Martini, *Invisible Enemies: The American War on Vietnam, 1975–2000* (Amherst: University of Massachusetts Press, 2007).
6. On the domestic narratives central to POW discourse, see Natasha Zaretsky, *No Direction Home: The American Family and the Fear of National Decline* (Chapel Hill: University of North Carolina Press, 2007), 25–70.
7. On the lengthy history of the term "fullest possible accounting," see Franklin, *M.I.A.*, 19–23.
8. This chapter does not offer a history of Andersonville or a general evaluation of it as a site of memory. See William Marvel, *Andersonville: The Last Depot* (Chapel Hill: University of North Carolina Press, 2006); Benjamin G. Cloyd, *Haunted by Atrocity: Civil War Prisons in American Memory* (Baton Rouge: Louisiana State University Press, 2010).
9. As Edwin Martini has noted, this has been a dominant theme in U.S. culture for the past four decades. *Invisible Enemies*, 7.
10. "Our Share, Nine Men," *Birmingham News*, May 27, 1966.
11. On the politics of military service in Vietnam and statistics about Alabama in particular, see Christian G. Appy, *Working-Class War: American Combat Soldiers in Vietnam* (Chapel Hill: University of North Carolina Press, 1993), esp. 14–15; statistics and place names are from Jay Ebert and Tom Holloway, "Vietnam Casualties by State and City or Town," Vietvet.org, n.d., www.vietvet.org.
12. "U.S. Troops Fight a Hanoi Regiment," *NYT*, May 30, 1966; Robert Moorefield, "U.S. Casualty Total Last Week at Record," *Birmingham News*, May 26, 1966; "Anti-Americanism

in Hue," *NYT*, May 28, 1966; "Monks, Nuns, Write LBJ in Blood," *Montgomery Advertiser*, May 27, 1966; "More Vietnam Suicides Reported," *WP*, May 30, 1966.

13. Paul Hoffman, "War Foes Stage Macabre Protest," *NYT*, May 31, 1966; Robert B. Semple Jr. "Pressure to Change Draft Is Gaining in Washington," *NYT*, May 30, 1966.
14. "U.S. Bogged Down in Vietnamese Mess," *Mobile Press-Register*, May 22, 1966.
15. "Johnson Calls U.S. Totally Committed in Vietnam War," *NYT*, May 27, 1966.
16. "Text of President Johnson's Arlington Speech," *NYT*, May 31, 1966.
17. "U.S. Viet War Dead 'Known,'" *Baltimore Sun*, May 29, 1966; Michael Sledge, *Soldier Dead: How We Recover, Identify, Bury, and Honor Our Military Fallen* (New York: Columbia University Press, 2005), 210. See also Allen, *Until the Last Man Comes Home*, 121–23.
18. "None Is Unknown to Me," *San Francisco Examiner*, May 29, 1966.
19. "A Nation's Heroes," *San Francisco Examiner*, May 29, 1966.
20. Dennis Higgins, "Viet Toll Underscores Solemnity of Rites to Mark Memorial Day," *PI*, May 27, 1966.
21. "Memorial Day, 1966," Editorial, *BG*, May 30, 1966.
22. "In Memoriam," Editorial, *NYT*, May 30, 1966.
23. James E. Westheider, *Fighting on Two Fronts: African Americans and the Vietnam War* (New York: New York University Press, 1997), 8; Jennifer C. James, *A Freedom Bought with Blood: African American War Literature from the Civil War to World War II* (Chapel Hill: University of North Carolina Press, 2007), 12, 188–89.
24. Westheider, *Fighting on Two Fronts*, 8.
25. Ibid., 9–10.
26. In general, African American newspapers were initially prowar. Lawrence Allen Eldridge, *Chronicles of a Two-Front War: Civil Rights and Vietnam in the African American Press* (Columbia: University of Missouri Press, 2011), 135–39.
27. Ibid., 134; Betty Washington, "Three Graduate from West Point," *Baltimore Afro-American*, May 24, 1966.
28. Betty Washington, "Negro Soldiers Did Their Part in the Civil War," *Chicago Daily Defender*, May 28–June3, 1966.
29. "Lest We Forget," *Baltimore Sun*, May 29, 1966; "Humphrey Says Hello," *PI*, May 31, 1966; "National Cemetery, Limekiln Pike and Haines St., Philadelphia," *PI*, May 29, 1966; "American Soldiers in South Viet Nam Pause to Honor Fallen Buddies . . . While Flags Decorate Headstones of Veterans in Arlington Cemetery," *Washington Evening Star*, May 30, 1966.
30. Charles Del Vechia, "With Full Honors," *WP*, May 30, 1966; Richard Corrigan, "Arlington Honor Guard Buried Near Tomb," *WP*, May 30, 1966.
31. Editorial cartoon, *Mobile Register*, May 30 1966. "'That They Have Not Died in Vain' Our Memorial Day Prayer," Baltimore *Afro-American*, May 24, 1966, 4; "Sir, Tell Them Ours Is a Country to Be Proud Of," *Chicago Daily Defender*, May 28–June 3, 1966.
32. See Westheider, *Fighting on Two Fronts*, 73; Eldridge, *Chronicle of a Two-Front War*, 70; Fran Leeper Buss, *Moisture of the Earth: Mary Robinson, Civil Rights and Textile Union Activist* (Ann Arbor: University of Michigan Press, 2009), 205–7; Taylor Branch, *At Canaan's Edge: America in the King Years, 1965–68* (New York: Simon and Schuster, 2006), 470–71.
33. "Taps to Sound for Green Beret," *Atlanta Journal*, May 30, 1966; Roger Hammer, "Wetumpka Soldier to Be Buried with Military Rites," *Atlanta Daily World*, May 29, 1966.
34. Harris, "Parents of Negro Soldier Decline Lot in City Cemetery," *Birmingham News*, May 27, 1966.

35. "Elmore County (Wetumka) Alabama, Annual Report of Branch Activities—1965," Branch Annual Reports, Alabama-Georgia, 1965, Series IV: Box C42, NAACP papers.
36. "Application for Charter of Elmore County, Alabama, Youth Council of the National Association for the Advancement of Colored People," April 3, 1968, Folder Youth Council, Elmore County, Ala., Box IV:E1; NAACP.
37. Westheider, *Fighting on Two Fronts*, 73.
38. Memorandum, May 25, 1966. Folder "Alabama," Box IX-3, NAACP.
39. "No Room in a Dixie Cemetery," *San Francisco Chronicle*, May 27, 1966; memorandum, May 25, 1966.
40. "U.S. Cemetery Takes Body of Negro GI," *WP*, May 27, 1966.
41. Gene Roberts, "Slain Negro G.I.'s Mother Charges Cemetery Bias," *NYT*, May 27, 1966.
42. On the Green Berets, see Mark Taylor, *The Vietnam War in History, Literature, and Film* (Tuscaloosa: University of Alabama Press, 2003), 37–43; Tom Englehardt, *The End of Victory Culture: Cold War America and the Disillusioning of a Generation* (New York: Basic Books, 1995), 162–63.
43. "Ala. Family Say Town Refuses to Bury Viet Hero," *Jet*, June 9, 1966; "Alabama Negro Buried with Military Honors," *Washington Evening Star*, May 30, 1966; "Dixie Negro Saved from Pauper's Burial," *PI*, May 28, 1966; "Negro GI Eulogy Recalls Affront," *Baltimore Sun*, May 30, 1966; "With Honor and Distinction," *Baltimore Afro-American*, June 11, 1966.
44. "Soldier Burial Site Upsets Negro Mother," *Augusta Chronicle*, May 27, 1966; also qtd. in Westheider, *Fighting on Two Fronts*, 73.
45. Mr. and Mrs. Jimmie Williams to The President, May 27, 1966, White House Central Files (hereafter WHCF) subject category ND 9-2-1 (National Defense, Burials), "ND 9-2-1 Burials 11/23/636/3/66," Box 49, LBJ.
46. Ibid.
47. Letter, Jamie McCracken to Lyndon B. Johnson, 5/27/66, Name File, WHCF, Box 234, "McCracken H-K," LBJ; Letter, Alice Wildermuth to Lyndon B. Johnson, 5/28/66, Name File, WHCF, Box 303, "Wild," LBJ.
48. Letter, John Wayne to Lyndon B. Johnson, 5/27/66, WHCF subject category ND 9-2-1 (National Defense, Burials), "ND 9-2-1 Burials 11/23/636/3/66," Box 49, LBJ.
49. Memo, Duggan to Cater, 5/31/66, WHCF ND (National Defense), Box 316, "ND 19/CO 312/ND 9 6/3/66–6/4/66," LBJ.
50. Douglas Cater to John Steadman, 6/3/66, WHCF subject category ND 9-2-1 (National Defense, Burials), "ND 9-2-1 Burials 11/23/636/3/66," Box 49, LBJ.
51. Harry McPherson to Mr. and Mrs. Williams, 5/28/66, WHCF subject category ND 9-2-1 (National Defense, Burials), "ND 9-2-1 Burials 11/23/636/3/66," Box 49, LBJ.
52. Ibid.
53. Bill Moyers to John Wayne, 5/28/66, WHCF subject category ND 9-2-1 (National Defense, Burials), "ND 9-2-1 Burials 11/23/636/3/66," Box 49, LBJ.
54. Ibid.; Westheider, *Fighting on Two Fronts* 73.
55. Eldridge suggests that the history of slavery was more significant. *Chronicles of a Two-Front War*, 70.
56. "Dixie Negro GI Saved from Pauper's Burial."
57. "GI to be Buried at Andersonville," *Columbus (Ga.) Ledger*, May 30, 1966; "All Is Quiet, Green Beret Laid to Rest," *Atlanta Daily World*, May 31, 1966.
58. "Taps, a Rifle Salute, a Resting Place for Pfc. Williams," *Augusta Chronicle*, May 30, 1966.

For similar sentiments, see Hammer, "Wetumpka Solider to Be Buried with Military Rites;" *Atlanta Daily World,* "All Is Quiet; Green Beret Laid to Rest"; "Negro G.I. Is Buried at Andersonville," *NYT,* May 31, 1966.

59. "Burial on Memorial Day," *LAT*, May 31, 1966; "All Is Quiet; Green Beret Laid to Rest."
60. "GI to Be Buried at Andersonville," *Columbus (Ga.) Ledger,* May 30, 1966.
61. "Taps, a Rifle Salute, a Resting Place for Pfc. Williams."
62. Letter, Alfred B. Fitt to Dorothy Liverpool, June 13, 1966, WHCF, Name File, "LIUB" Box 235, LBJ.
63. "A Place to Rest Is Found for a Soldier," *BG,* May 31, 1966.
64. "Negro G.I. Is Buried at Andersonville." A widely reprinted UPI story used similar language. See "Taps, a Rifle Salute, a Resting Place for Pfc. Williams."
65. Charles Poore, "Books of the Times," *NYT,* October 27, 1955.
66. "A Place to Rest Is Found for a Soldier."
67. "Mother Wins Burial Fight," *Baltimore Sun,* May 31, 1966.
68. "Negro Soldier Buried in Andersonville Grave," *Mobile Register,* May 31, 1966.
69. Ibid.
70. James Day, *The Vanishing Vision: The Inside Story of Public Television* (Berkeley: University of California Press, 1995), 266–67, 284; Donel Wayland Price, "A Description of the Development, Administration, Production Process, and Production Environment of the Public Television Drama Series: *Hollywood Television Theater*" (Ph.D. diss., University of Southern California, 1976), 216, 210. On the rationale for developing the series, its funding, and Freedman's selection, see Price, "A Description of the Development," 73–76, 81–82.
71. "Article 6—No Title," *NYT,* March 26, 1970, 77; "Thanks for a Great Year," Folder Los Angeles, KCET Channel 28, Box CPB 40, CPB.
72. Lewis Freedman, "How Far Is Andersonville from Vietnam?" *NYT,* May 17, 1970, 107. When the play premiered in Berlin, Levitt wrote an essay for the playbill making this connection. "Premiere in Berlin for 'Andersonville,'" *NYT,* November 25, 1960.
73. Brooks Atkinson, "Theatre: A Moral Issue; 'Andersonville Trial' of Civil War Staged," Review of Saul Levitt, *The Andersonville Trial, NYT,* December 29, 1959.
74. Ibid.
75. E. L. Forrester, "Andersonville Speech," May 30, 1967, Folder Memorial Day, Andersonville, 1967, Box 51, Subseries III; Francis E. Walter to E. L. Forrester, February 9, 1960, Box Folder 7, Box 55, Subseries IV, ELF.
76. "Andersonville Play Cancelled in Atlanta and Birmingham," *NYT,* September 29, 1960.
77. Scholars have made only passing references to this production's relationship to Vietnam. See Tom W. Hoffer and Richard Alan Nelson, "Docudrama on American Television," *Journal of the University Film Association* 30.2 (1978), 25.
78. Lewis Freedman to All Public Broadcast Service Affiliates, February 25, 1970, Folder Los Angeles, KCET Channel 28, Box CPB 40, NPBA.
79. On the My Lai massacre's larger history, see, among others, Kendrick Oliver, *The My Lai Massacre in American History and Memory* (Manchester: Manchester University Press, 2006); Michal R. Belknap, *The Vietnam War on Trial: The My Lai Massacre and the Court-Martial of Lieutenant Calley* (Lawrence: University Press of Kansas, 2002).
80. Edward F. Sherman, "Songmy 2: Some Knotty Legal Questions," *NYT,* December 7, 1969.
81. Oliver, *The My Lai Massacre in American History,* 9. On atrocity as a matter of policy, see Nick Turse, *Kill Anything That Moves: The Real American War in Vietnam* (New York: Metropolitan Books, 2013), 6.

82. Belknap, *The Vietnam War on Trial*, 130–31.
83. Clifton Daniel, "Songmy 1: Will a 'Lynching' Follow a 'Massacre'?," *NYT*, December 7, 1969, E3; Belknap, *The Vietnam War on Trial*, 119, 130; Oliver, *The My Lai Massacre in American History*, 49, 80.
84. Freedman to All Public Broadcast Service Affiliates.
85. Freedman to Ward Chamberlain Jr., March 23, 1970; Frank Goodman to Public Broadcast Service Stations, April 27, 1970, Folder Los Angeles, KCET Channel 28, Box CPB 40, NPBA.
86. Cecil Smith, "Scott to Debut as Director for TV," *Los Angeles Times*, n.d., encl. to Goodman to Public Broadcast Service Stations, April 27, 1970, Folder Los Angeles, California KCET Channel 28, Box CPB 40, CPB. This was apparently standard procedure at KCET regarding the series. Price, "A Description of the Development," 133.
87. "'The Andersonville Trial' Is Still Timely, Says Distinguished TV Producer Lewis Freedman," 1. Folder Hollywood TV Theatre Andersonville Trial Photos #27, Box 53, NPBA.
88. Ibid.
89. Ibid, 2.
90. Smith, "Scott to Debut as Director for TV."
91. PBS, "The Andersonville Trial to Kick Off Hollywood TV Theater," Press Release, Folder Los Angeles, KCET Channel 28, Box CPB 40, NPBA.
92. Kay Gardella, "Scott Makes the Switch in 'The Andersonville Trial,'" *New York Daily News*, May 12, 1970, Folder Los Angeles, California KCET Channel 28, Box CPB 40, NPBA.
93. Ibid.
94. Richard Hammer, "Is the Chain of Command the Chain of Guilt?" *NYT*, January 17, 1971. On the defense's efforts in this regard, see Belknap, *The Vietnam War on Trial*, 171–72; on its larger strategy, see 168–90.
95. Homer Bigart, "Task Force Chief Reported Mylai Action as 'Well Executed and Successful,'" *NYT*, January 14, 1971.
96. Oliver, *The My Lai Massacre in American History*, 106–7. For a broader survey of media coverage, testimony, and public sentiment, see ibid., 105–7.
97. "Suggested Spot Copy 2-5-71," Folder Hollywood TV Theatre Andersonville Trial Photos #27, Box 53, NPBA.
98. "The Andersonville Trial Returns to Public Television," Folder Hollywood Television Theatre 1970–71, Box 22:06; David Swanston, "Program Content," January 21, 1971, Folder Hollywood Television Theatre 1970–71, Box 22:06, NPBA.
99. *NYT*, "Display Ad 21," February 2, 1971, 22. See *Time*, December 5, 1969 and *Newsweek*, December 8, 1969.
100. Freedman, "How Far Is Andersonville from Vietnam?" *NYT*, May 17, 1970.
101. Ibid.
102. Ibid.
103. Paul Jones, "'Andersonville:' Scott Directs," *Atlanta Journal and Constitution*, May 17, 1970; Crabtree, "Trial at Andersonville," *Atlanta Journal and Constitution*, May 17, 1970.
104. Review of *The Andersonville Trial*, *Entertainment World*, May 15, 1970.
105. Jack Gould, "'Andersonville Trial' Is Revived on N.E.T.," review of *The Andersonville Trial*, *NYT*, May 18, 1970.
106. Bettelou Peterson, "'The Andersonville Trial,' Best TV Drama in Years," *Detroit Free Press*, May 15, 1970.

107. Ibid.
108. Ibid.
109. Percy Shain, "'Andersonville Trial'—Superb," *BG,* May 18, 1970.
110. "The Excuse of Obeying Orders," *BG,* May 19, 1970.
111. Price, "A Description of the Development," 6.
112. For background on the site's creation, see Cloyd, *Haunted by Atrocity,* 165–68; John Ricks, "Administrative History of Andersonville National Historic Site," 36–43, ANDE VF. On the army's desire to relinquish control of the site, see Alfred B. Fitt to Raymond L. Freeman, June 7, 1967, Box 121, Folder ANDE, RG79, NARA CP and Fitt to Richard B. Russell, September 16, 1964, Box 197, Folder 3, RBR; on the NPS's initial reluctance, see Director, NPS to Stuart Udall, March 6, 1967; and Regional Director, Southeast Region, to Director, January 13. 1966, Box 121, Folder ANDE, RG79, NARA CP. On the efforts of the regional planning commission, see Charles E. Campbell to Winston J. Stratton, January 13, 1969, Box 56, Folder 11, Subgroup X, Series XV, RBR; "Agenda for the April 24th Meeting With Secretary Udall," and Jimmy Carter to Richard B. Russell, March 28, 1967, Box 114, Folder 6, Subgroup C, Series XV, RBR.
113. John Jensen to Jean Swearingen, June 6, 1973, Box 7, Folder ANDE, RG 79, NARA CP.
114. Ibid.
115. Jensen to Swearingen, June 26, 1973 and Lowery, "Andersonville Planning Session," Box 7, Folder ANDE, RG 79, NARA CP.
116. Kenneth E. Foote, *Shadowed Ground: America's Landscapes of Violence and Tragedy* (Austin: University of Texas Press, 1997), 313. See also Cloyd, *Haunted by Atrocity,* 167.
117. Franklin, *M.I.A,* 48–49. See also Jeffrey Kimball, *Nixon's Vietnam War* (Lawrence: University Press of Kansas, 1998), 167–68.
118. Allen, *Until the Last Man Comes Home,* 49.
119. E. L. Forrester, "Andersonville Speech—May 30, 1967," 1, Box III.51, Folder 8, ELF. "Reconciliationist narrative" is David Blight's term. *Race and Reunion: The Civil War in American Memory* (Cambridge: Belknap Press of Harvard University Press, 2001), 4. See also "Memorial Day Through the Years at Andersonville," 15, ANDE VF.
120. Forrester, "Andersonville Speech," 1–2, 3.
121. Ibid., 4.
122. Zaretsky, *No Direction Home,* 27;
123. Forrester, "Andersonville Speech," 5.
124. Foote, *Shadowed Ground,* 313.
125. Cloyd, *Haunted by Atrocity,* 167.
126. Senate Committee on Insular Affairs, "Andersonville National Historic Site in the State of Georgia," 91st Cong., 2nd sess., 1970, S. Rep. 91-1258, 1.
127. Ibid., 2.
128. Jack Brinkley, "Memorial Day Ceremonies Sponsored by John D. Mathis, American Legion Post No. 2, Andersonville, Georgia, May 30, 1970," 1. Box 207, JBC.
129. Ibid., 6–7. On the hard hat protests, see John Prados, *Vietnam: The History of an Unwinnable War* (Lawrence: University Press of Kansas, 2009), 370–71.
130. "Memorial Day Through the Years at Andersonville," 16.
131. Ibid., 16–17.
132. R. W. Apple Jr. "Setting the Course on Vietnam: Indochina," *NYT,* April 8, 1973.
133. "Out of the Quagmire?" *NYT,* January 16, 1973.
134. Allen, *Until the Last Man Comes Home,* 55–56.

135. Stephen V. Roberts, "Ex-P.O.Ws Say Ordeal Was Not in Vain," *NYT*, February 24, 1973. On POW wives' evolving positions, see Zaretsky, *No Direction Home*, 45–46.
136. NPS, "Interpretive Prospectus, Andersonville National Historic Site, Georgia," July 23, 1974, 2, ANDE VF. Cloyd also notes antiwar sentiment in the prospectus. *Haunted by Atrocity*, 172.
137. NPS, "Andersonville National Historic Site Interpretive Prospectus," January 23, 1974, 4. ANDE.
138. Ibid., 7.
139. Ibid., 18.
140. Ricks, "Administrative History of Andersonville National Historic Site," 47.
141. Ibid., 48.
142. John H. Flister to Jack Brinkley, November 4, 1975, Box 234, JBC.
143. Cloyd, *Haunted by Atrocity*, 169–70.
144. Charles Hatcher, "Memorial Day Andersonville," Box 109, Series II.C, CHC.
145. Robin K. Burr to John H. Flister, June 19, 1977, ANDE VF.
146. Allen, *Until the Last Man Comes Home*, 179.
147. Ibid., 135.
148. Allen, *Until the Last Man Comes Home*, 2, 216–19; Franklin, *M.I.A.*, 11, 23, 35. See also Thomas M. Hawley, *Remains of War: Bodies, Politics, and the Search for American Soldiers Unaccounted for in Southeast Asia* (Durham: Duke University Press, 2005).
149. Allen, *Until the Last Man Comes Home*, 139–40; see also Franklin, *M.I.A.*, 122, 163.
150. Allen, *Until the Last Man Comes Home*, 1; Martini, *Invisible Enemies*, 24.
151. Cloyd, *Haunted by Atrocity*, 170–71.
152. Memorial Day Program, Andersonville NHS, May 27, 1985, Folder Memorial Day Through the Years, ANDE VF. Swindle would later direct Ross Perot's presidential campaign in 1992. Franklin, *M.I.A.*, 188.
153. "War Vets Honored at Impressive Memorial Day Ceremonies," *Americus Times-Recorder*, May 25, 1984, Folder Memorial Day Through the Years, ANDE VF; "Memorial Day Through the Years at Andersonville," 20.
154. "Memorial Day Through the Years at Andersonville," 22.
155. Superintendent's Annual Narrative Report for 1988, Folder Andersonville National Historic Site, Box 4, RG 79, NARA CP.
156. For more general accounts of this ceremony, see Cloyd, *Haunted by Atrocity*, 170–71, and "Memorial Day Through the Years at Andersonville," 22.
157. "Andersonville to Host Annual Memorial Day Service Sunday," *Americus Times Recorder*, May 27, 1998, Folder Memorial Day Through the Years, ANDE VF.
158. Charlotte Perkins, "Memorial Day Service Draws Over 800 to Andersonville," *Americus Times-Recorder*, May 30, 1988, Binder Press Releases Andersonville National Historic Site January 1988—Present, and "Memorial Day Through the Years at Andersonville," 22.
159. Perkins, "Memorial Day Service Draws Over 800 to Andersonville."
160. Allen, *Until the Last Man Comes Home*, 179–80; Franklin, *M.I.A.*, 97–102.
161. Perkins, "Memorial Day Service Draws Over 800 to Andersonville," and "Memorial Day Through the Years at Andersonville," 22.
162. "Andersonville Reunion," *Americus Times-Recorder*, May 30, 1988, 1, Folder Memorial Day Through the Years, ANDE VF.
163. Martini, *Invisible Enemies*, 184–85; Franklin, *M.I.A.*, 187; Rudy Hayes, "A'Ville Memorial Day Services Commemorate WWII 50th Anniversary," *Americus Times-Recorder*, May

25, 1992, Binder Press Releases Andersonville National Historic Site January 1988—Present, ANDE.

164. Stephen Jones, "Major General Lee Leads Andersonville Memorial Day Ceremony," *Macon County News Leader,* June 1, 2000. Andersonville NHS Articles 1997–2003, ANDE.
165. On normalization, see Martini, *Invisible Enemies,* 162–204.
166. Jim Stockdale, "Andersonville Memorial Day Speech—1994," 7, Folder Memorial Day Through the Years, ANDE VF.
167. This idea has long been central to the POW myth. Franklin, *M.I.A.,* 122.
168. Stockdale, "Andersonville Memorial Day Speech," 9–10.
169. Ibid., 10.
170. [Illegible] Harris, "Memorial Day Ceremony Urges Remembrance of Sacrifice," *Americus Times-Recorder,* May 26, 1998, Andersonville NHS Articles 1997–2003 Binder, ANDE.
171. Nan Gunn, "Impressive Memorial Day Services Feature Fighter Pilot Association Members," *Sumter Free Press,* May 28, 2003, n.p, Andersonville NHS Articles 1997–2003.
172. Fred Boyles to Chief, Cultural Resources Stewardship, SERO, January 20, 1999, "Park Annual Narrative Reports," Folder 4, Box 2635, RG79, NARA CP.
173. Ibid.
174. "Andersonville and Jimmy Carter National Historic Sites Annual Narrative Report 1999," Item D-39, NPS-DSC; "Superintendent's 2000 Annual Narrative Report," January 30, 2001, Item D-40, NPS-DSC. Cloyd notes this boom in attendance as well. *Haunted by Atrocity,* 177.
175. See Glenn Robbins, review of Andersonville NHS, *Journal of American History* 99.1 (2012), 277–79.
176. Cloyd, *Haunted by Atrocity,* 177, 179, 178, 181.
177. Barry Howard Ltd., *Final Exhibit Notebook: National Prisoner of War Museum,* October 1993, Book 1, ANDE, 3.1.G1b and 3.1.T1a.
178. Ibid., 3.1.G1b.
179. Ibid., 4.4.T1, 4.4.G1.
180. Ibid., 4.5.G1, 4.5.T1, and 3.3.T2a.
181. Ibid., 6.23.T1.
182. Ibid., 5.5.T3, 5.5.G1, 5.16.A1, 5.16.A2.
183. Ibid., 5.13.T1.
184. Ibid., 6.20.T1, 6.21.T1, 6.24.T1.
185. Ibid., 6.26.T1.
186. Barry Howard Ltd., *Final Exhibit Notebook: National Prisoner of War Museum,* October, 1993, Book 2, ANDE 7.6.T2, 7.6.T1.
187. Ibid., 7.1.T1a.
188. Tim Radford and Justin Radford, "National Prisoner of War Museum, Andersonville National Historic Site Exhibit Audiovisuals," February 25, 1997, (8.) Those Who Wait NPS-TV#620, NPS-DCC.
189. Ibid.
190. Ibid.
191. Susan Carruthers, *Cold War Captives: Imprisonment, Escape, and Brainwashing* (Berkeley: University of California Press, 2009), 191, 193. See also Robbins, "Review of National Prisoner of War Museum," 278.
192. Barry Howard Ltd., *Final Exhibit Notebook,* Book 2, 8.8.T1.
193. Ibid.

194. Ibid., 8.8.T1a. The original exhibit plan called for the use of the cover image from *Life*, October 20, 1967. Ibid., 8.1.G1b.
195. Ibid., 8.16.G1, 8.16.T2, 8.8.T2.
196. Ibid., 8.21.R1.
197. Radford and Radford, "National Prisoner of War Museum, Andersonville National Historic Site Exhibit Audiovisuals," February 25, 1997, (10) Hanoi Hilton—*Alcatraz*, NPS-AS #72, "The National Prisoner of War Memorial Museum."
198. *Final Exhibit Notebook*, Book 1, 2.1.T1a.
199. Richard J. Newman, "Museums: Honoring Prisoners of War," *U.S. News and World Report*, April 20, 1998, 14; Christina Nifong, "Tribute to POWs in Bricks and Mortar," *CSM*, April 10, 1998; Charles Seabrook, "Remembering the Horrors of War," *AJC*, March 30, 1998; AP, "Exhibit Honors Wartime Captives," *Orlando Sentinel*, March 30, 1998; George Coryell, "A Prison Once Called 'Hell on Earth' Becomes a Memorial to the Perseverance to Survive," *Baylife* (*Tampa Tribune*), April 26, 1998., Binder April 9, 1998, ANDE.
200. Franklin, *M.I.A.*, 133.
201. Ibid., 47, 134–35. See also Martini, *Invisible Enemies*, 56–57.
202. Querin Herlick, "Russian Roulette as Interrogation Technique," video interview, National Prisoner of War Museum, Andersonville.
203. Barry Howard Ltd., *Final Exhibit Notebook*, Book 2, 8.15.R1, 8.12.T2.
204. Ibid., 8.12.T1.
205. Franklin, *M.I.A.*, 48.
206. Barry Howard Ltd., *Final Exhibit Notebook*, Book 2, 8.12.T2; Franklin, *M.I.A.*, 133.
207. On this silence, see Marita Sturken, *Tangled Memories: The Vietnam War, the Aids Epidemic, and the Politics of Remembering* (Berkeley: University of California Press, 1998), 62–63. This affirmation is in keeping with Cloyd's larger critique that the museum "serves as an opportunity to celebrate liberty and the price we are willing to pay for it." *Haunted by Atrocity*, 179.
208. Doug Cumming, "Not Free to Grieve; Loved Ones of Vietnam MIAs Gather Again in Gnawing Hope," *AJC*, March 3, 1997.
209. Kimberly Ann Norris, "GSW Hosts POW/MIA Convocation," *Americus Times-Recorder*, September 15, 2010.
210. Victor Miller, "Call Leads to 'Relief' for Family of Dalton Vietnam-era MIA," *Dalton (Ga.) Daily Citizen*, July 31, 2008, http://daltondailycitizen.com.
211. Ibid.
212. Norris, "GSW Hosts POW/MIA Convocation."

2. "WE VETERANS OF MASS MURDER AND STUPIDITY"

1. James W. Hamilton, "Unusual Long-Term Sequelae of a Traumatic War Experience," *Bulletin of Menninger Clinic* 46.6 (1982), 539.
2. Ibid., 540.
3. On the history of PTSD, see Gerald Nicosia, *Home to War: A History of the Vietnam Veterans' Movement* (New York: Carroll and Graff, 2004), 202–9; Robert Jay Lifton, *Home from the War: Vietnam Veterans: Neither Victims Nor Executioners* (New York: Simon and Schuster, 1973); Patrick Hagopian, *The Vietnam War in American Memory: Veterans, Memorials, and the Politics of Healing* (Amherst: University of Massachusetts Press, 2009), 49–78; Wilbur J. Scott, *Vietnam Veterans since the War: The Politics of PTSD, Agent Orange, and the National Memorial* (Norman: University of Oklahoma Press, 2004).

4. Craig Van Dyke et al., "Post-Traumatic Stress Disorder: A Thirty-Year Delay in a World War II Veteran," *American Journal of Psychiatry* 132.9 (1985), 1071; Janet S. Richmond and James C. Beck, "Posttraumatic Stress Disorder in a World War II Veteran," Letter to the Editor, *American Journal of Psychiatry* 143 (1986), 1485–86; Robert Hierholzer et al., "Clinical Presentation of PTSD in World War II Combat Veterans," *Hospital and Community Psychiatry* 43.8 (1992), 818. Some of these accounts as well as others are also mentioned in Elizabeth Colerick Clipp and Glenn H. Elder, "The Aging Veteran of World War II: Psychiatric and Life Course Insights," in *Aging and Post-Traumatic Stress Disorder*, ed. Paul E. Ruskin and John A. Talbott, 27–28 (Washington, D.C.: American Psychiatric Publishers, 1996).
5. E. B. Sledge, *With the Old Breed: At Peleliu and Okinawa* (New York: Oxford University Press, 1990), 315; Paul Fussell, *Doing Battle: The Making of a Skeptic* (Boston: Back Bay Books, 1996), 242.
6. John Bodnar, *The "Good War" in American Memory* (Baltimore: Johns Hopkins University Press, 2010), 48–56, 238–39; Casey Clabough, "Confronting Traumatic Anxiety: William Manchester's *Goodbye, Darkness*," *War, Literature and the Arts* 16.1, 2 (2004). Jeremy Saucier also notes that "some representations of World War II (especially since the Vietnam War) depicted the war with increasing ambivalence." "Calls of Duty: The World War II Combat Video Game and the Construction of the 'Next Great Generation,'" MS in author's possession. Andrew J. Huebner identifies several revisionist Second World War films of the Vietnam era. *The Warrior Image: Soldiers in American Culture from the Second World War to the Vietnam Era* (Chapel Hill: University of North Carolina Press, 2008), 243–46.
7. Shoshana Felman and Dori Laub, *Testimony: Crises of Witnessing in Literature, Psychoanalysis, and History* (New York: Routledge, 1992), 63, 58. See also Leigh Gilmore, *The Limits of Autobiography: Trauma and Testimony* (Ithaca: Cornell University Press, 2001), 7; Jonathan Shay, *Achilles in Vietnam: Combat Trauma and the Undoing of Character* (New York: Atheneum, 1994), 188; Vamik Volkan, *Blind Trust: Large Groups and Their Leaders in Times of Crisis and Terror* (Charlottesville: Pitchstone Press, 2004), 32, 33, 39; Kalí Tal, *Worlds of Hurt: Reading the Literatures of Trauma* (Cambridge: Cambridge University Press, 1996), 115–16; Laurie Vickroy, *Trauma and Survival in Contemporary Fiction* (Charlottesville: University of Virginia Press, 2002), 13, 23, 25; and Kai Erikson, "Notes on Trauma and Community," in *Trauma: Explorations in Memory*, ed. Cathy Caruth, 194 (Baltimore: Johns Hopkins University Press, 1995).
8. Gilmore, *The Limits of Autobiography*, 6.
9. Philip H. Melling, *Vietnam in American Literature* (Boston: Twayne, 1990), 49; James Landers, *The Weekly War: Newsmagazines and Vietnam* (Columbia: University of Missouri Press, 2004), 5, 88–90; William M. Hammond, *Reporting Vietnam: Media and Military at War* (Lawrence: University Press of Kansas, 1999), 187, 193; Christian G. Appy, *Patriots: The Vietnam War Remembered from All Sides* (New York: Penguin Books, 2003), 238; Theodore Solotaroff, "Memoirs for Memorial Day," Review of *A Rumor of War*, by Philip Caputo, *New York Times Book Review*, May 29, 1977; Samuel Hynes, *The Soldiers' Tale: Bearing Witness to Modern War* (New York: Penguin Books, 1998), 212.
10. Merrill I. Lipton and William R. Schaeffer, "Post-Traumatic Stress Disorder in the Older Veteran," *Military Medicine* 151.10 (1986), 522.
11. Ibid., 522–23.
12. John L. Black and Terrence M. Keane, "Implosive Therapy in the Treatment of Combat-Related

Fears in a World War II Veteran," *Journal of Behavioral Therapy and Experimental Psychiatry* 13.2 (1982), 166, 163, 165.

13. U.S. Congress, Senate Committee on Veterans Affairs, *Veterans' Programs Extension and Improvement Act of 1981*, 97th Cong. 1st sess., 1981, 483.
14. Ibid.
15. House Subcommittee on Government Operations, *Diversion of Funds from Vietnam Veterans Readjustment Counseling Program*, 98th Cong., 2nd sess., 1984, 91; Senate Committee on Veterans Affairs, *Oversight of Post Traumatic Stress Disorder*, 100th Cong., 2nd sess., 1988, 261.
16. On Vet Centers, see Nicosia, *Home to War*, 517–20.
17. "For Many Vietnam Veterans, the Agonies of Battle Still Rage," AP, May 3, 1981.
18. U.S. Congress, Senate Committee on Veterans Affairs, *Diversion of Funds from Vietnam Veterans Readjustment Counseling Program*. 98th Cong., 2nd sess., 1984, 29.
19. "Center Aids Veterans Whose Problems Outlasted War," *NYT*, March 11, 1984.
20. Among the texts that challenge this narrative is Thomas Childers, *Soldier from the War Returning: The Greatest Generation's Troubled Homecoming from World War II* (Boston: Mariner Books, 2009).
21. Senate Committee on Veterans Affairs, *Diversion of Funds*, 91.
22. Hierholzer, "Clinical Presentation of PTSD," 816; Jack E. Games and Carl T. Hayden, "Abating the Trauma of World War II and Korean Conflict Veterans," *VA Practitioner* 8.7 (1991), 69; Charles G. Boyd and Kathryn M. Ward, "A PTSD Group for World War II and Korean Conflict Veterans," *VA Practitioner* 9.9 (1992), 99.
23. Some clinicians feared that older veterans who faced other physical and mental declines might experience PTSD differently. See Mary N. Summers et al., "Diagnosis of Later-Life PTSD among Elderly Combat Veterans," *Journal of Clinical Geropsychology* 2.2 (1996), 103; Clipp and Elder, "The Aging Veteran of World War II," 27.
24. Elizabeth Clipp and Glen Elder briefly discuss research comparing these populations. "The Aging Veteran of World War II," 35.
25. Jonathan R. T. Davidson et al., "Symptom and Comorbidity Patterns in World War II and Vietnam Veterans with Posttraumatic Stress Disorder," *Comprehensive Psychiatry* 31.2 (1990), 163.
26. Ibid., 165.
27. Ibid.; Clipp and Elder paraphrase these data, "The Aging Veteran of World War II," 35.
28. Davidson, et al., 167. Clipp and Elder paraphrase this conclusion. "The Aging Veteran of World War II," 35.
29. Alan Fontana et al., *The Long Journey Home: The First Progress Report on the Department of Veterans Affairs PTSD Clinical Teams Program* (West Haven, Conn.: Northeast Program Evaluation Center, Department of Veterans Affairs Medical Center, 1990), 14.
30. Ibid., 26. See also ibid., 14.
31. Alan Fontana et al., *The Long Journey Home III: The Third Progress Report on the Department of Veterans Affairs Specialized PTSD Programs* (West Haven, Conn.: Northeast Program Evaluation Center, 1993), 79.
32. Robert Rosenheck and Alan Fontana, "Long Term Sequelae of Combat in World War II, Korea, and Vietnam: A Comparative Study," in *Individual and Community Responses to Trauma and Disaster: The Structure of Human Chaos*, ed. Robert J. Ursano et al., (Cambridge: Cambridge University Press, 1994), 331, 333.
33. Ibid., 341.
34. Ibid., 346–47.

35. Ibid, 346.
36. Barbara F. Key et al., "Journey Out of the Night: Spiritual Renewal for Combat Veterans," *VA Practitioner* 11.1 (January 1994), 60.
37. House Committee on Veterans Affairs, Subcommittee on Hospitals and Healthcare, H.R. 4833, *A Bill to Authorize the VA to Provide Comprehensive Treatment Services to Veterans Suffering from Post-Traumatic-Stress Disorder, and the Veterans' Readjustment Counseling Program,* 98th Cong., 2nd sess., 1984, 52; House Committee on Veterans Affairs, Subcommittee on Hospitals and Healthcare, *Veterans' Administration Mental Health Programs,* 99th Cong., 1st sess., 61; *Oversight of PTSD,* 56–57; Vets Centers Meeting Notes, July 21, 1987, Folder 100th Congress Vet Center Info, Box 2, Senate Veterans Affairs Committee (Republican) Legislative Files—S. 1464/H.R. 2327, 100th Cong., RG 46, NARA.
38. U.S. Congress, Committee on Veterans Affairs, *Senate Report 102–118,* 102nd Cong., 1st sess., July 24, 1991.
39. House Committee on Veterans Affairs, Subcommittee on Hospitals and Healthcare, *Delivery of Mental Health Care Services and H.R. 3037,* 101st Cong. 2nd sess., 1990, 54, 182. See also *Oversight of PTSD,* 524, 547.
40. *Veterans' Administration Beneficiary Travel, Quality Assurance, and Readjustment Counseling Amendments of 1987,* S. 1464, on October 16, 1987, *CR* 133 pt. 162: 28205.
41. Veterans Administration Views on S. 1464, Folder S.14164/H.R. 2327 Senate Pass., Box 1: Senate Veterans Affairs Committee (Republican) Legislative Files—S. 1464/H.R. 2327, 100th Cong., RG 46, NARA.
42. Anthony J. Principi to Republican LA's for Veterans' Issues, July 16, 1987, Folder S. 1501 Cranston Vet Centers, Box 2, Senate Veterans Affairs Committee (Republican) Legislative Files—S. 1464/H.R. 2327, 100th Cong., RG 46, NARA.
43. Senator Murkowski of Alaska, speaking for Amendment 1007 on October 16, 1987, 100th Cong., 1st sess., *CR* 133, pt. 162, S14467.
44. Ibid.
45. Senator Helms of North Carolina, speaking for Amendment 1007 on October 16, 1987, 100th Cong., 1st sess., *CR* 133, pt. 162, S14491.
46. Senator Simpson of Wyoming, speaking for Amendment 1007 on October 16, 1987, 100th Cong., 1st sess., *CR* 133, pt. 162, S14491.
47. Ibid., S14492.
48. See Senator Cranston of California, Speaking in Favor of the Vietnam Veterans' Readjustment Counseling Program Preservation Act on July 15, 1987, 100th Cong., 1st sess., *CR* 133, pt. 117, S1068-69, and Cranston, Speaking in Favor of S.1464 on October 16, 1987, 100th Cong., 1st sess., *CR* 133, pt. 162, S1464-65.
49. Arthur Blank Jr. to Legislation and Policy Staff, March 29, 1988, Folder Readjustment / Vet Centers, Box 100-4, Committee on Veterans Affairs Oversight Files, 100th Cong., RG 46, NARA.
50. Ibid., 3.
51. Ibid.
52. Ibid. 4, 5.
53. Ibid., 5, 6.
54. Senator Cranston of California, speaking on the Veterans Administration Health Care Benefits Conference Report on April 28, 1988, 100th Cong., 2nd sess., *CR* 134, pt. 57: S5166.
55. Senator Cranston of California, speaking on S. 2100 on October 10, 1990, 101st Cong., 2nd sess. *CR* 136, pt. 134: S14877.

56. Ibid.; Senator Cranston of California, speaking on veterans programs, on March 21, 1991, 102nd Cong., 1st sess. *CR* 137, pt. 49: 7163.
57. Alan Simpson, Letter to the Editor, *Casper Star Tribune,* December 11, 1992, Folder 2, Box 52, AKSP.
58. "News from Senator Alan K. Simpson," March 29, 1988, 1. Folder 5, Box 50, AKSP.
59. Ibid., 3.
60. Claire Robb, et. al., "Attitudes Towards Mental Health Care in Younger and Older Adults: Similarities and Differences," *Aging & Mental Health* 7.2 (2003), 142–43. See also Jillian Zeitvogel Pino, "Age Group Differences in Older Adults' Attitudes Towards Psychotherapy and Willingness to Seek Help" (Psy.D. diss., Indiana University of Pennsylvania, 2012), 6.
61. Simpson to Colleagues, September 19, 1990, Folder 3, Box 516, AKSP. For Cranston's response; see Cranston to Colleagues, September 27, 1990, Folder 3, Box 516, AKS.
62. Senator Simpson of Wyoming, speaking on S. 2100 on October 10, 1990, 101st Cong., 2nd sess. *CR* 136, pt. 134: S.14883-84.
63. Edward J. Derwinski to Simpson, June 27, 1990, Folder 3, Box 516, AKS. This information appeared in Simpson's talking points the next day. Simpson, "Talking Points on Administration Objections," June 28, 1990, Folder 3, Box 516, AKS.
64. "Talking Points Support Murkowski Motion to Strike Readjustment Counseling Provisions for Korean and WWII Veterans," Folder 5, Box 516, AKS.
65. Senator Simpson of Wyoming, Speaking in Favor of Amendment 1359, on November 20, 1991. 102nd Cong., 1st sess. *CR* 137, pt. 172: S.17139.
66. Ibid., 17140.
67. Indeed, budgetary concerns seem to have been a fig leaf, as Republicans were aware that the expansion would entail "no cost" (Minority Staff to Minority Staff, Memorandum, June 20, 1990, 4–5, Folder 6-28-90 Markup: Mary's Memos Minority, Box 101-143 (Box 1 of 2), RG46, NARA.
68. Senate Committee on Veterans Affairs, *VA Mental Health Programs,* 103rd Cong., 1st sess., 1993, 7, 20, 21.
69. Ibid., 21.
70. Ibid.
71. Simpson to Dave, August 4, 1993, Folder 8, Box 479, AKS.
72. Ibid.
73. Andrea Stone, "Some WWII Vets Fight Enemy Within; Post-Traumatic Stress No Longer Suffered in Silence," *USA Today,* November 11, 1994; Francis X. Clines, "On Sunday; Unwelcome Memories Wake Dead," *NYT,* April 30, 1995. See also Bodnar, *The "Good War" in American Memory,* 215.
74. Lacy McCrary, "WWII Vets Are Reliving the Trauma," *PI,* August 3, 1995; Jane Gottlieb, "An Old Soldier Confronts His Anger," *Albany Times Union,* June 28, 1996.
75. Clines, "On Sunday."
76. Mitchell Landsberg, "Fifty Years Later, War Stress Ambushes World War II Vets," AP, August 6, 1995.
77. *South Bend Tribune,* "Even After 50 Years War Still Is Hell," August 17, 1995.
78. Senate Committee on Veterans Affairs, *Pending Legislation on Veterans Health Care,* 104th Cong., 1st sess., 1995, 25.
79. *Veterans' Health Care Eligibility Reform Act of 1996,* Public Law 104-262, 104th Cong., 2d sess. (October 9, 1996), 21.

80. Senator Akaka of Hawaii, speaking on H.R. 3118, on September 30, 1996, 104th Cong., 2d sess., *CR* 138: S12012.
81. Senator Simpson of Wyoming, speaking on "Veterans' Health Care Reform Act of 1996," on September 28, 1996, 104th Cong., 2d sess., *CR* 137, pt. 1: S11642-43.
82. Ibid., S11645.
83. Ibid.
84. Paul Fussell, *Wartime: Understanding and Behavior in the Second World War* (New York: Oxford University Press, 1989), ix.
85. David Streitfeld, "War and the Pity of War," *WP*, August 13, 1989.
86. Fussell, *Doing Battle*, n.p.
87. *NYT*, "Paperback Best Sellers," January 31, 1982.
88. Bodnar, *The 'Good War' in American Memory*, 48–56.
89. On the social struggles of returning veterans, see Childers, *Soldier from the War Returning*, 118, 129–31, 216–17.
90. See, among other examples, Audie Murphy, *To Hell and Back: The Classic Memoir of World War II by America's Most Decorated Soldier* (1949; repr., New York: Owl Books, 2002), 4, 15, 51, 99, 160, 174, 177, 202, 215, 217, 233–35, 241; Charles MacDonald, *Company Commander: The Classic Infantry Memoir of World War II* (1947; repr., Ithaca: Burford Books, 1999), 30, 74, 157.
91. The dominant remembrance is well documented. See, among others, Huebner, *The Warrior Image*, 142, 163.
92. On soldiers' experiences generally, see Gerald F. Linderman, *The World within War: America's Combat Experience in World War II* (New York: Free Press, 1997).
93. Ross Carter, *Those Devils in Baggy Pants* (New York: Signet, 1951), 28, 177, 179; Robert Leckie, *Helmet for My Pillow: From Parris Island to the Pacific* (New York: Bantam Books, 2010), 68, 134. See also Lester Atwell, *Private* (New York: Simon and Schuster, 1958), 216.
94. Carter, *Those Devils in Baggy Pants*, 24, 47–48; Atwell, *Private*, 119; James C. Fry, *Combat Soldier* (Washington, D.C.: National Press, 1968), 35, 79, 116.
95. See, for example, Fry, *Combat Soldier*, 11, 113–14, 139, 187; Atwell, *Private*, 166–67, 200; and Howard Randall, *Dirt and Doughfeet: Combat Experiences of a Rifle Platoon Leader* (New York: Exposition Press, 1955), 77, 104. See also Linderman, *The World within War*, 119, 125–32, 140.
96. Atwell, *Private*, 496; Linderman discusses this scene. *The World within War*, 130–31.
97. Carter, *Those Devils in Baggy Pants*, n.p.; Leckie, *Helmet for My Pillow*, 304; Randall, *Dirt and Doughfeet*, 113.
98. Atwell, *Private*, 153.
99. They are thus similar to what Huebner describes in contemporaneous film. *The Warrior Image*, 141.
100. Fry, *Combat Soldier*, 95; Atwell, *Private*, 275; Leckie, *Helmet for My Pillow*, 38, 86–87, 286. Similar scenes are in Atwell, *Private*, 279, and Randall, *Dirt and Doughfeet*, 52. Linderman cites very few passages that are exceptions. *The World within War*, 121, 140).
101. Elaine Scarry, *The Body in Pain: The Making and Unmaking of the World* (New York: Oxford University Press, 1985), 63.
102. Ibid., 72, 75, 80.
103. Carter, *Those Devils in Baggy Pants*, 60; Fry, *Combat Soldier*, 102; Randall, *Dirt and Doughfeet*, 57.
104. Leckie, *Helmet for My Pillow*, 82, 227.

105. Randall, *Dirt and Doughfeet,* 35, 62, 85.
106. Atwell, *Private,* 34.
107. Fry, *Combat Soldier,* 5; Randall, *Dirt and Doughfeet,* 42; and Atwell, *Private,* 153, 237.
108. Fry, *Combat Soldier,* 69. In contrast, see Philip Caputo, *A Rumor of War* (New York: Henry Holt, 1977), 128.
109. See Fry, *Combat Soldier,* 136, 159, 220, 336; Atwell, *Private,* 55, 153.
110. Atwell, *Private,* 110, 55. See also Randall, *Dirt and Doughfeet,* 74.
111. Linderman, *The World within War,* 71; see, more generally, 71–75.
112. Atwell, *Private,* 172. See also Fry, *Combat Soldier,* 31, 140.
113. Judith Butler, *Frames of War: When Is Life Grieveable?* (London: Verso, 2009), 15, 42–43; Fry, *Combat Soldier,* 136–37.
114. Fry, *Combat Soldier,* 173, 137, 31.
115. Randall, *Dirt and Doughfeet,* 43; Atwell, *Private,* 133.
116. Carter, *Those Devils in Baggy Pants,* 41.
117. Fry, *Combat Soldier,* 55. Only Atwell reflects on wartime injuries' long-term effects. *Private,* 262–63.
118. See Randall, *Dirt and Doughfeet,* 46–47; Atwell, *Private,* 491; Leckie, *Helmet for My* Pillow, 261–63; and Carter, *Those Devils in Baggy Pants,* 169–73.
119. Leckie, *Helmet for My Pillow,* 233.
120. Thomas Myers, *Walking Point: American Narratives of Vietnam* (New York: Oxford University Press, 1988), 72, and Tobey Herzog, *Vietnam War Stories: Innocence Lost* (London: Routledge, 1992), 13, discern this structure.
121. Caputo, *A Rumor of War,* 7; Sledge, *With the Old Breed,* 5.
122. Ron Kovic, *Born on the Fourth of July: A True Story of Innocence Lost and Courage Found* (New York: Pocket Books, 1975), 73; Sledge, *With the Old Breed,* 5.
123. Sledge, *With the Old Breed,* 10; O'Brien, *If I Die in a Combat Zone (Box Me Up and Ship Me Home)* (New York: Broadway Books, 1999), 43.
124. William Manchester, *Goodbye, Darkness: A Memoir of the Pacific War* (Boston: Little, Brown, 1980), 28; Caputo, *A Rumor of War,* 5.
125. Fussell, *Doing Battle,* 28; Kovic, *Born on the Fourth of July,* 55–56.
126. See Herzog, *Vietnam War Stories,* 72, and Hynes, *The Soldiers' Tale,* 191. Scarry, *The Body in Pain,* 65.
127. Caputo, *A Rumor of War,* 169.
128. Ibid., 119–20.
129. Butler, *Frames of War,* 25, 42–43; Caputo, *A Rumor of War,* 124.
130. O'Brien, *If I Die in a Combat Zone,* 112.
131. Ibid., 112–14.
132. Kovic, *Born on the Fourth of July,* 29, 34, 109, 31.
133. Melling, *Vietnam in American Literature,* 57–58.
134. Caputo, *A Rumor of War,* 128.
135. Myers, *Walking Point,* 96, 97.
136. This statement exemplifies Vickroy's definition. *Trauma and Survival in Contemporary Fiction,* 23. See also Tal, *Worlds of Hurt,* 116.
137. See, for example, Katherine Kinney, *Friendly Fire: American Images of the Vietnam War* (Oxford: Oxford University Press, 2000), 28, and Bates, *The Wars We Took to Vietnam,* 258.
138. Kovic, *Born on the Fourth of July,* 35.

139. Ibid., 165–66.
140. Manchester, *Goodbye, Darkness*, 186.
141. Fussell, *Doing Battle*, 123.
142. Manchester, *Goodbye, Darkness*, 6–7.
143. Caputo, *A Rumor of War*, 169–70.
144. O'Brien, *If I Die in a Combat Zone*, 113–14; Manchester, *Goodbye, Darkness*, 7.
145. Clabough notes that this scene reveals Manchester's "traumatic anxiety." "Confronting Traumatic Anxiety," 221.
146. On Manchester's fascination with his father's service, see ibid., 224–26.
147. Sledge, *With the Old Breed*, 117.
148. Fussell, *Doing Battle*, 105.
149. Manchester, *Goodbye, Darkness*, 388.
150. Sledge, *With the Old Breed*, 120; Leckie, *Helmet for My Pillow*, 86–87. On this practice more generally, sometimes quoting Sledge, see Hynes, *The Soldiers' Tale*, 192; John W. Dower, *War without Mercy: Race and Power in the Pacific War* (New York: Pantheon, 1987), 63–66 (on atrocities in the Pacific War more generally, see 66–67); Linderman, *The World within War*, 180–84; Bodnar, *The 'Good War' in American Memory*, 53.
151. Linderman, *The World within War*, 183.
152. Sledge, *With the Old Breed*, 152.
153. Michael Herr, *Dispatches* (New York: Vintage International, 1977), 99, 34; Caputo, *A Rumor of War*, 67; O'Brien, *If I Die in a Combat Zone*, 83.
154. Caputo, *A Rumor of War*, 67; Sledge, *With the Old Breed*, 153.
155. Sledge, *With the Old Breed*, 121; Caputo, *A Rumor of War*, 229.
156. Fussell, *Doing Battle*, 124.
157. *NYT*, "Transcript of Interview of Vietnam War Veteran on His Role in Alleged Massacre of Civilians at Songmy," November 25, 1969.
158. Fussell, *Doing Battle*, 124. Fussell early quotes Tobias Wolff; see also *Doing Battle*, 114.
159. Ibid., 108.
160. Kovic, *Born on the Fourth of July*, 166. On fatalism in the Second World War, see Linderman, *The World within War*, 83–89.
161. Fussell, *Doing Battle*, 163, 123; Kovic, *Born on the Fourth of July*, 166.
162. Kovic, *Born on the Fourth of July*, 165; Fussell, *Doing Battle*, 101.
163. Caputo, *A Rumor of War*, 332. On Kennedy's centrality to Vietnam memoirists' disillusionment, see John Hellman, *American Myth and the Legacy of Vietnam* (New York: Columbia University Press, 1986), 121.
164. Sledge, *With the Old Breed*, 146; Hynes calls these "recruiting office feelings." *The Soldiers' Tale*, 174.
165. Herzog, *Vietnam War Stories*, 73.
166. Sledge, *With the Old Breed*, 156.
167. Kovic, *Born on the Fourth of July*, 167.
168. Manchester, *Goodbye, Darkness*, 28–29.
169. Ibid., 382.
170. Ibid., 10. Clabough notes that Manchester's nightmares are archetypal symptoms of psychic trauma. "Confronting Traumatic Anxiety," 223.
171. Ibid., 395, 135.
172. Ibid., 200–201.
173. Herzog, *Vietnam War Stories*, 73.

174. O'Brien, *If I Die in a Combat Zone*, 175; Caputo, *A Rumor of War*, 223. Donald Ringnalda asserts that this moment summarizes O'Brien's criticisms of Vietnam. *Fighting and Writing the Vietnam War* (Jackson: University Press of Mississippi), 97.
175. Clabough, "Confronting Traumatic Anxiety," 230–31.
176. Kovic, *Born on the Fourth of July*, 223–24.
177. Kinney, *Friendly Fire*, 29.
178. Bodnar, *The 'Good War' in American Memory*, 49; Manchester, *Goodbye, Darkness*, 393–95.
179. Caputo, *A Rumor of War*, 22; Fussell, Doing *Battle*, 183, 237; E. B. Sledge, *China Marine: An Infantryman's Life after World War II* (New York: Oxford, 2002), 150–51.
180. Kovic, *Born on the Fourth of July*, 163; Sledge, *With the Old Breed*, 235; Sledge, *China Marine*, 151.
181. Sledge, *With the Old Breed*, 269; Caputo, *A Rumor of War*, 199.
182. Caputo, *A Rumor of War*, 4.
183. Manchester, *Goodbye, Darkness*, 262.
184. Fussell, *Doing Battle*, 183.
185. Ibid., 299.

3. "WE SEE A LOT OF PARALLELS BETWEEN THE MEN AT THE ALAMO AND OURSELVES"

1. Doralisa Pilarte, "Bush Helps Texas Remember the Alamo," AP, March 3, 1986. George H. W. Bush, "Excerpts from Remarks by Vice President George Bush, San Antonio Celebration of the Texas Sesquicentennial," 1. Folder "Original Press Releases 1/86–3/86," Box 1649, OA/ID 14920-008, Press Release Files, Press Office Series, George H. W. Bush Vice Presidential Records, George Bush Presidential Library, College Station, Texas.
2. UPI, "Bush Honors Alamo Heroes on Texas Independence Day," March 3, 1986.
3. James Coburn, "Support Growing for 'Last Patrol:' Big Crowd Expected at Alamo," *San Antonio Express News*. November 9, 1985.
4. Joe Vargo, "Vietnam Veterans End Vigil for 'Patrol Still Out,'" *Austin American-Statesman*, November 12, 1985; Jim Price, "Veterans in United Front at Alamo Plaza Ceremony," *San Antonio Express News*, November 12, 1985.
5. Wolfgang Schivelbusch, *The Culture of Defeat: On National Trauma, Mourning, and Recovery* (New York: Metropolitan Books, 2001), 6–7, 289.
6. Ibid., 13.
7. Ibid., 17.
8. Ibid., 58.
9. On the Vietnam syndrome and Reagan's invocation of it in these terms, see Patrick Hagopian, *The Vietnam War in American Memory: Veterans, Memorials, and the Politics of Healing* (Amherst: University of Massachusetts Press, 2009), 37–38, and Melani McAlister, *Epic Encounters: Culture, Media, and U.S. Interests in the Middle East, 1945–2000* (Berkeley: University of California Press, 2001), 186–87; Ronald Reagan, "Peace: Restoring the Margin of Safety: Address to the Veterans of Foreign Wars Convention, August 18, 1980," Ronald Reagan Presidential Library, www.reagan.utexas.edu.
10. Hagopian, *The Vietnam War in American Memory*, 39, 49; Reagan, "Peace: The Margin of Safety."
11. Holly Beachley Brear, "We Run the Alamo, and You Don't: Alamo Battles of Ethnicity and Gender," in Fitzhugh Brundage, ed. *Where These Memories Grow*, 299; Richard R. Flores, *Remembering the Alamo: Myth, Modernity, and the Master Symbol* (Austin: University

of Texas Press, 2002), ix; Edward Tabor Linenthal, *Sacred Ground: Americans and Their Battlefields,* 2d ed. (Urbana: University of Illinois Press, 1993), 55, 57.

12. On the marginalization of Latinos in the Alamo story, see Flores, *Remembering the Alamo,* 91; Beachley Brear, "We Run the Alamo and You Don't," 302; Linenthal, *Sacred Ground,* 70–78. Regarding Texans' desire for land, their attitudes toward slavery, and their actions during the battle, see H. W. Brands, *Lone Star Nation: How a Ragged Army of Volunteers Won the Battle for Texas Independence—and Changed America* (New York: Doubleday, 2004), 157, 169, 279, 340, 366–67, 379, and Phillip Thomas Tucker, *Exodus from the Alamo: The Anatomy of the Last Stand Myth* (Philadelphia: Casemate, 2010), 13, 15, 40, 253–301.
13. Linenthal, *Sacred Ground,* 63–64.
14. Ibid., 60; Randy Roberts and James S. Olsson, *A Line in the Sand: The Alamo in Blood and Memory* (New York: Touchstone, 2001), 242.
15. Linenthal, *Sacred Ground,* 57, 59; Flores, *Remembering the Alamo,* 154; Roberts and Olsson, *A Line in the Sand,* 282, 297.
16. Linenthal, *Sacred Ground,* 55–57.
17. Ibid., 62,
18. Ibid., 63–64. See also ibid., 57.
19. Ibid., 55.
20. On Alamo memory during the Cold War, see Roberts and Olsson, *A Line in the Sand,* 241–42, 271–72, and Linenthal, *Sacred Ground,* 59–62.
21. Here, I am following Kristin Ann Hass, *Sacrificing Soldiers on the National Mall* (Berkeley: University of California Press, 2013), 197–98.
22. AP, "Reagan Will Fight for Contra Aid," *San Antonio Express-News,* March 3, 1986.
23. On the Central America policy of the United States, see Hagopian, *The Vietnam War in American Memory,* 40–48; William M. LeoGrande, *Our Own Backyard: The United States and Central America, 1977–1992* (Chapel Hill: University of North Carolina Press, 1998); Roger Peace, *A Call to Conscience: The Anti-Contra War Campaign* (Amherst: University of Massachusetts Press, 2012).
24. Arthur Moczygemba, "Sandinistas Killing Miskitos, Indian Says; Freedom Fighter to Tell Story of Nicaraguan Betrayal," *San Antonio Express-News,* March 3, 1986.
25. Linenthal, *Sacred Ground,* 56–57. Here, I am also drawing on Benedict Anderson's comments about newspapers and the "imagined linkage" of events. *Imagined Communities: Reflections on the Origin and Spread of Nationalism* (London: Verso, 2002), 33.
26. UPI, "Washington News," March 4, 1986.
27. John B. Oakes, "No Illusions about Nicaragua, Please; U.S. Aid is Misguided," *NYT,* March 7, 1986.
28. Mike Coleman and Edward Walsh, "2 More House Panels Bar Contra Aid; Third Committee Backs It; Floor Vote Set for March 19," *WP,* March 7, 1986.
29. Anthony Lewis, "When Reagan Flees, Abroad at Home," *NYT,* March 10, 1985; see also Hagopian, *The Vietnam War in American Memory,* 40.
30. Ronald Reagan, "Address before a Joint Session of the Congress on Central America," April 27, 1983, Ronald Reagan Presidential Library, www.reagan.utexas.edu.
31. Steven S. Rosenfeld, "Democrats: Their Own Foreign Policy?," *WP,* May 9, 1986. Robert Busby, *Reagan and the Politics of the Iran-Contra Affair: The Politics of Presidential Recovery* (New York: St. Martin's Press, 1999), 55; James M. Scott, *Deciding to Intervene: The Reagan Doctrine and American Foreign Policy* (Durham: Duke University Press, 1996), 28–30.
32. Rick Marshall, "Nicaragua: A Test of Wills," *Defense and Foreign Affairs* XIV:12 (1986), 8.

33. Don Inman, "Vietnam and Central America . . . Light at the End of the Tunnel Vision," *VVA Veteran* 5.1 (1985), 27. See, among others, Jim Brown, "Making of a New Movie . . ." Letter, *VVA Veteran* 4.2 (1984), 22; Ralph McGehee, "Spy Story: A Former CIA Officer Tells What Went Wrong in Vietnam—and How It's Happening Again in Central America," *VVA Veteran* 5.6 (1985), 8–10; Joseph Puggelli, "*As I See It:* A Strategy for Latin America," *VVA Veteran* 4.8 (1984), 17.
34. "Vietnam Veterans to End Fast on US Latin Policy," *CSM,* October 17, 1986; Saundra Saperstein, "Medals of Valor Are Given Back in Protest," *WP,* October 10, 1986; "Veteran Returns Medal to Protest U.S. Policy," *WP,* July 30, 1986.
35. Duncan Spencer, "The Right Stuff Gone Wrong?," *VVA Veteran* 6.4 (1986), 13. On Liteky generally, see Hagopian, *The Vietnam War in American Memory,* 369.
36. Linenthal, *Sacred Ground,* 64.
37. McAlister, *Epic Encounters,* 186–87.
38. Reagan, "Peace: Restoring the Margin of Safety."
39. Ibid.
40. Hagopian, *The Vietnam War in American Memory,* 12.
41. Norman Podhoretz, "The New American Majority," *Commentary* 7.1 (1981), 20; Jeane Kirkpatrick, "U.S. Security and Latin America," *Commentary* 7.1 (1981), 30.
42 Norman Podhoretz, "The Future Danger," *Commentary* 8.4 (1981), 38–39.
43. Norman Podhoretz, *Why We Were in Vietnam* (New York: Simon and Schuster, 1982), 197.
44. Ibid., 210.
45. Podhoretz, "Vietnam: The Revised Standard Version," *Commentary* 7.4 (1984), 35.
46. Tod Lindberg, "Of Arms, Men and Monuments," *Commentary* 7.10 (1984), 56.
47. Carrier, "The Unknown Soldier," *VVA Veteran* 4.4 (1984), 22.
48. On Nixon's political rehabilitation, see John Herbers, "After Decade, Nixon Is Gaining Favor," *NYT,* August 5, 1984, and David Greenberg, *Nixon's Shadow: The History of an Image* (New York: W. W. Norton, 2003), 287–88. Bernard Gwertzman, "Books: Vietnam Debate," *NYT,* March 28, 1985; Robert A. Manning, "The New Nixon Is the Old Nixon in 'No More Vietnams.'" *VVA Veteran* 5.4 (1985), 23. For favorable reviews of Nixon's prescriptions, see James Chace, "How America 'Lost the Peace,'" *NYT,* April 7, 1985; Victor H. Krulak, "Nixon Looks Back on the Trials of Vietnam," *San Diego Union Tribune,* March 30, 1985; and review of Richard Nixon, *No More Vietnams, Arkansas Democrat-Gazette,* September 8, 1985.
49. Richard Nixon, *No More Vietnams* (New York: Arbor House, 1985), 46, 202.
50. Ibid., 128, 161.
51. Ibid., 210, 202.
52. Ibid., 97.
53. Ibid., 19, 14.
54. Reagan, "Peace: Restoring the Margin of Safety."
55. Nixon, *No More Vietnams,* 23, 210.
56. Ibid., 225.
57. Ibid., 221.
58. Ibid., 125.
59. Lindberg, "Of Arms, Men and Monuments," 55.
60. Patrick J. Buchanan, "The Contras Need Our Help," *WP,* March 5, 1986.
61. Podhoretz, "The Future Danger," 42.
62. Maggie Gallagher and Charles Bork, "The New Freedom Fighters," *Commentary* 12.9 (1985), 60.
63. Ibid., 60–61.

64. Podhoretz, "The Future Danger," 35.
65. Bush, "Excerpts from Remarks," 1.
66. Hagopian, *The Vietnam War in American Memory,* 39.
67. Ronald Reagan, "Message to the Congress on America's Agenda for the Future," February 6, 1986. Peters and Wooley, American Presidency Project, www.presidency.ucsb.edu.
68. Bush, "Excerpts from Remarks," 1–2.
69. David R. Lyons, "What's So Special about the Alamo?," *Discovery* (Brooks AFB, San Antonio, Texas), February 27, 1981, 2. DRTL VF 1981.
70. Diane Ackerman, "Remember the Alamo! A Poet Explores a Historic Landmark," *Parade,* July 12, 1987. DRTL VF 1987; Douglas A. Cohn, "The Alamo: 150 Years of Remembering," *Frederick (Md.) News Post,* March 7, 1986. DRTL VF 1986.
71. Gregory Curtis, ed. "The First Texan," in *Texas, Our Texas: 150 Moments that Made Us the Way We Are* (Austin: Texas Monthly Press, 1986), 37. The text of the letter is also available at "Letters from the Alamo: Micajah Autry," DRTL, http://thealamo.org.
72. Tucker, *Exodus from the Alamo,* 21. For the full text of the letter, see "Letters from the Alamo: Micajah Autry," DRTL, http://thealamo.org.
73. Bush, "Excerpts from Remarks," 2.
74. *Southern Living,* "Remembering the Texas Shrines," March 1986, 160–61. DRTL VF, 1986.
75. Brands, *Lone Star Nation,* 263–64.
76. Linenthal, *Sacred Ground,* 60; see also Tucker, *Exodus from the Alamo,* 78–138.
77. Clifford Pugh, "The Alamo: 13 Days That Shaped Texas History," *Magazine of the Houston Post,* February 23, 1986. DRTL VF, 1986.
78. Nixon, *No More Vietnams,* 97, 202.
79. Doug Harlan, "The Alamo—The Top Myth in Texas—Was a Real-Life Debacle," *SAL,* March 2, 1986. DRTL VF, 1986.
80. Ibid.
81. Podhoretz, *Why We Were in Vietnam,* 210.
82. Robert Reinhold, "Texans of the World Honor Alamo Heroes." *NYT,* March 7, 1986; Rick Marshall, "Nicaragua: A Test of Wills." *Defense and Foreign Affairs,* December, 1986. 8.
83. Ackerman, "Remember the Alamo!," 17.
84. Tim O'Brien, *If I Die in a Combat Zone* (New York: Broadway Books, 1999), 12; Christian Appy, *Working-Class War: American Combat Soldiers in Vietnam* (Chapel Hill: University of North Carolina Press, 1993), 60.
85. Appy, *Working-Class War,* 61–62.
86. Dan Goddard, "Myths of the Alamo," *San Antonio Express-News,* November 4, 1984. DRTL VF, 1984.
87. Frank Thompson, "Alamo Anniversary," *Southline,* September 17, 1986. DRTL VF 1986.
88. On the significance of sacrifice within traditional orthodox memory, see Linenthal, *Sacred Ground,* 62–64.
89. Sacrifice denotes "the destruction or surrender of something valued or desired for the sake of something having, or regarded as having, a higher or a more pressing claim," while risk denotes "the possibility of loss, injury, or other adverse or unwelcome circumstance" (*Oxford English Dictionary,* s.vv. "Sacrifice" and "Risk," www.oed.com.
90. "Excerpts from Remarks Made by the Vice President," 1.
91. Robert Reinhold, "Texans of the World Honor Alamo Heroes." *NYT,* March 7, 1986. Also qtd. in Linenthal, who points out that Fehrenbach "noted that the modern age would be 'baffled' by the Alamo if it did not understand courage and honor." *Sacred Ground,* 63.

92. Loydean Thomas, "Scholar: Alamo Battle a Sacrifice," *San Antonio Express News,* March 7, 1988. DRTL VF 1988.
93. Reagan, "Peace: The Margin of Safety"; Nixon, *No More Vietnams,* 14; Gallagher and Bork, "The New Freedom Fighters," 60–61.
94. Bush, "Excerpts from Remarks," 1.
95. Ibid.
96. Representative Wright of Texas, "A Letter from the Alamo," *CR,* March 2, 1982, 2698; Representative Fields of Texas, "The Sesquicentennial Celebration of Texas," *CR,* February 25, 1986, 2671; E. Suzanne Carter, and Larry D. Hodge, "The Republic of Texas, 1836," in *Texas 150th Celebration Program and Guide,* ed. E. Suzanne Carter, 42 (Austin: Texas Department of Parks and Recreation, 1986). For discussion of *Alamo: The Price of Freedom,* see Linenthal, *Sacred Ground,* 75–77.
97. Rene Lynn, "*Lone Star* to Become Series," *North San Antonio Times,* September 5, 1985. DRTL VF 1985.
98. Curtis, "The First Texan," 37; Carter and Hodge, "The Republic of Texas, 1836," 42.
99. Curtis, "The First Texan," 37.
100. Ibid.
101. Ibid.
102. Ibid.
103. Boyd, "The Battle for the Alamo," 29. By contrast, at least one article embraced the more traditional memory and argued that there was no military value to the battle. See Doug Harlan, "A Foolhardy, Yet Worthy, Way to Die," *Houston Post,* March 6, 1986. DRTL VF 1986.
104. Boyd, "The Battle for the Alamo," 31.
105. Ibid. Boyd is not unique in criticizing the Mexican army, which is frequently shown to be barbarous, and Santa Anna, who is often described as a dilettante. See Ackerman, "Remember the Alamo!," 14.
106. Boyd, "The Battle for the Alamo," 32.
107. Ibid.
108. Jane Gross, "City Opens Vietnam Veterans Tributes Today," *NYT,* May 6, 1985.
109. Judie Glave, "Domestic News," AP, May 6, 1985; *NYT,* "*Intrepid* Battling Financial Troubles," December 5, 1983.
110. H. R. Russell, "The Last Patrol," MJMartin Music, January 2000, www.mjmmusic.com.
111. Michael J. Martin, interview by author, August 1, 2012.
112. Ibid.; Jane Gross, "New York Pays Homage to Vietnam Veterans," *NYT,* May 7, 1985; William E. Geist, "About New York: The Ticker-Tape Parade They Finally Got," *NYT,* May 8, 1985.
113. Martin, interview by author.
114. Ibid.
115. Ibid.
116. James Coburn, "Last Patrol 'Home' at the Alamo," *San Antonio Express-News,* November 8, 1985.
117. Nancy Perdue, "Marching Vets Get to City," *SAL,* November 7, 1985; David McLemore, "Last Patrol's Journey; Veterans Prepare to Honor Comrades in San Antonio," November 11, 1985.
118. McLemore, "Last Patrol's Journey."
119. Hagopian, *The Vietnam War in American Memory,* 10; see also 140–41.

120. Ibid., 188–89, 162–63; Kristin Ann Hass, *Carried to the Wall: American Memory and the Vietnam Veterans Memorial* (Berkeley: University of California Press, 1996), 104; Appy, *Working-Class War*, 7.
121. "Probation Sentences in Synanon Rattlesnake Attack," UPI, November 21, 1980; "Self-Propelled Cannon Taken from U.S. Base," *NYT*, October 27, 1980.
122. Jeremy Kuzmarov, *The Myth of the Addicted Army: Vietnam and the Modern War on Drugs* (Amherst: University of Massachusetts Press, 2009), 161–65.
123. Art Harris, "A Belated Casualty of a Haunting War; Vietnam Veteran Is the Victim of a 10-Year, Belated Battle," *WP*, June 21, 1980.
124. Margaret Shapiro, "Md. Sniper Angry Victim of Vietnam," *WP*, November 15, 1980.
125. Philip Caputo, *A Rumor of War* (New York: Henry Holt, 1977), 3.
126. Robert Mason, *Chickenhawk* (London: Corgi 1998), 397, 399.
127. Stuart Smyth, "Back Home," *VVA Veteran* 2.1 (March-April 1982), 4.
128. "From the Editor . . ." *VVA Veteran* 1.1 (1980), 3.
129. See Gerald Nicosia, *Home to War: A History of the Vietnam Veterans' Movement* (New York: Carroll and Graff, 2004), passim; Hagopian, *The Vietnam War in American Memory*, 18, 141, as well as, among others, Dennis Rhoades, "Ups and Downs in Reagan Vets Budget," *VVA Veteran* 5.2 (1985), 4; "Congress Slams VA Cuts: Reagan 'Abandoning' Vets?," *VVA Veteran* 6.4 (1986), 23; "Combat Vets Go Jobless, Study Says," *VVA Veteran* 6.5 (1986), 25.
130. Caputo, *A Rumor of War*, 349–50, 223–24; see also Tobey C. Herzog, *Vietnam War Stories: Innocence Lost* (London: Routledge, 1992), 68. Mason, *Chickenhawk*, 397.
131. Nicosia, *Home to War*, 397–99, 416–18; "Firing for Effect, Not Results," *VVA Veteran* 5.2 (1985), 13.
132. Jeff Danziger, "A Memorial to the Last Ten Years," *VVA Veteran* 5.9 (1985), 4.
133. Hagopian, *The Vietnam War in American Memory*, 159.
134. Reagan, "Peace: Restoring the Margin of Safety."
135. Hagopian, *The Vietnam War in American Memory*, 189; UPI, "Washington News," May 21, 1984.
136. "Remarks of Congressman David Bonior. November 7, 1983. Shoreham Hotel, Washington, DC," *VVA Veteran* 3.6 (1983), 22.
137. Ibid.
138. Albin F. Irzyk, "They, Too, Were Heroes: Vietnam Veterans Are Finally Receiving Some Measure of Public Recognition for Their Service, But It Is Late and Little Enough in the View of a Professional Infantry Commander Who Led These Men in Battle and Found Them Courageous, Savvy, and Definitely Willing to Soldier," *VVA Veteran* 3.5 (1983), 5. See also Rick Herman, "My War, My Turn to Speak," *VVA Veteran* 4.1 (1984), 1; and Stout, "New York Vets Wowed by Viet Vets Homecoming," 5.
139. "'God, Were They Brave' Just Part of Alamo Legacy: Reverent Curator Traces the Legend," Unknown source. DRTL VF 1980.
140. "Regular Meeting of the City Council of the City of San Antonio Held in the Council Chamber, City Hall, on Thursday, August 8. 1985," 30. City of San Antonio, Office of the City Clerk, Municipal Archives and Records, https://webapps.sanantonio.gov.
141. "Regular Meeting of the City Council of the City of San Antonio Held in the Council Chamber, City Hall, on Thursday, October 3, 1985," 484. City of San Antonio, Office of the City Clerk, Municipal Archives and Records, https://webapps.sanantonio.gov.
142. "Ceremonial Items, October 3, 1985," Office of the City Clerk, City Council Ceremonials, 1939–2002, City of San Antonio, Office of the City Clerk, Municipal Archives and Records.

143. Bruce Franklin, *M.I.A., or Mythmaking in America: How and Why Belief in Live POWs Has Possessed a Nation* (New Brunswick: Rutgers University Press, 1992), 7; Hass, *Carried to the Wall*, 122.
144. Sheila Allee, "Vietnam Veterans' Odyssey Ends," *Dallas Morning Star*, November 8, 1985.
145. Coburn, "Support Growing for 'Last Patrol' "; Hagopian, *The Vietnam War in American Memory*, 154; "Tribute to War Veterans," Editorial, *Austin American Statesman*, November 11, 1985; Allee, "Vietnam Veterans' Odyssey Ends."
146. David McLemore, "Last Patrol's 'Journey'; Veterans Prepare to Honor Comrades in San Antonio," *Dallas Morning News*, November 11, 1985.
147. Jim Price, "Tears of War Flow in Song; Alamo Vigil Recalls Vietnam," *San Antonio Express-News*, November 11, 1985; McLemore, "Last Patrol's 'Journey' "; James Coburn, "Last Patrol 'Home' at Alamo; Enthusiastic Crowd Brings Tears to Vets," *San Antonio Express-News*, November 8, 1985; James Coburn, "Support Growing for 'Last Patrol'; Big Crowd Expected at Alamo," *San Antonio Express-News*, November 9, 1985.
148. Coburn, "Last Patrol 'Home' at Alamo"; Price, "Tears of War Flow in Song"; David McLemore, "Veterans Walk with Dignity," *Dallas Morning News*, November 12, 1985; McLemore, "Last Patrol's 'Journey.' "
149. McLemore, "Veterans Walk with Dignity"; Tim Griffin, "Anti-War Veterans Not Allowed in Parade," *San Antonio Express-News*, November 12, 1985; Jim Michaels, "Faith Is Kept; Veterans Honored," *SAL*, November 12, 1985.
150. Coburn, "Last Patrol 'Home' at Alamo."
151. Ibid; Allee, "Vietnam Veterans' Odyssey Ends."
152. Linenthal, *Sacred Ground*, 60.
153. Jim Michaels, "They Remembered MIAs at the Alamo," *SAL*, October 3, 1985.
154. Perdue, "Marching Vets Get to City."
155. McLemore, "Last Patrol's 'Journey.' "
156. As Linenthal notes, this is the defining heroic moment in the orthodox narrative. *Sacred Ground*, 61.
157. Mark Lane, "Five Points Necessary to Attain Legendary Status," in "Remember the Alamo: A Sesquicentennial Salute," Supplement to *North San Antonio Times*, *North Central Recorder-Times*, *Northeast Recorder Times*, and *Northwest Recorder Times*, February 20, 1986. DRTL VF 1986. Among texts that cite the Alamo as a precursor to ultimate victory in the Texas revolution, see Pugh, "The Alamo: 13 Days That Shaped Texas History"; Frank Thompson, "Alamo Anniversary," *Southline*, September 17, 1986. DRTL VF 1986; and Bill Gray, "Remembering . . . Remember What Happened 145 Years Ago This Month When an Old Church Became a Mission of Glory," *Friendsi Chevy Owners Magazine*, March, 1981. DRTL VF 1981.
158. Engelhardt, *The End of Victory Culture: Cold War America and the Disillusioning of a Generation*, 2nd ed. (Amherst: University of Massachusetts Press, 2007), 25.
159. The political evacuation of the Alamo in language familiar from Vietnam's remembrance is likewise apparent in a comment by the historian Joe B. Frantz: "The Alamo is a place where ordinary men were ennobled as they died gallantly for a cause, unclear though they were as to what the cause was all about." Reinhold, "Texans of the World Honor Alamo Heroes."
160. Beachley Brear, "We Run the Alamo and You Don't," 299.
161. Appy, *Working-Class War*, 242.
162. Mike Tolson, "Vietnam's Last Patrol in a Final Rendezvous," *SAL*, November 10, 1985.

This attitude is central to Martin's remembrance of the war. In 2012 he told me the war was "a lost cause, but we fought it anyway. We fought it for each other." Martin, interview by author.

163. McLemore, "Veterans Walk with Dignity."
164. Michaels, "Faith Is Kept."
165. McLemore, "Last Patrol's 'Journey.'"
166. Pierre Thomas, "Vietnam Veterans Who Returned Come Home to the Wall," *WP*, November 7, 1987.
167. Coburn, "Last Patrol 'Home' at Alamo"; Michael J. Martin, "The Last Patrol," Michel J. Martin Music Blog, comment posted on March 14, 2007, http://blogs.myspace.com. Martin drew on a historical document but performed a chronological sleight of hand, as Crockett had written the letter a month before he arrived at the Alamo. As Brands explains, Crockett expected to rekindle his political fortunes in Texas. *Lone Star Nation*, 332, 348. On the timing of the letter, see Stephen Harrigan, "The Last Days of David Crockett," *American History* 46.1 (2011), 28.
168. George Bruns and Tom Blackburn. "Ballad of Davy Crockett," Classic Western TV Shows, www.fiftiesweb.com. On the song's history, see Roberts and Olson, *A Line in the Sand*, 242.
169. Michael J. Martin, "I Am with My Friends," *Skyline*, compact disc, Struzbo Music, © 1983 M. J. Martin and (P) 1998 Struzbo Music.
170. Ibid.
171. Ibid.
172. Michael J. Martin, "I Ain't Here Alone," *Johnny Comes Marchin' Home*, compact disc, MJMartin, © 1982 M. J. Martin and (P) 1986 ASCAP.
173. Coburn, "Last Patrol 'Home' at Alamo."
174. McLemore, "Last Patrol's 'Journey.'"
175. Martin, interview by author.
176. Allee, "Vietnam Veterans' Odyssey Ends"; Coburn, "Last Patrol 'Home' at Alamo."
177. "Vietnam Vets Bring POW Drive to S.A.," *SAL*, October 1, 1985.
178. Michaels, "They Remembered MIAs at the Alamo."
179. Linenthal, *Sacred Ground*, 215, 60.
180. Joseph M. Puggelli, "July 4, 1984: Where Do We Go from Here?," *VVA Veteran* 4.6 (August 1984), 10.
181. Ibid.
182. Price, "Tears of War Flow in Song"; Alee, "Vietnam Veterans' Odyssey Ends."
183. McLemore, "Last Patrol's 'Journey'"; Coburn, "Last Patrol 'Home' at Alamo."
184. Thomas, "Vietnam Veterans Who Returned Come Home to the Wall."
185. Linenthal, *Sacred Ground*, 64; Linenthal writes that the Alamo "requires only that each generation's rededication is expressed in proper form" and notes that the proper form is "liv[ing] up to the heroic ideal." *Sacred Ground*, 58.
186. Ibid., 60–62.
187. Ibid., 62.
188. Price, "Veterans in United Front at Alamo Plaza Ceremony"; Joe Vargo, "Vietnam Veterans End Vigil for 'Patrol Still Out,'" *Austin American Statesman*, November 12, 1985.
189. Vargo, "Vietnam Veterans End Vigil." See also John Tackett, "Vietnam Veterans Pledge War on Suicide; Honor POWs, MIAs," *SAL*, November 12, 1985.
190. Martin, interview by author.

191. McLemore, "Veterans Walk with Dignity."
192. Ibid.
193. Vargo, "Vietnam Veterans End Vigil."
194. "As Shown at the Alamo, Vietnam Healing Begun," Editorial, *SAL*, November 12, 1985.
195. Martin, interview by author.

4. "WE SHOULD HAVE SAID NO"

1. William J. Clinton, "Address to the Nation on Airstrikes against Serbian Targets in the Federal Republic of Yugoslavia (Serbia and Montenegro), March 24, 1999," *PPP: WJC, 1999* (Washington: Government Printing Office, 2000), 1:451, 452.
2. Max Boot has termed this "the body bag syndrome." *The Savage Wars of Peace: Small Wars and the Rise of American Power* (New York: Basic Books, 2002), 327.
3. Patrick J. Buchanan, "The Mess They've Made," *WP*, April 13, 1999.
4. William J. Clinton, "Remarks at Georgetown University, November 8, 1999," in *PPP: WJC, 1999* (Washington: Government Printing Office, 2000), 2:2010; *Daily Oklahoman*, "Decidedly Deteriorating Clinton's Doctrine Is Ruining Our Military," November 14, 1999.
5. Peter Beinart, *The Icarus Syndrome: A History of American Hubris* (New York: Harper Collins, 2010), 277; John Shattuck, *Freedom on Fire: Human Rights Wars and America's Response* (Cambridge: Harvard University Press, 2003), 290, 295; quotation from Boot, *The Savage Wars of Peace*, 319.
6. Shattuck, *Freedom on Fire*, 285; Samantha Power, *A Problem from Hell: America and the Age of Genocide* (New York: Perennial, 2003), 503.
7. Andrew Bacevich, *The New American Militarism: How Americans Are Seduced by War* (London: Oxford University Press, 2005), 62, 3.
8. On comparisons to Vietnam, see, among others, Beinart, *The Icarus Syndrome*, 272.
9. Pat Oliphant, "Drawingboard," *LAT*, October 7, 1993; Cameron McWhirter, "Grieving Vet Asks: 'Why Are We There?,'" *Chicago Tribune*, October 6, 1993; Richard Millholland, editorial cartoon, *Chicago Tribune*, October 8, 1993; Anna Quindlen, "Admit Our Naiveté and Bring Soldiers Home from Somalia," *Chicago Tribune*, October 8, 1993.
10. George H. W. Bush, "Address to the Nation Announcing Allied Military Action in the Persian Gulf," *PPP:GHWB 1991*, 1:44.
11. Boot, *The Savage Wars of Peace*, 318–19.
12. John Marshall, "Witness to War; Heartfelt Book on Vietnam Reveals Courage and Sacrifice," review of *We Were Soldiers Once . . . and Young* by Hal C. Moore, *Seattle Post Intelligencer*, December 16, 1993.
13. Dave Moniz, "A Peacekeeping Mission Gone Wrong," review of *Black Hawk Down*, by Mark Bowden, *CSM*, March 11, 1999. The reviewer Bob Shacochis made the same point in "Birth of a Combat Classic: A Deadly Gauntlet in Somalia," review of *Black Hawk Down* by Mark Bowden, *New York Observer*, March 8, 1999.
14. Robert Scheer, "Imagine How Many Lives Could Have Been Saved If McNamara Had Released a Warning in 1967. Nation Paid for Bumbling and Secrecy," *San Jose Mercury News*, April 14, 1995.
15. "If Not Then, Why Now?" *St. Louis Post-Dispatch*, April 19, 1995.
16. For an overview of the response to *In Retrospect*, see Paul Hendrickson, *The Living and the Dead: Robert McNamara and Five Lives of a Lost War* (New York: Vintage, 1997), 376–80. That trust in government declined after Vietnam and Watergate has been well noted.

See, for example, James T. Patterson, *Grand Expectations: The United States, 1945–1974* (London: Oxford University Press, 1996), 782, and Bruce J. Schulman, *The Seventies: The Great Shift in American Culture, Society, and Politics* (New York: Free Press, 2001), 48, 51.

17. *USA Today,* "McNamara's Confession: Late But Pointed Lesson," April 10, 1995; see also A. Mark Woodward, "Vietnam Vindication: An Unwinnable War," *Bangor Daily News,* April 19, 1995.
18. M. J. Andersen, "McNamara's Unlearned Lesson," *Providence Journal,* April 22, 1995. See also "Had He Only Listened, McNamara's Memoir Would Be Different," *Austin American-Statesman,* April 11, 1995.
19. George H. W. Bush, "Radio Address to United States Armed Forces Stationed in the Persian Gulf Region," March 2, 1991, *PPP:GHWB,* 1:207.
20. James Carroll, *An American Requiem: God, My Father, and the War that Came Between Us* (New York: Houghton Mifflin, 1996), 220.
21. Susan Jeffords, *The Remasculinization of America: Gender and the Vietnam War* (Bloomington: University of Indiana Press, 1989), 8–12, 168, and *Hard Bodies: Hollywood Masculinity in the Reagan Era* (New Brunswick: Rutgers University Press, 1994), 34–41; Gregory A. Waller, "Rambo: Getting to Win This Time," in *From Hanoi to Hollywood: The Vietnam War in American Film,* ed. Linda Dittmar and Gene Michaud, 118, 125 (New Brunswick: Rutgers University Press, 1997); and Gaylyn Studlar and David Desser, "Never Having to Say You're Sorry: Rambo's Rewriting of the Vietnam War," in *From Hanoi to Hollywood,* 101–12.
22. Pat Aufderheide, "Good Soldiers," in *Seeing Through Movies,* ed. Mark Crispin Miller, 104–10 (New York: Pantheon Books, 1990); Judy Lee Kinney, "*Gardens of Stone, Platoon,* and *Hamburger Hill:* Rituals of Remembrance," in *Inventing Vietnam: The War in Film and Television,* ed. Michael Anderegg, 161 (Philadelphia: Temple University Press, 1991); and Harry W. Haines, "'They Were Called and They Went,'" in *From Hanoi to Hollywood,* 94–96; Stephen Kaplan, "The Undying Uncertainty of the Narrator in Tim O'Brien's *The Things They Carried,*" *Critique* 35.1 (1993), 46, and Daniel Robinson, "Getting it Right: The Short Fiction of Tim O'Brien," *Critique* 40.3 (1999), 258–59; Marita Sturken, *Tangled Memories: The Vietnam War, the AIDS Epidemic, and the Politics of Remembering* (Berkeley: University of California Press, 1998), 106.
23. Sturken, *Tangled Memories,* 106.
24. Wayne Karlin, *Wandering Souls Journeys with the Dead and Living in Vietnam* (New York: Nation Books, 2009), 6–7.
25. Sturken, *Tangled Memories,* 113; Aufderheide, "Good Soldiers," 87; see also Frank J. Wetta and Martin A. Novelli, "'Now a Major Motion Picture': War Films and Hollywood's New Patriotism," *Journal of Military History* 67.3 (2003), 866.
26. Michelle Kendrick, "Kicking the Vietnam Syndrome: CNN's and CBS's Video Narratives of the Persian Gulf War," in *Seeing Through the Media: The Persian Gulf War,* ed. Lauren Rabinovitz and Susan Jeffords, 71 (New Brunswick: Rutgers University Press, 1994). See also Jerry Lembke, *The Spitting Image: Myth, Memory, and the Legacy of Vietnam* (New York: New York University Press, 1998), 11–15.
27. Melani McAllister, *Epic Encounters: Culture, Media, and U.S. Interests in the Middle East, 1945–2000* (Berkeley: University of California Press, 2001), 237.
28. Robert Wilson, "The Ia Drang across a Vale of Years," review of *We Were Soldiers Once . . . and Young, USA Today,* November 13, 1992; Marshall, "Witness to War."
29. Leonard Bushkoff, "Tragic Ignorance in Vietnam," review of *We Were Soldiers Once . . .*

and Young by Hal C. Moore and Joseph Galloway and *After Tet: The Bloodiest Year in Vietnam* by Ronald Specter, *CSM*, November 30, 1992.

30. One reviewer noted this; see Richard Pyle, "*We Were Soldiers Once . . . and Young* Among the Best Vietnam War Books," review of *We Were Soldiers Once . . . and Young* by Hal C. Moore, AP, November 13, 1992.
31. Harold G. Moore and Joseph Galloway, *We Were Soldiers Once . . . and Young: Ia Drang—The Battle That Changed the War in Vietnam* (New York: Presidio Press, 1992), 9–10.
32. Ibid., 21, 22. At least one reviewer noted this, criticizing the authors for "substituting hagiography for biography" because "every soldier comes off as a battlefield superhero or instant hero." Gary A. Warner, "War Stories; A Frank Look Back at Vietnam," review of *We Were Soldiers Once . . . and Young*, by Hal C. Moore and Joseph Galloway, *Orange County Register*, November 15, 1992. On the representation of officers in Vietnam War films, see Sturken, *Tangled Memories*, 106.
33. Moore and Galloway, *We Were Soldiers Once*, 143; see also 137, 178–79, 280.
34. Ibid., 68.
35. "After Action Report, IA DRANG Valley Operation 1st Battalion, 7th Cavalry 14–16 November 1965," 5. Muir S. Fairchild Research Information Center, United States Air Force Air University, Maxwell AFB, Ala., www.au.af.mil; Moore and Galloway, *We Were Soldiers*, 123.
36. Moore and Galloway, *We Were Soldiers Once*, 171.
37. On war crimes, see ibid., 257, 274, 279, 284, 298, 303, 304, 308, 310, 313, 326; in this section I am following Frantz Fanon, *The Wretched of the Earth*, trans. Richard Philcox (New York: Grove Press, 2004), 6. Particularly significant is Moore's omission of any reference to such executions likely being due to lack of resources, information that was certainly available at the time of his writing; see Neil Sheehan *A Bright Shining Lie: John Paul Vann and America in Vietnam* (New York: Random House, 1988), 115.
38. Moore, *We Were Soldiers Once*, 153, 162, 133. On this language, see Elaine Scarry, *The Body in Pain: The Making and Unmaking of the World* (New York: Oxford University Press, 1985), 66, 74.
39. Moore, *We Were Soldiers Once*, 174.
40. Ibid., 164.
41. On tropes, see Jeffords, *The Masculinization of Amercia*, 10–12.
42. Ibid., 96–97; see also 19, 92, 171, 250, 275, 277.
43. Ibid., 190.
44. Christian G. Appy, *Patriots: The Vietnam War Remembered from All Sides* (New York: Penguin, 2004), 134.
45. Moore, *We Were Soldiers Once*, 107.
46. Ibid., 85.
47. Ibid., 166; see also 167.
48. Michel Foucault, *The Birth of the Clinic: An Archaeology of Medical Perception*, trans. A. M. Sheridan Smith (New York: Vintage, 1973), 143.
49. On precarity, see Judith Butler, *Frames of War: When Is Life Grievable?* (London: Verso, 2009), 25. On this phenomenon in other literatures, see Marianne Noble, "The Ecstasies of Sentimental Wounding in *Uncle Tom's Cabin*," *Yale Journal of Criticism* 10.2 (1997), 303.
50. Boot, *The Savage Wars of Peace*, 318–19; Moore, *We Were Soldiers Once*, 368–69; also 366.
51. Moore, *We Were Soldiers Once*, 370.
52. Fredrik Logevall, *Choosing War: The Lost Chance for Peace and the Escalation of the War in Vietnam* (Berkeley: University of California Press, 1999).

53. John Prados, *Vietnam: The History of an Unwinnable War* (Lawrence: University Press of Kansas, 2009), 139.
54. U.S. Army Command Information Unit, "Scrapbook for Fighting Men Too Busy to Keep Their Own! Special Presidential Unit Citation Issue," Folder Presidential Unit Citation Special Issue, Box 05-1CAVserS37, USAHEC.
55. Richard Fryklund, "Ia Drang Battle Indicates Enemy Can't Win," *(Washington) Sunday Star,* May 15, 1966, in U.S. Army Command Information Unit, "Scrapbook for Fighting Men Too Busy to Keep Their Own! Edition 5," Folder 5, Box 05-1CAVserS37, USAHEC.
56. United States Army, 1st Cavalry Division, *Combat Operations After Action Report, Pleiku Campaign: Pleiku Province, Republic of Vietnam, 23 Oct–26 Nov 1965*. [APO US Forces 96490]: Headquarters, 1st Cavalry Division (Airmobile), 1966, 124, USAHEC; W. C. Westmoreland, *Report on the War in Vietnam (As of 30 June 1968); Section II: Report on Operations in South Vietnam, January 1964–June 1968* (Washington: Government Printing Office, n.d.), 110, USAHEC.
57. Raymond R. Coffey, "Go Home? Col. Hal Would Rather Kill Reds," *Chicago Daily News,* July 27, 1966, in U.S. Army Command Information Unit, "Scrapbook for Fighting Men Too Busy to Keep Their Own! Edition 7," Folder 7, Box 05-1CAVserS37, USAHEC.
58. Moore and Galloway, *We Were Soldiers Once*, 374.
59. Both Moore and Kinnard, in their respective after-action reports, compliment the skill and courage of North Vietnamese soldiers. Kinnard writes that among "indices of high morale was the determination, aggressiveness and discipline of the troops facing US elements" and that "the close-in small arms fire of North Vietnamese regulars was characterized by unerring accuracy." *Combat Operations After Action Report,* 13. Moore writes that the enemy "appeared to be well-trained. He was aggressive" and "was a deadly shot." "After Action Report, IA DRANG Valley," 23. Kenneth R. Pierce attributes the description of the NVA as "the best light infantry in the world" to Bernard Fall. "The Battle of the Ia Drang Valley," *Military Review* 69.1 (1989), 87–97.
60. Robert McNamara with Brian Van De Mark, *In Retrospect: The Tragedy and Lessons of Vietnam,* (New York: Vintage, 1996), xx.
61. Ibid., 261; see also 330, 333.
62. Ibid., 243, 333.
63. On Project 100,000, see Christian G. Appy, *Working-Class War: American Combat Soldiers and Vietnam* (Chapel Hill: University of North Carolina Press, 1993), 32–33.
64. This exemplifies Jay Winter's concept of "*political* or *strategic* silence," one "chosen in order to suspend or truncate open conflict over the meaning of or justification for violence." "Remembering Injustice and the Social Construction of Silence," in *Democratic Narrative, History, and Memory,* ed. Carole A. Barbato and Laura L. Davis, 51 (Kent, Ohio: Kent State University Press, 2012).
65. "McNamara: Better Late Than Never," *WP,* April 13, 1995; see also "McNamara's Confession: Late But Pointed Lesson," *USA Today,* April 10, 1995.
66. A. M. Rosenthal, "Dole in Bosnia," *NYT,* April 18, 1995.
67. Elaine Sciolino, "Dole Offers Foreign Policy Initiatives," *NYT,* January 5, 1995.
68. Senator Dole of Kansas, speaking on the Fiftieth Anniversary of the United Nations, on June 26, 1995, 104th Cong., 1st sess., *CR* 141, pt.105:S9024-25.
69. Senator Lott of Mississippi, speaking for the Ia Drang Valley Military Awards Act, on June 26, 1995, 104th Cong., 1st sess., *CR* 141, pt.105:S9098.
70. National Security Review 30, June 15, 1992, GHWBPL, http://bushlibrary.tamu.edu.

71. George H. W. Bush, National Security Directive 74, November 24, 1992, GHWB, http://bushlibrary.tamu.edu.
72. George H. W. Bush, "Address to the Nation on the Situation in Somalia, December 4, 1992," *PPP:GHWB*, 1992, 2:2175–76. I have given a much briefer overview of the Somalia intervention and the subsequent policy debates that relies on some of the same sources in David Kieran, "'A Problem with Which We . . . Are Only Too Familiar': Adapting Contemporary and Historical Discourses of Race in the Popular Literature of the Somalia Intervention," in *The Theme of Cultural Adaptation in American History, Literature, and Film: Cases When the Discourse Changed*, ed. Laurence Raw, Tanfer Emin Tunc, and Gulriz Buken, 453–55 (Lewiston, N.Y.: Edwin Mellen Press, 2009).
73. Bush, "Address to the Nation on the Situation in Somali," 2175.
74. "Just Cause in Somalia," *AJC*, November 29, 1992.
75. Ted Koppel, "What Is the U.S. Military Role in Somalia?" *Nightline*. VHS (Oak Forest, Ill.: MPI Home Video, 1993).
76. Koppel, "Nightline in Somalia. [Day 3] What happened today?" *Nightline*. VHS (Oak Forest, Ill.: MPI Home Video, 1993).
77. Ibid.
78. Paul Alexander, "Was It Worth It? U.S. Troops Aren't Sure," AP, May 1, 1993; Cokie Roberts, "A Second Look at Operation Restore Hope," *Nightline*. VHS (Oak Forest, Ill.: MPI Home Video, 1993). For more positive accounts, see Peter Grier, "Somalia Mission Dubbed a Success," *CSM*, April 16, 1993, and Keith B. Richburg, "Forces Leaving Somalia See Job Well Done," *WP*, May 4, 1993.
79. Keith B. Richburg, "U.N.'s Somalia Envoy Exudes Can-Do Belief; Ex-Admiral Mending World Body's Image," *WP*, April 10, 1993.
80. Diana Jean Schemo, "Declare Victory, Hand Off, Slip Out, Cross Fingers," *NYT*, May 2, 1993. Aiken did not, in fact, say these exact words, and at least one scholar has argued that Aiken's suggestion has been taken out of context. See Mark A. Stoler, "What Did He *Really* Say? The 'Aiken Formula' for Vietnam Revisited," *Vietnam History* 46.2 (1978), 100-108; in 2005 a newspaper in Vermont reported that "Aiken never said the United States should declare victory and go home. [Former Aiken aide Stephen C.] Terry calls this 'journalistic short hand' for the senator's actual remarks" ("George Aiken in His Own Words," *Barre-Montpelier Times Argus*, February 13, 2005, www.timesargus.com.
81. William J. Clinton, "Remarks on Welcoming Military Personnel Returning from Somalia, May 5, 1993," *PPP:WJC* 1993, 1:565; Otis Pike, "TV Images of Anguish Aren't Good Reasons to Go to War," *CST*, April 20, 1993.
82. "Somalia: Clinton's Vietnam?" *New Orleans Times-Picayune*, October 6, 1993; Cal Thomas, "Come on Home," *New Orleans Times-Picayune*, October 7, 1993.
83. Paul Kirby, "Florida Lawmakers Call for Pull Out from Somalia," *States News Service*, October 5, 1993.
84. Senator Lautenberg of New Jersey, Speaking Against Operation Restore Hope, on October 5, 1993, 103rd Cong., 1st sess., *CR* 139 pt. 133: S13077-78; Representative Lazio of New York, Speaking Against Operation Restore Hope, on October 6, 1993, 103rd Cong., 1st sess., *CR* 139 pt. 134: H7521.
85. William J. Clinton, "Address to the Nation on Somalia, October 7, 1993," *PPP:WJC*, 1993, 2:1705.
86. Shattuck, *Freedom on Fire*, 89.
87. Shattuck, *Freedom on Fire*, 17, 41, 76, 286–87; Mark J. Lacy, "War, Cinema, and Moral

Anxiety," *Alternatives* 28 (2003), 618. Andrew Bacevich, *American Empire: The Realities and Consequences of U.S. Diplomacy* (Cambridge: Harvard University Press, 2002), 147; Beinart, *The Icarus Syndrome*, 274.

88. William J. Clinton, "The President's Radio Address, December 2, 1995" in *PPP: WJC*, 1995, 2:1832.
89. Ibid., 1833.
90. Senator Gregg of New Hampshire, Speaking Against Sending American Soldiers to Bosnia, on November 27, 1995, 104rd Cong., 1st sess., *CR* 141 pt. 187: S17517.
91. Representative Dornan of California, Speaking on Why We Should Not Be in Bosnia, on November 29, 1995, 104rd Cong., 1st sess., *CR* 141 pt. 189:H13791.
92. Senator Brown of Colorado, speaking for the Hutchison-Inhofe Resolution, on December 12, 1995, 104th Cong., 1st sess., *CR* 141 pt. 197:S18406.
93. Ibid.
94. Ibid.
95. Senator Smith of New Hampshire, speaking for the Hutchison-Inhofe Resolution, on December 12, 1995, 104th Cong., 1st sess., *CR* 141 pt. 197:S18418.
96. Ibid., S18420.
97. Ibid.
98. Senator Inhofe of Oklahoma, speaking on The Bosnia Issue, on December 12, 1995, 104th Cong., 1st sess., *CR* 141 pt. 197:S18400.
99. Ibid., S18401.
100. Senator Hutchison of Texas, speaking on The Bosnia Issue, on December 12, 1995, 104th Cong., 1st sess., *CR* 141 pt. 197:S18405.
101. Ibid.
102. Ibid.
103. Frank Newport, "Majority of Americans Want U.S. Troops Out of Bosnia," *Gallup*, July 25, 1997, www.gallup.com; Beinart, *The Icarus Syndrome*, 284.
104. Polad Rasch to Political Advisor to the CG, "Wehrkunde Conference, Remarks by SECDEF and Italian MOD," 9 February 1998, 1, 5, Folder 11, Box 1, Series I, EKS.
105. Notes on CODEL Gingrich Meeting at HQ SFOR, 31 May 1998, EKS, Box 1, Series I, Folder 16.
106. Beth Bailey, *America's Army: Making the All-Volunteer Force* (Cambridge: Harvard University Press, 2009), 200. As Bailey notes, this was also one of the army's busiest periods (199). On the Full-Spectrum Force, see Andrew J. Bacevich, *The New American Militarism: How Americans Are Seduced by War* (New York: Oxford University Press, 2005), 166–68, 172–74, and Bacevich, *American Empire*, 117–40.
107. "U.S. Army Europe: A Glimpse into the 21st Century," Oct 1997, EKS, Box 1, Series I, Folder 4. For a military history of this transition, see John Sloan Brown, *Kevlar Legions: The Transformation of the U.S. Army, 1989–2005* (Washington, D.C.: Center for Military History, United States Army, 2011).
108. Volney J. Warner, "Memorandum Thru Commander, 1st Armored Division, CMR 438," 19 Sep 1997, EKS, Box 1, Series I, Folder 3.
109. Peter J. Schifferle, *The Ia Drang Campaign 1965: A Successful Operational Campaign or a Mere Tactical Failure?* Fort Leavenworth, Kan.: School of Advanced Military Studies, United States Army Command and General Staff College, Second Term AY 93–94. USAHEC, 39–40.
110. See T. D. Vail, *Operation Restore and Continue Hope: Misuse of Military Power in Somalia.*

Personal Experience Monograph. USAWC, 2001, and Mark Van Drie, *Humanitarian Relief and Hunting Aideed: My Time with the U.S. Army Quick Reaction Force in Somalia.* Personal Experience Monograph (Hereafter: PEM), USAWC, April 20, 2000.

111. U.S. Army Center for Military History, *United States Forces Somalia After Action Report and Historical Overview, the United States Army in Somalia, 1992–1994,* 273, www.history.army.mil.
112. Ibid., 276.
113. Ibid., 241.
114. Beinart, *The Icarus Syndrome,* 287; Robert Burns, "Administration Restates Policy on Military Response in Kosovo," AP, March 5, 1998.
115. "Sometimes Peace Prevails," *AJC,* December 25, 1998; *Roanoke Times,* "Ethnic Cleansing Strikes at Kosovo," June 5, 1998.
116. "White House Says US Not Sending Troops to Kosovo," *White House Bulletin,* June 8, 1998; Brian Mitchell, "Step by Step into a Quagmire?" *Investor's Business Daily,* October 1, 1998; Jeanne Carter, "Lott Urges Action to End Fighting in Kosovo," AP, June 7, 1998.
117. Joseph Lieberman, "Transforming National Defense for the 21st Century: Opening Address before the U.S. Army Conference on Strategic Responsiveness," U.S. Army and Institute for Foreign Policy Analysis, Inc., the Fletcher School of Law and Diplomacy, Tufts University, and the Office of the Secretary of Defense for Net Assessment, November 2, 1999, 5, EKS Box 9, Series 1, Folder 5.
118. "Preparation Handbook for Meetings with Senators John Warner and Strom Thurmond, and with Mr. Les Brownlee, Regarding Shinseki's Confirmation as AC of S, 19 May 1999," Folder 9, Box 72, Series II, EKS. On the army's efforts to change its capacities during this period, see Bailey, *America's Army,* 230–33.
119. Memorandum for See Distribution, Planning Directive 1, 7 Dec 1999, Box 9, Series 1, Folder 6, EKS.
120. Richard Parker, "Lawmakers Criticize Extended Troop Stays," *PI,* March 7, 1998.
121. Harry Levins, "A New Front Flares in Yugoslavia's Ever-Spreading Civil War; More Talk of Intervention in a Place Most Americans Never Heard Of," *St. Louis Post-Dispatch,* March 8, 1998. On anxiety about casualties, see Boot, *The Savage Wars of Peace,* 326–28, and Beinart, *The Icarus Syndrome,* 287.
122. Senator Smith of New Hampshire, speaking against U.S. intervention in Kosovo, on March 23, 1999, 106th Cong., 1st sess., *CR* 145, pt. 46:S3072.
123. Senator Ashcroft of Missouri, speaking against U.S. intervention in Kosovo, on March 23, 1999, 106th Cong., 1st Sess., *CR* 145, pt. 46:S3071.
124. Senator Craig of Idaho, speaking against U.S. intervention in Kosovo, on March 23, 1999, 106th Cong., 1st Sess., *CR* 145, pt. 46:S3067.
125. Mark Gillespie, "Crisis in Kosovo: Questions and Answers about American Public Opinion," *Gallup,* April 16, 1999, www.gallup.com.
126. Stephen A. Klein, "Public Character and the Simulacrum: The Constitution of the Soldier Patriot and Citizen Agency in *Black Hawk Down,*" *Critical Studies in Media Communication* 22.5 (2005), 428, 436, 444.
127. Ibid., 436, 444; Lacy, "War, Cinema, and Moral Anxiety," 620–22.
128. Klein notes that the screenplay excised much of the political context included in Bowden's book (439).
129. Beinart, *The Icarus Syndrome,* 283.
130. Mark Bowden, *Black Hawk Down: A Story of Modern War* (New York: Signet, 2002), 37, 38.

131. Michael J. Durant with Steven Hartov, *In the Company of Heroes* (New York: New American Library, 2003), 146.
132. Martin Stanton, *Somalia on Five Dollars a Day: A Soldier's Story* (Novato, Calif.: Presidio Press, 2001), 4. One of Stanton's colleagues echoes this sentiment; see Van Drie, *Humanitarian Relief and Hunting Aideed,* 9–10.
133. Bowden, *Black Hawk Down,* 9, 183, 39. Officers share these assessments in Army War College monographs. See Philip Volpe, *"Medic! Medic!"—A Personal Experience Monograph.* PEM, USAWC, September 20, 1996, 8–9; Nicholas J. Anderson, *Personal Experience Monograph—Somalia.* PEM, USAWC, March 8, 2000, 2; T. D. Vail, *Operation Restore and Continue Hope: Misuse of Military Power in Somalia.* PEM, USAWC, 2001, 3; Van Drie, *Humanitarian Relief and Hunting Aideed,* 3, 8, 9, 10; and Volpe, "The Horrors of Combat," PEM, USAWC, May 29, 1996, 2.
134. Ibid., 38, 183.
135. Ibid., 39.
136. Matt Eversmann, "Operation Gothic Serpent," in *The Battle of Mogadishu: Firsthand Accounts from the Men of Task Force Ranger,* ed. Matt Eversmann and Dan Schilling, 6 (New York: Ballantine Books, 2004); see also Dan Schilling, "On Friendship and Firefights," ibid., 158–59.
137. Durant, *In the Company of Heroes,* 149.
138. Stanton, *Somalia on Five Dollars a Day,* 17.
139. Ibid., 18, 11; see also 19, 22–23, 24, 30–31.
140. On the post-Vietnam army's quality, see Bailey, *America's Army,* 36–37.
141. As Klein notes, "The ideal soldier is motivated solely by his dogged determination and look out for the welfare of his fellow soldier." "Public Character and the Simulacrum," 436.
142. Bowden, *Black Hawk Down,* 267.
143. Ibid., 325; see also 365.
144. Eversmann, "Operation Gothic Serpent," 33.
145. Tim Wilkinson, "Be Careful What You Wish For," in Eversmann and Schilling, *The Battle of Mogadishu,* 156.
146. Moore, *We Were Soldiers Once,* 95. The extent to which Moore revises this scene is evident; while he discusses Herrick "trying to get a defense organized," Dennis Deal's oral history calls him "aggressive to a fault" and argues that he "made a mistake" and died because of a "fourth grade playground trick." Moore, *We Were Soldiers,* 94; Appy, *Patriots,* 131.
147. On this, see Chris Hedges, *War Is a Force That Gives Us Meaning* (New York: Public Affairs Press, 2003), 38.
148. I have made a similar point elsewhere. See Kieran, "'A Problem with Which We . . . Are Only Too Familiar,'" 460–61. I am also in accord with Lacy's assessment of their portrayal in the film. "War, Cinema, and Moral Anxiety," 620.
149. Bowden, *Black Hawk Down,* 112. Fanon is instructive, writing that "savagery . . . manifests itself" in the native's preference for knives over guns "and in particular by the number of wounds, many of them inflicted unnecessarily after the victim's death." *The Wretched of the Earth,* 222.
150. Moore, *We Were Soldiers Once,* 115; Bowden, *Black Hawk Down,* 216.
151. Bowden, *Black Hawk Down,* 216.
152. Stanton, *Somalia on Five Dollars a Day,* 222.
153. Durant, *In the Company of Heroes,* 40.
154. Ibid., 127, 278; see also 190, 192, and Schilling, "On Friendship and Firefights," 192.

155. Here, Lacy's assertion that only American deaths receive attention is, though generally accurate, insufficiently complex. "War, Cinema, and Moral Anxiety," 620.
156. Bowden, *Black Hawk Down,* 187, 151; see also 67, 308, 359.
157. Ibid., 187.
158. Ibid., 257.
159. Ibid., 224, 267.
160. Ibid., 138.
161. Ibid., 332; see also 47, 78.
162. Lacy notes that this is likewise true of the film. "War, Cinema, and Moral Anxiety," 620. Only three passages describe Somali wounds in detail, and each exemplifies the total destruction of the enemy body by the American military's overwhelming power. Bowden, *Black Hawk Down,* 72, 147. See Kieran, "A Situation with Which We . . . Are Only Too Familiar," 460–61.
163. Bowden, *Black Hawk Down,* 201–2. Here as well I am following Scarry, *The Body In Pain,* 66.
164. Ibid., 98, 204, 262, 310, 311, 78.
165. Durant, *In the Company of Heroes,* 37.
166. Ibid., 75.
167. Lacy argues that the film likewise opposes humanitarian intervention. "War, Cinema, and Moral Anxiety," 621–22.
168. Bowden, *Black Hawk Down,* 408; see also 363–65, 394–95.
169. Stanton, *Somalia on Five Dollars a Day,* 258.
170. Schilling, "On Friendship and Firefights," 201.
171. Stanton, *Somalia on Five Dollars a Day,* xi.
172. Bowden, *Black Hawk* Down, 422.
173. Ibid., 397.
174. Stanton, *Somalia on Five Dollars a Day,* 69.
175. Bowden, *Black Hawk Down,* 409.
176. Ibid., 427.
177. Ibid., 428.

5. "IT'S ALMOST LIKE THE VIETNAM WALL"

1. Gregory Piatt, "5 Seabees Killed by Mortar Blast Were Floridians," *Florida Times-Union,* May 5, 2004.
2. Ibid. For a longer account of both attacks as well as Kubic's response to allegations made against him regarding the latter event, see Charles R. Kubic and James P. Rife, *Bridges to Baghdad: The U.S. Navy Seabees in the Iraq War* (Gettysburg, Pa.: Thomas Publications, 2009), 308–16.
3. Gregory Piatt, "Father Talked with Seabee Son Just before Attack," *Florida Times-Union,* May 6, 2004; AP, "Jacksonville Mourns Seabees Killed in Iraq," *Gainesville Sun,* May 5, 2004.
4. Ron Word, "Fla. Town Mourns 7 Sailors Killed in Iraq," AP, May 5, 2004.
5. FLNI ALB 9, 164.
6. Erika Doss, *Memorial Mania: Public Feeling in America* (Chicago: University of Chicago Press, 2010), 67; Kristin Ann Hass, *Carried to the Wall: American Memory and the Vietnam Veterans Memorial* (Berkeley: University of California Press, 1996), 5, 125. I do not discuss here the full breadth of personal expressions made at the memorial; on this, see Rhoda Schuler, "Pilgrimage to Shanksville, Pennsylvania: Where Heaven and Earth

Meet in American Civil Religion," paper presented at the North American Academy of Liturgy Liturgical Theology Seminar, New York, January 2004, 19. FLNI; and G. Robert Britten, "The Face of What Came After: Memorialization of September 11 in News Images and the Shanksville Site" (Ph.D. diss., University of Missouri, Columbia, 2008), 125–36; on Flight 93 staff's relationship with the curators of the Vietnam Veterans Memorial Collection, see 126–27.

7. Eric Draper, "The Road to Freedom," White House, http://georgewbush-whitehouse.archives.gov.
8. For the actions taken aboard Flight 93, see Thomas H. Kean et al., *The 9/11 Commission Report: Final Report of the National Commission on Terrorist Attacks upon the United States* (New York: W. W. Norton, 2004), 45. Other scholars share this view. See Elaine Scarry, qtd. in Marita Sturken, *Tourists of History: Memory, Kitsch, and Consumerism from Oklahoma City to Ground Zero* (Durham: Duke University Press, 2007), 78, and David Simpson, *9/11: The Culture of Commemoration* (Chicago: University of Chicago Press, 2006), 48.
9. Simpson, *9/11*, 48–49.
10. Here as well I am following Simpson's admonishment that patriotism was likely not a primary concern of those involved in the attacks. *9/11*, 48.
11. George W. Bush, "Graduation Speech at West Point, June 1, 2002," in John Ehrenberg et al., *The Iraq Papers* (Oxford: Oxford University Press, 2010), 66. For an analysis of the speech and the Bush doctrine, see Robert Singh, "The Bush Doctrine" in *The Bush Doctrine and the War on Terrorism: Global Reactions, Global Consequences*, ed. Mary Buckley and Robert Singh, 12–31 (New York: Routledge, 2006); Ehrenberg et al., *The Iraq Papers*, 54; Robert Swansbrough, *Test by Fire: The War Presidency of George W. Bush* (New York: Palgrave Macmillan, 2008), 131; and Thomas E. Ricks, *Fiasco: The American Military Adventure in Iraq* (New York: Penguin, 2007), 38–39.
12. Ron Suskind, *The One Percent Doctrine: Deep Inside America's Pursuits of Its Enemies Since 9/11* (New York: Simon and Schuster, 2006), 62.
13. Singh, "The Bush Doctrine," 18.
14. Condoleezza Rice, "Remarks on Terrorism and Foreign Policy, Johns Hopkins University, April 29, 2002," in Ehrenberg et al., *The Iraq Papers*, 64.
15. Ibid., 65.
16. Marita Sturken, "Masculinity, Courage, and Sacrifice," *Signs* 28.1 (2002), 444–45.
17. George W. Bush, "Address to the Nation from Atlanta on Homeland Security, November 8, 2001," *PPP:GWB 2001*, 1365. On this speech in particular and on "Let's roll" in general as a "frontier-grade battle cry," see Elle Kwok-Yin Ting, "Pax Americana: September 11 Memorialization and Nation-Building Mythologies" (Ph.D. diss., University of Western Ontario, 2009), 227.
18. James R. Edwards Jr., "We're Fighters," *National Review On-Line*, January 4, 2002.
19. Ibid.
20. Ibid.
21. Mark Steyn, "The Day America Fought Back: Lesson of Flight 93 Heroes an Example for Fighting Saddam," *CST*, September 8, 2002.
22. Ibid.
23. Karen DeYoung and Mike Allen, "Bush Shifts Strategy from Deterrence to Dominance," *WP*, September 21, 2002; "Best Sellers," *NYT*, September 22, 2002.
24. Simpson, *9/11*, 34, 23. The celebration of the passengers' and crew's ordinariness has been central to veneration at the crash site as well. Schuler, "Pilgrimage to Shanksville, Pennsylvania," 19.

25. Susan Jeffords, *Hard Bodies: Hollywood Masculinity in the Reagan Era* (New Brunswick: Rutgers University Press, 1994), 28, 32–38; Jeffords, *The Remasculinization of America: Gender and the Vietnam War* (Bloomington: Indiana University Press, 1989), 169, 10–12.
26. Jeffords, *Hard Bodies,* 185, 184.
27. Jere Longman: *Among the Heroes: Flight 93 and the Passengers and Crew Who Fought Back* (New York: Perennial, 2003), 121.
28. Ibid., 19, 123.
29. Ibid., 187.
30. Ibid., 56.
31. Jeffords, *Hard Bodies,* 28; Jeffords, *The Remasculinization of America,* 12.
32. Longman, *Among the Heroes,* 206. Such fantasizing also takes places at the memorial, though perhaps in less graphic terms. Schuler, "Pilgrimage to Shanksville, Pennsylvania," 19.
33. Longman, *Among the Heroes,* 135.
34. Ibid., 148, 178, 121, 123.
35. Ibid., 109.
36. Ibid.
37. Ibid., 113.
38. Ibid., 31, 54, 121.
39. Ibid., 124.
40. Stephen Robinson, "Let's Roll!," *London Daily Telegraph,* September 11, 2002.
41. Bob Dart, "A Year Later: Bush Joins Tribute to Flight 93's 'Stan,'" *AJC,* September 12, 2002. Erika Doss notes this quote as well. *Memorial Mania,* 167.
42. The weather has been so well noted as to become a trope in studies of the memorial. See Britten, "The Face of What Came After," 80.
43. FLNI ALB III, 10.
44. Sandy Wojcik, "Army Recruiters Renew Commitment to Country," *Somerset (Pa.) Daily American,* November 29, 2004.
45. FLNI ALB IV, 130.
46. FLNI ALB I, 190; FLNI ALB IV, 35; see also FLNI ALB V, 122, 144.
47. The history of the Vietnam Veterans Memorial is well documented. See Hass, *Carried to the Wall,* 7–33, and Patrick Hagopian, *The Vietnam War in American Memory: Veterans, Memorials, and the Politics of Healing* (Amherst: University of Massachusetts Press, 2010), 29–110.
48. Marita Sturken, *Tangled Memories: The Vietnam War, the AIDS Epidemic, and the Politics of Remembering* (Berkeley: University of California Press, 1998), 64.
49. Hagopian, *The Vietnam War in American* Memory, 369.
50. Doss, *Memorial Mania,* 154.
51. Kristin Ann Hass, *Sacrificing Soldiers on the National Mall* (Berkeley: University of California Press, 2013), 19–20.
52. Hass, *Carried to the Wall,* 89; see also 101.
53. Joseph Curl, "'A Struggle for Civilization'; Bush Helps the Nation Remember 9/11," *Washington Times,* September 12, 2006.
54. Thom Shanker, "Rumsfeld Marks 9/11 Crash Site with Medallion Given to Troops," *NYT,* March 28, 2006.
55. My discussion of how military awards are used to link disparate groups is indebted to Kyle Grimes, "The Entropics of Discourse" (1990).

56. CNN, "Poll: Pessimism about Iraq War Growing," CNN.com, March 16, 2006, www.cnn.com.
57. FLNI ALB II, 112.
58. FLNI ALB V, 153; n.p.
59. ALB IV, 57, 141.
60. ALB VIII, 20.
61. Ting, "Pax Americana," 211.
62. FLNI UCC Jul 11 2006, FLNI VCC 5-5-06 to 07-24-06; see also FLNI VCB XII, 50; FLNI VCB III, 123; FLNI UCC Aug 24, 2004; FLNI Exhibit Boxes, and FLNI VCC 061, Jun 6 2007; FLNI VCC 11-13-06 to 7-29-07.
63. FLNI UCC Aug 13, 2008; FLNI VCC 7-05-2008 to 8-20-2009.
64. FLNI UCC Apr 16, 2009; FLNI VCC 7-5-08 to 8-20-09.
65. FLNI VCB IV, 146; FLNI VCC 066 Jun 6 2007; FLNI VCC 11-13-06 to 7-29-07; see also FLNI UCC Mar 30, 2004; FLNI VCC 11-1-03 to 7-29-04.
66. FLNI UCC Nov 20, 2005; FLNI VCC 6-2-05 to 4-30-06; FLNI VCC 001, May 5, 2006; FLNI VCC 6-2-05 to 4-30-06; see also FLNI UCC May 15, 2004; FLNI VCC 11-1-03 to 7-29-04; FLNI VCC 003, Aug 28, 2004; FLNI VCC 8-7-04 to 5-29-05; and FLNI UCC Aug 4 2006; FLNI VCC 7-31-06 to 10-29-06.
67. Uncatalogued Item (UNCAT) FLNI SL 10-02-04, Group #2004.56; see also FLNI UCC Aug 7 2004; FLNI VCC 8-7-04 to 5-29-05. (NB: "SL" refers to the NPS's original cataloguing system, in which SL referred to Skyline Drive, the location of the Temporary Memorial and, thus, where the objects were collected; the numbers indicate the date on which the items were removed from the memorial.)
68. FLNI VCB 8, 52; FLNI VCB XI, 7; FLNI VCB XIV, 85; see also FLNI UCC Jul 31 2005; FLNI VCC 6-2-05 to 4-30-06; FLNI UCC Jun 19 2006; VCC 5-5-06 to 7-24-06.
69. FLNI UCC Jul 27 2005; FLNI VCC 6-2-05 to 4-30-06.
70. FLNI UCC Apr 6, 2008; FLNI VCC 8-11-07 to 5-27-08; FLNI UCC Aug 12 2006, 7-31-06 to 10-29-06; FLNI VCC 054, Jul 14, 2007; FLNI VCC 11-13-06 to 7-29-07; FLNI VCB V, 79; FLNI VCC 001, Sept 6 2004; FLNI VCC 8-7-04 to 5-29-05.
71. UNCAT, Exhibit Boxes, FLNI.
72. Britten also discusses this item and notes that it is evidence that "the [Flight 93] story, once considered speculation, is now so widely accepted that it has been engineered into the current 'War on Terror' narrative." "The Face of What Came After," 130, 174.
73. Doss discusses what she calls "the usual cheap stuff of memorials" and observes, "Temporary memorials rarely feature precious materials." *Memorial Mania,* 70, 72.
74. Sturken, *Tangled Memories,* 64. See also Hass, *Carried to the Wall,* 95. Many of the nonmilitary visitors are likewise "speaking to the dead," as Schuler discovered. "Pilgrimage to Shanksville, Pennsylvania," 30.
75. UNCAT, SL 9-23-06 and SL 10-01-06, Group # 2006.44 and 2006.47.
76. UNCAT, SL 08-05-04, Group #2004.36; UNCAT SL 09-28-04, Group #2004.53; UNCAT, SL 2-16-06, SL2-22-06, Group #2006.06/2006.07.
77. Hass, *Carried to the Wall,* 98. John Prados, *Vietnam: The Unwinnable War* (Lawrence: University Press of Kansas, 2010), 4; Hagopian, *The Vietnam War in American Memory,* 369.
78. UNCAT, SL-11-27-06, Group 2006.55, FLNI.
79. UNCAT Item. FLNI Exhibit Boxes.
80. Grimes, "The Entropics of Discourse," 423.
81. Ibid.
82. Erika Doss writes, "The material culture of grief . . . demonstrated the faith that Americans

place in *things* to negotiate complex moments and events." "Spontaneous Memorials and Contemporary Modes of Mourning in America," *Material Religion* 2.3 (2006), 299.

83. Grimes, "The Entropics of Discourse," 423.
84. UNCAT, Folder SL 6-26-04, Group 2004.5-2004.33, Box SL 2-17-04 to 7-11-04, FLNI; see also FLNI UCC Jul 5, 2008; FLNI VCC 7-05-08 to 8-20-09; FLNI ALB 2, 82.
85. FLNI ALB VI, 104.
86. FLNI UCC May 23, 2008; FLNI VCC 8-11-07 to 5-27-08.
87. FLNI ALB 1, 110. See also FLNI ALB VI, 144.
88. Even Mark Bingham, whose homosexuality has been celebrated in this narrative, is celebrated for his heteronormativity and masculine toughness.
89. FLNI UCC Aug 28, 2007; FLNI VCC 8-11-07 to 5-27-08.
90. UNCAT, FLNI-82, SL 8-15-06, Group #2006.33.
91. UNCAT, FLNI SL 9-5-06, Group #2006.41.
92. The debate over interrogation methods and torture is too vast a topic for this chapter. See Phillipe Sands, *Torture Team: Rumsfeld's Memo and the Betrayal of American Values* (New York: Palgrave Macmillan, 2008); Amy Kaplan, "Where Is Guantánamo?" *American Quarterly* 57.3 (2005), 831–58; Jameel Jaffer and Amrit Singh, *Administration of Torture* (New York: Columbia University Press, 2007).
93. FLNI UCC April 30, 2006; FLNI VCC 6-2-05 to 4-30-06.
94. FLNI UCC Jul 10, 2004; FLNI VCC 11-1-03 to 7-29-04.
95. FLNI UCC Oct 17, 2005, FLNI VCC 06-02-05 to 04-30-06.
96. FLNI 2521, Box 67, FLNI.
97. Doss, *Memorial Mania*, 98, 71.
98. FLNI ALB 2, 189; FLNI ALB 4, 106; FLNI ALB 5, 62; FLNI ALB 7, 127; FLNI ALB 4, 85.
99. Hagopian, *The Vietnam War in American Memory*, 141.
100. FLNI ALB 5, 67.
101. See FLNI ALB 4, 3, 4.
102. FLNI 8, Folder 2, Box 1, FLNI.
103. FLNI 2225, Box 38; FLNI ALB 5, 66–67.
104. UNCAT, SL 05-21-04, Group 2004.23, FLNI; Prados, *Vietnam*, 112–14.
105. FLNI 7414, Folder 40, Box 18; FLNI 295, Folder 39, Box 1, FLNI.
106. Flight 93 Record of Remembrance, Folder Fundraising Campaign Comments 2005–2007, Box Archives: Fundraising Campaign Comments, 2005–2007, FLNI.
107. That veterans have adopted this role is evident in one veteran's declaration that he was "Standing guard" (FLNI VCB I, 174); on the Last Firebase, see Hagopian, *The Vietnam War in American Memory*, 194.
108. Adam Shaffer, e-mail message to the author, July 7, 2010.
109. Jay Winter, "Thinking about Silence," in *Shadows of War: A Social History of Silence in the Twentieth Century*, ed. Efret Ben-Ze'ev, Ruth Ginio, and Jay Winter, 4 (Cambridge: Cambridge University Press, 2010).
110. Pierre Bourdieu, *Outline of a Theory of Practice*, trans. Richard Nice, 17th ed. (Cambridge: Cambridge University Press, 2003), 78, 168.
111. FLNI ALB I, 37.
112. H. Bruce Franklin, *MIA, or Mythmaking in America: How and Why Belief in Live POWs Has Possessed a Nation* (New Brunswick: Rutgers University Press, 1993), 3–4.
113. Thomas M. Hawley, *The Remains of War: Bodies, Politics, and the Search for American Soldiers Unaccounted for in Southeast Asia* (Durham: Duke University Press, 2005), 4. See

also Michael J. Allen, *Until the Last Man Comes Home: POWs, MIAs, and the Unending Vietnam War* (Chapel Hill: University of North Carolina Press, 2009), 139–40, 248; Franklin, *M.I.A.*, 156.

114. Hawley, *The Remains of War*, 82; Allen, *Until the Last Man Comes Home*, 85–86, 244–45; Franklin, *M.I.A.*, 99–104.
115. Hawley, *The Remains of War*, 81–114.
116. Ibid., 24.
117. See, for example, Peter Perl, "Hallowed Ground," *WP*, May 12, 2002, and Alessandra Stanley, "Looking Back on a Tragedy with Energy and Respect," *NYT*, September 12, 2006.
118. Sara Rimer, "Public Lives; Where Death Mostly Tiptoed, It Rushed Violently In," *NYT*, September 22, 2001; Sue Ann Pressly, "Site of Crash is 'Hallowed Ground'; In a PA Field, Thousands Pay Homage to Where America First Fought Back," *WP*, September 11, 2002. See also Schuler, "Pilgrimage to Shanksville, Pennsylvania," 21.
119. Rimer, "Public Lives"; Longman, *Among the Heroes*, 260; Perl, "Hallowed Ground."
120. Mary Niederberger, "3 Caskets Are to Be Buried at Flight 93 Site Today," *PPG*, September 12, 2011.
121. Rick Hampson and Martha T. Moore, "9/11 Put Anonymous Faces on the Front Page of History," *USA Today*, September 8, 2006; Hawley, *The Remains of War*, 49. See also Hass, *Carried to the Wall*, 105–6, 121.
122. DoubleACS, "Attleboro POW-MIA 9/11 Remembrance 2007," September 15, 2007, www.doubleacs.com.
123. UNCAT, FLNI 55-66, SL 2-16-06 and SL 2-22-06, Groups #2006.06 and 2006.07.
124. UNCAT, FLNI-80, SL 7-24-06, Group 2006.31.
125. UNCAT, SL9-18-06.
126. Clinton W. Taylor, "Monumental Failure," *American Spectator On-Line*, January 4, 2006, http://spectator.org.
127. Jonathan V. Last, "The Memorials We Deserve," *Weekly Standard*, May 28, 2007, www.weeklystandard.com.
128. "The Week," *National Review*, October 10, 2005.
129. Flight 93 National Memorial Internal Design Competition, "Stage II Jury Report," September 7, 2005, 5–11, www.nps.gov.
130. Alec Rawls, "Crescent of Betrayal: Dishonoring the Heroes of Flight 93," 2007, www.crescentofbetrayal.com; Amy Worden, "Fighting to Build a Flight 93 Memorial in a Violated Land," *PI*, September 11, 2007; Doss, *Memorial Mania*, 79. For an overview of the controversy, see Doss, *Memorial Mania*, 176–79, and Ting, "Pax Americana," 213–14. For a catalogue of Rawls's claims and the NPS's response, see Paula Reed Ward, "Flight 93 Memorial Draws a New Round of Criticism," *PPG*, August 18, 2007. See also Ann C. Mulkern, "Tancredo Rips Sept. 11 Memorial," *Denver Post*, September 14, 2005.
131. Doss, *Memorial Mania*, 179; Paula Reed Ward, "Flight 93 Memorial Crescent Now a Circle," *PPG*, December 1, 2005.
132. Doss, *Memorial Mania*, 178.
133. Lisa Fabrizio, "Flights of Fancy," *American Spectator On-Line*, April 19, 2006, http://spectator.org.
134. Taylor, "Monumental Failure."
135. Sturken, *Tangled Memories*, 58.
136. Representative Cubin of Wyoming, Speaking on Behalf of H.R. 3917 on July 22, 2002, 107th Cong., 2nd sess., *CR* 148, pt.100: H5003.

137. The survey aimed to provide the members of the task force with a sense of public sentiments as they began the design competition. The survey received 385 responses via mail and the memorial's website, and additional responses were gathered through a public open house in Shanksville and a workshop held in San Francisco with family members (Flight 93 National Memorial, "Summary of Public Comments, Task Force and Family Workshops as of December, 31, 2003," n.d., copy in author's possession.)
138. Flight 93 Mission Statement Public Comments 2004, FLNI.
139. Ibid.
140. Ibid. Representative comments include the following: "It *should not* be a wall such as the memorials in Washington, D.C." and "I feel that a simple granite wall would not convey enough for the future generations to actually be able to visualize what happened that day."
141. Ibid.
142. Ibid.
143. Ibid. On Fonda's legacy in relation to the Vietnam War, see Jerry Lembcke, *Hanoi Jane: War, Sex, and Fantasies of Betrayal* (Amherst: University of Massachusetts Press, 2010).
144. Paula Reed Ward, "Flight 93 Memorial Design Contest Starts Sept. 11," *PPG*, July 31, 2004.
145. NPS, *Flight 93 National Memorial: An International Design Competition*, 7.
146. Flight 93 Memorial Task Force and Advisory Commission, "Flight 93 National Memorial Mission Statement," NPS, July 2004, 1, www.nps.gov.
147. NPS, *Flight 93 National Memorial: An International Design Competition*, 12; "Flight 93 National Memorial: An International Design Competition," DVD, 0:51.
148. Sturken notes a similar phenomenon in the competition for the World Trade Center Memorial. *Tourists of History*, 264.
149. Design 39-730, Flight 93 Memorial Design Competition Entries. NPS, www.flight93memorialproject.org.
150. Designs 27-508, 25-476, 27-511, 28-523, Flight 93 Memorial Design Competition Entries.
151. Doss, *Memorial Mania*, 133. The elements of the Vietnam Veterans Memorial are themselves entirely original, as the naming of the dead has long been a feature of war memorials. Hass, *Carried to the Wall*, 55–56, Simpson, *9/11*, 79; Hagopian, *The Vietnam War in American Memory*, 232; Doss, *Memorial Mania*, 239–40.
152. See, among others, Hass, *Carried to the Wall* 14, 15; Edwin A. Martini, *Invisible Enemies: The American War on Vietnam, 1975–2000* (Amherst: University of Massachusetts Press, 2007), 214, 216, 208; Sturken, *Tangled Memories*, 75; Doss, *Memorial Mania*, 240.
153. On the design elements of the Vietnam Veterans Memorial, see Sturken, *Tangled Memories*, 50–55; Hass, *Carried to the Wall*, 12–20; Martini, *Invisible Enemies*, 208–13.
154. Erika Doss, "Death, Art, and Memory in the Public Sphere: The Visual and Material Culture of Grief in Contemporary America," *Mortality* 7.1 (2002), 65; Sturken, *Tangled Memories*, 51.
155. Sturken, *Tangled Memories*, 58–59. Martini, citing Hass, makes a similar observation. *Invisible Enemies*, 208.
156. Sturken, *Tangled Memories*, 72. See also Hass, *Carried to the Wall*, 15.
157. Flight 93 National Memorial, "Summary of Public Comments, Task Force and Family Workshops as of December, 31, 2003"; Mission Statement Public Comments, 2004, FLNI.
158. Design 19-361, "Flight 93 Memorial Design Competition Overview."
159. Design 31-601, 35-674, 33-626.
160. Design 30-561, 06-119, 40-748, "Flight 93 Memorial Design Competition Overview."
161. Sturken, *Tangled Memories*, 46; Hagopian, *The Vietnam War in American Memory*, 358.

162. Design 31-595, "Flight 93 Memorial Design Competition Overview."
163. Design 38-717, "Flight 93 Memorial Design Competition Overview."
164. Sturken, *Tangled Memories*, 72.
165. Design 36-682, "Flight 93 Memorial Design Competition Overview."
166. Design 17-326, "Flight 93 Memorial Design Competition Overview." David Simpson notes that the World Trade Center memorial will also be aligned with the path of the hijacked airliner, though he argues that this alignment serves a different purpose. *9/11*, 83.
167. Britten, "The Face of What Came After," 126.
168. Design 34-642, "Flight 93 Memorial Design Competition Overview."
169. FLNI UCC and FLNI UCC Design Competition Stage II Public Comments.
170. FLNI UCC, Design Competition Stage II Public Comments.
171. FLNI UCC, Design Competition Stage II Public Comments.
172. FLNI UCC, Design Competition Stage II Public Comments.
173. Here, I am in accord with Ting, who writes, "The Flight 93 memorial space will not tolerate elements that are unfriendly to its heroic definitions" and "reminds those still standing what the fight is about and why it needs to continue," though she does not connect this impulse to the revision of the Wall's design elements. "Pax Americana," 214–15.
174. "Stage II Jury Report," 5.
175. Devin Zuber, "Flânerie at Ground Zero: Aesthetic Countermemories in Lower Manhattan," *American Quarterly* 58.2 (2006), 271.
176. Paula Reed Ward, "Flight 93 Marker Design Picked; Maple Trees, Wind Chimes Honor Those Who Died," *PPG*, September 8, 2005.
177. Barbara Black, e-mail to the author, August 2, 2013.
178. John Bodnar, *Remaking America: Public Memory, Commemoration, and Patriotism in the Twentieth Century* (Princeton: Princeton University Press, 1992), 13–14.
179. "Stage II Jury Report," 6.
180. For a description of a similar experience at the Wall, see Hass, *Carried to the Wall*, 14.
181. Ibid.
182. On the World War II Memorial, see Doss, *Memorial Mania*, 187–252.

6. "THE LESSONS OF HISTORY"

1. Bruce Springsteen, "Last to Die," *Magic*, compact disc, Columbia Music, © 2007 Bruce Springsteen and (P) 2007 Columbia.
2. Senator Kerry of Massachusetts, Speaking on "The Strategy in Iraq," on January 24, 2007, 110th Cong., 1st sess., *CR* 153, pt. 14:S1034; Senator Kerry of Massachusetts, Speaking on Amendment 2091, on July 12, 2007, 110th Cong., 1st sess., *CR* 153, pt. 111:S9108.
3. Jeffrey M. Jones, "Public Optimism about U.S. Troop Surge in Iraq Improves but Remains Low," *Gallup*, August 8, 2007, www.gallup.com.
4. "The Names of the Dead," *NYT*, September 28, 2007; James Risen, "State Dept. Tallies 56 Shootings Involving Blackwater on Diplomatic Guard Duty," *NYT*, September 28, 2007; Paul Von Zielbauer, "Testimony in Court-Martial Describes a Sniper-Squad Pressed to Raise Body Count," *NYT*, September 28, 2007.
5. For similar lists of shared qualities, see Jeffrey Record, "Leaving Vietnam: Insights for Iraq?," *Diplomatic History* 34.3 (2010), 567–68, and Marc J. Selverstone, "Editor's Introduction: The Politics of Troop Withdrawal," *Diplomatic History* 34.3 (2010), 461–62.
6. Both Fick and Mullaney have published articles and opinion pieces in major national publications and have emerged as something of public figures. As an informal measure,

the fact that each of these books remains, as of February 1, 2011, among the top sixty books of all genres dealing with the Iraq war sold by Amazon.com (they are also among the top ten memoirs; Fick's *One Bullet Away* remains Amazon's highest-selling Iraq war memoir) indicates their continuing cultural impact.

7. In making this argument, I am following Philip Melling's point that "the Vietnam veteran came to be regarded as a genuine witness whose right to testify publicly was seen as a worthwhile calling," that "personal narrative was an act of revelation and duty," and that "the autobiographies of the Vietnam veteran are statements of revelation"; I also take Tobey Herzog's point that the attention these texts pay to atrocity is central to their capacity to "raise moral issues" related to the war. Philip H. Melling, *Vietnam in American Literature* (Boston: Twayne, 1990), 49, 54, 60; Tobey C. Herzog, *Vietnam War Stories: Innocence Lost* (London: Routledge, 1992), 75. I also extend N. E. Anderson's recognition that Nathaniel Fick is "not writing his memoir from a void; he has read, and by reading, he has coded, both consciously and subconsciously, means of articulating his perceptions." "Writing War: An Analysis and Deconstruction of the Contemporary Combat Memoir in Nathaniel Fick's *One Bullet Away*," *War, Literature and the Arts* 21 (2009), 68–84, 78.
8. Many scholars have made this observation. See, for example, Mark Atwood Lawrence, "Too Late or Too Soon? Debating the Withdrawal from Vietnam in the Age of Iraq," *Diplomatic History* 34.3 (2010), 589–90; Jeffrey Record, "Leaving Vietnam: Insights for Iraq?," *Diplomatic History* 34.3 (2010), 567; *Iraq and the Lessons of Vietnam*, ed. Lloyd C. Gardner and Marilyn Young (New York: New Press, 2007).
9. Rick Rogers, "Charges against Marines Detailed; Documents Released in Haditha Slayings," *San Diego Union-Tribune*, December 30, 2006; Marsha Mercer, "Abuse Images Are Branded on a Nation's Minds, Hearts," *Richmond Times-Dispatch*, May 9, 2004. See also Cynthia Enloe, *Nimo's War, Emma's War: Making Feminist Sense of the Iraq War* (Berkeley: University of California Press, 2010), 72–73.
10. David Fitzgerald, "Vietnam, Iraq, and the Rebirth of Counterinsurgency," *Irish Studies in International Affairs* 21 (2010), 155.
11. Gian Gentile, *Wrong Turn: America's Deadly Embrace of Counterinsurgency* (New York: New Press, 2013), 13.
12. Ibid., 157–58; *CSM*, "What to Read on Iraq," June 27, 2007; John Nagl, *Counterinsurgency Lessons from Malaya and Vietnam: Learning to Eat Soup With a Knife* (Westport: Praeger, 2002), xiv, 205. For a critical assessment of Nagl, see Gentile, *Wrong Turn*, 21.
13. George W. Bush, "Address to the Nation on Military Operations in Iraq, January 10, 2007," *PPP:GWB 2007* (Washington, D.C.: Government Printing Office, 2008), 1:17. On clear and hold, see Lewis Sorley, *A Better War: The Unexamined Victories and Final Tragedy of America's Last Years in Vietnam* (Orlando: Harcourt, 1999), and Lawrence, "Too Late or Too Soon?," 592–94. On the popularity of Abrams among those who praised counterinsurgency during the Iraq war, see Fitzgerald, "Vietnam, Iraq and the Rebirth of Counterinsurgency," 153–54 and Gentile, *Wrong Turn*, 20–21. David Elliot notes that clear and hold was invoked prior to 2006 as well and offers a useful critique of the theory's application to Vietnam and Iraq. "Parallel Wars: Can the Lessons of Vietnam be Applied to Iraq?," in *Iraq and the Lessons of Vietnam*, 29–30.
14. Robert G. Kaiser, "Trapped by Hubris, Again," *WP*, January 14, 2007. See also Robert K. Brigham, "The Time to Negotiate Is Now," *WP*, January 14, 2007.
15. Leslie H. Gelb and Richard K. Betts, "We're Fighting Not to Lose," *WP*, January 14, 2007.

16. Gail Russell Chaddock, "Democrats Aim to Exploit GOP Split over War," *CSM*, January 17, 2007.
17. Representative Ellison of Minnesota, Speaking on The War in Iraq, on January 11, 2007, 110th Cong., 1st sess., *CR* 153, pt. 6:H411.
18. Martin Luther King Jr., "A Time to Break the Silence," in *A Testament of Hope: The Essential Writings of Martin Luther King, Jr.* ed. James M. Washington, 239 (New York: HarperOne, 1986).
19. On reaction to the speech, see Taylor Branch, *At Canaan's Edge: America in the King Years, 1965–68* (New York: Simon and Schuster, 2006), 594–97; Mitchell K. Hall, *Because of Their Faith: CALCAV and Religious Opposition to the Vietnam War* (New York: Columbia University Press, 1990), 43–44; Vincent Harding, *Martin Luther King: The Inconvenient Hero* (Maryknoll, N.Y.: Orbis, 2008), 67; Michael Eric Dyson, *I May Not Get There with You: The True Martin Luther King, Jr.* (New York: Free Press, 2000), 61–62; and Edward P. Morgan, "The Good, the Bad, and the Forgotten: Media Culture and Public Memory of the Civil Rights Movement," in *The Civil Rights Movement in American Memory*, ed. Renee C. Romano and Leigh Raiford, 152 (Athens: University of Georgia Press, 2006).
20. Hall, *Because of Their Faith*, 43.
21. Dyson, "I May Not Get There with You," 55, 76.
22. Jonathan Weisman and Dan Balz, "Democrats Aim to Block Funds for Plan," *WP*, January 11, 2007.
23. Representative Jackson-Lee of Texas, Speaking on The War in Iraq, on January 11, 2007, 110th Cong., 1st sess., *CR* 153, pt. 6:H411.
24. Thomas J. Lueck, "Echoing King in New York, Edwards Calls for War's End," *NYT*, January 15, 2007.
25. Robert E. Pierre, "Residents Ensure King Gets His Day; Grass-Roots Peace Walk Is Precursor to Official Parade," *WP*, January 12, 2007; "Digest," *St. Louis Post-Dispatch*, January 16, 2007; John Iwasaki, "Pint-Size Boy Fills the Stage with Passion at Martin Luther King, Jr. Rally," *Seattle Post Intelligencer*, January 16, 2007; Terry Dickson, "Parade Honors Coretta, Too, to Keep Dream Alive," *Florida Times-Union*, (Jacksonville), January 16, 2007; Louis Hansen, "On Day Honoring Pacifist, Troops Join in Dissent of War," *Virginian-Pilot*, January 16, 2007.
26. Colbert I. King, "From Dr. King, a Reminder on Iraq," *WP*, January 13, 2007.
27. "Remembering King's Message of Peace; His Words against War Remain Powerful," *Minneapolis Star Tribune*, January 15, 2007.
28. Bob Herbert, "The Lost Voice of Protest," *NYT*, January 18, 2007; Cynthia Tucker, "Our Opinion: King's Voice of Peace Resounds Amid Iraq Woes," *AJC*, January 14, 2007; Michael Paul Williams, "More than Ever, America Needs King," *Richmond Times-Dispatch*, January 15, 2007; *CST*, "Lightning Rod: Three Takes on MLK: Doomed to Repeat?: Taking on the Hot Topics of the Day," January 16, 2007; Jesse Jackson, "Doomed to Repeat?" *CST*, January 16, 2007; "Rev. King on Ending War," Editorial, *Capital Times* (Madison), January 15, 2007; Scott Stroud, "Leaders Should Take Faith beyond Stump, Reconcile It With War," *San Antonio Express News*, January 20, 2007; Kevin Graman, "The War for Rights; Couple Sees Important Lessons in King's Perspective on Vietnam," *(Spokane) Spokesman-Review*, January 15, 2007; Paula Kaufman, "Remember the Struggle; Let Us Rededicate Ourselves to Solving the Nation's Problems," *Charleston Gazette*, January 15, 2007.
29. Julian E. Zelizer, "Congress and the Politics of Troops Withdrawal," *Diplomatic History* 34.3 (2010), 540; Frank Newport, "Martin Luther King, Jr.: Revered More after Death than

Before; Americans Chose King as Second Most Admired Person of Century in 1999," *Gallup,* January 16, 2006, www.gallup.com.

30. Melvin Small, "Bring the Boys Home Now! Antiwar Activism and Withdrawal From Vietnam—and Iraq," *Diplomatic History* 34.3 (2010), 544–45; Lawrence, "Too Late or Too Soon?" 590. See also Hector Amaya, "Latino Immigrants in the American Discourses of Citizenship and Nationalism during the Iraqi War," *Critical Discourse Studies* 4.3 (2007), 239.
31. Senator Durbin of Illinois, Speaking in Iraq, on January 17, 2007, 110th Cong., 1st sess., *Cong. Rec.* 153, pt. 9:S634–35.
32. Senator Byrd of West Virginia, Speaking on Senate Resolution 39, on January 24, 2007, 110th Cong., 1st sess., *Cong. Rec.* 153, pt. 14:S1074.
33. Representative McDermott of Washington, Speaking on "Ending the Iraq War," February 6, 2007, 110th Cong., 1st sess., *Cong. Rec.* 153, pt. 22:H1237.
34. Representative McDermott of Washington, Speaking on the Iraq War Supplemental Funding Bill, on March 22, 2007, 110th Cong., 1st sess., *Cong. Rec.* 153, pt. 50:H2932.
35. Senator Tester of Montana, Speaking on Procedural Tactics on February 7, 2007, 110th Cong., 1st sess., *CR* 153, pt. 23:S1673.
36. Representative Kennedy of Rhode Island, Speaking against the Iraq Surge, on February 14, 2007, 110th Cong., 1st sess., *CR* 153, pt. 28:H1664.
37. Representative Skelton of Missouri, speaking on the Iraq War Resolution, on February 16, 2007, 110th Cong., 1st sess., *CR* 153, pt. 30:H1799; Senator Menendez of New Jersey, Speaking in Favor of the Levin-Reid Amendment, on July 11, 2007, 110th Cong., 1st sess., *CR* 153, pt. 110:S8992, and Speaking on July 17, 2007, 110th Cong., 1st sess., *CR* 153, pt. 114:S9364.
38. Zelizer, "Congress and the Politics of Troop Withdrawal," 530.
39. Frank Newport et al., "Gallup Poll Review: Key Points about Public Opinion in Iraq," *Gallup,* August 14, 2007, www.gallup.com.
40. Prados, *Vietnam: The History of an Unwinnable War* (Lawrence: University Press of Kansas, 2009), xi.
41. George W. Bush, "Remarks at the Veterans of Foreign Wars National Convention in Kansas City, Missouri, August 22, 2007," *PPP:GWB* 2007, 2:1103–4; Lawrence offers a similar summary of the speech and analysis of this quote. "Too Late or Too Soon?," 590–91.
42. "Kerry Statement on Bush Speech to the VFW," John Kerry—United States Senator for Massachusetts: Press Room, http://kerry.senate.gov. See also Jim Rutenberg et al, "Bush Declares that 'Free Iraq' Is within Reach," *NYT,* August 23, 2007.
43. Michael A. Fletcher, "Bush Compares Iraq to Vietnam; He Says Pullout Would be Disastrous," *WP,* August 23, 2007.
44. Max Boot, "Another Vietnam?," Editorial, *WSJ,* August 24, 2007; Norman Podhoretz, "'America the Ugly,'" *WSJ,* September 11, 2007; *Rocky Mountain News,* "The Value of the Vietnam Analogy," Editorial, August 25, 2007; Jim Wooten, "Our Opinion: President Is Right to Follow History in Iraq," Editorial, *AJC,* August 26, 2007. In Congress, see Representative Wamp of Tennessee on "The Situation in Iraq," on September 5, 2007, 110th Cong., 1st sess., *CR* 153, pt. 130:H10139; Senator Bond of Missouri, speaking on Iraq, on September 6, 2007, 110th Cong., 1st sess., *CR* 153, pt. 131:S11134; Representative Poe of Texas, speaking on "Planned Defeat by Withdrawal," on September 6, 2007, 110th Cong., 1st sess., *CR* 153, pt. 131:H10199; and Senator McCain of Arizona speaking on the National Defense Authorization Act, on September 18, 2007, 110th Cong., 1st sess., *CR* 153, pt. 138:S11634.
45. "The Problem Isn't Mr. Maliki," Editorial, *NYT,* August 24, 2007; "Bush's Vietnam: Myopia

and Pandering Won't Change Iraq's Reality," Editorial, *PPG*, August 24, 2007; Andrew Greeley, "True or False: Can Bush Tell the Difference?" *CST*, September 5, 2007.

46. *PI*, "Iraq vs. Vietnam; A Different Twist," Editorial, August 26, 2007; Eugene Robinson, "Good Morning, Vietnam!" *WP*, September 4, 2007. Slightly more charitable editorials condemned Bush's "shaky grasp of history," noted historians' skepticism of Bush's claims, argued that Bush's assertion that the United States should have stayed in Vietnam was simply foolhardy, and suggested that regardless of the president's opinion on Southeast Asia, arguing that a U.S. withdrawal might lead to chaotic violence overlooked the reality of such chaos in Iraq. Jim Hoagland, "Bush's Vietnam Blunder," *WP*, August 24, 2007; "Invoking Vietnam; Bush's Selective Reading of History a Smokescreen," *Dallas Morning News*, August 24, 2007; Thom Shanker, "Historians Question Bush's Reading of Lessons of Vietnam for Iraq," *NYT*, August 23, 2007; Michael Tackett, "Bush Cites Past Wars for Lessons on Iraq; But Historians Say Vietnam, Japan Analogies Flawed," *Chicago Tribune*, August 23, 2007. See also Sheryl Gay Stolberg and Jim Rutenberg, "A Step Away from Maliki," *NYT*, August 22, 2007; David Jackson and Matt Kelley, "Bush to Discuss Vietnam's Legacy in Speech on Iraq," *USA Today*, August 22, 2007; Sally Kalson, "The Real Lesson of Vietnam: Bush Looks to Asia's Past Agony to Prolong Iraq's Present Suffering," *PPG*, August 26, 2007; Stephen Karalekas, Letter to the Editor, *WP*, August 24, 2007; Zay N. Smith, "Who Needs Friends?" *CST*, August 23, 2007; *LAT*, "Bush's Vietnam Problem," Editorial, August 23, 2007.
47. E. J. Dionne Jr., "For Now, the Maliki Primary," *WP*, August 24, 2007; "More Realism, Less Spin," Editorial, *NYT*, August 31, 2007.
48. "Back to Vietnam," Editorial, *BG*, August 24, 2007.
49. Mike Lukovich, cartoon, *AJC*, August 23, 2007.
50. For an overview of the Senate hearings, see Thomas Ricks, *The Gamble: General David Petraeus and the American Military Adventure in Iraq, 2006–08* (New York: Penguin, 2009), 243–51; Joseph Carroll, "Americans More Positive than Negative in Views of Gen. Petraeus," *Gallup*, August 14, 2007, www.gallup.com.
51. Thom Shanker, "The Struggle for Iraq: Rehearsals and Early Reviews: The Time Has Come, the General's Here: Petraeus Preps for Testimony on Iraq," *NYT*, September 8, 2007. See also Kathy Kiely, "Progress Report Due to Congress Today; Petraeus: Scholar's Intellect Meets Warrior's Intensity," *USA Today*, September 10, 2007.
52. David E. Sanger, "2 Officials Cite Long-Term Need for U.S. in Iraq," *NYT*, September 12, 2007; Calvin Woodward, "Petraeus Joins Generals Called by Congress," AP, September 10, 2007; Peter Baker and Thomas E. Ricks, "Petraeus Returns to War that Is Now His Own," *WP*, September 13, 2007. Smaller papers also raised the comparison. See Julian E. Barnes. "Gen. Petraeus Brings Savvy to Report," *Topeka Capital-Journal*, September 9. 2007; Mike Soraghan, "All Eyes on Gen. Petraeus," *The Hill*, September 11, 2007; Burt Constable, "Another Tuesday, Sept. 11, and Bush Is Our Quarterback," *Chicago Daily Herald*, September 11, 2007; "The General's Skewed Report," Editorial, *Chattanooga Free Press*, September 11, 2007; Bob Deans, "General Tells Panel He Supports Troop Cuts," *Austin American-Statesman*, September 11, 2007; Evan Lehmann, "Kerry, Kennedy Press Petraeus on Iraq," *Lowell (Mass.) Sun*, September 12, 2007. For letters to the editor, see Letter to the Editor, *CSM*, September 12, 2007; John Blaisdell, Letter to the Editor, *San Antonio Express News*, September 23, 2007; John Bedecarre, Letter to the Editor, *Contra Costa Times*, October 2, 2007; Richard E. Saunier, Letter to the Editor, *Santa Fe New Mexican*, September 22, 2007; Bob Hannah, Letter to the Editor, *Las Vegas Review Journal*, September 18, 2007; Rich Broderick, "Petraeus' Report Nothing but Political Theater,"

Albany Times-Union, September 17, 2007; Joe Gallagher, Letter to the Editor, *Daily News of Los Angeles*, September 14, 2007; and Carlos T. Mock, "Bush's Iraq Strategy Echoes the Failures in Vietnam War," *CST*, September 12, 2007.

53. John Darkow, "General Information," *Columbia (Mo.) Daily Tribune*, September 11, 2007, Daryl Cagle's Politicalcartoons.com store.

54. Petraeus's integrity was indeed challenged publicly by MoveOn.org, which ran newspaper ads that changed the general's name to Betray-Us. Ricks, *The Gamble*, 245–46.

55. Senate Committee on Foreign Relations, *Iraq: The Crocker-Petraeus Report*, 110th Cong., 1st sess., 2007, 55; House Committee on Armed Forces and House Committee on Foreign Affairs, *The Status of the War and Political Developments in Iraq*, 110th Cong., 1st sess., 2007, 72–73. For coverage of and responses to these comparisons, see Karen DeYoung and Thomas E. Ricks, "The General's Long View Could Cut Withdrawal Debate Short," *WP*, September 11, 2007; Susan Page, "A Mixed Reception, With No Sign of Consensus on War," *USA Today*, September 11, 2007; David S. Cloud and Thom Shanker, "Petraeus Warns against Quick Pullback in Iraq," *NYT*, September 11, 2007; Peter Baker and Jonathan Weisman, "Petraeus Backs Initial Pullout; General Praises Progress, Warns Against 'Rushing to Failure,'" *WP*, September 11, 2007; and Dale Eisman, "Time to Bring Some Home, Top General in Iraq Says," *(Norfolk) Virginian-Pilot*, September 11, 2007; Ken Allard, "Democrats' Criticism a Poor Response to General's Message," *San Antonio Express-News*, September 13, 2007; Mark Moyar, "Optimism and War," Editorial, *New York Sun*, September 18, 2007.

56. U.S. House of Representatives, "The Status of the War and Political Developments in Iraq," Joint Hearing before the Committee on Armed Services Meeting Jointly With Committee on Foreign Affairs, 110th Cong., 1st sess., September 10, 2007 (Washington: Government Printing Office, 2008), 12–13. William Westmoreland, Address to a Joint Session of Congress, April 28, 1967, 90th Cong., 1st Sess., *CR* 113, pt. 9:1153–54; House of Representatives, "The Status of the War and Political Developments in Iraq," 14; H. D. S. Greenway, "Pickup Game That Is Iraq War Continues," *Seattle Post-Intelligencer*, September 21, 2007; Carolyn Lochhead, "Upbeat Assessment Buys Bush Some Time," *San Francisco Chronicle*, September 11, 2007.

57. Ricks, *The Gamble*, 244, 251. The hearings did improve Petraeus's public standing and momentarily increased support for his plan. In the long run, however, they did little to change public sentiment about the war, and Vietnam comparisons continued unabated. See Frank Newport, "Public: Situation in Iraq Getting Worse for U.S.; Six in Ten Say War Was a Mistake," *Gallup*, October 18, 2007, www.gallup.com. See also "Out of Iraq—Who Will Lead?," Editorial, *San Francisco Chronicle*, September 23, 3007. For references to Iraq as Vietnam, see *SFC*, "Out of Iraq—Who Will Lead?," Editorial, September 23, 2007; "V-AQI Day?," Editorial, *St. Louis Post-Dispatch*, October 16, 2007; David Ignatius, "Dividing Iraq to Save It," *WP*, October 4, 2007; Jim Hoagland, "Deploying for 'The New Normal,'" *WP*, October 21, 2007; Carol Marin, "Vietnam Lessons Lost in Iraq War—We Shouldn't Once Again Wait Too Long to Admit Our Mistake and Leave," *CST*, September 23, 2007.

58. Ricks, *The Gamble*, 251.

59. Jeffrey M. Jones, "In U.S., More Optimism about Iraq, Less about Afghanistan; New High of 42% Say War in Afghanistan a Mistake," Gallup, March 18, 2009, www.gallup.com; Small, "Bring the Boys Home Now!," 552.

60. See, for example, John Barry et al. "Obama's Vietnam," *Newsweek*, February 1, 2009.

61. Lawrence, "Too Late or Too Soon?," 599; Jim Hoagland, "Behind the Afghan Strategy," *WP*, March 22, 2009; Bob Woodward, *Obama's Wars* (New York: Simon and Shuster, 2010), 129–30. Among the articles that mentioned the administration's use of this book

are Peter Baker, "Inside the Situation Room: How a War Plan Evolved," *NYT*, December 6, 2009; Matt Bai, "Escalations: How Afghanistan Might Be Vietnam—and Obama the Real Kennedy," *NYT*, November 1, 2009; Frank Rich, "Obama at the Precipice," Editorial, *NYT*, September 27, 2009; Peter Spiegel and Jonathan Weisman, "Behind Afghan War Debate, A Battle of Two Books Rages," *WSJ*, October 7, 2009; Gordon Lubold, "More Troops in Afghanistan? Naysayers Gain Clout with Obama," *CSM*, October 9, 2009; and Eugene Robinson, "Bring the Troops Home," Editorial, *WP*, October 27, 2009.

62. "Afghan Troop Plan Risks Repeat of Past Mistakes," Editorial, *USA Today*, January 28, 2009; see also Jack Kelly, "Obama's Vietnam? Pouring More Troops into Afghanistan Isn't Going to Help," *PPG*, February 1, 2009.
63. Ralph Peters, "The Mendacity of Hope; The U.S. Essentially Has Four Options—From Best to Worst—Going Forward in Afghanistan," *USA Today*, February 24, 2009.
64. Representative Obey of Wisconsin, Speaking on the Supplemental Appropriations Act, 2009, on May 14, 2009, *CR* 155, pt. 74:H5622.
65. See, for example, Representative McKeon of California, Speaking Against the McGovern Amendment, June 25, 2009, *CR* 155, pt. 97:H7339.
66. Representative Jones of North Carolina, Speaking in Favor of H.R. 2404, May 18, 2009, *CR* 155, pt. 76:H5693. On Jones's personal habits and changing attitude on the Iraq war, see Robert Dreyfuss, "The Three Conversions of Walter B. Jones: From Freedom Fries to Marine Funerals, a Southern Republican's Road to Damascus," *Mother Jones*, January/February 2006, http://motherjones.com.
67. Representative Jones of North Carolina, Speaking in Favor of H.R. 2404, May 18, 2009. *CR* 155, pt. 76:H5694.
68. Andrew Bacevich, "To Die for a Mystique," *American Conservative*, May 18, 2009, www.theamericanconservative.com.
69. Representative Jones of North Carolina, Speaking on U.S. Strategy in Afghanistan, May 21, 2009, *CR* 155, pt. 79:H5985.
70. Representative Jones of North Carolina, "To Die for a Mystique," on June 23, 2009, *Cong. Rec.* 155, pt. 95:H7117. See also Representative Jones of North Carolina, Speaking in Favor of the McGovern Amendment, on June 25, 2009, *CR* 155, pt. 95:97H7338–39.
71. Representative Jones of North Carolina, "Military Strategy for Afghanistan," on October 27, 2009, *CR* 155, pt. 157:H11834.
72. John Harwood, "Obama Rejects Afghanistan–Vietnam Comparison," *NYT*, September 15, 2009. See Paul R. Pillar, "Who's Afraid of a Terrorist Haven?" Editorial, *WP*, September 16, 2009; "Vietnam Redux? A General Seeks More Troops for an Uncertain War," Editorial, *PPG*, September 24, 2009; Robert Scheer, "U.S. Clings to Failed Afghanistan Policy," *CST*, November 6, 2009; "Afghan Strategy: Exit: Our View: Mr. Obama Approaches His JFK Moment in Afghanistan," Editorial, *St. Louis Post-Dispatch*, November 13, 2009; and Jim Hoagland, "Afghanistan: The Speech You'll Miss," *WP*, November 29, 2009.
73. Tim Burke, Letter to the Editor, *NYT*, September 4, 2009.
74. Bob Herbert, "Reliving the Past," *NYT*, September 5, 2009; Jack Kelly, "Pretending in Afghanistan; It's Not a Real Country and We Can't Make It One," Editorial, *PPG*, September 6, 2009.
75. See, for example, Ross K. Baker, "A War President's Delicate Footing," *USA Today*, September 29, 2009; Jack Kelly, "Obama Dithers Toward an Afghan Defeat; A Half-Measure Plan Won't Do the Job," Editorial, *PPG*, October 11, 2009; *Washington Times*, "Vietnam Myths Haunt Afghanistan," Editorial, November 11, 2009.

76. Daryl Cagle, "Ghost of LBJ Haunts Obama," MSNBC.com, September 30, 2009, www.politicalcartoons.com.
77. "Obama's Afghan Policy Speech at West Point," *WP*, December 1, 2009.
78. Peter Baker and Adam Nagourney, "Two Messages for Two Sides," *NYT*, December 2, 2009.
79. See, for example, Sheryl Gay Stohlberg and Helene Cooper, "Obama Speeds Troops, Vows to Start Pullout in 2011," *NYT*, December 2, 2009.
80. Bob Herbert, "A Tragic Mistake," *NYT*, December 1, 2009.
81. John Baer, "This Troop-Surge Talk Has a Familiar Ring," *Philadelphia Daily News*, December 2, 2009; Representative Poe of Texas, "Conditional Commitment," on December 2, 2009, *CR* 155, pt. 177:H13389.
82. On Poe's habit of speaking first each morning, see Jennifer Steinhauer, "This Texan Always Wants the First Word," *NYT*, March 11, 2009.
83. Representative Kucinich of Ohio, "Our Presence in Afghanistan Not Wanted," on December 2, 2009, *CR* 155, pt. 177:H13389. For similar sentiments, see Representative Doggett of Texas, "Wider War Not a Path to Peace and Security," on December 2, 2009, *CR* 155, pt. 177:H13390–91; Representative Pingree of Maine, "Jobs and the Economy," on December 2, 2009, *CR* 155, pt. 177:H13392; Representative McGovern of Massachusetts, "The Wrong Decision on Afghanistan," on December 2, 2009, *CR* 155, pt. 177:H13443–44.
84. Kristin Ann Hass, *Sacrificing Soldiers on the National Mall* (Berkeley: University of California Press, 2013), 198; see also Andrew Bacevich, *The Limits of Power: The End of American Exceptionalism* (New York: Henry Holt, 2009), 131.
85. Hass, *Sacrificing Soldiers on the National Mall*, 198.
86. O'Brien, *If I Die in a Combat Zone (Box Me Up and Ship Me Home)* (1975; repr., New York: Broadway, 1999), 22.
87. Ibid., 11–12, 21, 50.
88. Donovan Campbell, *Joker One: A Marine Platoon's Story of Courage, Leadership, and Brotherhood* (New York: Random House, 2009), 9.
89. Ibid., 9.
90. Ibid., 36–37.
91. On these inequalities, see Christian G. Appy, *Working-Class War: American Combat Soldiers and Vietnam* (Chapel Hill: University of North Carolina Press, 1993).
92. Here, I am following Hector Amaya's provocative claim that "failing to address this debate carries benefits, for it allows writers and speakers to imagine that the choosing of the military is a matter of patriotism and evidence of love for the nation. . . . These ideas leave unexplored the social structure of America, where it is evident that the armed forces are increasingly targeting Latinos." "Latino Immigrants in the American Discourses of Citizenship," 245; more generally, see 243–45.
93. Philip Caputo, *A Rumor of War* (New York: Henry Holt, 1996), 27–28.
94. Beth Bailey shows that the Iraq and Afghanistan wars in fact did not unfairly exploit either the poor or the nonwhite. *America's Army: Building the All-Volunteer Force* (Cambridge: Harvard University Press, 2009), 258–59.
95. Caputo, *A Rumor of War*, 5–6. Vietnam memoirists' initial idealism has been widely noted. See, for example, Milton J. Bates, *The Wars We Took to Vietnam: Cultural Conflict and Storytelling* (Berkeley: University of California Press, 1996), 36, and Tobey C. Herzog, *Vietnam War Stories: Innocence Lost* (London: Routledge, 1992), 32, 38, 66–69.
96. Nathaniel Fick, *One Bullet Away: The Making of a Marine Officer* (New York: Houghton Mifflin, 2005), 4–5. Anderson notes the romanticism of this passage. "Writing War," 70.

97. Herzog, *Vietnam War Stories*, 68–69.
98. Caputo, *A Rumor of War*, 119–20. Likewise, Herzog writes, "Typical of grunts in modern war, Caputo and his men also encounter the horrible destruction caused by the impact of modern war technology on the fragile human body." *Vietnam War Stories*, 72.
99. Caputo, *A Rumor of War*, 123, 124.
100. Judith Butler, *Frames of War: When Is Life Grievable?* (London: Verso, 2009), 42–43.
101. Herzog, *Vietnam War Stories*, 75. See also Philip D. Beidler, *American Literature and the Experience of Vietnam* (Athens: University of Georgia Press, 1982), 162.
102. Fick, *One Bullet Away*, 272.
103. Anderson, "Writing War," 78. This scene offers yet another inversion of Caputo. Whereas Caputo describes a U.S. soldier executing an injured Viet Cong soldier with his pistol, Fick refuses to do the same. Caputo, *A Rumor of War*, 118; Fick, *One Bullet Away*, 272.
104. Caputo, *A Rumor of War*, 124.
105. Fick, *One Bullet Away*, 273.
106. Anderson, "Writing War," 78; Butler, *Frames of War*, 42.
107. Caputo, *A Rumor of War*, 128; Fick, *One Bullet Away*, 273. Anderson argues that "this description writes into the convention of understanding war as a game, the Test." "Writing War," 78. See also *A Rumor of War*, 124.
108. Craig Mullaney, *The Unforgiving Minute: A Soldier's Education* (New York: Penguin, 2009), 299–300. Mullaney tells his readers that he has memorized that diameter of an American rifle round on pages 27–28.
109. Ibid. For a similar passage, see Campbell, *Joker One*, 187. Notably, this passage, too, evokes Caputo, *A Rumor of War*, 162.
110. The terms *precarity* and *grievability* are Butler's. See *Frames of War*, passim.
111. Herzog, *Vietnam War Stories*, 75; Philip D. Beidler, *Re-Writing America: Vietnam Authors in Their Generation* (Athens: University of Georgia Press, 1991), 81.
112. Caputo, *A Rumor of War*, 228–29.
113. Ibid., 110, 90.
114. O'Brien, *If I Die in a Combat Zone*, 119–20; see also 84.
115. Campbell, *Joker One*, 189–90.
116. Herzog, *Vietnam War Stories*, 146; Bates, *The Wars We Took to Vietnam*, 36.
117. On the civilian death toll, see also Enloe, *Nimos's War, Emma's War*, 221–22.
118. Moni Basu and Gayle White, "US Defends Bombing Mosque," *Cox News Service*, April 7, 2004. Campbell sets the date of these orders on April 6. *Joker One*, 189.
119. Trudy Rubin, "A Growing Impatience with the U.S. among Iraqis," *The Record* (Bergen County, N.J.), April 11, 2004; Bassem Mroue, "Civilian Deaths Anger Fallujah Refugees," AP, April 19, 2004; and Ian Fisher, "Attack in Iraq: Many Versions, Obscure Truth," *NYT*, April 26, 2004. That same month Howard Zinn complained in a piece profiling him that "the American media practices 'self-censorship,' leaving the headlines to the number of troops killed on a given day and downplaying the thousands of civilian casualties, women and children killed amid the violence." Philip Read, "A View of Inglorious War," *Newark Star-Ledger*, April 28, 2004.
120. See, for example, Maureen Dowd, "No Way to Make Wrong Terms Seem Right," *(Albany) Times Union*, April 8, 2004; Matthew Schofield, "As Death Toll Grows, So Does Anti-U.S. Feeling," *St. Paul Pioneer Press*, April 11, 2004; and Eric Schmitt and Thom Shanker, "A Full Range of Technology Is Applied to Bomb Falluja," *NYT*, April 30, 2004.
121. Caputo, *A Rumor of War*, 126.

122. Michael Herr, *Dispatches* (New York: Vintage, 1991), 198–99.
123. Ibid., 200.
124. Fick, *One Bullet Away,* 272; Mullaney, *The Unforgiving Minute,* 300.
125. Brian Hartman, "Did Troops Trade Photos of Iraq Dead for Porn?," *ABC News,* September 28, 2005, http://abcnews.go.com; William Yardley, "Drug Use Cited in the Killings of 3 Civilians; Testimony in Afghan Case—Tapes Aired," *NYT,* September 28, 2010; David Zucchino, "Marine Pleads Guilty to Urinating on Afghan Corpses," *LAT,* January 16, 2013.
126. See, for example, Melling, *Vietnam in American Literature,* 62; Thomas Myers, *Walking Point: American Narratives of Vietnam* (New York: Oxford University Press, 1988), 90; and Ringnalda, *Fighting and Writing the Vietnam War* (Jackson: University Press of Mississippi), 94–97.
127. O'Brien, *If I Die in a Combat Zone,* 18, 168.
128. Caputo, *A Rumor of War,* 332, 334–35.
129. Campbell, *Joker One,* 299.
130. Elisabeth Bumiller, "A Well-Written War, Told in the First Person," *NYT,* February 8, 2010.
131. Fick, *One Bullet Away,* 241. He makes a similar rhetorical move on 220.
132. Mullaney, *The Unforgiving Minute,* 362.
133. Jay Winter, "Remembering Injustice and the Social Construction of Silence," in *Democratic Narrative, History, and Memory,* ed. Carole A. Barbato and Laura L. Davis, 51 (Kent, Ohio: Kent State University Press, 2012).
134. On this role for the veteran, see Melling, *Vietnam in American Literature,* 49.
135. Fick, *One Bullet Away,* 368.
136. Caputo, *A Rumor of War,* 4.
137. Fick, *One Bullet Away,* 361, 363.
138. Campbell, *Joker One,* 305.
139. Mullaney, *The Unforgiving Minute,* 348; Caputo, *A Rumor of War,* 246. I have addressed Mullaney's PTSD more fully in "'We Combat Veterans Have a Responsibility to Ourselves and to Our Families:' Domesticity and the Politics of PTSD." Forthcoming in *American Studies* 53.2 (2014).
140. Fick, *One Bullet Away,* 369.
141. Ibid., 368–69.
142. Errol Morris, "*The Fog of War:* Transcript," Errol Morris: Film, www.errolmorris.com.
143. See, for example, George W. Bush, "The President's News Conference with Prime Minister Ayad Allawi of Iraq, September 23, 2004," *PPP:GWB,* 2005, 2180; "Remarks at McDill Air Force Base in Tampa, Florida, June 16, 2004," *PPP:GWB,* 2005, 1062; and "Remarks at Fort Lewis, Washington, June 18, 2004," *PPP:GWB,* 2005, 1087.
144. Caputo, *A Rumor of War,* 326.
145. Fick, *One Bullet Away,* 369. Anderson argues that this passage represents the fulfillment of Fick's construction of his experience as "the Test of War." "Writing War," 73.
146. George W. Bush, "The President's News Conference," March 6, 2003, *PPP:GWB,* 2004, 250.
147. O'Brien suggests a similar disinterest in the war among his men, though the antiwar sentiment of his memoir is clear (80). Elaine Scarry posits that if this were the "primary goal . . . he would have led those comrades to another geography." Scarry, *The Body in Pain: The Making and Unmaking of the World* (New York: Oxford University Press, 1985), 65.
148. Bailey, *America's Army,* 253.
149. Ibid., 206.
150. Ibid., 36–37.

151. Ibid., 200–201.
152. Fick, *One Bullet Away,* 5. Here, I am building on Anderson's discussion, which I note above, of Fick's decision to join the marines as a rite of passage equal to a variety of other adventures a young person might undertake (72). Yet Fick's comment here seems to belie his equation of the two.
153. Mullaney, *The Unforgiving Minute,* 13, 16–17.
154. Ibid., 17–18.
155. Campbell does not date his enlistment, though he notes that he "it took a year and a half," time which included "toiling away on staff intelligence work in Iraq throughout the summer and fall of 2003." He took command of his platoon on October 15, 2003. *Joker One,* 11–13. That would put his enlistment, conservatively, at April 2002.
156. Campbell, *Joker One,* 9.
157. Ibid.
158. Each is white, enters the military as an officer, and possesses an elite education: both Fick and Campbell are Ivy League graduates, and each is the child of professionals; Mullaney, despite his blue-collar upbringing, attends Oxford as a Rhodes Scholar before taking command of a platoon. As Bailey has shown, this is not representative of the military more broadly, even though "by the 1990s, the army not only presented itself as a site of equal opportunity and inclusion, but came close to matching its claims." *America's Army,* 213, 215, 219.
159. Campbell, *Joker One,* 8.
160. Ibid., 300.
161. Campbell casts the war as a triumph of Christian morality; his celebration of love follows his discussion of faith and hope, a section clearly based on I Corinthians 13:13. The Iraq war thus becomes, in Campbell's narration, not, as Vietnam was for Caputo, an experience in which an emphatically Christian American morality was lost, but one in which it was discovered.
162. Caputo, *A Rumor of War,* 224.
163. Campbell, *Joker One,* 8, 10.
164. Mullaney, *The Unforgiving Minute,* 380.
165. Caputo, *A Rumor of War,* xxi.
166. See, for example, Enloe, *Nimo's War, Emma's War,* 72–73; Rick Rogers, "Charges against Marines Detailed; Documents Released in Haditha Slayings," *San Diego Union-Tribune,* December 30, 2006; Rick Rogers and Mark Sauer, "Plot Detailed at Court-Martial; Marines Killed Iraqi When Suspect Couldn't be Found, Corpsman Testifies," *San Diego Union-Tribune,* October 7, 2006; Linda Feldmann, "Abuse Photos Harden US War Divide," *CSM,* May 10, 2004, and Elizabeth Sullivan, "There's No Escape from Those Photos," *Cleveland Plain Dealer,* May 6, 2004; Bailey, *America's Army,* 229, 249–55.

AFTERWORD

1. Barack Obama, "Interview with Fareed Zakaria on CNN's 'Global Public Square,'" July 13, 2008, John T. Woolley and Gerhard Peters, *The American Presidency Project,* www.presidency.ucsb.edu.
2. Barack Obama, "Remarks Commemorating the 50th Anniversary of the Vietnam War," May 28, 2012, 1. *Compilation of Presidential Documents* (Washington, D.C.: Government Printing Office, 2012), www.gpo.gov.
3. Ibid.

4. Ibid.
5. Iraq Body Count, www.iraqbodycount.org; Simon Rogers and Monica Chalabi, "Afghanistan Civilian Casualties," DataBlog, *The Guardian*, April 12, 2013, www.theguardian.com; Brad Knickerbocker, "Iraq War 10 Years Later: Was It Worth It?" *CSM*, March 17, 2013; Kevin Sieff, "An Ancient Treatment for Modern Ills," *WP*, October 24, 2012; Lourdes Garcia-Navarro, "Treating Iraqi Children for PTSD," *NPR News*, August 25, 2008, www.npr.org.
6. Gregg Zoraya, "Recent War Vets Face Hiring Obstacle: PTSD Bias," *USA Today*, April 9, 2013; Mark Davis, "Filmmaker Focuses on Brain-Injured Troops," *AJC*, May 12, 2013; Zoraya, "Study: Military Substance Abuse at 'Crisis' Levels," *USA Today*, September 18, 2012; Zoraya, "Troops Stay Mum on Mental Health," *USA Today*, July 3, 2013. See also Adam Glantz, *The War Comes Home: Washington's Battle against America's Veterans* (Berkeley: University of California Press, 2010).
7. I am not alone in leveling critiques of this sort. Kristin Ann Hass argues that this has been a trend in American memorialization more generally since the Vietnam War. *Sacrificing Soldiers on the National Mall* (Berkeley: University of California Press, 2013), 197–98.
8. Warodometer, "Iran War Odometer Sticker," Café Press, www.cafepress.com.
9. For a sampling of articles that suggested a potential conflict with Iran, see Seymour M. Hersh, "Preparing the Battlefield," *New Yorker*, July 7, 2008, www.newyorker.com; Matthew Rotschild, "Bush's Iran War Plans," *The Progressive*, October 2007, http://progressive.org; Wesley Clark, "The Next War," *WP*, September 16, 2007; Michael E. Ruane, "Antiwar Protesters Decry Handling of Iran," *WP*, September 26, 2007; and David Ignatius, "A Way Out for Iran," *WP*, October 7, 2007.
10. Thomas Friedman, "Syria is Iraq," *NYT*, July 24, 2012.
11. Ibid.
12. National Public Radio, "Transcript and Audio: Vice Presidential Debate," October 11, 2012, www.npr.org.
13. Josh Gerstein, "Mattis Skittish on Syria," *Politico*, July 20, 2013, www.politico.com.
14. Ibid.
15. Doyle McManus, "America Turns Skeptical," *LAT*, September 15, 2013. See also Carol Morello, "In Norfolk, Sentiment Is Clear; 'We've Had Enough of War,' " *WP*, September 14, 2013; Ernesto Londono and Craig Whitlock, "Syria Crisis Reveals Obama's Strained Ties With Military," *WP*, September 19, 2013.
16. M. Kay Gartrell, Letter to the Editor, *WP*, September 22, 2013.
17. Ron Charles, "Iraq Tales to Battle for Honors," *WP*, October 11, 2012.
18. Joe Dziemianowicz, " 'Water' Pours on the Drama," review of Quiara Alegría Hudes, *Water by the Spoonful*, *New York Daily News*, January 9, 2013.

INDEX

A native of Reading, Massachusetts, David Kieran is a visiting assistant professor of American Studies at Franklin & Marshall College in Lancaster, Pennsylvania. He earned a bachelor's degree in English from Connecticut College and a doctorate in American Studies at the George Washington University. He was previously a post-doctoral fellow in the American Culture Studies Program at Washington University in St. Louis. He and his wife, Emma Gilmore Kieran, live in Lancaster, Pennsylvania.